CORE STATUTES ON
INSOLVENCY LAW
AND
CORPORATE RESCUE

CORE STATUTES ON INSOLVENCY LAW AND CORPORATE RESCUE

Edited by

John Tribe

KPMG Lecturer in Restructuring

Kingston Law School, Kingston University

palgrave
macmillan

Published 2008 by
PALGRAVE MACMILLAN
Houndmills, Basingstoke, Hampshire RG21 6XS and
175 Fifth Avenue, New York, N.Y. 10010
Companies and representatives throughout the world

PALGRAVE MACMILLAN is the global academic imprint of the Palgrave Macmillan division of St. Martin's Press, LLC and of Palgrave Macmillan Ltd. Macmillan® is a registered trademark in the United States, United Kingdom and other countries. Palgrave is a registered trademark in the European Union and other countries.

ISBN-13: 978–0–230–22049–2 paperback
ISBN-10:   0–230–22049–5 paperback

This book is printed on paper suitable for recycling and made from fully managed and sustained forest sources. Logging, pulping and manufacturing processes are expected to conform to the environmental regulations of the country of origin.

A catalogue record for this book is available from the British Library.

A catalog record for this book is available from the Library of Congress.

10 9 8 7 6 5 4 3 2 1
17 16 15 14 13 12 11 10 09 08

Typeset by Style Photosetting Ltd, Mayfield, East Sussex
Printed and bound in Great Britain by
Cromwell Press Ltd, Trowbridge, Wiltshire

FOREWORD

In the last 25 years or so insolvency law and practice have been the subject of massive changes. The first and most important, at least in legal terms, came as a result of the passing of the Insolvency Act 1986, which not only codified and modernised existing legislation but introduced sweeping changes and greater emphasis on the rescue and rehabilitation of both companies and individuals in financial difficulty. The second major change has been commercial and social, the increased use of insolvency mechanisms, not just by companies but by individuals who have been entering into voluntary arrangements or even embracing bankruptcy on an unprecedented scale.

The result is that insolvency is no longer, as it was until fairly recently, the preserve of a small number of specialist law and accountancy firms, often practising at what was regarded as the grubby end of the market, but is part of the mainstream of legal and financial life. That in turn has resulted in its being studied academically, at both undergraduate and postgraduate level, as well as practically, not least of all for the JIEB examinations, now a required step on the path to becoming a licensed insolvency practitioner.

The growth of interest in insolvency law has also resulted in the publication of numerous insolvency textbooks, guides to and commentaries on the insolvency legislation. So why another?

This work offers at least two advantages which others cannot claim. First, it is not only up to date, as any law book must be, but it also covers the historical sweep of the law on insolvency from the sixteenth century to the present day. This will be of interest not only to legal historians but to anyone who wishes to have an understanding of the roots and foundations of our system of dealing with debt. Secondly, it comes at an affordable price, something which will commend it to the student as well as to the practitioner who is looking for value for money.

It is a pleasure to commend it to all with an interest in insolvency law, whether as student, practitioner or, as many of us always really are, both.

Stephen Baister
Chief Bankruptcy Registrar
Royal Courts of Justice, The Strand, WC2A 2LL
June 2008

PREFACE

This set of insolvency and corporate rescue statutes and statutory instruments has been drawn together to provide an accessible and inexpensive set of materials for both undergraduate and postgraduate university courses in insolvency law and corporate rescue. For some time the extremely good annotated, professionally focused statute books on the subject have been the only pure sources for insolvency statute coverage for the discerning student.[1] These materials have usually been beyond the reach of the typical undergraduate as they are intended for a professional audience. Recourse to company law statute books has been the preferred second choice option. This is of course unsatisfactory, as these books invariably do not include provisions on the personal side of the subject. This collection will address this lacuna and it may also be of use to those studying for the Joint Insolvency Examinations (JIEB).[2]

Materials that relate to personal insolvency, corporate insolvency and restructuring practice have been included, as well as some portions of early modern bankruptcy statutes. This allows the student reader to engage with the statutory foundations of the subject and the sources of some of the main ideas that still dominate intellectual discussion, if not practical insolvency law and practice, eg pari passu (supposed) equality of treatment, compositions and debtor discharge. Some early modern statutory material has also been included that demonstrates the punishment and treatment that early modern debtors received, such as pillorying, ear loss and hanging. Where appropriate, spelling and style have been modernised for ease of understanding.[3] Statutes and Interregnum Ordinances relating to imprisonment for debt and the amelioration of debtor prisoners have not been included because of space constraints.[4] Similarly, Scottish insolvency laws have not been included in this edition (eg the Bankruptcy (Scotland) Act 1985 (c 66), the Bankruptcy and Diligence etc (Scotland) Act 2007 (asp 3) and the parts of the Insolvency Act 1986 which appertain to insolvency law in Scotland).

In more recent times there have been some fundamental changes to the statutory landscape of insolvency law and related areas following the seminal Cork Report[5] and the enactment of the main statute, the Insolvency Act 1986 (which is included as amended). There have been a number of subsequent Acts that have amended the principal statute, most notably the Enterprise Act 2002.[6] It was initially hoped that the salient provisions in this statute, as well as other amending statutes (the two Insolvency Acts of 1994 and the Insolvency Act 2000), could also be included as enacted (in part) so as to provide the undergraduate student with a clear understanding of their effect on the main statute. This has not been possible because of space constraints, but any future edition may be able to carry what would amount to this slight repetition. The Company Directors Disqualification Act 1986 public protection provisions are included.[7] Relevant parts of the Companies Act 1985 and Companies Act 2006 find a place

---

1.   eg Milman, D & Sealy, L, *Sealy & Milman: Annotated Guide to the Insolvency Legislation* (2 volumes), 10th edn (Sweet & Maxwell Ltd, 2007) (hereafter referred to as Sealy & Milman). See also Keay, A & Doyle, L, *Insolvency Legislation: Annotations and Commentary*, 2nd edn (Jordans Publishing Ltd, 2007) (hereafter referred to as Keay & Doyle).

2.   Please note that this collection is edited and that due to space constraints some sections and rules have been edited out of both the Acts and the rules. The 1986 Act and rules are not reproduced in their entirety.

3.   To be clear, the Acts reproduced in this volume with the years of Royal Asset, 1543, 1571, 1604, 1623, 1697, 1705, 1976, are *no longer in force* and are reproduced here for historical interest and discussion only.

4.   On these debtor relief statutes during the seventeenth century and particularly the ordinances of the interregnum, see Tribe, J, *'Punishment without Crime' – An Historical Examination of the Treatment of Debtors and the use of Punishment in English Insolvency Law during the Seventeenth Century* (PhD thesis, University College London, University of London (forthcoming)). For access to the primary source materials, see Firth, CH & Rait, RS (eds), *Acts and Ordinances of the Interregnum 1642–1660*, Vol III (HMSO, 1911).

5.   *Insolvency Law and Practice, Report of the Review Committee*, Cmnd 8558 (HMSO, 1982); see also *A Revised Framework for Insolvency Law*, Cmnd 91775 (HMSO, 1984).

6.   For an excellent summary on the personal side, see Walters, A, *Personal insolvency law after the Enterprise Act: an appraisal* (2005) JCLS 2005, 5(1), 65–104. For an excellent summary on the corporate side, see Fletcher, IF, *UK corporate rescue: recent developments – changes to administrative receivership, administration, and company voluntary arrangements – the Insolvency Act 2000, the White Paper 2001, and the Enterprise Act 2002* (2004) EBOR 5(1), 119–151.

7.   On this reform, see Walters, A and Davis-White, M, *Directors' disqualification and bankruptcy restrictions*, 2nd edn (Sweet & Maxwell, 2005).

because of the small company definitions (for CVAs), schemes of arrangement and striking off provisions.[8] European harmonisation activities also necessitate the inclusion of the EC Regulation on Insolvency Proceedings.[9] Personal insolvency law and practice will be impacted by the Tribunals, Courts and Enforcement Act 2007 and the Debt Management Schemes and Debt Relief Order provisions that the Act brings in to force.[10] These have therefore been included.

Insolvency law and practice is heavily influenced in the practical sense by the main statutory instrument, the Insolvency Rules 1986 and professional guidance. Relevant parts of the Insolvency Rules have been included in truncated form in this collection. The current reform activity regarding the Insolvency Rules 1986 will give rise to a new set of Insolvency Rules. The future legislative reform picture looks interesting and a number of reform initiatives are on the horizon.[11] These reforms will hopefully feature in any future editions of this collection.

Tutors are most welcome to contact the editor if any material has not been included that they would find useful in subsequent editions, or of course to highlight any possible omissions or lack of precision. Every attempt has been made to cite the law as amended (where appropriate) up to and including 31 May 2008.

John Tribe
KPMG Lecturer in Restructuring, Kingston Law School, Kingston University
June 2008
j.tribe@kingston.ac.uk

---

8.   For more detailed coverage of the company law provisions, see the sister text in this core statute series: Ervine, C, *Core Statutes on Company Law 2008–09* (Palgrave Macmillan, 2008). See also Dine, J & Koutsias, M, *Company Law*, 6th edn (Palgrave Macmillan, 2007).
9.   On this regulation, see Fletcher, IF, Moss, G & Issacs, S (eds), *The EC Regulation on Insolvency Proceedings: A Commentary and Annotated Guide* (Oxford University Press, 2002).
10.   On these recent changes, see McKenzie Skene & Walters, A, *Consuming Passions: Benchmarking Consumer Bankruptcy Law Systems*, in Omar, PJ (ed), *International Insolvency Law: Themes and Perspectives* (Ashgate, 2008), at pp 135–70.
11.   On past reform documentation from the Insolvency Service that has led to the statutory amendments contained in this collection, see, *inter alia, Company Voluntary Arrangements and Administration Orders. A Consultative document* (DTI, 1993); *Revised Proposals for a New Company Voluntary Arrangement* (DTI, 1995); *A Review of Company Rescue and Business Reconstruction Mechanisms, A Report by the Review Group, Insolvency Service* (May 2000); *Bankruptcy: A Fresh Start* (DTI, 2000); *Productivity and Enterprise: Insolvency – A Second Chance*, Cm 5234 (DTI, The Insolvency Service; TSO, July 2001); *Relief for the Indebted – an Alternative to Bankruptcy?* (DTI, 2005); *Improving Individual Voluntary Arrangements* (DTI, 2005); *Bankruptcy: proposals for reform of the debtor petition process* (DTI, 2007). These and more insolvency reform documents are available online via the Insolvency Service website (http://www.insolvency.gov.uk/).

ABOUT THE EDITOR

John Tribe is the *KPMG Lecturer in Restructuring* at Kingston Law School, Kingston University. He teaches company law, insolvency law and equity and trusts at undergraduate and postgraduate level. John has also taught company law as a visiting lecturer at Beijing Normal University and insolvency law as a guest teacher at the London School of Economics and Political Science, University of London. John has undertaken three funded research projects for the Insolvency Service (an executive agency of the Department for Business, Enterprise and Regulatory Reform) and gave evidence before the Scottish Parliament on the Bankruptcy and Diligence etc (Scotland) Bill during its passage through the committee stage. John is an editorial board member of the Butterworths journal, 'Corporate Rescue and Insolvency', and is a member of the academic advisory group of the Insolvency Lawyers Association. He is the author of a practitioners' text on personal insolvency law (Tribe, J, Daniels, P & Morgan, S, *Personal Insolvency – A User's Guide* (Jordans Publishing Ltd), which will be published in late 2008.

ACKNOWLEDGEMENTS

The Publisher and Editor would like to gratefully acknowledge the following sources from which this collection has been drawn:

- Queen's Printers Copy Statutes, Her Majesty's Stationery Office, Crown Copyright. Crown copyright material is reproduced with kind permission of the Controller of Her Majesty's Stationery Office.

- The UK Statute Law Database, Ministry of Justice, Crown Copyright. Crown copyright material is reproduced with kind permission of the Controller of Her Majesty's Stationery Office. Caution must be exercised with this digital resource as, at the time of collation (April and May 2008), the source was out of date with the latest statutory changes.

- *The Statutes at Large from the first year of King James the First to the tenth year of the Reign of King William the Third, to which is prefixed a Table of the Titles of all the Publick and Private Statutes during that Time.* Volume the Third. Printed by Charles Eyre and Andrew Strahan, Printers to the King's Most Excellent Majesty; and by William Woodfall and Andrew Strahan, Law Printers to the King's Most Excellent Majesty, London, MDCCLXXXVI.

- *The Statutes at Large, from the Tenth Year of the Reign of King William the Third, to the End of the Reign of Queen Anne, to which is prefixed a Table of the Titles of all the Publick and Private Statutes during the Time.* Volume the Fourth. Printed by Charles Eyre and Andrew Strahan, Printers to the King's Most Excellent Majesty; and by William Woodfall and Andrew Strahan, Law Printers to the King's Most Excellent Majesty, London, MDCCLXXXVI.

- Council Regulation (EC) No 1346/2000 of 29 May 2000 on Insolvency Proceedings is reproduced from the Official Journal with kind permission of the European Commission.

The Editor would like to gratefully acknowledge the help and support of the series commissioning editor, Jasmin Naim, of Palgrave Macmillan, and the series project manager, David Stott, for their help in getting the manuscript into shape and for smoothly piloting the manuscript through the production process. The Editor is also grateful to the anonymous proposal reviewers for their comments on the proposed material and for their suggestions for additional inclusion of material not considered at the proposal stage. The Editor is also particularly grateful to Chief Registrar Stephen Baister for his foreword to this volume and for his support of the *Muir Hunter Museum of Bankruptcy*. The Editor is also grateful to Professors Fletcher, Graham, Milman, Finch and Walters for their ongoing kindness and encouragement. Finally, the Editor is grateful to KPMG LLP for its continued support for the *KPMG Lectureship in Restructuring*. The usual caveats apply in terms of any errors or omissions in the text.

TABLE OF CONTENTS

PART ONE: STATUTES

AN ACT AGAINST SUCH PERSONS AS DO MAKE BANKRUPTS 1543
(34 & 35 Hen VIII, c 4)[1]

Where divers and sundry persons craftily obtaining into their hands great substance of other mens goods, do suddenly flee to parts unknown, or keep their houses, not minding to pay or restore to any their creditors, their debts and duties, but at their own wills and pleasures consume the substance obtained by credit of other men, for their own pleasure and delicate living, against all reason, equity and good conscience:

I.

... the lord Chancellor ... to order the same for true satisfaction and payment of the said creditors: that is to say, to every of the said creditors, a portion, rate and rate like, according to the quantity of their debts ...

V.

... all goods, chattels, lands, tenements and debts of every such offender shall be by the order and direction of the said lords employed and distributed amongst his creditors equally and indifferently rate for rate, in like manner and form as is afore declared.

AN ACT TOUCHING ORDERS FOR BANKRUPTS 1571
(Stat 13 Eliz I, c 7)[2]

Forasmuch as notwithstanding the statute made against bankrupts in the thirty-fourth year of the reign of our late sovereign lord King Henry the Eighth, those kind of persons have and do still increase into great and excessive numbers, and are like more to do, if some better provision be not made for the repression of them, and doe a plain declaration to be made and set forth, who is and ought to be taken and deemed for a bankrupt:

(2)   ... That if any merchant or other person, using or exercising the trade of merchandize by way of bargaining, exchange, rechange, bartry, cheviance, or otherwise, in gross or retail,

(3)   or seeking his or her trade of living by buying and selling ...

...

(6)   ... begin to keep his or her house or houses; or otherwise to absent him or herself;

(7)   to take sanctuary;

(8)   to suffer him or herself willingly to be arrested for any debt or other thing ...

(9)   hath or will suffer him or herself to be outlawed, or yield him or herself to prison, or depart from his or her dwelling-house or houses,

(10)   to the intent or purpose to defraud or hinder any of his or her creditors ... shall be reputed, deemed and taken for a bankrupt.

II.

... That the lord chancellor ... shall have full power and authority by commission under the great seal of England, to name, assign and appoint such wise and honest discreet persons as to him shall seem good ...

---

1.   Professor David Graham QC has posited that the widely held view that this statute received Royal Assent in 1542 is erroneous (Graham, D, *The formative years of English Insolvency Law – 1543 to 1603* (1995) (Phoenix, December 1995, Issue 21, pp 23 to 25)). See also Elton, G, *Reform and Renewal: Thomas Cromwell and the Common Weal* (Cambridge, 1973) at p 149. More work on the primary source documentation of the period is required to resolve this issue definitively. For an argument in favour of the Act being carried over in to 1543 see Lehmberg, SE, *The Later Parliaments of Henry VIII 1536-1547* (Cambridge University Press, 1977) at p 181.

2.   Unlike 34 & 35 Hen VIII, c. 4 (1543), there is little debate over the year of Royal assent and passage of the second early modern bankruptcy statute (Stat 13 Eliz I, c. 7 (1571)). See: Elton, GR, *The Parliament of England 1559-1581* (Cambridge University Press, Cambridge, 1986) at p. 297, which for example puts the Act at 1571. See also: Elton, GR, *Studies in Tudor and Stuart Politics and Government. Volume III: Papers and Reviews 1973-1981* (Cambridge University Press, Cambridge, 1983) at p 146n for an exposition of the passage of the Act.

(10)   or otherwise to order the same for true satisfaction and payment of the said creditors; that is to say, to every of the said creditors a portion, rate and rate like, according to the quantity of his or their debts …

AN ACT FOR THE BETTER RELIEF OF THE CREDITORS AGAINST SUCH AS SHALL BECOME BANKRUPTS 1604
(1 Jac, c 15)

FOR that frauds and deceits, as new diseases, daily increase amongst such as live by buying and selling, to the hindrance of traffick and mutual commerce, and to the general hurt of the realm, by such as wickedly and wilfully become bankrupts; (2) and for that the description of a bankrupt in former statutes is not so fully expressed, nor the power given thereby to the commissioners for bankrupts so large, as is meet in such cases of deceit, to prevent the deceitful actions of bankrupts.

VI.

And for that the practices of bankrupts of late are so secret and so subtil, as they can very hardly be found out or brought to light; (2) and for that the former statute, giving power to the commissioners to examine others than the bankrupts, hath not fully or sufficiently authorised them to examine the said bankrupt upon oath …

IX.

And that if upon his, her or their examination, it shall appear that he, she or they have committed any wilful or corrupt perjury, tending to the hurt or damage of the creditors of the said bankrupt, to the value of ten pounds of lawful money of England, or above, the party so offending shall or may thereof be indicted in any of the King's majesty's courts of record, and being lawfully convicted thereof shall stand upon the pillory in some publick place by the space of two hours, and have one of his ears nailed to the pillory and cut off.

XVII.

… the commissioners shall distribute the goods, lands and debts of the offenders or any of them, by force of the aforementioned statute of the thirteenth year of the reign of our late sovereign lady Queen Elizabeth …

AN ACT FOR THE FURTHER DESCRIPTION OF A BANKRUPT AND RELIEF OF CREDITORS AGAINST SUCH AS SHALL BECOME BANKRUPTS AND FOR INFLICTING CORPORAL PUNISHMENT UPON THE BANKRUPTS IN SOME SPECIAL CASES 1623
(21 Jac 1, c 19)

Forasmuch as daily experience showeth, that the number and multitude of bankrupts do increase more and more, and also the frauds and deceits invented and practised for the avoiding and deluding the penalties of the good laws in that behalf already made, and the remedy by them provided: (2) and for that divers defects are daily found in the former statutes made against bankrupts, both in the description of a bankrupt, as also in the power given to the commissioners for the discovery and distributing the bankrupts estate, to the great encouragement of evil-minded persons, the hindrance of traffick and commerce, the great decay, overthrow and undoing of many clothiers, by whom many thousands of the natural-born subjects of this realm be from time t time in all parts of this kingdom set on work: all which do tend to the general hurt of this realm …

(3)   … That all and singular the aforesaid statutes and laws heretofore made against bankrupts, and for relief of creditors, shall be in all things largely and beneficially construed and expounded for the aid, help and relief of the creditors of such person or persons as already be or hereafter shall become bankrupt …

V.

… but some doubt hath been made whether the commissioners have power to examine the wives of the bankrupts touching the same, by reason whereof the bankrupts wives do daily conceal and convey away, and cause to be conveyed away, much part of their husbands monies, wares, goods, merchandize and other estate, to person or persons unknown to any but such wives, by reason whereof much of the bankrupts estate is concealed and detained from creditors … the said commissioners … have power and authority to examine upon oath the wife or wives of all and every such bankrupt …

VII.

… if any bankrupt … be found fraudulently or deceitfully to have conveyed away his or her goods, chattels, lands, tenements, offices, fees, rents or annuities … to the end and purpose to hinder the execution of this statute … or to defraud, delay or hinder his or her creditors of the same, and shall not upon his or her examination discover unto the said commissioners and … deliver unto the said commissioners all that estate … [the bankrupt] may be indicted … and if upon such indictment or indictments the bankrupt be thereof convicted, he or she so convicted shall be set upon the pillory in some publick place for the space of two hours, and have one of his or her ears nailed to the pillory and cut off.

IX.

And for the better division and distribution of the lands, tenements, hereditaments, goods, chattels and other estate of such bankrupt to and amongst his creditors … and that all and every creditor and creditors having security for his or their several debts … whereof there is no execution or extent served … before such time as he or she shall or do become bankrupt … shall not be relieved upon any such judgment, statute, recognisance, specialty, attachments or other security for any more than a rateable part of their just and due debts, with the other creditors of the said bankrupt.

X.

(5)　　And for that it often falls out, that many persons before they become bankrupts, do convey their goods to other men upon good consideration, yet still do keep the same, and are reputed the owners thereof, and dispose the same as their own:

AN ACT FOR RELIEF OF CREDITORS, BY MAKING COMPOSITIONS WITH THEIR DEBTORS IN CASE TWO THIRDS IN NUMBER AND VALUE DO AGREE 1697 (8&9 WmIII, c 18)[1]

Whereas many debtors disabled by Losses and Misfortunes to pay their whole Debts, are often willing to make What Satisfaction they can for the same, so as they may enjoy their Liberty upon Reasonable Agreements or Compositions; But some … Creditors insisting on their whole Debts … Incapacitated to make any Composition with Debtors despairing to see and end to their Troubles, Transport themselves and their Effects beyond the Sea, or consume the same in Prisons, or pretended Priviledged Places to their utter Ruin, and become useless to the Government, their families, a burden to their Relations, or the Parishes they live in and all their Creditors lose what may be had for their debts: for remedy whereof, Be it Enacted … That is shall be lawful to and for Two Third parts or more in number and value of all real creditors … to make such Agreements they shall think fit and reasonable with any of their Debtors, who being unable to pay their whole Debt …

1.　Repealed in the following year (William III, cap XXIX, 1698), *An Act to Repeal the Act made the last session of Parliament, Intituled An Act for Relief of Creditors, by majority Composition with their Debtors, in case Two thirds in Number and Value do Agree.*

AN ACT TO PREVENT FRAUDS FREQUENTLY COMMITTED BY BANKRUPTS 1705
(4 & 5 Anne, c 17)

Whereas many persons have and do daily become bankrupt, not so much by reason of losses and unavoidable misfortunes, as to the intent to defraud and hinder their creditors of their just debts and duties to them due and owing; for the prevention thereof …

… in all things conform to the several statutes already made concerning bankrupts, and also upon such examination fully and truly disclose and discover how, and in what manner, and to whom, and upon what consideration, he, she or they hath or have disposed, assigned or transferred any of his, her or their goods, wares, merchandizes, money or other effects or estate, and all books, papers and writings relating thereunto … as at the time of such examination shall be in his, her or their possession, custody or power(his, her of their, and his her and their wives and childrens necessary wearing apparel only accepted) then he, she or they the said bankrupt in case of any default or wilful omission therein, or in any the premises, and being thereof lawfully lawfully convicted by indictment or information, shall suffer as a felon, without the benefit of clergy.

VII.

… Allowance to all and every person and person so becoming bankrupt as aforesaid, who shall within the time limited by this act surrender him, her, or themselves to the major part of the commissioners therein named and in all things confirm as in and by this act is directed, shall be allowed the sum of five pounds per centum out of the neat product of all the state that shall be recovered in and received on such discovery, which shall be paid unto him by the assignee or assignees of the said commissioners … and shall be discharged from all debts by him, her, or them due and owing at the time that he, she, or they did become bankrupt;

XVIII

… That is such person or persons so voluntarily surrendering him, her or themselves, shall afterwards neglect or omit to discover and deliver and his , her or their estates and effects, and in every thing act and do as in this act is directed, every such person or persons shall be taken and adjudged to be a fraudulent bankrupt within the true intent and meaning of this act, and thereof being lawfully convicted, shall suffer as a felon without benefit of clergy.

XX.

And whereas commissioners of bankrupts have been often executed with great expense in eating and drinking, at the meetings of the commissioners, or some of them therein named, to the great prejudice of the bankrupts and their creditors; be it further enacted by the authority aforesaid, That there shall not be paid or allowed by the creditors, or out of the estate of the bankrupts, any monies whatsoever for expences in eating or drinking of the commissioners …

AN ACT FOR THE ABOLITION OF IMPRISONMENT FOR DEBT, FOR THE PUNISHMENT OF FRAUDULENT DEBTORS, AND FOR OTHER PURPOSES (DEBTORS ACT 1869)
(1869, c 62)

PART 1
ABOLITION OF IMPRISONMENT FOR DEBT

4   With the exceptions herein-after mentioned, no person shall, after the commencement of this Act, be arrested or imprisoned for making default in payment of a sum of money … that no person shall be imprisoned in any case excepted from the operation of this section for a longer period than one year …

INSOLVENCY ACT 1976
(1976, c 60)

...

(2) Where the court makes an order under subsection (1) above, then, if the debtor is or has been adjudged bankrupt in the proceedings and—
   (a) is not discharged in respect of the adjudication under section 26 of the said Act of 1914 before the fifth anniversary of the date of the adjudication; and
   (b) the adjudication is not annulled before the anniversary under section 21(2) or 29 of that Act, the same results shall ensure as if the court had on that anniversary granted him an absolute order of discharge in respect of the adjudication under the said section 26.

...

COMPANIES ACT 1985
(1985, c 6)

247   Qualification of company as small or medium-sized
   (1) A company qualifies as small or medium-sized in relation to a financial year if the qualifying conditions are met—
   (a) in the case of the company's first financial year, in that year, and
   (b) in the case of any subsequent financial year, in that year and the preceding year.
   (2) A company shall be treated as qualifying as small or medium-sized in relation to a financial year—
   (a) if it so qualified in relation to the previous financial year under subsection (1) above or was treated as so qualifying under paragraph (b) below; or
   (b) if it was treated as so qualifying in relation to the previous year by virtue of paragraph (a) and the qualifying conditions are met in the year in question.
   (3) The qualifying conditions are met by a company in a year in which it satisfies two or more of the following requirements—

Small company	
1. Turnover	Not more than £2.8million
2. Balance sheet total	Not more than £1.4 million
3. Number of employees	Not more than 50
Medium-sized company	
1. Turnover	Not more than £11.2 million
2. Balance sheet total	Not more than £5.6 million
3. Number of employees	Not more than 250

   (4) For a period which is a company's financial year but not in fact a year the maximum figures for turnover shall be proportionately adjusted.
   (5) The balance sheet total means—
   (a) where in the company's accounts Format 1 of the balance sheet formats set out in Part I of Schedule 4 or Part I of Schedule 8 is adopted, the aggregate of the amounts shown in the balance sheet under the headings corresponding to items A to D in that Format, and
   (b) where Format 2 is adopted, the aggregate of the amounts shown under the general heading "Assets".
   (6) The number of employees means the average number of persons employed by the company in the year (determined on a monthly basis).

That number shall be determined by applying the method of calculation prescribed by paragraph 56(2) and (3) of Schedule 4 for determining the corresponding number required to be stated in a note to the company's accounts.

395 Certain charges void if not registered

(1)   Subject to the provisions of this Chapter, a charge created by a company registered in England and Wales and being a charge to which this section applies is, so far as any security on the company's property or undertaking is conferred by the charge, void against the liquidator or administrator and any creditor of the company, unless the prescribed particulars of the charge together with the instrument (if any) by which the charge is created or evidenced, are delivered to or received by the registrar of companies for registration in the manner required by this Chapter within 21 days after the date of the charge's creation.

(2)   Subsection (1) is without prejudice to any contract or obligation for repayment of the money secured by the charge; and when a charge becomes void under this section, the money secured by it immediately becomes payable.

396 Charges which have to be registered

(1)   Section 395 applies to the following charges—
   (a)   a charge for the purpose of securing any issue of debentures,
   (b)   a charge on uncalled share capital of the company,
   (c)   a charge created or evidenced by an instrument which, if executed by an individual, would require registration as a bill of sale,
   (d)   a charge on land (wherever situated) or any interest in it, but not including a charge for any rent or other periodical sum issuing out of the land,
   (e)   a charge on book debts of the company,
   (f)   a floating charge on the company's undertaking or property,
   (g)   a charge on calls made but not paid,
   (h)   a charge on a ship or aircraft, or any share in a ship,
   (j)   a charge on goodwill, or on any intellectual property.

(2)   Where a negotiable instrument has been given to secure the payment of any book debts of a company, the deposit of the instrument for the purpose of securing an advance to the company is not, for purposes of section 395, to be treated as a charge on those book debts.

(3)   The holding of debentures entitling the holder to a charge on land is not for purposes of this section deemed to be an interest in land.

(3A) The following are "intellectual property" for the purposes of this section—
   (a)   any patent, trade mark ..., registered design, copyright or design right;
   (b)   any licence under or in respect of any such right.

(4)   In this Chapter, "charge" includes mortgage.

PART XIII
ARRANGEMENTS AND RECONSTRUCTIONS

425 Power of company to compromise with creditors and members

(1)   Where a compromise or arrangement is proposed between a company and its creditors, or any class of them, or between the company and its members, or any class of them, the court may on the application of the company or any creditor or member of it or, in the case of a company being wound up or an administration order being in force in relation to a company, of the liquidator or administrator, order a meeting of the creditors or class of creditors, or of the members of the company or class of members (as the case may be), to be summoned in such manner as the court directs.

(2)   If a majority in number representing three-fourths in value of the creditors or class of creditors or members or class of members (as the case may be), present and voting either in person or by proxy at the meeting, agree to any compromise or arrangement, the compromise or arrangement, if sanctioned by the court, is binding on all creditors or the class of creditors or on the members or class of members (as the case may be), and also on the company or, in the case of a company in the course of being wound up, on the liquidator and contributories of the company.

(3)   The court's order under subsection (2) has no effect until an office copy of it has been delivered to the registrar of companies for registration; and a copy of every such order shall be annexed to every copy of the company's memorandum issued after the order has been made or, in the case of a company not having a memorandum, of every copy so issued of the instrument constituting the company or defining its constitution.

(4)   If a company makes default in complying with subsection (3), the company and every officer of it who is in default is liable to a fine.

...

(6)   In this section and the next—
   (a)   "company" means any company liable to be wound up under this Act, and
   (b)   "arrangement" includes a reorganisation of the company's share capital by the consolidation of shares of different classes or by the division of shares into shares of different classes, or by both of those methods.

426   Information as to compromise to be circulated

(1)   The following applies where a meeting of creditors or any class of creditors, or of members or any class of members, is summoned under section 425.

(2)   With every notice summoning the meeting which is sent to a creditor or member there shall be sent also a statement explaining the effect of the compromise or arrangement and in particular stating any material interests of the directors of the company (whether as directors or as members or as creditors of the company or otherwise) and the effect on those interests of the compromise or arrangement, in so far as it is different from the effect on the like interests of other persons.

(3)   In every notice summoning the meeting which is given by advertisement there shall be included either such a statement as above-mentioned or a notification of the place at which, and the manner in which, creditors or members entitled to attend the meeting may obtain copies of the statement.

...

(5)   Where a notice given by advertisement includes a notification that copies of a statement explaining the effect of the compromise or arrangement proposed can be obtained by creditors or members entitled to attend the meeting, every such creditor or member shall, on making application in the manner indicated by the notice, be furnished by the company free of charge with a copy of the statement.

...

427   Provisions for facilitating company reconstruction or amalgamation

(1)   The following applies where application is made to the court under section 425 for the sanctioning of a compromise or arrangement proposed between a company and any such persons as are mentioned in that section.

(2)   If it is shown—
   (a)   that the compromise or arrangement has been proposed for the purposes of, or in connection with, a scheme for the reconstruction of any company or companies, or the amalgamation of any two or more companies, and
   (b)   that under the scheme the whole or any part of the undertaking or the property of any company concerned in the scheme ("a transferor company") is to be transferred to another company ("the transferee company"),
   the court may, either by the order sanctioning the compromise or arrangement or by any subsequent order, make provision for all or any of the following matters.

(3)   The matters for which the court's order may make provision are—
   (a)   the transfer to the transferee company of the whole or any part of the undertaking and of the property or liabilities of any transferor company,
   (b)   the allotting or appropriation by the transferee company of any shares, debentures, policies or other like interests in that company which under the compromise or arrangement are to be allotted or appropriated by that company to or for any person,
   (c)   the continuation by or against the transferee company of any legal proceedings pending by or against any transferor company,

   (d) the dissolution, without winding up, of any transferor company,
   (e) the provision to be made for any persons who, within such time and in such manner as the court directs, dissent from the compromise or arrangement,
   (f) such incidental, consequential and supplemental matters as are necessary to secure that the reconstruction or amalgamation is fully and effectively carried out.
(4) If an order under this section provides for the transfer of property or liabilities, then—
   (a) that property is by virtue of the order transferred to, and vests in, the transferee company, and
   (b) those liabilities are, by virtue of the order, transferred to and become liabilities of that company;
and property (if the order so directs) vests freed from any charge which is by virtue of the compromise or arrangement to cease to have effect.

...

INSOLVENCY ACT 1986
(1986, c 45)

PART I
COMPANY VOLUNTARY ARRANGEMENTS

The proposal

1 Those who may propose an arrangement

(1) The directors of a company (other than one for which an administration order is in force, or which is being wound up) may make a proposal under this Part to the company and to its creditors for a composition in satisfaction of its debts or a scheme of arrangement of its affairs (from here on referred to, in either case, as a "voluntary arrangement").

(2) A proposal under this Part is one which provides for some person ("the nominee") to act in relation to the voluntary arrangement either as trustee or otherwise for the purpose of supervising its implementation; and the nominee must be a person who is qualified to act as an insolvency practitioner or authorised to act as nominee, in relation to the voluntary arrangement.

(3) Such a proposal may also be made—
   (a) where an administration order is in force in relation to the company, by the administrator, and
   (b) where the company is being wound up, by the liquidator.

(4) In this Part "company" means—
   (a) a company within the meaning of section 735(1) of the Companies Act 1985,
   (b) a company incorporated in an EEA State other than the United Kingdom; or
   (c) a company not incorporated in an EEA State but having its centre of main interests in a member State other than Denmark.

(5) In subsection (4), in relation to a company, 'centre of main interests' has the same meaning as in the EC Regulation and, in the absence of proof to the contrary, is presumed to be the place of its registered office (within the meaning of that Regulation).

...

1A Moratorium

(1) Where the directors of an eligible company intend to make a proposal for a voluntary arrangement, they may take steps to obtain a moratorium for the company.

(2) The provisions of Schedule A1 to this Act have effect with respect to—
   (a) companies eligible for a moratorium under this section,
   (b) the procedure for obtaining such a moratorium,
   (c) the effects of such a moratorium, and

(d)   the procedure applicable (in place of sections 2 to 6 and 7) in relation to the approval and implementation of a voluntary arrangement where such a moratorium is or has been in force.

2   Procedure where nominee is not the liquidator or administrator

(1)   This section applies where the nominee under section 1 is not the liquidator or administrator of the company and the directors do not propose to take steps to obtain a moratorium under section 1A for the company.

(2)   The nominee shall, within 28 days (or such longer period as the court may allow) after he is given notice of the proposal for a voluntary arrangement, submit a report to the court stating—

     (a)   whether, in his opinion, the proposed voluntary arrangement has a reasonable prospect of being approved and implemented,

     (aa)   whether, in his opinion, meetings of the company and of its creditors should be summoned to consider the proposal, and

     (b)   if in his opinion such meetings should be summoned, the date on which, and time and place at which, he proposes the meetings should be held.

(3)   For the purposes of enabling the nominee to prepare his report, the person intending to make the proposal shall submit to the nominee—

     (a)   a document setting out the terms of the proposed voluntary arrangement, and

     (b)   a statement of the company's affairs containing—

         (i)   such particulars of its creditors and of its debts and other liabilities and of its assets as may be prescribed, and

         (ii)   such other information as may be prescribed.

(4)   The court may—

     (a)   on an application made by the person intending to make the proposal, in a case where the nominee has failed to submit the report required by this section or has died, or

     (b)   on an application made by that person or the nominee, in a case where it is impracticable or inappropriate for the nominee to continue to act as such,

direct that the nominee be replaced as such by another person qualified to act as an insolvency practitioner, or authorised to act as nominee, in relation to the voluntary arrangement.

3   Summoning of meetings

(1)   Where the nominee under section 1 is not the liquidator or administrator, and it has been report to the court that such meetings as are mentioned in section 2(2) should be summoned, the person making the report shall (unless the court otherwise directs) summon those meetings for the time, date and place proposed in the report.

(2)   Where the nominee is the liquidator or administrator, he shall summon meetings of the company and of its creditors to consider the proposal for such a time, date and place as he thinks fit.

(3)   The persons to be summoned to a creditors' meeting under this section are every creditor of the company of whose claim and address the person summoning the meeting is aware.

Consideration and implementation of proposal

4   Decisions of meetings

(1)   The meetings summoned under section 3 shall decide whether to approve the proposed voluntary arrangement (with or without modifications).

(2)   The modifications may include one conferring the functions proposed to be conferred on the nominee on another person qualified to act as an insolvency practitioner or authorised to act as nominee, in relation to the voluntary arrangement.

But they shall not include any modification by virtue of which the proposal ceases to be a proposal such as is mentioned in section 1.

(3)   A meeting so summoned shall not approve any proposal or modification which affects the right of a secured creditor of the company to enforce his security, except with the concurrence of the creditor concerned.

(4) Subject as follows, a meeting so summoned shall not approve any proposal or modification under which—

    (a) any preferential debt of the company is to be paid otherwise than in priority to such of its debts as are not preferential debts, or

    (b) a preferential creditor of the company is to be paid an amount in respect of a preferential debt that bears to that debt a smaller proportion than is borne to another preferential debt by the amount that is to be paid in respect of that other debt.

However, the meeting may approve such a proposal or modification with the concurrence of the preferential creditor concerned.

(5) Subject as above, each of the meetings shall be conducted in accordance with the rules.

(6) After the conclusion of either meeting in accordance with the rules, the chairman of the meeting shall report the result of the meeting to the court, and, immediately after reporting to the court, shall give notice of the result of the meeting to such persons as may be prescribed.

…

4A   Approval of arrangement

(1) This section applies to a decision, under section 4, with respect to the approval of a proposed voluntary arrangement.

(2) The decision has effect if, in accordance with the rules—

    (a) it has been taken by both meetings summoned under section 3, or

    (b) (subject to any order made under subsection (4)) it has been taken by the creditors' meeting summoned under that section.

(3) If the decision taken by the creditors' meeting differs from that taken by the company meeting, a member of the company may apply to the court.

(4) An application under subsection (3) shall not be made after the end of the period of 28 days beginning with—

    (a) the day on which the decision was taken by the creditors' meeting, or

    (b) where the decision of the company meeting was taken on a later day, that day.

…

(6) On an application under subsection (3), the court may—

    (a) order the decision of the company meeting to have effect instead of the decision of the creditors' meeting, or

    (b) make such other order as it thinks fit.

5   Effect of approval

(1) This section applies where a decision approving a voluntary arrangement has effect under section 4A.

(2) The voluntary arrangement—

    (a) takes effect as if made by the company at the creditors' meeting, and

    (b) binds every person who in accordance with the rules—

    (i) was entitled to vote at that meeting (whether or not he was present or represented at it), or

    (ii) would have been so entitled if he had had notice of it,

as if he were a party to the voluntary arrangement.

(2A) If—

    (a) when the arrangement ceases to have effect any amount payable under the arrangement to a person bound by virtue of subsection (2)(b)(ii) has not been paid, and

    (b) the arrangement did not come to an end prematurely, the company shall at that time become liable to pay to that person the amount payable under the arrangement.

(3) Subject as follows, if the company is being wound up or an administration order is in force, the court may do one or both of the following, namely—

    (a) by order stay or sist all proceedings in the winding up or discharge the administration order;

    (b) give such directions with respect to the conduct of the winding up or the administration as it thinks appropriate for facilitating the implementation of the voluntary arrangement.

(4) The court shall not make an order under subsection (3)(a)—

(a) at any time before the end of the period of 28 days beginning with the first day on which each of the reports required by section 4(6) has been made to the court, or

(b) at any time when an application under the next section or an appeal in respect of such an application is pending, or at any time in the period within which such an appeal may be brought.

...

6 Challenge of decisions

(1) Subject to this section, an application to the court may be made, by any of the persons specified below, on one or both of the following grounds, namely—

(a) that a voluntary arrangement which has effect under section unfairly prejudices the interests of a creditor, member or contributory of the company;

(b) that there has been some material irregularity at or in relation to either of the meetings.

(2) The persons who may apply under this section are—

(a) a person entitled, in accordance with the rules, to vote at either of the meetings;

(aa) a person who would have been entitled, in accordance with the rules, to vote at the creditors' meeting if he had had notice of it

(b) the nominee or any person who has replaced him under section 2(4) or 4(2); and

(c) if the company is being wound up or an administration order is in force, the liquidator or administrator.

...

(3) An application under this section shall not be made

(a) after the end of the period of 28 days beginning with the first day on which each of the reports required by section 4(6) has been made to the court or

(b) in the case of a person who was not given notice of the creditors' meeting, after the end of the period of 28 days beginning with the day on which he became aware that the meeting had taken place,

but (subject to that) an application made by a person within subsection (2)(aa) on the ground that the voluntary arrangement prejudices his interests may be made after the arrangement has ceased to have effect, unless it came to an end prematurely.

(4) Where on such an application the court is satisfied as to either of the grounds mentioned in subsection (1), it may do one or both of the following, namely—

(a) revoke or suspend any decision approving the voluntary arrangement which has effect under section 4A or, in a case falling within subsection (1)(b), any decision taken by the meeting in question which has effect under that section;

(b) give a direction to any person for the summoning of further meetings to consider any revised proposal the person who made the original proposal may make or, in the case falling within subsection (1)(b), a further company or (as the case may be) creditors' meeting to reconsider the original proposal.

(5) Where at any time after giving a direction under subsection (4)(b) for the summoning of meetings to consider a revised proposal the court is satisfied that the person who made the original proposal does not intend to submit a revised proposal, the court shall revoke the direction and revoke or suspend any decision approving the voluntary arrangement which has effect under section 4A.

(6) In a case where the court, on an application under this section with respect to any meeting—

(a) gives a direction under subsection (4)(b), or

(b) revokes or suspends an approval under subsection (4)(a) or (5),

the court may give such supplemental directions as it thinks fit and, in particular, directions with respect to things done under the voluntary arrangement since it took effect.

(7) Except in pursuance of the preceding provisions of this section, decision taken at a meeting summoned under section 3 is not invalidated by any irregularity at or in relation to the meeting.

...

6A   False representations, etc

(1)   If, for the purpose of obtaining the approval of the members or creditors of a company to a proposal for a voluntary arrangement, a person who is an officer of the company—

(a)   makes any false representation, or

(b)   fraudulently does, or omits to do, anything,

he commits an offence.

(2)   Subsection (1) applies even if the proposal is not approved.

(3)   For purposes of this section "officer" includes a shadow director.

(4)   A person guilty of an offence under this section is liable to imprisonment or a fine, or both.

7   Implementation of proposal

(1)   This section applies where a voluntary arrangement has effect under section 4A.

(2)   The person who is for the time being carrying out in relation to the voluntary arrangement the functions conferred—

(a)   on the nominee by virtue of the approval given at one or both of the meetings summoned under section 3

(b)   by virtue of section 2(4) or 4(2) on a person other than the nominee, shall be known as the supervisor of the voluntary arrangement.

(3)   If any of the company's creditors or any other person is dissatisfied by any act, omission or decision of the supervisor, he may apply to the court; and on the application the court may—

(a)   confirm, reverse or modify any act or decision of the supervisor,

(b)   give him directions, or

(c)   make such other order as it thinks fit.

(4)   The supervisor—

(a)   may apply to the court for directions in relation to any particular matter arising under the voluntary arrangement, and

(b)   is included among the persons who may apply to the court for the winding up of the company or for an administration order to be made in relation to it.

(5)   The court may, whenever—

(a)   it is expedient to appoint a person to carry out the functions of the supervisor, and

(b)   it is inexpedient, difficult or impracticable for an appointment to be made without the assistance of the court,

make an order appointing a person who is qualified to act as an insolvency practitioner or authorised to act as supervisor, in relation to the voluntary arrangement, either in substitution for the existing supervisor or to fill a vacancy.

(6)   The power conferred by subsection (5) is exercisable so as to increase the number of persons exercising the functions of supervisor or, where there is more than one person exercising those functions, so as to replace one or more of those persons.

7A   Prosecution of delinquent officers of company

(1)   This section applies where a moratorium under section 1A has been obtained for a company or the approval of a voluntary arrangement in relation to a company has taken effect under section 4A or paragraph 36 of Schedule A1.

(2)   If it appears to the nominee or supervisor that any past or present officer of the company has been guilty of any offence in connection with the moratorium or, as the case may be, voluntary arrangement for which he is criminally liable, the nominee or supervisor shall forthwith—

(a)   report the matter to the appropriate authority, and

(b)   provide the appropriate authority with such information and give the authority such access to and facilities for inspecting and taking copies of documents (being information or documents in the possession or under the control of the nominee or supervisor and relating to the matter in question) as the authority requires.

In this subsection, "the appropriate authority" means—

(i)   in the case of a company registered in England and Wales, the Secretary of State, and

...

(3)   Where a report is made to the Secretary of State under subsection (2), he may, for the purpose of investigating the matter reported to him and such other matters relating to the affairs of the company as appear to him to require investigation, exercise any of the powers which are exercisable by inspectors appointed under section 431 or 432 of the Companies Act to investigate a company's affairs.

(4)   For the purpose of such an investigation any obligation imposed on a person by any provision of the Companies Act to produce documents or give information to, or otherwise to assist, inspectors so appointed is to be regarded as an obligation similarly to assist the Secretary of State in his investigation.

(5)   An answer given by a person to a question put to him in exercise of the powers conferred by subsection (3) may be used in evidence against him.

(6)   However, in criminal proceedings in which that person is charged with an offence to which this subsection applies—

(a)   no evidence relating to the answer may be adduced, and

(b)   no question relating to it may be asked,

by or on behalf of the prosecution, unless evidence relating to it is adduced, or a question relating to it is asked, in the proceedings by or on behalf of that person.

...

(8)   Where a prosecuting authority institutes criminal proceedings following any report under subsection (2), the nominee or supervisor, and every officer and agent of the company past and present (other than the defendant or defender), shall give the authority all assistance in connection with the prosecution which he is reasonably able to give.

For this purpose—

"agent" includes any banker or solicitor of the company and any person employed by the company as auditor, whether that person is or is not an officer of the company,

"prosecuting authority" means the Director of Public Prosecutions ... or the Secretary of State.

(9)   The court may, on the application of the prosecuting authority, direct any person referred to in subsection (8) to comply with that subsection if he has failed to do so.

7B   Arrangements coming to an end prematurely

For the purposes of this Part, a voluntary arrangement the approval of which has taken effect under section 4A or paragraph 36 of Schedule A1 comes to an end prematurely if, when it ceases to have effect, it has not been fully implemented in respect of all persons bound by the arrangement by virtue of section 5(2)(b)(i) or, as the case may be, paragraph 37(2)(b)(i) of Schedule A1.

PART II

ADMINISTRATION

Making etc. of administration order

8   Schedule B1 to this Act (which makes provision about the administration of companies) shall have effect.

...

PART III

RECEIVERSHIP

CHAPTER I

RECEIVERS AND MANAGERS (ENGLAND AND WALES)

Preliminary and general provisions

29   Definitions

(1)   It is hereby declared that, except where the context otherwise requires—

(a)   any reference in the Companies Act or this Act to a receiver or manager of the property of a company, or to a receiver of it, includes a receiver or manager, or (as the case may be) a receiver of part only of that property and a receiver only of the income arising from the property or from part of it; and

(b)   any reference in the Companies Act or this Act to the appointment of a receiver or manager under powers contained in an instrument includes an appointment made under powers which, by virtue of any enactment, are implied in and have effect as if contained in an instrument.

(2)   In this Chapter "administrative receiver" means—

(a)   a receiver or manager of the whole (or substantially the whole) of a company's property appointed by or on behalf of the holders of any debentures of the company secured by a charge which, as created, was a floating charge, or by such a charge and one or more other securities; or

(b)   a person who would be such a receiver or manager but for the appointment of some other person as the receiver of part of the company's property.

30   Disqualification of body corporate from acting as receiver

A body corporate is not qualified for appointment as receiver of the property of a company, and any body corporate which acts as such a receiver is liable to a fine.

31   Disqualification of bankrupt

(1)   A person commits an offence if he acts as receiver or manager of the property of a company on behalf of debenture holders while—

(a)   he is an undischarged bankrupt, or

(b)   a bankruptcy restrictions order is in force in respect of him.

(2)   A person guilty of an offence under subsection (1) shall be liable to imprisonment, a fine or both.

(3)   This section does not apply to a receiver or manager acting under an appointment made by the court.

32   Power for court to appoint official receiver

Where application is made to the court to appoint a receiver on behalf of the debenture holders or other creditors of a company which is being wound up by the court, the official receiver may be appointed.

Receivers and managers appointed out of court

33   Time from which appointment is effective

(1)   The appointment of a person as a receiver or manager of a company's property under powers contained in an instrument—

(a)   is of no effect unless it is accepted by that person before the end of the business day next following that on which the instrument of appointment is received by him or on his behalf, and

(b)   subject to this, is deemed to be made at the time at which the instrument of appointment is so received.

(2)   This section applies to the appointment of two or more persons as joint receivers or managers of a company's property under powers contained in an instrument, subject to such modifications as may be prescribed by the rules.

34   Liability for invalid appointment

Where the appointment of a person as the receiver or manager of a company's property under powers contained in an instrument is discovered to be invalid (whether by virtue of the invalidity of the instrument or otherwise), the court may order the person by whom or on whose behalf the appointment was made to indemnify the person appointed against any liability which arises solely by reason of the invalidity of the appointment.

35 Application to court for directions

(1) A receiver or manager of the property of a company appointed under powers contained in an instrument, or the persons by whom or on whose behalf a receiver or manager has been so appointed, may apply to the court for directions in relation to any particular matter arising in connection with the performance of the functions of the receiver or manager.

(2) On such an application, the court may give such directions, or may make such order declaring the rights of persons before the court or otherwise, as it thinks just.

36 Court's power to fix remuneration

(1) The court may, on an application made by the liquidator of a company, by order fix the amount to be paid by way of remuneration to a person who, under powers contained in an instrument, has been appointed receiver or manager of the company's property.

(2) The court's power under subsection (1), where no previous order has been made with respect thereto under the subsection—

    (a) extends to fixing the remuneration for any period before the making of the order or the application for it,

    (b) is exercisable notwithstanding that the receiver or manager has died or ceased to act before the making of the order or the application, and

    (c) where the receiver or manager has been paid or has retained for his remuneration for any period before the making of the order any amount in excess of that so fixed for that period, extends to requiring him or his personal representatives to account for the excess or such part of it as may be specified in the order.

...

37 Liability for contracts, etc

(1) A receiver or manager appointed under powers contained in an instrument (other than an administrative receiver) is, to the same extent as if he had been appointed by order of the court—

    (a) personally liable on any contract entered into by him in the performance of his functions (except in so far as the contract otherwise provides) and on any contract of employment adopted by him in the performance of those functions, and

    (b) entitled in respect of that liability to indemnity out of the assets.

(2) For the purposes of subsection (1)(a), the receiver or manager is not to be taken to have adopted a contract of employment by reason of anything done or omitted to be done with 14 days after his appointment.

(3) Subsection (1) does not limit any right to indemnity which the receiver or manager would have apart from it, nor limit his liability on contracts entered into without authority, nor confer any right to indemnity in respect of that liability.

(4) Where at any time the receiver or manager so appointed vacates office—

    (a) his remuneration and any expenses properly incurred by him, and

    (b) any indemnity to which he is entitled out of the assets of the company,

shall be charged on and paid out of any property of the company which is in his custody or under his control at that time in priority to any charge or other security held by the person by or on whose behalf he was appointed.

38 Receivership accounts to be delivered to registrar

(1) Except in the case of an administrative receiver, every receiver or manager of a company's property who has been appointed under powers contained in an instrument shall deliver to the registrar of companies for registration the requisite accounts of his receipts and payments.

(2) The accounts shall be delivered within one month (or such longer period as the registrar may allow) after the expiration of 12 months from the date of his appointment and of every subsequent period of 6 months, and also within one month after he ceases to act as receiver or manager.

(3) The requisite accounts shall be an abstract in the prescribed form showing—

    (a) receipts and payments during the relevant period of 12 or 6 months, or

(b) where the receiver or manager ceases to act, receipts and payments during the period from the end of the period of 12 or 6 months to which the last preceding abstract related (or, if no preceding abstract has been delivered under this section, from the date of his appointment) up to the date of his so ceasing, and the aggregate amount of receipts and payments during all preceding periods since his appointment.

...

(5) A receiver or manager who makes default in complying with this section is liable to a fine and, for continued contravention, to a daily default fine.

Provisions applicable to every receivership

39 Notification that receiver or manager appointed

(1) When a receiver or manager of the property of a company has been appointed, every invoice, order for goods or business letter issued by or on behalf of the company or the receiver or manager or the liquidator of the company, being a document on or in which the company's name appears, shall contain a statement that a receiver or manager has been appointed.

(2) If default is made in complying with this section, the company and any of the following persons, who knowingly and wilfully authorises or permits the default, namely, any officer of the company, any liquidator of the company and any receiver or manager, is liable to a fine.

40 Payment of debts out of assets subject to floating charge

(1) The following applies in the case of a company, where a receiver is appointed on behalf of the holders of any debentures of the company secured by a charge which, as created, was a floating charge.

(2) If the company is not at the time in course of being wound up, its preferential debts (within the meaning given to that expression by section 386 in Part XII) shall be paid out of the assets coming to the hands of the receiver in priority to any claims for principal or interest in respect of the debentures.

(3) Payments made under this section shall be recouped, as far as may be, out of the assets of the company available for payment of general creditors.

41 Enforcement of duty to make returns

(1) If a receiver or manager of a company's property—

(a) having made default in filing, delivering or making any return, account or other document, or in giving any notice, which a receiver or manager is by law required to file, deliver, make or give, fails to make good the default within 14 days after the service on him of a notice requiring him to do so, or

(b) having been appointed under powers contained in an instrument, has, after being required at any time by the liquidator of the company to do so, failed to render proper accounts of his receipts and payments and to vouch them and pay over to the liquidator the amount properly payable to him,

the court may, on an application made for the purpose, make an order directing the receiver or manager (as the case may be) to make good the default within such time as may be specified in the order.

(2) In the case of the default mentioned in subsection (1)(a), application to the court may be made by any member or creditor of the company or by the registrar of companies; and in the case of the default mentioned in subsection (1)(b), the application shall be made by the liquidator.

In either case the court's order may provide that all costs of and incidental to the application shall be borne by the receiver or manager, as the case may be.

...

Administrative receivers: general

42   General powers

(1)   The powers conferred on the administrative receiver of a company by the debentures by virtue of which he was appointed are deemed to include (except in so far as they are inconsistent with any of the provisions of those debentures) the powers specified in Schedule 1 to this Act.

(2)   In the application of Schedule 1 to the administrative receiver of a company—

    (a)   the words "he" and "him" refer to the administrative receiver, and

    (b)   references to the property of the company are to the property of which he is or, but for the appointment of some other person as the receiver of part of the company's property, would be the receiver or manager.

(3)   A person dealing with the administrative receiver in good faith and for value is not concerned to inquire whether the receiver is acting within his powers.

43   Power to dispose of charged property, etc

(1)   Where, on an application by the administrative receiver, the court is satisfied that the disposal (with or without other assets) of any relevant property which is subject to a security would be likely to promote a more advantageous realisation of the company's assets than would otherwise be effected, the court may by order authorise the administrative receiver to dispose of the property as if it were not subject to the security.

(2)   Subsection (1) does not apply in the case of any security held by the person by or on whose behalf the administrative receiver was appointed, or of any security to which a security so held has priority.

(3)   It shall be a condition of an order under this section that—

    (a)   the net proceeds of the disposal, and

    (b)   where those proceeds are less than such amount as may be determined by the court to be the net amount which would be realised on a sale of the property in the open market by a willing vendor, such sums as may be required to make good the deficiency,

shall be applied towards discharging the sums secured by the security.

(4)   Where a condition imposed in pursuance of subsection (3) relates to two or more securities, that condition shall require the net proceeds of the disposal and, where paragraph (b) of that subsection applies, the sums mentioned in that paragraph to be applied towards discharging the sums secured by those securities in the order of their priorities.

(5)   An office copy of an order under this section shall, within 14 days of the making of the order, be sent by the administrative receiver to the registrar of companies.

(6)   If the administrative receiver without reasonable excuse fails to comply with subsection (5), he is liable to a fine and, for continued contravention, to a daily default fine.

(7)   In this section "relevant property", in relation to the administrative receiver, means the property of which he is or, but for the appointment of some other person as the receiver of part of the company's property, would be the receiver or manager.

44   Agency and liability for contracts

(1)   The administrative receiver of a company—

    (a)   is deemed to be the company's agent, unless and until the company goes into liquidation;

    (b)   is personally liable on any contract entered into by him in the carrying out of his functions (except in so far as the contract otherwise provides) and, to the extent of any qualifying liability,]on any contract of employment adopted by him in the carrying out of those functions; and

    (c)   is entitled in respect of that liability to an indemnity out of the assets of the company.

(2)   For the purposes of subsection (1)(b) the administrative receiver is not to be taken to have adopted a contract of employment by reason of anything done or omitted to be done within 14 days after his appointment.

(2A)   For the purposes of subsection (1)(b), a liability under a contract of employment is a qualifying liability if—

    (a) it is a liability to pay a sum by way of wages or salary or contribution to an occupational pension scheme,

    (b) it is incurred while the administrative receiver is in office, and

    (c) it is in respect of services rendered wholly or partly after the adoption of the contract.

(2B) Where a sum payable in respect of a liability which is a qualifying liability for the purposes of subsection (1)(b) is payable in respect of services rendered partly before and partly after the adoption of the contract, liability under subsection (1)(b) shall only extend to so much of the sum as is payable in respect of services rendered after the adoption of the contract.

(2C) For the purposes of subsections (2A) and (2B)—

    (a) wages or salary payable in respect of a period of holiday or absence from work through sickness or other good cause are deemed to be wages or (as the case may be) salary in respect of services rendered in that period, and

    (b) a sum payable in lieu of holiday is deemed to be wages or (as the case may be) salary in respect of services rendered in the period by reference to which the holiday entitlement arose.

(2D) In subsection (2C)(a), the reference to wages or salary payable in respect of a period of holiday includes any sums which, if they had been paid, would have been treated for the purposes of the enactments relating to social security as earnings in respect of that period.

(3) This section does not limit any right to indemnity which the administrative receiver would have apart from it, nor limit his liability on contracts entered into or adopted without authority, nor confer any right to indemnity in respect of that liability.

45   Vacation of office

(1) An administrative receiver of a company may at any time be removed from office by order of the court (but not otherwise) and may resign his office by giving notice of his resignation in the prescribed manner to such persons as may be prescribed.

(2) An administrative receiver shall vacate office if he ceases to be qualified to act as an insolvency practitioner in relation to the company.

(3) Where at any time an administrative receiver vacates office—

    (a) his remuneration and any expenses properly incurred by him, and

    (b) any indemnity to which he is entitled out of the assets of the company,

shall be charged on and paid out of any property of the company which is in his custody or under his control at that time in priority to any security held by the person by or on whose behalf he was appointed.

(4) Where an administrative receiver vacates office otherwise than by death, he shall, within 14 days after his vacation of office, send a notice to that effect to the registrar of companies.

(5) If an administrative receiver without reasonable excuse fails to comply with subsection (4), he is liable to a fine and, for continued contravention, to a daily default fine.

Administrative receivers: ascertainment and investigation of company's affairs

46   Information to be given by administrative receiver

(1) Where an administrative receiver is appointed, he shall—

    (a) forthwith send to the company and publish in the prescribed manner a notice of his appointment, and

    (b) within 28 days after his appointment, unless the court otherwise directs, send such a notice to all the creditors of the company (so far as he is aware of their addresses).

(2) This section and the next do not apply in relation to the appointment of an administrative receiver to act—

    (a) with an existing administrative receiver, or

    (b) in place of an administrative receiver dying or ceasing to act,

except that, where they apply to an administrative receiver who dies or ceases to act before they have been fully complied with, the references in this section and the next to the administrative receiver include (subject to the next subsection) his successor and any continuing administrative receiver.

(3) If the company is being wound up, this section and the next apply notwithstanding that the administrative receiver and the liquidator are the same person, but with any necessary modifications arising from that fact.

(4) If the administrative receiver without reasonable excuse fails to comply with this section, he is liable to a fine and, for continued contravention, to a daily default fine.

47 Statement of affairs to be submitted

(1) Where an administrative receiver is appointed, he shall forthwith require some or all of the persons mentioned below to make out and submit to him a statement in the prescribed form as to the affairs of the company.

(2) A statement submitted under this section shall be verified by affidavit by the persons required to submit it and shall show—

    (a) particulars of the company's assets, debts and liabilities;

    (b) the names and addresses of its creditors;

    (c) the securities held by them respectively;

    (d) the dates when the securities were respectively given; and

    (e) such further or other information as may be prescribed.

(3) The persons referred to in subsection (1) are—

    (a) those who are or have been officers of the company;

    (b) those who have taken part in the company's formation at any time within one year before the date of the appointment of the administrative receiver;

    (c) those who are in the company's employment, or have been in its employment within that year, and are in the administrative receiver's opinion capable of giving the information required;

    (d) those who are or have been within that year officers of or in the employment of a company which is, or within that year was, an officer of the company.

In this subsection "employment" includes employment under a contract for services.

(4) Where any persons are required under this section to submit a statement of affairs to the administrative receiver, they shall do so (subject to the next subsection) before the end of the period of 21 days beginning with the day after that on which the prescribed notice of the requirement is given to them by the administrative receiver.

(5) The administrative receiver, if he thinks fit, may—

    (a) at any time release a person from an obligation imposed on him under subsection (1) or (2), or

    (b) either when giving notice under subsection (4) or subsequently, extend the period so mentioned;

and where the administrative receiver has refused to exercise a power conferred by this subsection, the court, if it thinks fit, may exercise it.

(6) If a person without reasonable excuse fails to comply with any obligation imposed under this section, he is liable to a fine and, for continued contravention, to a daily default fine.

48 Report by administrative receiver

(1) Where an administrative receiver is appointed, he shall, within 3 months (or such longer period as the court may allow) after his appointment, send to the registrar of companies, to any trustees for secured creditors of the company and (so far as he is aware of their addresses) to all such creditors a report as to the following matters, namely—

    (a) the events leading up to his appointment, so far as he is aware of them;

    (b) the disposal or proposed disposal by him of any property of the company and the carrying on or proposed carrying on by him of any business of the company;

    (c) the amounts of principal and interest payable to the debenture holders by whom or on whose behalf he was appointed and the amounts payable to preferential creditors; and

    (d) the amount (if any) likely to be available for the payment of other creditors.

(2) The administrative receiver shall also, within 3 months (or such longer period as the court may allow) after his appointment, either—

(a)   send a copy of the report (so far as he is aware of their addresses) to all unsecured creditors of the company; or

(b)   publish in the prescribed manner a notice stating an address to which unsecured creditors of the company should write for copies of the report to be sent to them free of charge,

and (in either case), unless the court otherwise directs, lay a copy of the report before a meeting of the company's unsecured creditors summoned for the purpose on not less than 14 days' notice.

(3)   The court shall not give a direction under subsection (2) unless—

(a)   the report states the intention of the administrative receiver to apply for the direction, and

(b)   a copy of the report is sent to the persons mentioned in paragraph (a) of that subsection, or a notice is published as mentioned in paragraph (b) of that subsection, not less than 14 days before the hearing of the application.

(4)   Where the company has gone or goes into liquidation, the administrative receiver—

(a)   shall, within 7 days after his compliance with subsection (1) or, if later, the nomination or appointment of the liquidator, send a copy of the report to the liquidator, and

(b)   where he does so within the time limited for compliance with subsection (2), is not required to comply with that subsection.

(5)   A report under this section shall include a summary of the statement of affairs made out and submitted to the administrative receiver under section 47 and of his comments (if any) upon it.

(6)   Nothing in this section is to be taken as requiring any such report to include any information the disclosure of which would seriously prejudice the carrying out by the administrative receiver of his functions.

(7)   Section 46(2) applies for the purposes of this section also.

(8)   If the administrative receiver without reasonable excuse fails to comply with this section, he is liable to a fine and, for continued contravention, to a daily default fine.

49   Committee of creditors

(1)   Where a meeting of creditors is summoned under section 48, the meeting may, if it thinks fit, establish a committee ("the creditors' committee") to exercise the functions conferred on it by or under this Act.

(2)   If such a committee is established, the committee may, on giving not less than 7 days' notice, require the administrative receiver to attend before it at any reasonable time and furnish it with such information relating to the carrying out by him of his functions as it may reasonably require.

...

CHAPTER III
RECEIVERS' POWERS IN GREAT BRITAIN AS A WHOLE

72   Cross-border operation of receivership provisions

(1)   A receiver appointed under the law of either part of Great Britain in respect of the whole or any part of any property or undertaking of a company and in consequence of the company having created a charge which, as created, was a floating charge may exercise his powers in the other part of Great Britain so far as their exercise is not inconsistent with the law applicable there.

(2)   In subsection (1) "receiver" includes a manager and a person who is appointed both receiver and manager.

CHAPTER IV
PROHIBITION OF APPOINTMENT OF ADMINISTRATIVE RECEIVER

72A   Floating charge holder not to appoint administrative receiver

(1)   The holder of a qualifying floating charge in respect of a company's property may not appoint an administrative receiver of the company.

...
(3) In subsections (1) and (2)—
     "holder of a qualifying floating charge in respect of a company's property" has the same meaning as in paragraph 14 of Schedule B1 to this Act, and
     "administrative receiver" has the meaning given by section 251.
(4) This section applies—
     (a) to a floating charge created on or after a date appointed by the Secretary of State by order made by statutory instrument, and
     (b) in spite of any provision of an agreement or instrument which purports to empower a person to appoint an administrative receiver (by whatever name).
(5) An order under subsection (4)(a) may—
     (a) make provision which applies generally or only for a specified purpose;
     (b) make different provision for different purposes;
     (c) make transitional provision.
(6) This section is subject to the exceptions specified in sections 72B to 72G

72B First exception: capital market

(1) Section 72A does not prevent the appointment of an administrative receiver in pursuance of an agreement which is or forms part of a capital market arrangement if—
     (a) a party incurs or, when the agreement was entered into was expected to incur, a debt of at least £50 million under the arrangement, and
     (b) the arrangement involves the issue of a capital market investment.
(2) In subsection (1)—
     "capital market arrangement" means an arrangement of a kind described in paragraph 1 of Schedule 2A, and
     "capital market investment" means an investment of a kind described in paragraph 2 or 3 of that Schedule.

72C Second exception: public-private partnership

(1) Section 72A does not prevent the appointment of an administrative receiver of a project company of a project which—
     (a) is a public-private partnership project, and
     (b) includes step-in rights.
(2) In this section "public-private partnership project" means a project—
     (a) the resources for which are provided partly by one or more public bodies and partly by one or more private persons, or
     (b) which is designed wholly or mainly for the purpose of assisting a public body to discharge a function.
(3) In this section—
     "step-in rights" has the meaning given by paragraph 6 of Schedule 2A, and
     "project company" has the meaning given by paragraph 7 of that Schedule.

72D Third exception: utilities

72D Third exception: utilities (1) Section 72A does not prevent the appointment of an administrative receiver of a project company of a project which—
     (a) is a utility project, and
     (b) includes step-in rights.
(2) In this section—
     (a) "utility project" means a project designed wholly or mainly for the purpose of a regulated business,
     (b) "regulated business" means a business of a kind listed in paragraph 10 of Schedule 2A,
     (c) "step-in rights" has the meaning given by paragraph 6 of that Schedule, and
     (d) "project company" has the meaning given by paragraph 7 of that Schedule.

72DA Exception in respect of urban regeneration projects

    (1)   Section 72A does not prevent the appointment of an administrative receiver of a project company of a project which—

        (a)   is designed wholly or mainly to develop land which at the commencement of the project is wholly or partly in a designated disadvantaged area outside Northern Ireland, and

        (b)   includes step-in rights.

    (2)   In subsection (1) "develop" means to carry out—

        (a)   building operations,

        (b)   any operation for the removal of substances or waste from land and the levelling of the surface of the land, or

        (c)   engineering operations in connection with the activities mentioned in paragraph (a) or (b).

    (3)   In this section—

        "building" includes any structure or erection, and any part of a building as so defined, but does not include plant and machinery comprised in a building,

        "building operations" includes—

        (a)   demolition of buildings,

        (b)   filling in of trenches,

        (c)   rebuilding,

        (d)   structural alterations of, or additions to, buildings and

        (e)   other operations normally undertaken by a person carrying on business as a builder,

        "designated disadvantaged area" means an area designated as a disadvantaged area under section 92 of the Finance Act 2001,

        "engineering operations" includes the formation and laying out of means of access to highways,

        "project company" has the meaning given by paragraph 7 of Schedule 2A,

        "step-in rights" has the meaning given by paragraph 6 of that Schedule,

        "substance" means any natural or artificial substance whether in solid or liquid form or in the form of a gas or vapour, and

        "waste" includes any waste materials, spoil, refuse or other matter deposited on land.

72E Fourth exception: project finance

    (1)   Section 72A does not prevent the appointment of an administrative receiver of a project company of a project which—

        (a)   is a financed project, and

        (b)   includes step-in rights.

    (2)   In this section—

        (a)   a project is "financed" if under an agreement relating to the project a project company incurs, or when the agreement is entered into is expected to incur, a debt of at least £50 million for the purposes of carrying out the project,

        (b)   "project company" has the meaning given by paragraph 7 of Schedule 2A, and

        (c)   "step-in rights" has the meaning given by paragraph 6 of that Schedule.

72F Fifth exception: financial market

Section 72A does not prevent the appointment of an administrative receiver of a company by virtue of—

    (a)   a market charge within the meaning of section 173 of the Companies Act 1989,

    (b)   a system-charge within the meaning of the Financial Markets and Insolvency Regulations 1996,

    (c)   a collateral security charge within the meaning of the Financial Markets and Insolvency (Settlement Finality) Regulations 1999.

72G Sixth exception: registered social landlord

Section 72A does not prevent the appointment of an administrative receiver of a company which is registered as a social landlord under Part I of the Housing Act 1996 …

72GA Exception in relation to protected railway companies etc

Section 72A does not prevent the appointment of an administrative receiver of—

(a) a company holding an appointment under Chapter I of Part II of the Water Industry Act 1991,

(b) a protected railway company within the meaning of section 59 of the Railways Act 1993 (including that section as it has effect by virtue of section 19 of the Channel Tunnel Rail Link Act 1996, or

(c) a licence company within the meaning of section 26 of the Transport Act 2000.

...

PART IV
WINDING UP OF COMPANIES REGISTERED UNDER THE COMPANIES ACTS
CHAPTER I
PRELIMINARY

Modes of winding up

73 Alternative modes of winding up

(1) The winding up of a company, within the meaning given to that expression by section 735 of the Companies Act, may be either voluntary (Chapters II, III, IV and V in this Part) or by the court (Chapter VI).

...

Contributories

74 Liability as contributories of present and past members

(1) When a company is wound up, every present and past member is liable to contribute to its assets to any amount sufficient for payment of its debts and liabilities, and the expenses of the winding up, and for the adjustment of the rights of the contributories among themselves.

(2) This is subject as follows—

(a) a past member is not liable to contribute if he has ceased to be a member for one year or more before the commencement of the winding up;

(b) a past member is not liable to contribute in respect of any debt or liability of the company contracted after he ceased to be a member;

(c) a past member is not liable to contribute, unless it appears to the court that the existing members are unable to satisfy the contributions required to be made by them in pursuance of the Companies Act and this Act;

(d) in the case of a company limited by shares, no contribution is required from any member exceeding the amount (if any) unpaid on the shares in respect of which he is liable as a present or past member;

(e) nothing in the Companies Act or this Act invalidates any provision contained in a policy of insurance or other contract whereby the liability of individual members on the policy or contract is restricted, or whereby the funds of the company are alone made liable in respect of the policy or contract;

(f) a sum due to any member of the company (in his character of a member) by way of dividends, profits or otherwise is not deemed to be a debt of the company, payable to that member in a case of competition between himself and any other creditor not a member of the company, but any such sum may be taken into account for the purpose of the final adjustment of the rights of the contributories among themselves.

(3) In the case of a company limited by guarantee, no contribution is required from any member exceeding the amount undertaken to be contributed by him to the company's assets in the event of its being wound up; but if it is a company with a share capital, every member of it is liable (in addition to the amount so undertaken to be contributed to the assets), to contribute to the extent of any sums unpaid on shares held by him.

75 Directors, etc with unlimited liability

(1) In the winding up of a limited company, any director or manager (whether past or present) whose liability is under the Companies Act unlimited is liable, in addition to his liability (if any) to contribute as an ordinary member, to make a further contribution as if he were at the commencement of the winding up a member of an unlimited company.

(2) However—

(a) a past director or manager is not liable to make such further contribution if he has ceased to hold office for a year or more before the commencement of the winding up;

(b) a past director or manager is not liable to make such further contribution in respect of any debt or liability of the company contracted after he ceased to hold office;

(c) subject to the company's articles, a director or manager is not liable to make such further contribution unless the court deems it necessary to require that contribution in order to satisfy the company's debts and liabilities, and the expenses of the winding up.

76 Liability of past directors and shareholders

(1) This section applies where a company is being wound up and—

(a) it has under Chapter VII of Part V of the Companies Act (redeemable shares; purchase by a company of its own shares) made a payment out of capital in respect of the redemption or purchase of any of its own shares (the payment being referred to below as "the relevant payment"), and

(b) the aggregate amount of the company's assets and the amounts paid by way of contribution to its assets (apart from this section) is not sufficient for payment of its debts and liabilities, and the expenses of the winding up.

(2) If the winding up commenced within one year of the date on which the relevant payment was made, then—

(a) the person from whom the shares were redeemed or purchased, and

(b) the directors who signed the statutory declaration made in accordance with section 173(3) of the Companies Act for purposes of the redemption or purchase (except a director who shows that he had reasonable grounds for forming the opinion set out in the declaration,

are, so as to enable that insufficiency to be met, liable to contribute to the following extent to the company's assets.

(3) A person from whom any of the shares were redeemed or purchased is liable to contribute an amount not exceeding so much of the relevant payment as was made by the company in respect of his shares; and the directors are jointly and severally liable with that person to contribute that amount.

(4) A person who has contributed any amount to the assets in pursuance of this section may apply to the court for an order directing any other person jointly and severally liable in respect of that amount to pay him such amount as the court thinks just and equitable.

…

…

78 Unlimited company formerly limited

(1) This section applies in the case of a company being wound up which was at some former time registered as limited but has been re-registered as unlimited under section 49 of the Companies Act (or the former corresponding provision, section 43 of the Companies Act 1967).

(2) A person who, at the time when the application for the company to be re-registered was lodged, was a past member of the company and did not after that again become a member of it is not liable to contribute to the assets of the company more than he would have been liable to contribute had the company not been re-registered.

79 Meaning of "contributory"

(1) In this Act and the Companies Act the expression "contributory" means every person liable to contribute to the assets of a company in the event of its being wound up, and for the

purposes of all proceedings for determining, and all proceedings prior to the final determination of, the persons who are to be deemed contributories, includes any person alleged to be a contributory.

(2) The reference in subsection (1) to persons liable to contribute to the assets does not include a person so liable by virtue of a declaration by the court under section 213 (imputed responsibility for company's fraudulent trading) or section 214 (wrongful trading) in Chapter X of this Part.

...

80 Nature of contributory's liability

The liability of a contributory creates a debt (in England and Wales in the nature of a speciality) accruing due from him at the time when his liability commenced, but payable at the times when calls are made for enforcing the liability.

81 Contributories in case of death of a member

(1) If a contributory dies either before or after he has been placed on the list of contributories, his personal representatives, and the heirs ... are liable in a due course of administration to contribute to the assets of the company in discharge of his liability and are contributories accordingly.

(2) Where the personal representatives are placed on the list of contributories, the heirs ... need not be added, but they may be added as and when the court thinks fit.

(3) If in England and Wales the personal representatives make default in paying any money ordered to be paid by them, proceedings may be taken for administering the estate of the deceased contributory and for compelling payment out of it of the money due.

82 Effect of contributory's bankruptcy

(1) The following applies if a contributory becomes bankrupt, either before or after he has been placed on the list of contributories.

(2) His trustee in bankruptcy represents him for all purposes of the winding up, and is a contributory accordingly.

(3) The trustee may be called on to admit to proof against the bankrupt's estate, or otherwise allow to be paid out of the bankrupt's assets in due course of law, any money due from the bankrupt in respect of his liability to contribute to the company's assets.

(4) There may be proved against the bankrupt's estate the estimated value of his liability to future calls as well as calls already made.

...

CHAPTER II
VOLUNTARY WINDING UP (INTRODUCTORY AND GENERAL)

Resolutions for, and commencement of, voluntary winding up

84 Circumstances in which company may be wound up voluntarily

(1) A company may be wound up voluntarily—

(a) when the period (if any) fixed for the duration of the company by the articles expires, or the event (if any) occurs, on the occurrence of which the articles provide that the company is to be dissolved, and the company in general meeting has passed a resolution requiring it be wound up voluntarily;

(b) if the company resolves by special resolution that it be wound up voluntarily;

(c) if the company resolves by extraordinary resolution to the effect that it cannot by reason of its liabilities continue its business, and that it is advisable to wind up.

(2) In this Act the expression "a resolution for voluntary winding up" means a resolution passed under any of the paragraphs of subsection (1).

(2A) Before a company passes a resolution for voluntary winding up it must give written notice of the resolution to the holder of any qualifying floating charge to which section 72A applies.

(2B) Where notice is given under subsection (2A) a resolution for voluntary winding up may be passed only—

      (a)   after the end of the period of five business days beginning with the day on which the notice was given, or

      (b)   if the person to whom the notice was given has consented in writing to the passing of the resolution.

  (3)   A resolution passed under paragraph (a) of subsection (1), as well as a special resolution under paragraph (b) and an extraordinary resolution under paragraph (c), is subject to section 380 of the Companies Act (copy of resolution to be forwarded to registrar of companies within 15 days).

...

85   Notice of resolution to wind up

  (1)   When a company has passed a resolution for voluntary winding up, it shall, within 14 days after the passing of the resolution, give notice of the resolution by advertisement in the Gazette.

  (2)   If default is made in complying with this section, the company and every officer of it who is in default is liable to a fine and, for continued contravention, to a daily default fine.

      For purposes of this subsection the liquidator is deemed an officer of the company.

86   Commencement of winding up

A voluntary winding up is deemed to commence at the time of the passing of the resolution for voluntary winding up.

Consequences of resolution to wind up

87   Effect on business and status of company

  (1)   In case of a voluntary winding up, the company shall from the commencement of the winding up cease to carry on its business, except so far as may be required for its beneficial winding up.

  (2)   However, the corporate state and corporate powers of the company, notwithstanding anything to the contrary in its articles, continue until the company is dissolved.

88   Avoidance of share transfers, etc after winding-up resolution

Any transfer of shares, not being a transfer made to or with the sanction of the liquidator, and any alteration in the status of the company's members, made after the commencement of a voluntary winding up, is void.

Declaration of solvency

89   Statutory declaration of solvency

  (1)   Where it is proposed to wind up a company voluntarily, the directors (or, in the case of a company having more than two directors, the majority of them) may at a directors' meeting make a statutory declaration to the effect that they have made a full inquiry into the company's affairs and that, having done so, they have formed the opinion that the company will be able to pay its debts in full, together with interest at the official rate (as defined in section 251), within such period, not exceeding 12 months from the commencement of the winding up, as may be specified in the declaration.

  (2)   Such a declaration by the directors has no effect for purposes of this Act unless—

      (a)   it is made within the 5 weeks immediately preceding the date of the passing of the resolution for winding up, or on that date but before the passing of the resolution, and

      (b)   it embodies a statement of the company's assets and liabilities as at the latest practicable date before the making of the declaration.

  (3)   The declaration shall be delivered to the registrar of companies before the expiration of 15 days immediately following the date on which the resolution for winding up is passed.

  (4)   A director making a declaration under this section without having reasonable grounds for the opinion that the company will be able to pay its debts in full, together with interest at the official rate, within the period specified is liable to imprisonment or a fine, or both.

  (5)   If the company is wound up in pursuance of a resolution passed within 5 weeks after the making of the declaration, and its debts (together with interest at the official rate) are not

paid or provided for in full within the period specified, it is to be presumed (unless the contrary is shown) that the director did not have reasonable grounds for his opinion.

...

90   **Distinction between "members'" and "creditors'" voluntary winding up**

A winding up in the case of which a directors' statutory declaration under section 89 has been made is a "members' voluntary winding up"; and a winding up in the case of which such a declaration has not been made is a "creditors' voluntary winding up".

CHAPTER III
MEMBERS' VOLUNTARY WINDING UP

91   **Appointment of liquidator**

(1) In a members' voluntary winding up, the company in general meeting shall appoint one or more liquidators for the purpose of winding up the company's affairs and distributing its assets.

(2) On the appointment of a liquidator all the powers of the directors cease, except so far as the company in general meeting or the liquidator sanctions their continuance.

92   **Power to fill vacancy in office of liquidator**

(1) If a vacancy occurs by death resignation or otherwise in the office of liquidator appointed by the company, the company in general meeting may, subject to any arrangement with its creditors, fill the vacancy.

(2) For that purpose a general meeting may be convened by any contributory or, if there were more liquidators than one, by the continuing liquidators.

(3) The meeting shall be held in manner provided by this Act or by the articles, or in such manner as may, on application by any contributory or by the continuing liquidators, be determined by the court.

93   **General company meeting at each year's end**

(1) Subject to sections 96 and 102, in the event of the winding up continuing for more than one year, the liquidator shall summon a general meeting of the company at the end of the first year from the commencement of the winding up, and of each succeeding year, or at the first convenient date within 3 months from the end of the year or such longer period as the Secretary of State may allow.

(2) The liquidator shall lay before the meeting an account of his acts and dealings, and of the conduct of the winding up, during the preceding year.

(3) If the liquidator fails to comply with this section, he is liable to a fine.

94   **Final meeting prior to dissolution**

(1) As soon as the company's affairs are fully wound up, the liquidator shall make up an account of the winding up showing how it has been conducted and the company's property has been disposed of, and thereupon shall call a general meeting of the company for the purpose of laying before it the account, and giving an explanation of it.

(2) The meeting shall be called by advertisement in the Gazette, specifying its time, place and object and published at least one month before the meeting.

(3) Within one week after the meeting, the liquidator shall send to the registrar of companies a copy of the account, and shall make a return to him of the holding of the meeting and of its date.

(4) If the copy is not sent or the return is not made in accordance with subsection (3), the liquidator is liable to a fine and, for continued contravention, to a daily default fine.

(5) If a quorum is not present at the meeting, the liquidator shall, in *lieu* of the return mentioned above, make a return that the meeting was duly summoned and that no quorum was present; and upon such a return being made, the provisions of subsection (3) as to the making of the return are deemed complied with.

(6) If the liquidator fails to call a general meeting of the company as required by subsection (1), he is liable to a fine.

95   Effect of company's insolvency

(1)   This section applies where the liquidator is of the opinion that the company will be unable to pay its debts in full (together with interest at the official rate) within the period stated in the directors' declaration under section 89.

(2)   The liquidator shall—

(a)   summon a meeting of creditors for a day not later than the 28th day after the day on which he formed that opinion;

(b)   send notices of the creditors' meeting to the creditors by post not less than 7 days before the day on which that meeting is to be held;

(c)   cause notice of the creditors' meeting to be advertised once in the Gazette and once at least in 2 newspapers circulating in the relevant locality (that is to say the locality in which the company's principal place of business in Great Britain was situated during the relevant period); and

(d)   during the period before the day on which the creditors' meeting is to be held, furnish creditors free of charge with such information concerning the affairs of the company as they may reasonably require;

and the notice of the creditors' meeting shall state the duty imposed by paragraph (d) above.

(3)   The liquidator shall also—

(a)   make out a statement in the prescribed form as to the affairs of the company;

(b)   lay that statement before the creditors' meeting; and

(c)   attend and preside at that meeting.

(4)   The statement as to the affairs of the company shall be verified by affidavit by the liquidator and shall show—

(a)   particulars of the company's assets, debts and liabilities;

(b)   the names and addresses of the company's creditors;

(c)   the securities held by them respectively;

(d)   the dates when the securities were respectively given; and

(e)   such further or other information as may be prescribed.

(5)   Where the company's principal place of business in Great Britain was situated in different localities at different times during the relevant period, the duty imposed by subsection (2)(c) applies separately in relation to each of those localities.

(6)   Where the company had no place of business in Great Britain during the relevant period, references in subsections (2)(c) and (5) to the company's principal place of business in Great Britain are replaced by references to its registered office.

(7)   In this section "the relevant period" means the period of 6 months immediately preceding the day on which were sent the notices summoning the company meeting at which it was resolved that the company be wound up voluntarily.

(8)   If the liquidator without reasonable excuse fails to comply with this section, he is liable to a fine.

96   Conversion to creditors' voluntary winding up

As from the day on which the creditors' meeting is held under section 95, this Act has effect as if—

(a)   the directors' declaration under section 89 had not been made; and

(b)   the creditors' meeting and the company meeting at which it was resolved that the company be wound up voluntarily were the meetings mentioned in section 98 in the next Chapter; and accordingly the winding up becomes a creditors' voluntary winding up.

CHAPTER IV

CREDITORS' VOLUNTARY WINDING UP

97   Application of this Chapter

(1)   Subject as follows, this Chapter applies in relation to a creditors' voluntary winding up.

(2)   Sections 98 and 99 do not apply where, under section 96 in Chapter III, a members' voluntary winding up has become a creditors' voluntary winding up.

98   Meeting of creditors

    (1)   The company shall—

        (a)   cause a meeting of its creditors to be summoned for a day not later than the 14th day after the day on which there is to be held the company meeting at which the resolution for voluntary winding up is to be proposed;

        (b)   cause the notices of the creditors' meeting to be sent by post to the creditors not less than 7 days before the day on which that meeting is to be held; and

        (c)   cause notice of the creditors' meeting to be advertised once in the Gazette and once at least in two newspapers circulating in the relevant locality (that is to say the locality in which the company's principal place of business in Great Britain was situated during the relevant period).

    (2)   The notice of the creditors' meeting shall state either—

        (a)   the name and address of a person qualified to act as an insolvency practitioner in relation to the company who, during the period before the day on which that meeting is to be held, will furnish creditors free of charge with such information concerning the company's affairs as they may reasonably require; or

        (b)   a place in the relevant locality where, on the two business days falling next before the day on which that meeting is to be held, a list of the names and addresses of the company's creditors will be available for inspection free of charge.

    (3)   Where the company's principal place of business in Great Britain was situated in different localities at different times during the relevant period, the duties imposed by subsections (1)(c) and (2)(b) above apply separately in relation to each of those localities.

    (4)   Where the company had no place of business in Great Britain during the relevant period, references in subsections (1)(c) and (3) to the company's principal place of business in Great Britain are replaced by references to its registered office.

    (5)   In this section "the relevant period" means the period of 6 months immediately preceding the day on which were sent the notices summoning the company meeting at which it was resolved that the company be wound up voluntarily.

    (6)   If the company without reasonable excuse fails to comply with subsection (1) or (2), it is guilty of an offence and liable to a fine.

99   Directors to lay statement of affairs before creditors

    (1)   The directors of the company shall—

        (a)   make out a statement in the prescribed form as to the affairs of the company;

        (b)   cause that statement to be laid before the creditors' meeting under section 98; and

        (c)   appoint one of their number to preside at that meeting;

    and it is the duty of the director so appointed to attend the meeting and preside over it.

    (2)   The statement as to the affairs of the company shall be verified by affidavit by some or all of the directors and shall show—

        (a)   particulars of the company's assets, debts and liabilities;

        (b)   the names and addresses of the company's creditors;

        (c)   the securities held by them respectively;

        (d)   the dates when the securities were respectively given; and

        (e)   such further or other information as may be prescribed.

    (3)   If—

        (a)   the directors without reasonable excuse fail to comply with subsection (1) or (2); or

        (b)   any director without reasonable excuse fails to comply with subsection (1), so far as requiring him to attend and preside at the creditors' meeting,

    the directors are or (as the case may be) the director is guilty of an offence and liable to a fine.

100   Appointment of liquidator

    (1)   The creditors and the company at their respective meetings mentioned in section 98 may nominate a person to be liquidator for the purpose of winding up the company's affairs and distributing its assets.

(2)   The liquidator shall be the person nominated by the creditors or, where no person has been so nominated, the person (if any) nominated by the company.

(3)   In the case of different persons being nominated, any director, member or creditor of the company may, within 7 days after the date on which the nomination was made by the creditors, apply to the court for an order either—

(a)   directing that the person nominated as liquidator by the company shall be liquidator instead of or jointly with the person nominated by the creditors, or

(b)   appointing some other person to be liquidator instead of the person nominated by the creditors.

101   Appointment of liquidation committee

(1)   The creditors at the meeting to be held under section 98 or at any subsequent meeting may, if they think fit, appoint a committee ("the liquidation committee") of not more than 5 persons to exercise the functions conferred on it by or under this Act.

(2)   If such a committee is appointed, the company may, either at the meeting at which the resolution for voluntary winding up is passed or at any time subsequently in general meeting, appoint such number of persons as they think fit to act as members of the committee, not exceeding 5.

(3)   However, the creditors may, if they think fit, resolve that all or any of the persons so appointed by the company ought not to be members of the liquidation committee; and if the creditors so resolve—

(a)   the persons mentioned in the resolution are not then, unless the court otherwise directs, qualified to act as members of the committee; and

(b)   on any application to the court under this provision the court may, if it thinks fit, appoint other persons to act as such members in place of the persons mentioned in the resolution.

...

102   Creditors' meeting where winding up converted under s 96

Where, in the case of a winding up which was under section 96 in Chapter III, converted to a creditors' voluntary winding up, a creditors' meeting is held in accordance with section 95, any appointment made or committee established by that meeting is deemed to have been made or established by a meeting held in accordance with section 98 in this Chapter.

103   Cesser of directors' powers

On the appointment of a liquidator, all the powers of the directors cease, except so far as the liquidation committee (or, if there is no such committee, the creditors) sanction their continuance.

104   Vacancy in office of liquidator

If a vacancy occurs, by death, resignation or otherwise, in the office of a liquidator (other than a liquidator appointed by, or by the direction of, the court), the creditors may fill the vacancy.

105   Meetings of company and creditors at each year's end

(1)   If the winding up continues for more than one year, the liquidator shall summon a general meeting of the company and a meeting of the creditors at the end of the first year from the commencement of the winding up, and of each succeeding year, or at the first convenient date within 3 months from the end of the year or such longer period as the Secretary of State may allow.

(2)   The liquidator shall lay before each of the meetings an account of his acts and dealings and of the conduct of the winding up during the preceding year.

(3)   If the liquidator fails to comply with this section, he is liable to a fine.

(4)   Where under section 96 a members' voluntary winding up has become a creditors' voluntary winding up, and the creditors' meeting under section 95 is held 3 months or less before the end of the first year from the commencement of the winding up, the liquidator is not required by this section to summon a meeting of creditors at the end of that year.

106   Final meeting prior to dissolution

(1)   As soon as the company's affairs are fully wound up, the liquidator shall make up an account of the winding up, showing how it has been conducted and the company's property has been disposed of, and thereupon shall call a general meeting of the company and a meeting of the creditors for the purpose of laying the account before the meetings and giving an explanation of it.

(2)   Each such meeting shall be called by advertisement in the Gazette specifying the time, place and object of the meeting, and published at least one month before it.

(3)   Within one week after the date of the meetings (or, if they are not held on the same date, after the date of the later one) the liquidator shall send to the registrar of companies a copy of the account, and shall make a return to him of the holding of the meetings and of their dates.

(4)   If the copy is not sent or the return is not made in accordance with subsection (3), the liquidator is liable to a fine and, for continued contravention, to a daily default fine.

(5)   However, if a quorum is not present at either such meeting, the liquidator shall, in lieu of the return required by subsection (3), make a return that the meeting was duly summoned and that no quorum was present; and upon such return being made the provisions of that subsection as to the making of the return are, in respect of that meeting, deemed complied with.

(6)   If the liquidator fails to call a general meeting of the company or a meeting of the creditors as required by this section, he is liable to a fine.

CHAPTER V
PROVISIONS APPLYING TO BOTH KINDS OF VOLUNTARY WINDING UP

107   Distribution of company's property

Subject to the provisions of this Act as to preferential payments, the company's property in a voluntary winding up shall on the winding up be applied in satisfaction of the company's liabilities *pari passu* and, subject to that application, shall (unless the articles otherwise provide) be distributed among the members according to their rights and interests in the company.

108   Appointment or removal of liquidator by the court

(1)   If from any cause whatever there is no liquidator acting, the court may appoint a liquidator.

(2)   The court may, on cause shown, remove a liquidator and appoint another.

109   Notice by liquidator of his appointment

(1)   The liquidator shall, within 14 days after his appointment, publish in the Gazette and deliver to the registrar of companies for registration a notice of his appointment in the form prescribed by statutory instrument made by the Secretary of State.

(2)   If the liquidator fails to comply with this section, he is liable to a fine and, for continued contravention, to a daily default fine.

110   Acceptance of shares, etc, as consideration for sale of company property

(1)   This section applies, in the case of a company proposed to be, or being, wound up voluntarily, where the whole or part of the company's business or property is proposed to be transferred or sold—

(a)   to another company ("the transferee company"), whether or not the latter is a company within the meaning of the Companies Act or

(b)   to a limited liability partnership (the "transferee limited liability partnership").

(2)   With the requisite sanction, the liquidator of the company being, or proposed to be, wound up ("the transferor company") may receive, in compensation or part compensation for the transfer or sale—

(a)   in the case of the transferee company, shares, policies or other like interests in the transferee company for distribution among the members of the transferor company, or

(b)   in the case of the transferee limited liability partnership, membership in the transferee limited liability partnership for distribution among the members of the transferor company.

(3) The sanction requisite under subsection (2) is—

    (a) in the case of a members' voluntary winding up, that of a special resolution of the company, conferring either a general authority on the liquidator or an authority in respect of any particular arrangement, and

    (b) in the case of a creditors' voluntary winding up, that of either the court or the liquidation committee.

(4) Alternatively to subsection (2), the liquidator may (with that sanction) enter into any other arrangement whereby the members of the transferor company may—

    (a) in the case of the transferee company, in *lieu* of receiving cash, shares, policies or other like interests (or in addition thereto) participate in the profits of, or receive any other benefit from, the transferee company, or

    (b) in the case of the transferee limited liability partnership, in lieu of receiving cash or membership (or in addition thereto), participate in some other way in the profits of, or receive any other benefit from, the transferee limited liability partnership.

(5) A sale or arrangement in pursuance of this section is binding on members of the transferor company.

(6) A special resolution is not invalid for purposes of this section by reason that it is passed before or concurrently with a resolution for voluntary winding up or for appointing liquidators; but, if an order is made within a year for winding up the company by the court, the special resolution is not valid unless sanctioned by the court.

111 Dissent from arrangement under s 110

(1) This section applies in the case of a voluntary winding up where, for the purposes of section 110(2) or (4), there has been passed a special resolution of the transferor company providing the sanction requisite for the liquidator under that section.

(2) If a member of the transferor company who did not vote in favour of the special resolution expresses his dissent from it in writing, addressed to the liquidator and left at the company's registered office within 7 days after the passing of the resolution, he may require the liquidator either to abstain from carrying the resolution into effect or to purchase his interest at a price to be determined by agreement or by arbitration under this section.

(3) If the liquidator elects to purchase the member's interest, the purchase money must be paid before the company is dissolved and be raised by the liquidator in such manner as may be determined by special resolution.

...

112 Reference of questions to court

(1) The liquidator or any contributory or creditor may apply to the court to determine any question arising in the winding up of a company, or to exercise, as respects the enforcing of calls or any other matter, all or any of the powers which the court might exercise if the company were being wound up by the court.

(2) The court, if satisfied that the determination of the question or the required exercise of power will be just and beneficial, may accede wholly or partially to the application on such terms and conditions as it thinks fit, or may make such other order on the application as it thinks just.

(3) A copy of an order made by virtue of this section staying the proceedings in the winding up shall forthwith be forwarded by the company, or otherwise as may be prescribed, to the registrar of companies, who shall enter it in his records relating to the company.

...

114 No liquidator appointed or nominated by company

(1) This section applies where, in the case of a voluntary winding up, no liquidator has been appointed or nominated by the company.

(2) The powers of the directors shall not be exercised, except with the sanction of the court or (in the case of a creditors' voluntary winding up) so far as may be necessary to secure compliance with sections 98 (creditors' meeting) and 99 (statement of affairs), during the period before the appointment or nomination of a liquidator of the company.

(3) Subsection (2) does not apply in relation to the powers of the directors—

    (a)   to dispose of perishable goods and other goods the value of which is likely to diminish if they are not immediately disposed of, and

    (b)   to do all such other things as may be necessary for the protection of the company's assets.

(4) If the directors of the company without reasonable excuse fail to comply with this section, they are liable to a fine.

115 Expenses of voluntary winding up

All expenses properly incurred in the winding up, including the remuneration of the liquidator, are payable out of the company's assets in priority to all other claims.

116 Saving for certain rights

The voluntary winding up of a company does not bar the right of any creditor or contributory to have it wound up by the court; but in the case of an application by a contributory the court must be satisfied that the rights of the contributories will be prejudiced by a voluntary winding up.

CHAPTER VI

WINDING UP BY THE COURT

Jurisdiction (England and Wales)

117 High Court and county court jurisdiction

(1) The High Court has jurisdiction to wind up any company registered in England and Wales.

(2) Where the amount of a company's share capital paid up or credited as paid up does not exceed £120,000, then (subject to this section) the county court of the district in which the company's registered office is situated has concurrent jurisdiction with the High Court to wind up the company.

...

(4) The Lord Chancellor may, with the concurrence of the Lord Chief Justice, by order in a statutory instrument exclude a county court from having winding-up jurisdiction, and for the purposes of that jurisdiction may attach its district, or any part thereof, to any other county court, and may by statutory instrument revoke or vary any such order.

In exercising the powers of this section, the Lord Chancellor shall provide that a county court is not to have winding-up jurisdiction unless it has for the time being jurisdiction for the purposes of Parts VIII to XI of this Act (individual insolvency).

(5) Every court in England and Wales having winding-up jurisdiction has for the purposes of that jurisdiction all the powers of the High Court; and every prescribed officer of the court shall perform any duties which an officer of the High Court may discharge by order of a judge of that court or otherwise in relation to winding up.

(6) For the purposes of this section, a company's "registered office" is the place which has longest been its registered office during the 6 months immediately preceding the presentation of the petition for winding up.

(7) This section is subject to Article 3 of the EC Regulation (jurisdiction under EC Regulation).

...

118 Proceedings taken in wrong court

(1) Nothing in section 117 invalidates a proceeding by reason of its being taken in the wrong court.

(2) The winding up of a company by the court in England and Wales, or any proceedings in the winding up, may be retained in the court in which the proceedings were commenced, although it may not be the court in which they ought to have been commenced.

119 Proceedings in county court; case stated for High Court

(1) If any question arises in any winding-up proceedings in a county court which all the parties to the proceedings, or which one of them and the judge of the court, desire to have determined in the first instance in the High Court, the judge shall state the facts in the form of a special case for the opinion of the High Court.

(2) Thereupon the special case and the proceedings (or such of them as may be required) shall
     be transmitted to the High Court for the purposes of the determination.

...

Grounds and effect of winding-up petition

122   Circumstances in which company may be wound up by the court

(1) A company may be wound up by the court if—

    (a) the company has by special resolution resolved that the company be wound up by the
        court.

    (b) being a public company which was registered as such on its original incorporation, the
        company has not been issued with a certificate under section 117 of the Companies
        Act (public company share capital requirements) and more than a year has expired
        since it was so registered,

    ...

    (d) the company does not commence its business within a year from its incorporation or
        suspends its business for a whole year,

    (e) except in the case of a private company limited by shares or by guarantee, the number
        of members is reduced below 2,

    (f) the company is unable to pay its debts,

    (fa) at the time at which a moratorium for the company under section 1A comes to an end,
        no voluntary arrangement approved under Part I has effect in relation to the company.

    (g) the court is of the opinion that it is just and equitable that the company should be
        wound up.

...

For this purpose a creditor's security is deemed to be in jeopardy if the Court is satisfied that events
have occurred or are about to occur which render it unreasonable in the creditor's interests that the
company should retain power to dispose of the property which is subject to the floating charge.

123   Definition of inability to pay debts

(1) A company is deemed unable to pay its debts—

    (a) if a creditor (by assignment or otherwise) to whom the company is indebted in a sum
        exceeding £750 then due has served on the company, by leaving it at the company's
        registered office, a written demand (in the prescribed form) requiring the company to
        pay the sum so due and the company has for 3 weeks thereafter neglected to pay the
        sum or to secure or compound for it to the reasonable satisfaction of the creditor, or

    (b) if, in England and Wales, execution or other process issued on a judgment, decree or
        order of any court in favour of a creditor of the company is returned unsatisfied in
        whole or in part, or

    ...

    (d) if, in Northern Ireland, a certificate of unenforceability has been granted in respect of a
        judgment against the company, or

    (e) if it is proved to the satisfaction of the court that the company is unable to pay its debts
        as they fall due.

(2) A company is also deemed unable to pay its debts if it is proved to the satisfaction of the
     court that the value of the company's assets is less than the amount of its liabilities, taking
     into account its contingent and prospective liabilities.

    ...

124   Application for winding up

(1) Subject to the provisions of this section, an application to the court for the winding up of a
     company shall be by petition presented either by the company, or the directors, or by any
     creditor or creditors (including any contingent or prospective creditor or creditors),
     contributory or contributories, or by a liquidator (within the meaning of Article 2(b) of the
     EC Regulation) appointed in proceedings by virtue of Article 3(1) of the EC Regulation or a
     temporary administrator (within the meaning of Article 38 of the EC Regulation), or by the

designated officer for a magistrates' court in the exercise of the power conferred by section 87A of the Magistrates' Courts Act 1980 (enforcement of fines imposed on companies) or by all or any of those parties, together or separately.

(2) Except as mentioned below, a contributory is not entitled to present a winding-up petition unless either—

(a) the number of members is reduced below 2, or

(b) the shares in respect of which he is a contributory, or some of them, either were originally allotted to him, or have been held by him, and registered in his name, for at least 6 months during the 18 months before the commencement of the winding up, or have devolved on him through the death of a former holder.

(3) A person who is liable under section 76 to contribute to a company's assets in the event of its being wound up may petition on either of the grounds set out in section 122(1)(f) and (g), and subsection (2) above does not then apply; but unless the person is a contributory otherwise than under section 76, he may not in his character as contributory petition on any other ground.

...

(3A) A winding-up petition on the ground set out in section 122(1)(fa) may only be presented by one or more creditors.

(4) A winding-up petition may be presented by the Secretary of State—

(a) if the ground of the petition is that in section 122(1)(b) or (c), or

(b) in a case falling within section 124A or 124B below.

(4AA)A winding up petition may be presented by the Financial Services Authority in a case falling within section 124C(1) or (2).

(4A) A winding-up petition may be presented by the Regulator of Community Interest Companies in a case falling within section 50 of the Companies (Audit, Investigations and Community Enterprise) Act 2004.

(5) Where a company is being wound up voluntarily in England and Wales, a winding-up petition may be presented by the official receiver attached to the court as well as by any other person authorised in that behalf under the other provisions of this section; but the court shall not make a winding-up order on the petition unless it is satisfied that the voluntary winding up cannot be continued with due regard to the interests of the creditors or contributories.

124A   Petition for winding up on grounds of public interest

(1) Where it appears to the Secretary of State from—

(a) any report made or information obtained under Part XIV (except section 448A) of the Companies Act 1985 (company investigations, &c.),

(b) any report made by inspectors under—

(i) section 167, 168, 169 or 284 of the Financial Services and Markets Act 2000, or

(ii) where the company is an open-ended investment company (within the meaning of that Act), regulations made as a result of section 262(2)(k) of that Act;

(bb) any information or documents obtained under section 165, 171, 172, 173 or 175 of that Act,

(c) any information obtained under section 2 of the Criminal Justice Act 1987 or section 52 of the Criminal Justice (Scotland) Act 1987 (fraud investigations), or

(d) any information obtained under section 83 of the Companies Act 1989 (powers exercisable for purpose of assisting overseas regulatory authorities),

that it is expedient in the public interest that a company should be wound up, he may present a petition for it to be wound up if the court thinks it just and equitable for it to be so.

(2) This section does not apply if the company is already being wound up by the court.

124B   Petition for winding up of SE

(1) Where—

(a) an SE whose registered office is in Great Britain is not in compliance with Article 7 of Council Regulation (EC) No 2157/2001 on the Statute for a European company (the "EC Regulation") (location of head office and registered office), and

(b) it appears to the Secretary of State that the SE should be wound up, he may present a petition for it to be wound up if the court thinks it is just and equitable for it to be so.

(2) This section does not apply if the SE is already being wound up by the court.

(3) In this section "SE" has the same meaning as in the EC Regulation.

124C Petition for winding up of SCE

(1) Where, in the case of an SCE whose registered office is in Great Britain—

(a) there has been such a breach as is mentioned in Article 73(1) of Council Regulation (EC) No 1435/2003 on the Statute for a European Cooperative Society (SCE) (the "European Cooperative Society Regulation") (winding up by the court or other competent authority), and

(b) it appears to the Financial Services Authority that the SCE should be wound up,

the Authority may present a petition for the SCE to be wound up if the court thinks it is just and equitable for it to be so.

(2) Where, in the case of an SCE whose registered office is in Great Britain—

(a) the SCE is not in compliance with Article 6 of the European Cooperative Society Regulation (location of head office and registered office, and

(b) it appears to the Financial Service Authority that the SCE should be wound up,

the Authority may present a petition for the SCE to be wound up if the court thinks it is just and equitable for it to be so.

(3) This section does not apply if the SCE is already being wound up by the court.

(4) In this section "SCE" has the same meaning as in the European Cooperative Society Regulation.

125 Powers of court on hearing of petition

(1) On hearing a winding-up petition the court may dismiss it, or adjourn the hearing conditionally or unconditionally, or make an interim order, or any other order that it thinks fit; but the court shall not refuse to make a winding-up order on the ground only that the company's assets have been mortgaged to an amount equal to or in excess of those assets, or that the company has no assets.

(2) If the petition is presented by members of the company as contributories on the ground that it is just and equitable that the company should be wound up, the court, if it is of opinion—

(a) that the petitioners are entitled to relief either by winding up the company or by some other means, and

(b) that in the absence of any other remedy it would be just and equitable that the company should be wound up,

shall make a winding-up order; but this does not apply if the court is also of the opinion both that some other remedy is available to the petitioners and that they are acting unreasonably in seeking to have the company wound up instead of pursuing that other remedy.

126 Power to stay or restrain proceedings against company

(1) At any time after the presentation of a winding-up petition, and before a winding-up order has been made, the company, or any creditor or contributory, may—

(a) Where any action or proceeding against the company is pending in the High Court or Court of Appeal in England and Wales or Northern Ireland, apply to the court in which the action or proceeding is pending for a stay of proceedings therein, and

(b) Where any other action or proceeding is pending against the company, apply to the court having jurisdiction to wind up the company to restrain further proceedings in the action or proceeding;

and the court to which application is so made may (as the case may be) stay, sist or restrain the proceedings accordingly on such terms as it thinks fit.

...

127 Avoidance of property dispositions, etc

(1) In a winding up by the court, any disposition of the company's property, and any transfer of shares, or alteration in the status of the company's members, made after the commencement of the winding up is, unless the court otherwise orders, void.

(2)   This section has no effect in respect of anything done by an administrator of a company while a winding-up petition is suspended under paragraph 40 of Schedule B1.

128   Avoidance of attachments, etc

(1)   Where a company registered in England and Wales is being wound up by the court, any attachment, sequestration, distress or execution put in force against the estate or effects of the company after the commencement of the winding up is void.

...

Commencement of winding up

129   Commencement of winding up by the court

(1)   If, before the presentation of a petition for the winding up of a company by the court, a resolution has been passed by the company for voluntary winding up, the winding up of the company is deemed to have commenced at the time of the passing of the resolution; and unless the court, on proof of fraud or mistake, directs otherwise, all proceedings taken in the voluntary winding up are deemed to have been validly taken.

(1A) Where the court makes a winding-up order by virtue of paragraph 13(1)(e) of Schedule B1, the winding up is deemed to commence on the making of the order.

(2)   In any other case, the winding up of a company by the court is deemed to commence at the time of the presentation of the petition for winding up.

130   Consequences of winding-up order

(1)   On the making of a winding-up order, a copy of the order must forthwith be forwarded by the company (or otherwise as may be prescribed) to the registrar of companies, who shall enter it in his records relating to the company.

(2)   When a winding-up order has been made or a provisional liquidator has been appointed, no action or proceeding shall be proceeded with or commenced against the company or its property, except by leave of the court and subject to such terms as the court may impose.

(3)   When an order has been made for winding up a company registered under section 680 of the Companies Act, no action or proceeding shall be commenced or proceeded with against the company or its property or any contributory of the company, in respect of any debt of the company, except by leave of the court, and subject to such terms as the court may impose.

(4)   An order for winding up a company operates in favour of all the creditors and of all contributories of the company as if made on the joint petition of a creditor and of a contributory.

Investigation procedures

131   Company's statement of affairs

(1)   Where the court has made a winding-up order or appointed a provisional liquidator, the official receiver may require some or all of the persons mentioned in subsection (3) below to make out and submit to him a statement in the prescribed form as to the affairs of the company.

(2)   The statement shall be verified by affidavit by the persons required to submit it and shall show—

(a)   particulars of the company's assets, debts and liabilities;

(b)   the names and addresses of the company's creditors;

(c)   the securities held by them respectively;

(d)   the dates when the securities were respectively given; and

(e)   such further or other information as may be prescribed or as the official receiver may require.

(3)   The persons referred to in subsection (1) are—

(a)   those who are or have been officers of the company;

(b)   those who have taken part in the formation of the company at any time within one year before the relevant date;

      (c)   those who are in the company's employment, or have been in its employment within that year, and are in the official receiver's opinion capable of giving the information required;

      (d)   those who are or have been within that year officers of, or in the employment of, a company which is, or within that year was, an officer of the company.

(4)   Where any persons are required under this section to submit a statement of affairs to the official receiver, they shall do so (subject to the next subsection) before the end of the period of 21 days beginning with the day after that on which the prescribed notice of the requirement is given to them by the official receiver.

(5)   The official receiver, if he thinks fit, may—

      (a)   at any time release a person from an obligation imposed on him under subsection (1) or (2) above; or

      (b)   either when giving the notice mentioned in subsection (4) or subsequently, extend the period so mentioned;

and where the official receiver has refused to exercise a power conferred by this subsection, the court, if it thinks fit, may exercise it.

(6)   In this section—

"employment" includes employment under a contract for services; and "the relevant date" means—

      (a)   in a case where a provisional liquidator is appointed, the date of his appointment; and

      (b)   in a case where no such appointment is made, the date of the winding-up order.

(7)   If a person without reasonable excuse fails to comply with any obligation imposed under this section, he is liable to a fine and, for continued contravention, to a daily default fine.

…

132 Investigation by official receiver

(1)   Where a winding-up order is made by the court in England and Wales, it is the duty of the official receiver to investigate—

      (a)   if the company has failed, the causes of the failure; and

      (b)   generally, the promotion, formation, business, dealings and affairs of the company,

and to make such report (if any) to the court as he thinks fit.

(2)   The report is, in any proceedings, *prima facie* evidence of the facts stated in it.

133 Public examination of officers

(1)   Where a company is being wound up by the court, the official receiver … may at any time before the dissolution of the company apply to the court for the public examination of any person who—

      (a)   is or has been an officer of the company; or

      (b)   has acted as liquidator or administrator of the company or as receiver or manager …; or

      (c)   not being a person falling within paragraph (a) or (b), is or has been concerned, or has taken part, in the promotion, formation or management of the company.

(2)   Unless the court otherwise orders, the official receiver … shall make an application under subsection (1) if he is requested in accordance with the rules to do so by—

      (a)   one-half, in value, of the company's creditors; or

      (b)   three-quarters, in value, of the company's contributories.

(3)   On an application under subsection (1), the court shall direct that a public examination of the person to whom the application relates shall be held on a day appointed by the court; and that person shall attend on that day and be publicly examined as to the promotion, formation or management of the company or as to the conduct of its business and affairs, or his conduct or dealings in relation to the company.

(4)   The following may take part in the public examination of a person under this section and may question that person concerning the matters mentioned in subsection (3), namely—

      (a)   the official receiver;

      (b)   the liquidator of the company;

    (c)   any person who has been appointed as special manager of the company's property or business;

    (d)   any creditor of the company who has tendered a proof ...;

    (e)   any contributory of the company.

134   Enforcement of s 133

(1)   If a person without reasonable excuse fails, at any time to attend his public examination under section 133, he is guilty of a contempt of court and liable to be punished accordingly.

(2)   In a case where a person without reasonable excuse fails at any time to attend his examination under section 133 or there are reasonable grounds for believing that a person has absconded, or is about to abscond, with a view to avoiding or delaying his examination under that section, the court may cause a warrant to be issued to a constable or prescribed officer of the court—

    (a)   for the arrest of that person; and

    (b)   for the seizure of any books, papers, records, money or goods in that person's possession.

(3)   In such a case the court may authorise the person arrested under the warrant to be kept in custody, and anything seized under such a warrant to be held, in accordance with the rules, until such time as the court may order.

Appointment of liquidator

135   Appointment and powers of provisional liquidator

(1)   Subject to the provisions of this section, the court may, at any time after the presentation of a winding-up petition, appoint a liquidator provisionally.

(2)   In England and Wales, the appointment of a provisional liquidator may be made at any time before the making of a winding-up order; and either the official receiver or any other fit person may be appointed.

    ...

(4)   The provisional liquidator shall carry out such functions as the court may confer on him.

(5)   When a liquidator is provisionally appointed by the court, his powers may be limited by the order appointing him.

136   Functions of official receiver in relation to office of liquidator

(1)   The following provisions of this section have effect, subject to section 140 below, on a winding-up order being made by the court in England and Wales.

(2)   The official receiver, by virtue of his office, becomes the liquidator of the company and continues in office until another person becomes liquidator under the provisions of this Part.

(3)   The official receiver is, by virtue of his office, the liquidator during any vacancy.

(4)   At any time when he is the liquidator of the company, the official receiver may summon separate meetings of the company's creditors and contributories for the purpose of choosing a person to be liquidator of the company in place of the official receiver.

(5)   It is the duty of the official receiver—

    (a)   as soon as practicable in the period of 12 weeks beginning with the day on which the winding-up order was made, to decide whether to exercise his power under subsection (4) to summon meetings, and

    (b)   if in pursuance of paragraph (a) he decides not to exercise that power, to give notice of his decision, before the end of that period, to the court and to the company's creditors and contributories, and

    (c)   (whether or not he has decided to exercise that power) to exercise his power to summon meetings under subsection (4) if he is at any time requested, in accordance with the rules, to do so by one-quarter, in value, of the company's creditors; and accordingly, where the duty imposed by paragraph (c) arises before the official receiver has performed a duty imposed by paragraph (a) or (b), he is not required to perform the latter duty.

(6)   A notice given under subsection (5)(b) to the company's creditors shall contain an explanation of the creditors' power under subsection (5)(c) to require the official receiver to summon meetings of the company's creditors and contributories.

137   Appointment by Secretary of State

(1)   In a winding up by the court in England and Wales the official receiver may, at any time when he is the liquidator of the company, apply to the Secretary of State for the appointment of a person as liquidator in his place.

(2)   If meetings are held in pursuance of a decision under section 136(5)(a), but no person is chosen to be liquidator as a result of those meetings, it is the duty of the official receiver to decide whether to refer the need for an appointment to the Secretary of State.

(3)   On an application under subsection (1), or a reference made in pursuance of a decision under subsection (2), the Secretary of State shall either make an appointment or decline to make one.

(4)   Where a liquidator has been appointed by the Secretary of State under subsection (3), the liquidator shall give notice of his appointment to the company's creditors or, if the court so allows, shall advertise his appointment in accordance with the directions of the court.

(5)   In that notice or advertisement the liquidator shall—

    (a)   state whether he proposes to summon a general meeting of the company's creditors under section 141 below for the purpose of determining (together with any meeting of contributories) whether a liquidation committee should be established under that section, and

    (b)   if he does not propose to summon such a meeting, set out the power of the company's creditors under that section to require him to summon one.

...

139   Choice of liquidator at meetings of creditors and contributories

(1)   This section applies where a company is being wound up by the court and separate meetings of the company's creditors and contributories are summoned for the purpose of choosing a person to be liquidator of the company.

(2)   The creditors and the contributories at their respective meetings may nominate a person to be liquidator.

(3)   The liquidator shall be the person nominated by the creditors or, where no person has been so nominated, the person (if any) nominated by the contributories.

(4)   In the case of different persons being nominated, any contributory or creditor may, within 7 days after the date on which the nomination was made by the creditors, apply to the court for an order either—

    (a)   appointing the person nominated as liquidator by the contributories to be a liquidator instead of, or jointly with, the person nominated by the creditors; or

    (b)   appointing some other person to be liquidator instead of the person nominated by the creditors.

140   Appointment by the court following administration or voluntary arrangement

(1)   Where a winding-up order is made immediately upon the appointment of an administrator ceasing to have effect, the court may appoint as liquidator of the company the person whose appointment as administrator has ceased to have effect.

(2)   Where a winding-up order is made at a time when there is a supervisor of a voluntary arrangement approved in relation to the company under Part I, the court may appoint as liquidator of the company the person who is the supervisor at the time when the winding-up order is made.

(3)   Where the court makes an appointment under this section, the official receiver does not become the liquidator as otherwise provided by section 136(2), and he has no duty under section 136(5)(a) or (b) in respect of the summoning of creditors' or contributories' meetings.

Liquidation committees

141   Liquidation committee (England and Wales)

(1)   Where a winding-up order has been made by the court in England and Wales and separate meetings of creditors and contributories have been summoned for the purpose of choosing a person to be liquidator, those meetings may establish a committee ("the liquidation committee") to exercise the functions conferred on it by or under this Act.

(2)   The liquidator (not being the official receiver) may at any time, if he thinks fit, summon separate general meetings of the company's creditors and contributories for the purpose of determining whether such a committee should be established and, if it is so determined, of establishing it.

  The liquidator (not being the official receiver) shall summon such a meeting if he is requested, in accordance with the rules, to do so by one-tenth, in value, of the company's creditors.

(3)   Where meetings are summoned under this section, or for the purpose of choosing a person to be liquidator, and either the meeting of creditors or the meeting of contributories decides that a liquidation committee should be established, but the other meeting does not so decide or decides that a committee should not be established, the committee shall be established in accordance with the rules, unless the court otherwise orders.

(4)   The liquidation committee is not to be able or required to carry out its functions at any time when the official receiver is liquidator; but at any such time its functions are vested in the Secretary of State except to the extent that the rules otherwise provide.

(5)   Where there is for the time being no liquidation committee, and the liquidator is a person other than the official receiver, the functions of such a committee are vested in the Secretary of State except to the extent that the rules otherwise provide.

...

The liquidator's functions

143   General functions in winding up by the court

(1)   The functions of the liquidator of a company which is being wound up by the court are to secure that the assets of the company are got in, realised and distributed to the company's creditors and, if there is a surplus, to the persons entitled to it.

(2)   It is the duty of the liquidator of a company which is being wound up by the court in England and Wales, if he is not the official receiver—

(a)   to furnish the official receiver with such information,

(b)   to produce to the official receiver, and permit inspection by the official receiver of, such books, papers and other records, and

(c)   to give the official receiver such other assistance,

as the official receiver may reasonably require for the purposes of carrying out his functions in relation to the winding up.

144   Custody of company's property

(1)   When a winding-up order has been made, or where a provisional liquidator has been appointed, the liquidator or the provisional liquidator (as the case may be) shall take into his custody or under his control all the property and things in action to which the company is or appears to be entitled.

  ...

145   Vesting of company property in liquidator

(1)   When a company is being wound up by the court, the court may on the application of the liquidator by order direct that all or any part of the property of whatsoever description belonging to the company or held by trustees on its behalf shall vest in the liquidator by his official name; and thereupon the property to which the order relates vests accordingly.

(2)   The liquidator may, after giving such indemnity (if any) as the court may direct, bring or defend in his official name any action or other legal proceeding which relates to that

property or which it is necessary to bring or defend for the purpose of effectually winding up the company and recovering its property.

146   Duty to summon final meeting

(1)   Subject to the next subsection, if it appears to the liquidator of a company which is being wound by the court that the winding up of the company is for practical purposes complete and the liquidator is not the official receiver, the liquidator shall summon a final general meeting of the company's creditors which—

(a)   shall receive the liquidator's report of the winding up, and

(b)   shall determine whether the liquidator should have his release under section 174 in Chapter VII of this Part.

(2)   The liquidator may, if he thinks fit, give the notice summoning the final general meeting at the same time as giving notice of any final distribution of the company's property but, if summoned for an earlier date, that meeting shall be adjourned (and, if necessary, further adjourned) until a date on which the liquidator is able to report to the meeting that the winding up of the company is for practical purposes complete.

(3)   In the carrying out of his functions in the winding up it is the duty of the liquidator to retain sufficient sums from the company's property to cover the expenses of summoning and holding the meeting required by this section.

General powers of court

147   Power to stay or sist winding up

(1)   The court may at any time after an order for winding up, on the application either of the liquidator or the official receiver or any creditor or contributory, and on proof to the satisfaction of the court that all proceedings in the winding up ought to be stayed or sisted, make an order staying or sisting the proceedings, either altogether or for a limited time, on such terms and conditions as the court thinks fit.

(2)   The court may, before making an order, require the official receiver to furnish to it a report with respect to any facts or matters which are in his opinion relevant to the application.

(3)   A copy of every order made under this section shall forthwith be forwarded by the company, or otherwise as may be prescribed, to the registrar of companies, who shall enter it in his records relating to the company.

148   Settlement of list of contributories and application of assets

(1)   As soon as may be after making a winding-up order, the court shall settle a list of contributories, with power to rectify the register of members in all cases where rectification is required in pursuance of the Companies Act or this Act, and shall cause the company's assets to be collected, and applied in discharge of its liabilities.

(2)   If it appears to the court that it will not be necessary to make calls on or adjust the rights of contributories, the court may dispense with the settlement of a list of contributories.

(3)   In settling the list, the court shall distinguish between persons who are contributories in their own right and persons who are contributories as being representatives of or liable for the debts of others.

149   Debts due from contributory to company

(1)   The court may, at any time after making a winding-up order, make an order on any contributory for the time being on the list of contributories to pay, in manner directed by the order, any money due from him (or from the estate of the person who he represents) to the company, exclusive of any money payable by him or the estate by virtue of any call in pursuance of the Companies Act or this Act.

(2)   The court in making such an order may—

(a)   in the case of an unlimited company, allow to the contributory by way of set-off any money due to him or the estate which he represents from the company on any independent dealing or contract with the company, but not any money due to him as a member of the company in respect of any dividend or profit, and

(b)   in the case of a limited company, make to any director or manager whose liability is unlimited or to his estate the like allowance.

(3)   In the case of any company, whether limited or unlimited, when all the creditors are paid in full (together with interest at the official rate), any money due on any account whatever to a contributory from the company may be allowed to him by way of set-off against any subsequent call.

150   Power to make calls

(1)   The court may, at any time after making a winding-up order, and either before or after it has ascertained the sufficiency of the company's assets, make calls on all or any of the contributories for the time being settled on the list of the contributories to the extent of their liability, for payment of any money which the court considers necessary to satisfy the company's debts and liabilities, and the expenses of winding up, and for the adjustment of the rights of the contributories among themselves, and make an order for payment of any calls so made.

(2)   In making a call the court may take into consideration the probability that some of the contributories may partly or wholly fail to pay it.

151   Payment into bank of money due to company

(1)   The court may order any contributory, purchaser or other person from whom money is due to the company to pay the amount due into the Bank of England (or any branch of it) to the account of the liquidator instead of to the liquidator, and such an order may be enforced in the same manner as if it had directed payment to the liquidator.

(2)   All money and securities paid or delivered into the Bank of England (or branch) in the event of a winding up by the court are subject in all respects to the orders of the court.

152   Order on contributory to be conclusive evidence

(1)   An order made by the court on a contributory is conclusive evidence that the money (if any) thereby appearing to be due or ordered to be paid is due, but subject to any right of appeal.

(2)   All other pertinent matters stated in the order are to be taken as truly stated as against all persons and in all proceedings ... against the heritable estate of a deceased contributory; and in that case the order is only *prima facie* evidence for the purpose of charging his heritable estate, unless his heirs or legatees of heritage were on the list of contributories at the time of the order being made.

153   Power to exclude creditors not proving in time

The court may fix a time or times within which creditors are to prove their debts or claims or to be excluded from the benefit of any distribution made before those debts are proved.

154   Adjustment of rights of contributories

The court shall adjust the rights of the contributories among themselves and distribute any surplus among the persons entitled to it.

155   Inspection of books by creditors, etc

(1)   The court may, at any time after making a winding-up order, make such order for inspection of the company's books and papers by creditors and contributories as the court thinks just; and any books and papers in the company's possession may be inspected by creditors and contributories accordingly, but not further or otherwise.

(2)   Nothing in this section excludes or restricts any statutory rights of a government department or person acting under the authority of a government department.

...

156   Payment of expenses of winding up

The court may, in the event of the assets being insufficient to satisfy the liabilities, make an order as to the payment out of the assets of the expenses incurred in the winding up in such order of priority as the court thinks just.

...

158   Power to arrest absconding contributory

The court, at any time either before or after making a winding-up order, on proof of probable cause for believing that a contributory is about to quit the United Kingdom or otherwise to abscond or to remove or conceal any of his property for the purpose of evading payment of calls, may cause the contributory to be arrested and his books and papers and moveable personal property to be seized and him and them to be kept safely until such time as the court may order.

159   Powers of court to be cumulative

Powers conferred by this Act and the Companies Acts on the court are in addition to, and not in restriction of, any existing powers of instituting proceedings against a contributory or debtor of the company, or the estate of any contributory or debtor, for the recovery of any call or other sums.

160   Delegation of powers to liquidator (England and Wales)

(1) Provision may be made by rules for enabling or requiring all or any of the powers and duties conferred and imposed on the court in England and Wales by the Companies Act and this Act in respect of the following matters—

(a) the holding and conducting of meetings to ascertain the wishes of creditors and contributories,

(b) the settling of lists of contributories and the rectifying of the register of members where required, and the collection and application of the assets,

(c) the payment, delivery, conveyance, surrender or transfer of money, property, books or papers to the liquidator,

(d) the making of calls,

(e) the fixing of a time within which debts and claims must be proved,

to be exercised or performed by the liquidator as an officer of the court, and subject to the court's control.

(2) But the liquidator shall not, without the special leave of the court, rectify the register of members, and shall not make any call without either that special leave or the sanction of the liquidation committee.

...

CHAPTER VII
LIQUIDATORS

Preliminary

163   Style and title of liquidators

The liquidator of a company shall be described—

(a) where a person other than the official receiver is liquidator, by the style of "the liquidator" of the particular company, or

(b) where the official receiver is liquidator, by the style of "the official receiver and liquidator" of the particular company;

and in neither case shall he be described by an individual name.

164   Corrupt inducement affecting appointment

A person who gives, or agrees or offers to give, to any members or creditor of a company any valuable consideration with a view to securing his own appointment or nomination, or to securing or preventing the appointment or nomination of some person other than himself, as the company's liquidator is liable to a fine.

Liquidator's powers and duties

165   Voluntary winding up

(1) This section has effect where a company is being wound up voluntarily, but subject to section 166 below in the case of a creditors' voluntary winding up.

(2) The liquidator may—

  (a) in the case of a members' voluntary winding up, with the sanction of an special resolution of the company, and

  (b) in the case of a creditors' voluntary winding up, with the sanction of the court or the liquidation committee (or, if there is no such committee, a meeting of the company's creditors),

exercise any of the powers specified in Part I of Schedule 4 to this Act (payment of debts, compromise of claims, etc.).

(3) The liquidator may, without sanction, exercise either of the powers specified in Part II of that Schedule (institution and defence of proceedings; carrying on the business of the company) and any of the general powers specified in Part III of that Schedule.

(4) The liquidator may—

  (a) exercise the court's power of settling a list of contributories (which list is prima facie evidence of the liability of the persons named in it to be contributories),

  (b) exercise the court's power of making calls,

  (c) summon general meetings of the company for the purpose of obtaining its sanction by special resolution or for any other purpose he may think fit.

(5) The liquidator shall pay the company's debts and adjust the rights of the contributories among themselves.

(6) Where the liquidator in exercise of the powers conferred on him by this Act disposes of any property of the company to a person who is connected with the company (within the meaning of section 249 in Part VII), he shall, if there is for the time being a liquidation committee, give notice to the committee of that exercise of his powers.

166 Creditors' voluntary winding up

(1) This section applies where, in the case of a creditors' voluntary winding up, a liquidator has been nominated by the company.

(2) The powers conferred on the liquidator by section 165 shall not be exercised, except with the sanction of the court, during the period before the holding of the creditors' meeting under section 98 in Chapter IV.

(3) Subsection (2) does not apply in relation to the power of the liquidator—

  (a) to take into his custody or under his control all the property to which the company is or appears to be entitled;

  (b) to dispose of perishable goods and other goods the value of which is likely to diminish if they are not immediately disposed of; and

  (c) to do all such other things as may be necessary for the protection of the company's assets.

(4) The liquidator shall attend the creditors' meeting held under section 98 and shall report to the meeting on any exercise by him of his powers (whether or not under this section or under section 112 or 165).

(5) If default is made—

  (a) by the company in complying with subsection (1) or (2) of section 98, or

  (b) by the directors in complying with subsection (1) or (2) of section 99,

the liquidator shall, within 7 days of the relevant day, apply to the court for directions as to the manner in which that default is to be remedied.

(6) "The relevant day" means the day on which the liquidator was nominated by the company or the day on which he first became aware of the default, whichever is the later.

(7) If the liquidator without reasonable excuse fails to comply with this section, he is liable to a fine.

167 Winding up by the court

(1) Where a company is being wound up by the court, the liquidator may—

  (a) with the sanction of the court or the liquidation committee, exercise any of the powers specified in Parts I and II of Schedule 4 to this Act (payment of debts; compromise of claims, etc.; institution and defence of proceedings; carrying on of the business of the company), and

  (b) with or without that sanction, exercise any of the general powers specified in Part III of that Schedule.

(2) Where the liquidator (not being the official receiver), in exercise of the powers conferred on him by this Act—

  (a) disposes of any property of the company to a person who is connected with the company (within the meaning of section 249 in Part VII), or

  (b) employs a solicitor to assist him in the carrying out of his functions,

he shall, if there is for the time being a liquidation committee, give notice to the committee of that exercise of his powers.

(3) The exercise by the liquidator in a winding up by the court of the powers conferred by this section is subject to the control of the court, and any creditor or contributory may apply to the court with respect to any exercise or proposed exercise of any of those powers.

168 Supplementary powers (England and Wales)

(1) This section applies in the case of a company which is being wound up by the court in England and Wales.

(2) The liquidator may summon general meetings of the creditors or contributories for the purpose of ascertaining their wishes; and it is his duty to summon meetings at such times as the creditors or contributories by resolution (either at the meeting appointing the liquidator or otherwise) may direct, or whenever requested in writing to do so by one-tenth in value of the creditors or contributories (as the case may be).

(3) The liquidator may apply to the court (in the prescribed manner) for directions in relation to any particular matter arising in the winding up.

(4) Subject to the provisions of this Act, the liquidator shall use his own discretion in the management of the assets and their distribution among the creditors.

(5) If any person is aggrieved by an act or decision of the liquidator, that person may apply to the court; and the court may confirm, reverse or modify the act or decision complained of, and make such order in the case as it thinks just.

. . .

(5C) Where the court makes an order for the winding up of an insolvent partnership under—

  (a) section 72(1)(a) of the Financial Services Act 1986;

  (b) section 92(1)(a) of the Banking Act 1987; or

  (c) section 367(3)(a) of the Financial Services and Markets Act 2000,

the court may make an order as to the future conduct of the winding up proceedings, and any such order may apply any provisions of the Insolvent Partnerships Order 1994 with any necessary modifications.

. . .

170 Enforcement of liquidator's duty to make returns, etc

(1) If a liquidator who has made any default—

  (a) in filing, delivering or making any return, account or other document, or

  (b) in giving any notice which he is by law required to file, deliver, make or give,

fails to make good the default within 14 days after the service on him of a notice requiring him to do so, the court has the following powers.

(2) On an application made by any creditor or contributory of the company, or by the registrar of companies, the court may make an order directing the liquidator to make good the default within such time as may be specified in the order.

(3) The court's order may provide that all costs of and incidental to the application shall be borne by the liquidator.

(4) Nothing in this section prejudices the operation of any enactment imposing penalties on a liquidator in respect of any such default as is mentioned above.

Removal; vacation of office

171   Removal, etc (voluntary winding up)

(1)   This section applies with respect to the removal from office and vacation of office of the liquidator of a company which is being wound up voluntarily.

(2)   Subject to the next subsection, the liquidator may be removed from office only by an order of the court or—

    (a)   in the case of a members' voluntary winding up, by a general meeting of the company summoned specially for that purpose, or

    (b)   in the case of a creditors' voluntary winding up, by a general meeting of the company's creditors summoned specially for that purpose in accordance with the rules.

(3)   Where the liquidator was appointed by the court under section 108 in Chapter V, a meeting such as is mentioned in subsection (2) above shall be summoned for the purpose of replacing him only if he thinks fit or the court so directs or the meeting is requested, in accordance with the rules—

    (a)   in the case of a members' voluntary winding up, by members representing not less than one-half of the total voting rights of all the members having at the date of the request a right to vote at the meeting, or

    (b)   in the case of a creditors' voluntary winding up, by not less than one-half, in value, of the company's creditors.

(4)   A liquidator shall vacate office if he ceases to be a person who is qualified to act as an insolvency practitioner in relation to the company.

(5)   A liquidator may, in the prescribed circumstances, resign his office by giving notice of his resignation to the registrar of companies.

(6)   Where—

    (a)   in the case of a members' voluntary winding up, a final meeting of the company has been held under section 94 in Chapter III, or

    (b)   in the case of a creditors' voluntary winding up, final meetings of the company and of the creditors have been held under section 106 in Chapter IV,

the liquidator whose report was considered at the meeting or meetings shall vacate office as soon as he has complied with subsection (3) of that section and has given notice to the registrar of companies that the meeting or meetings have been held and of the decisions (if any) of the meeting or meetings.

172   Removal, etc (winding up by the court)

(1)   This section applies with respect to the removal from office and vacation of office of the liquidator of a company which is being wound up by the court, or of a provisional liquidator.

(2)   Subject as follows, the liquidator may be removed from office only by an order of the court or by a general meeting of the company's creditors summoned specially for that purpose in accordance with the rules; and a provisional liquidator may be removed from office only by an order of the court.

(3)   Where—

    (a)   the official receiver is liquidator otherwise than in succession under section 136(3) to a person who held office as a result of a nomination by a meeting of the company's creditors or contributories, or

    (b)   the liquidator was appointed by the court otherwise than under section 139(4)(a) or 140(1), or was appointed by the Secretary of State,

a general meeting of the company's creditors shall be summoned for the purpose of replacing him only if he thinks fit, or the court so directs, or the meeting is requested, in accordance with the rules, by not less than one-quarter, in value, of the creditors.

(4)   If appointed by the Secretary of State, the liquidator may be removed from office by a direction of the Secretary of State.

(5)   A liquidator or provisional liquidator, not being the official receiver, shall vacate office if he ceases to be a person who is qualified to act as an insolvency practitioner in relation to the company.

(6)   A liquidator may, in the prescribed circumstances, resign his office by giving notice of his resignation to the court.

...

(8)   Where a final meeting has been held under section 146 (liquidator's report on completion of winding up), the liquidator whose report was considered at the meeting shall vacate office as soon as he has given notice to the court and the registrar of companies that the meeting has been held and of the decisions (if any) of the meeting.

Release of liquidator

173   Release (voluntary winding up)

(1)   This section applies with respect to the release of the liquidator of a company which is being wound up voluntarily.

(2)   A person who has ceased to be a liquidator shall have his release with effect from the following time, that is to say—

    (a)   in the case of a person who has been removed from office by a general meeting of the company or by a general meeting of the company's creditors that has not resolved against his release or who has died, the time at which notice is given to the registrar of companies in accordance with the rules that that person has ceased to hold office;

    (b)   in the case of a person who has been removed from office by a general meeting of the company's creditors that has resolved against his release, or by the court, or who has vacated office under section 171(4) above, such time as the Secretary of State may, on the application of that person, determine;

    (c)   in the case of a person who has resigned, such time as may be prescribed;

    (d)   in the case of a person who has vacated office under subsection (6)(a) of section 171, the time at which he vacated office;

    (e)   in the case of a person who has vacated office under subsection (6)(b) of that section—

       (i)   if the final meeting of the creditors referred to in that subsection has resolved against that person's release, such time as the Secretary of State may, on an application by that person, determine, and

       (ii)   if that meeting has not resolved against that person's release, the time at which he vacated office.

...

(4)   Where a liquidator has his release under subsection (2), he is, with effect from the time specified in that subsection, discharged from all liability both in respect of acts or omissions of his in the winding up and otherwise in relation to his conduct as liquidator.

But nothing in this section prevents the exercise, in relation to a person who has had his release under subsection (2), of the court's powers under section 212 of this Act (summary remedy against delinquent directors, liquidators, etc.).

174   Release (winding up by the court)

(1)   This section applies with respect to the release of the liquidator of a company which is being wound up by the court, or of a provisional liquidator.

(2)   Where the official receiver has ceased to be liquidator and a person becomes liquidator in his stead, the official receiver has his release with effect from the following time, that is to say—

    (a)   in a case where that person was nominated by a general meeting of creditors or contributories, or was appointed by the Secretary of State, the time at which the official receiver gives notice to the court that he has been replaced;

    (b)   in a case where that person is appointed by the court, such time as the court may determine.

(3)   If the official receiver while he is a liquidator gives notice to the Secretary of State that the winding up is for practical purposes complete, he has his release with effect from such time as the Secretary of State may determine.

(4)   A person other than the official receiver who has ceased to be a liquidator has his release with effect from the following time, that is to say—

(a)   in the case of a person who has been removed from office by a general meeting of creditors that has not resolved against his release or who has died, the time at which notice is given to the court in accordance with the rules that that person has ceased to hold office;

(b)   in the case of a person who has been removed from office by a general meeting of creditors that has resolved against his release, or by the court or the Secretary of State, or who has vacated office under section 172(5) or (7), such time as the Secretary of State may, on an application by that person, determine;

(c)   in the case of a person who has resigned, such time as may be prescribed;

(d)   in the case of a person who has vacated office under section 172(8)—

(i)   if the final meeting referred to in that subsection has resolved against that person's release, such time as the Secretary of State may, on an application by that person, determine, and

(ii)   if that meeting has not so resolved, the time at which that person vacated office.

(5)   A person who has ceased to hold office as a provisional liquidator has his release with effect from such time as the court may, on an application by him, determine.

(6)   Where the official receiver or a liquidator or provisional liquidator has his release under this section, he is, with effect from the time specified in the preceding provisions of this section, discharged from all liability both in respect of acts or omissions of his in the winding up and otherwise in relation to his conduct as liquidator or provisional liquidator.

But nothing in this section prevents the exercise, in relation to a person who has had his release under this section, of the court's powers under section 212 (summary remedy against delinquent directors, liquidators, etc.).

...

CHAPTER VIII
PROVISIONS OF GENERAL APPLICATION IN WINDING UP

Preferential debts

175   Preferential debts (general provision)

(1)   In a winding up the company's preferential debts (within the meaning given by section 386 in Part XII) shall be paid in priority to all other debts.

(2)   Preferential debts—

(a)   rank equally among themselves after the expenses of the winding up and shall be paid in full, unless the assets are insufficient to meet them, in which case they abate in equal proportions; and

(b)   so far as the assets of the company available for payment of general creditors are insufficient to meet them, have priority over the claims of holders of debentures secured by, or holders of, any floating charge created by the company, and shall be paid accordingly out of any property comprised in or subject to that charge.

176   Preferential charge on goods distrained

(1)   This section applies where a company is being wound up by the court in England and Wales, and is without prejudice to section 128 (avoidance of attachments, etc.).

(2)   Where any person (whether or not a landlord or person entitled to rent) has distrained upon the goods or effects of the company in the period of 3 months ending with the date of the winding-up order, those goods or effects, or the proceeds of their sale, shall be charged for the benefit of the company with the preferential debts of the company to the extent that the company's property is for the time being insufficient for meeting them.

(3)   Where by virtue of a charge under subsection (2) any person surrenders any goods or effects to a company or makes a payment to a company, that person ranks, in respect of the amount of the proceeds of sale of those goods or effects by the liquidator or (as the case may be) the amount of the payment, as a preferential creditor of the company, except as against so much of the company's property as is available for the payment of preferential creditors by virtue of the surrender or payment.

176ZA Payment of expenses of winding up (England and Wales)

(1)   The expenses of winding up in England and Wales, so far as the assets of the company available for payment of general creditors are insufficient to meet them, have priority over any claims to property comprised in or subject to any floating charge created by the company and shall be paid out of any such property accordingly.

(2)   In subsection (1)—
    (a)   the reference to assets of the company available for payment of general creditors does not include any amount made available under section 176A(2)(a);
    (b)   the reference to claims to property comprised in or subject to a floating charge is to the claims of—
        (i)   the holders of debentures secured by, or holders of, the floating charge, and
        (ii)   any preferential creditors entitled to be paid out of that property in priority to them.

(3)   Provision may be made by rules restricting the application of subsection (1), in such circumstances as may be prescribed, to expenses authorised or approved—
    (a)   by the holders of debentures secured by, or holders of, the floating charge and by any preferential creditors entitled to be paid in priority to them, or
    (b)   by the court.

(4)   References in this section to the expenses of the winding up are to all expenses properly incurred in the winding up, including the remuneration of the liquidator.

176A Share of assets for unsecured creditors

(1)   This section applies where a floating charge relates to property of a company—
    (a)   which has gone into liquidation,
    (b)   which is in administration,
    (c)   of which there is a provisional liquidator, or
    (d)   of which there is a receiver.

(2)   The liquidator, administrator or receiver—
    (a)   shall make a prescribed part of the company's net property available for the satisfaction of unsecured debts, and
    (b)   shall not distribute that part to the proprietor of a floating charge except in so far as it exceeds the amount required for the satisfaction of unsecured debts.

(3)   Subsection (2) shall not apply to a company if—
    (a)   the company's net property is less than the prescribed minimum, and
    (b)   the liquidator, administrator or receiver thinks that the cost of making a distribution to unsecured creditors would be disproportionate to the benefits.

(4)   Subsection (2) shall also not apply to a company if or in so far as it is disapplied by—
    (a)   a voluntary arrangement in respect of the company, or
    (b)   a compromise or arrangement agreed under section 425 of the Companies Act (compromise with creditors and members).

(5)   Subsection (2) shall also not apply to a company if—
    (a)   the liquidator, administrator or receiver applies to the court for an order under this subsection on the ground that the cost of making a distribution to unsecured creditors would be disproportionate to the benefits, and
    (b)   the court orders that subsection (2) shall not apply.

(6)   In subsections (2) and (3) a company's net property is the amount of its property which would, but for this section, be available for satisfaction of claims of holders of debentures secured by, or holders of, any floating charge created by the company.

(7) An order under subsection (2) prescribing part of a company's net property may, in particular, provide for its calculation—
    (a) as a percentage of the company's net property, or
    (b) as an aggregate of different percentages of different parts of the company's net property.

(8) An order under this section—
    (a) must be made by statutory instrument, and
    (b) shall be subject to annulment pursuant to a resolution of either House of Parliament.

(9) In this section—
"floating charge" means a charge which is a floating charge on its creation and which is created after the first order under subsection (2)(a) comes into force, and
"prescribed" means prescribed by order by the Secretary of State.

(10) An order under this section may include transitional or incidental provision.

Special managers

177 Power to appoint special manager

(1) Where a company has gone into liquidation or a provisional liquidator has been appointed, the court may, on an application under this section, appoint any person to be the special manager of the business or property of the company.

(2) The application may be made by the liquidator or provisional liquidator in any case where it appears to him that the nature of the business or property of the company, or the interests of the company's creditors or contributories or members generally, require the appointment of another person to manage the company's business or property.

(3) The special manager has such powers as may be entrusted to him by the court.

(4) The court's power to entrust powers to the special manager includes power to direct that any provision of this Act that has effect in relation to the provisional liquidator or liquidator of a company shall have the like effect in relation to the special manager for the purposes of the carrying out by him of any of the functions of the provisional liquidator or liquidator.

(5) The special manager shall—
    (a) give such security ... as may be prescribed;
    (b) prepare and keep such accounts as may be prescribed; and
    (c) produce those accounts in accordance with the rules to the Secretary of State or to such other persons as may be prescribed.

Disclaimer (England and Wales only)

178 Power to disclaim onerous property

(1) This and the next two sections apply to a company that is being wound up in England and Wales.

(2) Subject as follows, the liquidator may, by the giving of the prescribed notice, disclaim any onerous property and may do so notwithstanding that he has taken possession of it, endeavoured to sell it, or otherwise exercised rights of ownership in relation to it.

(3) The following is onerous property for the purposes of this section—
    (a) any unprofitable contract, and
    (b) any other property of the company which is unsaleable or not readily saleable or is such that it may give rise to a liability to pay money or perform any other onerous act.

(4) A disclaimer under this section—
    (a) operates so as to determine, as from the date of the disclaimer, the rights, interests and liabilities of the company in or in respect of the property disclaimed; but
    (b) does not, except so far as is necessary for the purpose of releasing the company from any liability, affect the rights or liabilities of any other person.

(5) A notice of disclaimer shall not be given under this section in respect of any property if—
    (a) a person interested in the property has applied in writing to the liquidator or one of his predecessors as liquidator requiring the liquidator or that predecessor to decide whether he will disclaim or not, and

(b)   the period of 28 days beginning with the day on which that application was made, or such longer period as the court may allow, has expired without a notice of disclaimer having been given under this section in respect of that property.

(6)   Any person sustaining loss or damage in consequence of the operation of a disclaimer under this section is deemed a creditor of the company to the extent of the loss or damage and accordingly may prove for the loss or damage in the winding up.

179   Disclaimer of leaseholds

(1)   The disclaimer under section 178 of any property of a leasehold nature does not take effect unless a copy of the disclaimer has been served (so far as the liquidator is aware of their addresses) on every person claiming under the company as underlessee or mortgagee and either—

(a)   no application under section 181 below is made with respect to that property before the end of the period of 14 days beginning with the day on which the last notice served under this subsection was served; or

(b)   where such an application has been made, the court directs that the disclaimer shall take effect.

(2)   Where the court gives a direction under subsection (1)(b) it may also, instead of or in addition to any order it makes under section 181, make such orders with respect to fixtures, tenant's improvements and other matters arising out of the lease as it thinks fit.

180   Land subject to rentcharge

(1)   The following applies where, in consequence of the disclaimer under section 178 of any land subject to a rentcharge, that land vests by operation of law in the Crown or any other person (referred to in the next subsection as "the proprietor").

(2)   The proprietor and the successors in title of the proprietor are not subject to any personal liability in respect of any sums becoming due under the rentcharge except sums becoming due after the proprietor, or some person claiming under or through the proprietor, has taken possession or control of the land or has entered into occupation of it.

181   Powers of court (general)

(1)   This section and the next apply where the liquidator has disclaimed property under section 178.

(2)   An application under this section may be made to the court by—

(a)   any person who claims an interest in the disclaimed property, or

(b)   any person who is under any liability in respect of the disclaimed property, not being a liability discharged by the disclaimer.

(3)   Subject as follows, the court may on the application make an order, on such terms as it thinks fit, for the vesting of the disclaimed property in, or for its delivery to—

(a)   a person entitled to it or a trustee for such a person, or

(b)   a person subject to such a liability as is mentioned in subsection (2)(b) or a trustee for such a person.

(4)   The court shall not make an order under subsection (3)(b) except where it appears to the court that it would be just to do so for the purpose of compensating the person subject to the liability in respect of the disclaimer.

(5)   The effect of any order under this section shall be taken into account in assessing for the purpose of section 178(6) the extent of any loss or damage sustained by any person in consequence of the disclaimer.

(6)   An order under this section vesting property in any person need not be completed by conveyance, assignment or transfer.

...

Execution, attachment ...

183 Effect of execution or attachment (England and Wales)

(1) Where a creditor has issued execution against the goods or land of a company or has attached any debt due to it, and the company is subsequently wound up, he is not entitled to retain the benefit of the execution or attachment against the liquidator unless he has completed the execution or attachment before the commencement of the winding up.

(2) However—

    (a) if a creditor has had notice of a meeting having been called at which a resolution for voluntary winding up is to be proposed, the date on which he had notice is substituted, for the purpose of subsection (1), for the date of commencement of the winding up;

    (b) a person who purchases in good faith under a sale by the enforcement officer or other officer charged with the execution of the writ any goods of a company on which execution has been levied in all cases acquires a good title to them against the liquidator; and

    (c) the rights conferred by subsection (1) on the liquidator may be set aside by the court in favour of the creditor to such extent and subject to such terms as the court thinks fit.

(3) For purposes of this Act—

    (a) an execution against goods is completed by seizure and sale, or by the making of a charging order under section 1 of the Charging Orders Act 1979;

    (b) an attachment of a debt is completed by receipt of the debt; and

    (c) an execution against land is completed by seizure, by the appointment of a receiver, or by the making of a charging order under section 1 of the Act above-mentioned.

(4) In this section, "goods" includes all chattels personal; and "enforcement officer" means an individual who is authorised to act as an enforcement officer under the Courts Act 2003.

...

184 Duties of officers charged with execution of writs and other processes (England and Wales)

(1) The following applies where a company's goods are taken in execution and, before their sale or the completion of the execution (by the receipt or recovery of the full amount of the levy), notice is served on the enforcement officer, or other officer, charged with execution of the writ or other process, that a provisional liquidator has been appointed or that a winding-up order has been made, or that a resolution for voluntary winding up has been passed.

(2) The enforcement officer or other officer shall, on being so required, deliver the goods and any money seized or received in part satisfaction of the execution to the liquidator; but the costs of execution are a first charge on the goods or money so delivered, and the liquidator may sell the goods, or a sufficient part of them, for the purpose of satisfying the charge.

(3) If under an execution in respect of a judgment for a sum exceeding £500 a company's goods are sold or money is paid in order to avoid sale, the enforcement officer or other officer shall deduct the costs of the execution from the proceeds of sale or the money paid and retain the balance for 14 days.

(4) If within that time notice is served on the enforcement officer or other officer of a petition for the winding up of the company having been presented, or of a meeting having been called at which there is to be proposed a resolution for voluntary winding up, and an order is made or a resolution passed (as the case may be), the enforcement officer or other officer shall pay the balance to the liquidator, who is entitled to retain it as against the execution creditor.

(5) The rights conferred by this section on the liquidator may be set aside by the court in favour of the creditor to such extent and subject to such terms as the court thinks fit.

(6) In this section, "goods" includes all chattels personal; and "enforcement officer" means an individual who is authorised to act as an enforcement officer under the Courts Act 2003.

(7) The money sum for the time being specified in subsection (3) is subject to increase or reduction by order under section 416 in Part XV.

...

•••

Miscellaneous matters

186   Rescission of contracts by the court

(1)   The court may, on the application of a person who is, as against the liquidator, entitled to the benefit or subject to the burden of a contract made with the company, make an order rescinding the contract on such terms as to payment by or to either party of damages for the non-performance of the contract, or otherwise as the court thinks just.

(2)   Any damages payable under the order to such a person may be proved by him as a debt in the winding up.

187   Power to make over assets to employees

(1)   On the winding up of a company (whether by the court or voluntarily), the liquidator may, subject to the following provisions of this section, make any payment which the company has, before the commencement of the winding up, decided to make under section 247 of the Companies Act 2006 of the Companies Act (power to provide for employees or former employees on cessation or transfer of business).

(2)   The liquidator may, after the winding up has commenced, make any such provision as is mentioned in section 247(1) if—

(a)   the company's liabilities have been fully satisfied and provision has been made for the expenses of the winding up,

(b)   the exercise of the power has been sanctioned by a resolution of the company, and

(c)   any requirements of the company's memorandum or articles as to the exercise of the power conferred by section 247(1) are complied with.

(3)   Any payment which may be made by a company under this section (that is, a payment after the commencement of its winding up) may be made out of the company's assets which are available to the members on the winding up.

(4)   On a winding up by the court, the exercise by the liquidator of his powers under this section is subject to the court's control, and any creditor or contributory may apply to the court with respect to any exercise or proposed exercise of the power.

(5)   Subsections (1) and (2) above have effect notwithstanding anything in any rule of law or in section 107 of this Act (property of company after satisfaction of liabilities to be distributed among members).

188   Notification that company is in liquidation

(1)   When a company is being wound up, whether by the court or voluntarily—

(a)   every invoice, order for goods, business letter or order form (whether in hard copy, electronic or any other form) issued by or on behalf of the company, or a liquidator of the company or a receiver or manager of the company's property, being a document on or in which the name of the company appears, and

(b)   all the company's websites,

must contain a statement that the company is being wound up.

(2)   If default is made in complying with this section, the company and any of the following persons who knowingly and wilfully authorises or permits the default, namely, any officer of the company, any liquidator of the company and any receiver or manager, is liable to a fine.

189   Interest on debts

(1)   In a winding up interest is payable in accordance with this section on any debt proved in the winding up, including so much of any such debt as represents interest on the remainder.

(2)   Any surplus remaining after the payment of the debts proved in a winding up shall, before being applied for any other purpose, be applied in paying interest on those debts in respect of the periods during which they have been outstanding since the company went into liquidation.

(3)   All interest under this section ranks equally, whether or not the debts on which it is payable rank equally.

(4)   The rate of interest payable under this section in respect of any debt ("the official rate" for the purposes of any provision of this Act in which that expression is used) is whichever is the greater of—

    (a)   the rate specified in section 17 of the Judgments Act 1838 on the day on which the company went into liquidation, and

    (b)   the rate applicable to that debt apart from the winding up.

...

190   Documents exempt from stamp duty

(1)   In the case of a winding up by the court, or of a creditors' voluntary winding up, the following has effect as regards exemption from duties chargeable under the enactments relating to stamp duties.

(2)   If the company is registered in England and Wales, the following documents are exempt from stamp duty—

    (a)   every assurance relating solely to freehold or leasehold property, or to any estate, right or interest in, any real or personal property, which forms part of the company's assets and which, after the execution of the assurance, either at law or in equity, is or remains part of those assets, and

    (b)   every writ, order, certificate, or other instrument or writing relating solely to the property of any company which is being wound up as mentioned in subsection (1), or to any proceeding under such a winding up.

    "Assurance" here includes deed, conveyance, assignment and surrender.

...

191   Company's books to be evidence

Where a company is being wound up, all books and papers of the company and of the liquidators are, as between the contributories of the company, *prima facie* evidence of the truth of all matters purporting to be recorded in them.

192   Information as to pending liquidations

(1)   If the winding up of a company is not concluded within one year after its commencement, the liquidator shall, at such intervals as may be prescribed, until the winding up is concluded, send to the registrar of companies a statement in the prescribed form and containing the prescribed particulars with respect to the proceedings in, and position of, the liquidation.

(2)   If a liquidator fails to comply with this section, he is liable to a fine and, for continued contravention, to a daily default fine.

...

194   Resolutions passed at adjourned meetings

Where a resolution is passed at an adjourned meeting of a company's creditors or contributories, the resolution is treated for all purposes as having been passed on the date on which it was in fact passed, and not as having been passed on any earlier date.

195   Meetings to ascertain wishes of creditors or contributories

(1) The court may—

    (a)   as to all matters relating to the winding up of a company, have regard to the wishes of the creditors or contributories (as proved to it by any sufficient evidence), and

    (b)   if it thinks fit, for the purpose of ascertaining those wishes, direct meetings of the creditors or contributories to be called, held and conducted in such manner as the court directs, and appoint a person to Act as chairman of any such meeting and report the result of it to the court.

(2)   In the case of creditors, regard shall be had to the value of each creditor's debt.

(3)   In the case of contributories, regard shall be had to the number of votes conferred on each contributory by the Companies Act or the articles.

196   Judicial notice of court documents

In all proceedings under this Part, all courts, judges and persons judicially acting, and all officers, judicial or ministerial, of any court, or employed in enforcing the process of any court shall take judicial notice—

(a)   of the signature of any officer of the High Court or of a county court in England and Wales, … or of the High Court in Northern Ireland, and also

(b)   of the official seal or stamp of the several offices of the High Court in England and Wales or Northern Ireland …, appended to or impressed on any document made, issued or signed under the provisions of this Act or the Companies Act, or any official copy of such a document.

197   Commission for receiving evidence

(1)   When a company is wound up in England and Wales …, the court may refer the whole or any part of the examination of witnesses—

(a)   to a specified county court in England and Wales, or

…

(c)   to the High Court in Northern Ireland or a specified Northern Ireland County Court, ("specified" meaning specified in the order of the winding-up court).

(2)   Any person exercising jurisdiction as a judge of the court to which the reference is made … shall then, by virtue of this section, be a commissioner for the purpose of taking the evidence of those witnesses.

…

(4)   The examination so taken shall be returned or reported to the court which made the order in such manner as that court requests.

(5)   This section extends to Northern Ireland.

…

200   Affidavits etc in United Kingdom and overseas

(1)   An affidavit required to be sworn under or for the purposes of this Part may be sworn in the United Kingdom, or elsewhere in Her Majesty's dominions, before any court, judge or person lawfully authorised to take and receive affidavits, or before any of Her Majesty's consuls or vice-consuls in any place outside Her dominions.

(2)   All courts, judges, justices, commissioners and persons acting judicially shall take judicial notice of the seal or stamp or signature (as the case may be) of any such court, judge, person, consul or vice-consul attached, appended or subscribed to any such affidavit, or to any other document to be used for the purposes of this Part.

CHAPTER IX
DISSOLUTION OF COMPANIES AFTER WINDING UP

201   Dissolution (voluntary winding up)

(1)   This section applies, in the case of a company wound up voluntarily, where the liquidator has sent to the registrar of companies his final account and return under section 94 (members' voluntary) or section 106 (creditors' voluntary).

(2)   The registrar on receiving the account and return shall forthwith register them; and on the expiration of 3 months from the registration of the return the company is deemed to be dissolved.

(3)   However, the court may, on the application of the liquidator or any other person who appears to the court to be interested, make an order deferring the date at which the dissolution of the company is to take effect for such time as the court thinks fit.

(4)   It is the duty of the person on whose application an order of the court under this section is made within 7 days after the making of the order to deliver to the registrar an office copy of

the order for registration; and if that person fails to do so he is liable to a fine and, for continued contravention, to a daily default fine.

202   Early dissolution (England and Wales)

(1)   This section applies where an order for the winding up of a company has been made by the court in England and Wales.

(2)   The official receiver, if—

(a)   he is the liquidator of the company, and

(b)   it appears to him—

(i)   that the realisable assets of the company are insufficient to cover the expenses of the winding up, and

(ii)   that the affairs of the company do not require any further investigation,

may at any time apply to the registrar of companies for the early dissolution of the company.

(3)   Before making that application, the official receiver shall give not less than 28 days' notice of his intention to do so to the company's creditors and contributories and, if there is an administrative receiver of the company, to that receiver.

(4)   With the giving of that notice the official receiver ceases (subject to any directions under the next section) to be required to perform any duties imposed on him in relation to the company, its creditors or contributories by virtue of any provision of this Act, apart from a duty to make an application under subsection (2) of this section.

(5)   On the receipt of the official receiver's application under subsection (2) the registrar shall forthwith register it and, at the end of the period of 3 months beginning with the day of the registration of the application, the company shall be dissolved.

However, the Secretary of State may, on the application of the official receiver or any other person who appears to the Secretary of State to be interested, give directions under section 203 at any time before the end of that period.

203   Consequence of notice under s 202

(1)   Where a notice has been given under section 202(3), the official receiver or any creditor or contributory of the company, or the administrative receiver of the company (if there is one) may apply to the Secretary of State for directions under this section.

(2)   The grounds on which that application may be made are—

(a)   that the realisable assets of the company are sufficient to cover the expenses of the winding up;

(b)   that the affairs of the company do require further investigation; or

(c)   that for any other reason the early dissolution of the company is inappropriate.

(3)   Directions under this section—

(a)   are directions making such provision as the Secretary of State thinks fit for enabling the winding up of the company to proceed as if no notice had been given under section 202(3), and

(b)   may, in the case of an application under section 202(5), include a direction deferring the date at which the dissolution of the company is to take effect for such period as the Secretary of State thinks fit.

(4)   An appeal to the court lies from any decision of the Secretary of State on an application for directions under this section.

(5)   It is the duty of the person on whose application any directions are given under this section, or in whose favour an appeal with respect to an application for such directions is determined, within 7 days after the giving of the directions or the determination of the appeal, to deliver to the registrar of companies for registration such a copy of the directions or determination as is prescribed.

(6)   If a person without reasonable excuse fails to deliver a copy as required by subsection (5), he is liable to a fine and, for continued contravention, to a daily default fine.

...

205   Dissolution otherwise than under ss 202-204

(1)   This section applies where the registrar of companies receives—

(a)   a notice served for the purposes of section 172(8) (final meeting of creditors and vacation of office by liquidator), or

(b)   a notice, from the official receiver that the winding up of a company by the court is complete.

(2)   The registrar shall, on receipt of the notice, forthwith register it; and, subject as follows, at the end of the period of 3 months beginning with the day of the registration of the notice, the company shall be dissolved.

(3)   The Secretary of State may, on the application of the official receiver or any other person who appears to the Secretary of State to be interested, give a direction deferring the date at which the dissolution of the company is to take effect for such period as the Secretary of State thinks fit.

(4)   An appeal to the court lies from any decision of the Secretary of State on an application for a direction under subsection (3);

...

(6)   It is the duty of the person—

(a)   on whose application a direction is given under subsection (3);

(b)   in whose favour an appeal with respect to an application for such a direction is determined; or

(c)   on whose application an order is made under subsection (5),

within 7 days after the giving of the direction, the determination of the appeal or the making of the order, to deliver to the registrar for registration such a copy of the direction, determination or order as is prescribed.

(7)   If a person without reasonable excuse fails to deliver a copy as required by subsection (6), he is liable to a fine and, for continued contravention, to a daily default fine.

CHAPTER X

MALPRACTICE BEFORE AND DURING LIQUIDATION; PENALISATION OF COMPANIES AND COMPANY OFFICERS; INVESTIGATIONS AND PROSECUTIONS

Offences of fraud, deception, etc

206   Fraud, etc in anticipation of winding up

(1)   When a company is ordered to be wound up by the court, or passes a resolution for voluntary winding up, any person, being a past or present officer of the company, is deemed to have committed an offence if, within the 12 months immediately preceding the commencement of the winding up, he has—

(a)   concealed any part of the company's property to the value of £500 or more, or concealed any debt due to or from the company, or

(b)   fraudulently removed any part of the company's property to the value of £500 or more, or

(c)   concealed, destroyed, mutilated or falsified any book or paper affecting or relating to the company's property or affairs, or

(d)   made any false entry in any book or paper affecting or relating to the company's property or affairs, or

(e)   fraudulently parted with, altered or made any omission in any document affecting or relating to the company's property or affairs, or

(f)   pawned, pledged or disposed of any property of the company which has been obtained on credit and has not been paid for (unless the pawning, pledging or disposal was in the ordinary way of the company's business).

(2)   Such a person is deemed to have committed an offence if within the period above mentioned he has been privy to the doing by others of any of the things mentioned in paragraphs (c), (d) and (e) of subsection (1); and he commits an offence if, at any time after the commencement of the winding up, he does any of the things mentioned in paragraphs (a) to

(f) of that subsection, or is privy to the doing by others of any of the things mentioned in paragraphs (c) to (e) of it.

(3)   For purposes of this section, "officer" includes a shadow director.

(4)   It is a defence—

    (a)   for a person charged under paragraph (a) or (f) of subsection (1) (or under subsection (2) in respect of the things mentioned in either of those two paragraphs) to prove that he had no intent to defraud, and

    (b)   for a person charged under paragraph (c) or (d) of subsection (1) (or under subsection (2) in respect of the things mentioned in either of those two paragraphs) to prove that he had no intent to conceal the state of affairs of the company or to defeat the law.

(5)   Where a person pawns, pledges or disposes of any property in circumstances which amount to an offence under subsection (1)(f), every person who takes in pawn or pledge, or otherwise receives, the property knowing it to be pawned, pledged or disposed of in such circumstances, is guilty of an offence.

(6)   A person guilty of an offence under this section is liable to imprisonment or a fine, or both.

...

207   Transactions in fraud of creditors

(1)   When a company is ordered to be wound up by the court or passes a resolution for voluntary winding up, a person is deemed to have committed an offence if he, being at the time an officer of the company—

    (a)   has made or caused to be made any gift or transfer of, or charge on, or has caused or connived at the levying of any execution against, the company's property, or

    (b)   has concealed or removed any part of the company's property since, or within 2 months before, the date of any unsatisfied judgment or order for the payment of money obtained against the company.

(2)   A person is not guilty of an offence under this section—

    (a)   by reason of conduct constituting an offence under subsection (1)(a) which occurred more than 5 years before the commencement of the winding up, or

    (b)   if he proves that, at the time of the conduct constituting the offence, he had no intent to defraud the company's creditors.

(3)   A person guilty of an offence under this section is liable to imprisonment or a fine, or both.

208   Misconduct in course of winding up

(1)   When a company is being wound up, whether by the court or voluntarily, any person, being a past or present officer of the company, commits an offence if he—

    (a)   does not to the best of his knowledge and belief fully and truly discover to the liquidator all the company's property, and how and to whom and for what consideration and when the company disposed of any part of that property (except such part as has been disposed of in the ordinary way of the company's business), or

    (b)   does not deliver up to the liquidator (or as he directs) all such part of the company's property as is in his custody or under his control, and which he is required by law to deliver up, or

    (c)   does not deliver up to the liquidator (or as he directs) all books and papers in his custody or under his control belonging to the company and which he is required by law to deliver up, or

    (d)   knowing or believing that a false debt has been proved by any person in the winding up, fails to inform the liquidator as soon as practicable, or

    (e)   after the commencement of the winding up, prevents the production of any book or paper affecting or relating to the company's property or affairs.

(2)   Such a person commits an offence if after the commencement of the winding up he attempts to account for any part of the company's property by fictitious losses or expenses; and he is deemed to have committed that offence if he has so attempted at any meeting of the company's creditors within the 12 months immediately preceding the commencement of the winding up.

(3)   For purposes of this section, "officer" includes a shadow director.

(4)   It is a defence—

    (a)   for a person charged under paragraph (a), (b) or (c) of subsection (1) to prove that he had no intent to defraud, and

    (b)   for a person charged under paragraph (e) of that subsection to prove that he had no intent to conceal the state of affairs of the company or to defeat the law.

(5)   A person guilty of an offence under this section is liable to imprisonment or a fine, or both.

209   Falsification of company's books

(1)   When a company is being wound up, an officer or contributory of the company commits an offence if he destroys, mutilates, alters or falsifies any books, papers or securities, or makes or is privy to the making of any false or fraudulent entry in any register, book of account or document belonging to the company with intent to defraud or deceive any person.

(2)   A person guilty of an offence under this section is liable to imprisonment or a fine, or both.

210   Material omissions from statement relating to company's affairs

(1)   When a company is being wound up, whether by the court or voluntarily, any person, being a past or present officer of the company, commits an offence if he makes any material omission in any statement relating to the company's affairs.

(2)   When a company has been ordered to be wound up by the court, or has passed a resolution for voluntary winding up, any such person is deemed to have committed that offence if, prior to the winding up, he has made any material omission in any such statement.

(3)   For purposes of this section, "officer" includes a shadow director.

(4)   It is a defence for a person charged under this section to prove that he had no intent to defraud.

(5)   A person guilty of an offence under this section is liable to imprisonment or a fine, or both.

211   False representations to creditors

(1)   When a company is being wound up, whether by the court or voluntarily, any person, being a past or present officer of the company—

    (a)   commits an offence if he makes any false representation or commits any other fraud for the purpose of obtaining the consent of the company's creditors or any of them to an agreement with reference to the company's affairs or to the winding up, and

    (b)   is deemed to have committed that offence if, prior to the winding up, he has made any false representation, or committed any other fraud, for that purpose.

(2)   For purposes of this section, "officer" includes a shadow director.

(3)   A person guilty of an offence under this section is liable to imprisonment or a fine, or both.

Penalisation of directors and officers

212   Summary remedy against delinquent directors, liquidators, etc

(1)   This section applies if in the course of the winding up of a company it appears that a person who—

    (a)   is or has been an officer of the company,

    (b)   has acted as liquidator or administrative receiver of the company, or

    (c)   not being a person falling within paragraph (a) or (b), is or has been concerned, or has taken part, in the promotion, formation or management of the company,

has misapplied or retained, or become accountable for, any money or other property of the company, or been guilty of any misfeasance or breach of any fiduciary or other duty in relation to the company.

(2)   The reference in subsection (1) to any misfeasance or breach of any fiduciary or other duty in relation to the company includes, in the case of a person who has acted as liquidator of the company, any misfeasance or breach of any fiduciary or other duty in connection with the carrying out of his functions as liquidator of the company.

(3)   The court may, on the application of the official receiver or the liquidator, or of any creditor or contributory, examine into the conduct of the person falling within subsection (1) and compel him—

      (a)   to repay, restore or account for the money or property or any part of it, with interest at such rate as the court thinks just, or

      (b)   to contribute such sum to the company's assets by way of compensation in respect of the misfeasance or breach of fiduciary or other duty as the court thinks just.

(4)   The power to make an application under subsection (3) in relation to a person who has acted as liquidator of the company is not exercisable, except with the leave of the court, after he has had his release.

(5)   The power of a contributory to make an application under subsection (3) is not exercisable except with the leave of the court, but is exercisable notwithstanding that he will not benefit from any order the court may make on the application.

213   Fraudulent trading

(1)   If in the course of the winding up of a company it appears that any business of the company has been carried on with intent to defraud creditors of the company or creditors of any other person, or for any fraudulent purpose, the following has effect.

(2)   The court, on the application of the liquidator may declare that any persons who were knowingly parties to the carrying on of the business in the manner above-mentioned are to be liable to make such contributions (if any) to the company's assets as the court thinks proper.

214   Wrongful trading

(1)   Subject to subsection (3) below, if in the course of the winding up of a company it appears that subsection (2) of this section applies in relation to a person who is or has been a director of the company, the court, on the application of the liquidator, may declare that that person is to be liable to make such contribution (if any) to the company's assets as the court thinks proper.

(2)   This subsection applies in relation to a person if—

      (a)   the company has gone into insolvent liquidation,

      (b)   at some time before the commencement of the winding up of the company, that person knew or ought to have concluded that there was no reasonable prospect that the company would avoid going into insolvent liquidation, and

      (c)   that person was a director of the company at that time;

but the court shall not make a declaration under this section in any case where the time mentioned in paragraph (b) above was before 28th April 1986.

(3)   The court shall not make a declaration under this section with respect to any person if it is satisfied that after the condition specified in subsection (2)(b) was first satisfied in relation to him that person took every step with a view to minimising the potential loss to the company's creditors as (assuming him to have known that there was no reasonable prospect that the company would avoid going into insolvent liquidation) he ought to have taken.

(4)   For the purposes of subsections (2) and (3), the facts which a director of a company ought to know or ascertain, the conclusions which he ought to reach and the steps which he ought to take are those which would be known or ascertained, or reached or taken, by a reasonably diligent person having both—

      (a)   the general knowledge, skill and experience that may reasonably be expected of a person carrying out the same functions as are carried out by that director in relation to the company, and

      (b)   the general knowledge, skill and experience that that director has.

(5)   The reference in subsection (4) to the functions carried out in relation to a company by a director of the company includes any functions which he does not carry out but which have been entrusted to him.

(6)   For the purposes of this section a company goes into insolvent liquidation if it goes into liquidation at a time when its assets are insufficient for the payment of its debts and other liabilities and the expenses of the winding up.

(7)   In this section "director" includes a shadow director.

(8)   This section is without prejudice to section 213.

214A   Adjustment of withdrawals

    (1)   This section has effect in relation to a person who is or has been a member of a limited liability partnership where, in the course of the winding up of that limited liability partnership, it appears that subsection (2) of this section applies in relation to that person.

    (2)   This subsection applies in relation to a person if—

        (a)   within the period of two years ending with the commencement of the winding up, he was a member of the limited liability partnership who withdrew property of the limited liability partnership, whether in the form of a share of profits, salary, repayment of or payment of interest on a loan to the limited liability partnership or any other withdrawal of property, and

        (b)   it is proved by the liquidator to the satisfaction of the court that at the time of the withdrawal he knew or had reasonable grounds for believing that the limited liability partnership—

            (i)   was at the time of the withdrawal unable to pay its debts within the meaning of section 123 of the Act, or

            (ii)   would become so unable to pay its debts after the assets of the limited liability partnership had been depleted by that withdrawal taken together with all other withdrawals (if any) made by any members contemporaneously with that withdrawal or in contemplation when that withdrawal was made.

    (3)   Where this section has effect in relation to any person the court, on the application of the liquidator, may declare that that person is to be liable to make such contribution (if any) to the limited liability partnership's assets as the court thinks proper.

    (4)   The court shall not make a declaration in relation to any person the amount of which exceeds the aggregate of the amounts or values of all the withdrawals referred to in subsection (2) made by that person within the period of 2 years referred to in that subsection.

    (5)   The court shall not make a declaration under this section with respect to any person unless that person knew or ought to have concluded that after each withdrawal referred to in subsection (2) there was no reasonable prospect that the limited liability partnership would avoid going into insolvent liquidation.

    (6)   For the purposes of subsection (5) the facts which a member ought to know or ascertain, the conclusions which he ought to reach and the steps which he ought to have taken are those which would be known or ascertained, or reached or taken, by a reasonably diligent person having both:

        (a)   the general knowledge, skill and experience that may reasonably be expected of a person carrying out the same functions as are carried out by that member in relation to the limited liability partnership, and

        (b)   the general knowledge, skill and experience that that member has.

    (7)   For the purposes of this section a limited liability partnership goes into insolvent liquidation if it goes into liquidation at a time when its assets are insufficient for the payment of its debts and other liabilities and the expenses of the winding up.

    (8)   In this section "member" includes a shadow member.

    (9)   This section is without prejudice to section 214.

215   Proceedings under ss 213, 214

    (1)   On the hearing of an application under section 213 or 214, the liquidator may himself give evidence or call witnesses.

    (2)   Where under either section the court makes a declaration, it may give such further directions as it thinks proper for giving effect to the declaration; and in particular, the court may—

        (a)   provide for the liability of any person under the declaration to be a charge on any debt or obligation due from the company to him, or on any mortgage or charge or any interest in a mortgage or charge on assets of the company held by or vested in him, or any person on his behalf, or any person claiming as assignee from or through the person liable or any person acting on his behalf, and

(b) from time to time make such further order as may be necessary for enforcing any charge imposed under this subsection.

(3) For the purposes of subsection (2), "assignee"—

(a) includes a person to whom or in whose favour, by the directions of the person made liable, the debt, obligation, mortgage or charge was created, issued or transferred or the interest created, but

(b) does not include an assignee for valuable consideration (not including consideration by way of marriage[or the formation of a civil partnership]1) given in good faith and without notice of any of the matters on the ground of which the declaration is made.

(4) Where the court makes a declaration under either section in relation to a person who is a creditor of the company, it may direct that the whole or any part of any debt owed by the company to that person and any interest thereon shall rank in priority after all other debts owed by the company and after any interest on those debts.

(5) Sections 213 and 214 have effect notwithstanding that the person concerned may be criminally liable in respect of matters on the ground of which the declaration under the section is to be made.

216 Restriction on re-use of company names

(1) This section applies to a person where a company ("the liquidating company") has gone into insolvent liquidation on or after the appointed day and he was a director or shadow director of the company at any time in the period of 12 months ending with the day before it went into liquidation.

(2) For the purposes of this section, a name is a prohibited name in relation to such a person if—

(a) it is a name by which the liquidating company was known at any time in that period of 12 months, or

(b) it is a name which is so similar to a name falling within paragraph (a) as to suggest an association with that company.

(3) Except with leave of the court or in such circumstances as may be prescribed, a person to whom this section applies shall not at any time in the period of 5 years beginning with the day on which the liquidating company went into liquidation—

(a) be a director of any other company that is known by a prohibited name, or

(b) in any way, whether directly or indirectly, be concerned or take part in the promotion, formation or management of any such company, or

(c) in any way, whether directly or indirectly, be concerned or take part in the carrying on of a business carried on (otherwise than by a company) under a prohibited name.

(4) If a person acts in contravention of this section, he is liable to imprisonment or a fine, or both.

(5) In subsection (3) "the court" means any court having jurisdiction to wind up companies; and on an application for leave under that subsection, the Secretary of State or the official receiver may appear and call the attention of the court to any matters which seem to him to be relevant.

(6) References in this section, in relation to any time, to a name by which a company is known are to the name of the company at that time or to any name under which the company carries on business at that time.

(7) For the purposes of this section a company goes into insolvent liquidation if it goes into liquidation at a time when its assets are insufficient for the payment of its debts and other liabilities and the expenses of the winding up.

(8) In this section "company" includes a company which may be wound up under Part V of this Act.

217 Personal liability for debts, following contravention of s 216

(1) A person is personally responsible for all the relevant debts of a company if at any time—

(a) in contravention of section 216, he is involved in the management of the company, or

(b) as a person who is involved in the management of the company, he acts or is willing to act on instructions given (without the leave of the court) by a person whom he knows at that time to be in contravention in relation to the company of section 216.

(2) Where a person is personally responsible under this section for the relevant debts of a company, he is jointly and severally liable in respect of those debts with the company and any other person who, whether under this section or otherwise, is so liable.

(3) For the purposes of this section the relevant debts of a company are—

(a) in relation to a person who is personally responsible under paragraph (a) of subsection (1), such debts and other liabilities of the company as are incurred at a time when that person was involved in the management of the company, and

(b) in relation to a person who is personally responsible under paragraph (b) of that subsection, such debts and other liabilities of the company as are incurred at a time when that person was acting or was willing to act on instructions given as mentioned in that paragraph.

(4) For the purposes of this section, a person is involved in the management of a company if he is a director of the company or if he is concerned, whether directly or indirectly, or takes part, in the management of the company.

(5) For the purposes of this section a person who, as a person involved in the management of a company, has at any time acted on instructions given (without the leave of the court) by a person whom he knew at that time to be in contravention in relation to the company of section 216 is presumed, unless the contrary is shown, to have been willing at any time thereafter to act on any instructions given by that person.

(6) In this section "company" includes a company which may be wound up under Part V.

Investigation and prosecution of malpractice

218　Prosecution of delinquent officers and members of company

(1) If it appears to the court in the course of a winding up by the court that any past or present officer, or any member, of the company has been guilty of any offence in relation to the company for which he is criminally liable, the court may (either on the application of a person interested in the winding up or of its own motion) direct the liquidator to refer the matter

(a) in the case of a winding up in England and Wales, to the Secretary of State, and

　...

(2) ...

(3) If in the case of a winding up by the court in England and Wales it appears to the liquidator, not being the official receiver, that any past or present officer of the company, or any member of it, has been guilty of an offence in relation to the company for which he is criminally liable, the liquidator shall report the matter to the official receiver.

(4) If it appears to the liquidator in the course of a voluntary winding up that any past or present officer of the company, or any member of it, has been guilty of an offence in relation to the company for which he is criminally liable, he shall forthwith report the matter—

(a) in the case of a winding up in England and Wales, to the Secretary of State, and

　...

(5) Where a report is made to the Secretary of State under subsection (4) he may, for the purpose of investigating the matter reported to him and such other matters relating to the affairs of the company as appear to him to require investigation, exercise any of the powers which are exercisable by inspectors appointed under section 431 or 432 of the Companies Act to investigate a company's affairs.

(6) If it appears to the court in the course of a voluntary winding up that—

(a) any past or present officer of the company, or any member of it, has been guilty as above-mentioned, and

(b) no report with respect to the matter has been made by the liquidator under subsection (4), the court may (on the application of any person interested in the winding up or of its own motion) direct the liquidator to make such a report.

On a report being made accordingly, this section has effect as though the report had been made in pursuance of subsection (4).

219   Obligations arising under s 218

(1)   For the purpose of an investigation by the Secretary of State in consequence of a report made to him under section 218(4), any obligation imposed on a person by any provision of the Companies Act to produce documents or give information to, or otherwise to assist, inspectors appointed as mentioned in section 218(5) is to be regarded as an obligation similarly to assist the Secretary of State in his investigation.

(2)   An answer given by a person to a question put to him in exercise of the powers conferred by section 218(5) may be used in evidence against him.

(2A) However, in criminal proceedings in which that person is charged with an offence to which this subsection applies—

(a)   no evidence relating to the answer may be adduced, and

(b)   no question relating to it may be asked,

by or on behalf of the prosecution, unless evidence relating to it is adduced, or a question relating to it is asked, in the proceedings by or on behalf of that person.

(2B) Subsection (2A) applies to any offence other than—

(a)   an offence under section 2 or 5 of the Perjury Act 1911 (false statements made on oath otherwise than in judicial proceedings or made otherwise than on oath), or

...

(3)   Where criminal proceedings are instituted by the Director of Public Prosecutions, ... or the Secretary of State following any report or reference under section 218, it is the duty of the liquidator and every officer and agent of the company past and present (other than the defendant or defender) to give to the Director of Public Prosecutions, ... or the Secretary of State (as the case may be) all assistance in connection with the prosecution which he is reasonably able to give.

For this purpose "agent" includes any banker or solicitor of the company and any person employed by the company as auditor, whether that person is or is not an officer of the company.

(4)   If a person fails or neglects to give assistance in the manner required by subsection (3), the court may, on the application of the Director of Public Prosecutions, ... or the Secretary of State (as the case may be) direct the person to comply with that subsection; and if the application is made with respect to a liquidator, the court may (unless it appears that the failure or neglect to comply was due to the liquidator not having in his hands sufficient assets of the company to enable him to do so) direct that the costs shall be borne by the liquidator personally.

PART V
WINDING UP OF UNREGISTERED COMPANIES

220   Meaning of "unregistered company"

(1)   For the purposes of this Part, the expression "unregistered company" includes any association and any company, with the following exceptions—

(a)   ...

(b)   a company registered in any part of the United Kingdom under the Joint Stock Companies Acts or under the legislation (past or present) relating to companies in Great Britain.

...

221   Winding up of unregistered companies

(1)   Subject to the provisions of this Part, any unregistered company may be wound up under this Act; and all the provisions of this Act and the Companies Act about winding up apply to

an unregistered company with the exceptions and additions mentioned in the following subsections.

(2)   If an unregistered company has a principal place of business situated in Northern Ireland, it shall not be wound up under this Part unless it has a principal place of business situated in England and Wales ..., or in both England and Wales ...

(3)   For the purpose of determining a court's winding-up jurisdiction, an unregistered company is deemed—

(a)   to be registered in England and Wales ..., according as its principal place of business is situated in England and Wales ..., or

(b)   if it has a principal place of business situated in both countries, to be registered in both countries;

and the principal place of business situated in that part of Great Britain in which proceedings are being instituted is, for all purposes of the winding up, deemed to be the registered office of the company.

(4)   No unregistered company shall be wound up under this Act voluntarily, except in accordance with the EC Regulation.

(5)   The circumstances in which an unregistered company may be wound up are as follows—

(a)   if the company is dissolved, or has ceased to carry on business, or is carrying on business only for the purpose of winding up its affairs;

(b)   if the company is unable to pay its debts;

(c)   if the court is of opinion that it is just and equitable that the company should be wound up.

...

222   Inability to pay debts: unpaid creditor for £750 or more

(1)   An unregistered company is deemed (for the purposes of section 221) unable to pay its debts if there is a creditor, by assignment or otherwise, to whom the company is indebted in a sum exceeding £750 then due and—

(a)   the creditor has served on the company, by leaving at its principal place of business, or by delivering to the secretary or some director, manager or principal officer of the company, or by otherwise serving in such manner as the court may approve or direct, a written demand in the prescribed form requiring the company to pay the sum due, and

(b)   the company has for 3 weeks after the service of the demand neglected to pay the sum or to secure or compound for it to the creditor's satisfaction.

(2)   The money sum for the time being specified in subsection (1) is subject to increase or reduction by regulations under section 417 in Part XV; but no increase in the sum so specified affects any case in which the winding-up petition was presented before the coming into force of the increase.

223   Inability to pay debts: debt remaining unsatisfied after action brought

An unregistered company is deemed (for the purposes of section 221) unable to pay its debts if an action or other proceeding has been instituted against any member for any debt or demand due, or claimed to be due, from the company, or from him in his character of member, and—

(a)   notice in writing of the institution of the action or proceeding has been served on the company by leaving it at the company's principal place of business (or by delivering it to the secretary, or some director, manager or principal officer of the company, or by otherwise serving it in such manner as the court may approve or direct), and

(b)   the company has not within 3 weeks after service of the notice paid, secured or compounded for the debt or demand, or procured the action or proceeding to be stayed or sisted, or indemnified the defendant or defender to his reasonable satisfaction against the action or proceeding, and against all costs, damages and expenses to be incurred by him because of it.

224   Inability to pay debts: other cases

(1)   An unregistered company is deemed (for purposes of section 221) unable to pay its debts—

(a)   if in England and Wales execution or other process issued on a judgment, decree or order obtained in any court in favour of a creditor against the company, or any member of it as such, or any person authorised to be sued as nominal defendant on behalf of the company, is returned unsatisfied;

...

(c) if in Northern Ireland a certificate of unenforceability has been granted in respect of any judgment, decree or order obtained as mentioned in paragraph (a);

(d) if it is otherwise proved to the satisfaction of the court that the company is unable to pay its debts as they fall due.

(2) An unregistered company is also deemed unable to pay its debts if it is proved to the satisfaction of the court that the value of the company's assets is less than the amount of its liabilities, taking into account its contingent and prospective liabilities.

225 Oversea company may be wound up though dissolved

(1) Where a company incorporated outside Great Britain which has been carrying on business in Great Britain ceases to carry on business in Great Britain, it may be wound up as an unregistered company under this Act, notwithstanding that it has been dissolved or otherwise ceased to exist as a company under or by virtue of the laws of the country under which it was incorporated.

(2) This section is subject to the EC Regulation.

...

227 Power of court to stay, sist or restrain proceedings

The provisions of this Part with respect to staying, sisting or restraining actions and proceedings against a company at any time after the presentation of a petition for winding up and before the making of a winding-up order extend, in the case of an unregistered company, where the application to stay, sist or restrain is presented by a creditor, to actions and proceedings against any contributory of the company.

228 Actions stayed on winding-up order

Where an order has been made for winding up an unregistered company, no action or proceeding shall be proceeded with or commenced against any contributory of the company in respect of any debt of the company, except by leave of the court, and subject to such terms as the court may impose.

229 Provisions of this Part to be cumulative

(1) The provisions of this Part with respect to unregistered companies are in addition to and not in restriction of any provisions in Part IV with respect to winding up companies by the court; and the court or liquidator may exercise any powers or do any act in the case of unregistered companies which might be exercised or done by it or him in winding up companies formed and registered under the Companies Act.

(2) However, an unregistered company is not, except in the event of its being wound up, deemed to be a company under the Companies Act, and then only to the extent provided by this Part of this Act.

PART VI

MISCELLANEOUS PROVISIONS APPLYING TO COMPANIES WHICH ARE INSOLVENT OR IN LIQUIDATION

Office-holders

230 Holders of office to be qualified insolvency practitioners

(1) ...

(2) Where an administrative receiver of a company is appointed, he must be a person who is so qualified.

(3) Where a company goes into liquidation, the liquidator must be a person who is so qualified.

(4) Where a provisional liquidator is appointed, he must be a person who is so qualified.

(5) Subsections (3) and (4) are without prejudice to any enactment under which the official receiver is to be, or may be, liquidator or provisional liquidator.

231   Appointment to office of two or more persons

(1)   This section applies if an appointment or nomination of any person to the office of administrative receiver, liquidator or provisional liquidator—

(a)   relates to more than one person, or

(b)   has the effect that the office is to be held by more than one person.

(2)   The appointment or nomination shall declare whether any act required or authorised under any enactment to be done by the ... administrative receiver, liquidator or provisional liquidator is to be done by all or any one or more of the persons for the time being holding the office in question.

232   Validity of office-holder's acts

The acts of an individual as administrative receiver, liquidator or provisional liquidator of a company are valid notwithstanding any defect in his appointment, nomination or qualifications.

Management by administrators, liquidators, etc

233   Supplies of gas, water, electricity, etc

(1)   This section applies in the case of a company where—

(a)   the company enters administration, or

(b)   an administrative receiver is appointed, or

(ba)   a moratorium under section 1A is in force, or,

(c)   a voluntary arrangement approved under Part I, has taken effect, or

(d)   the company goes into liquidation, or

(e)   a provisional liquidator is appointed;

and "the office-holder" means the administrator, the administrative receiver, the nominee, the supervisor of the voluntary arrangement, the liquidator or the provisional liquidator, as the case may be.

(2)   If a request is made by or with the concurrence of the office-holder for the giving, after the effective date, of any of the supplies mentioned in the next subsection, the supplier—

(a)   may make it a condition of the giving of the supply that the office-holder personally guarantees the payment of any charges in respect of the supply, but

(b)   shall not make it a condition of the giving of the supply, or do anything which has the effect of making it a condition of the giving of the supply, that any outstanding charges in respect of a supply given to the company before the effective date are paid.

(3)   The supplies referred to in subsection (2) are—

(a)   a supply of gas by a gas supplier within the meaning of Part I of the Gas Act 1986:

(b)   a supply of electricity by an electricity supplier within the meaning of Part I of the Electricity Act 1989,

(c)   a supply of water by a water undertaker ...

(d)   a supply of communications services by a provider of a public electronic communications service.

(4)   "The effective date" for the purposes of this section is whichever is applicable of the following dates—

(a)   the date on which the company entered administration,

(b)   the date on which the administrative receiver was appointed (or, if he was appointed in succession to another administrative receiver, the date on which the first of his predecessors was appointed),

(ba)   the date on which the moratorium came into force,

(c)   the date on which the voluntary arrangement took effect,

(d)   the date on which the company went into liquidation,

(e)   the date on which the provisional liquidator was appointed.

(5)   The following applies to expressions used in subsection (3)—

(a)   ...

(b)   ...

...

(d) 'communications services' do not include electronic communications services to the extent that they are used to broadcast or otherwise transmit programme services (within the meaning of the Communications Act 2003).

234 Getting in the company's property

(1) This section applies in the case of a company where—
   (a) the company enters administration,
   (b) an administrative receiver is appointed, or
   (c) the company goes into liquidation, or
   (d) a provisional liquidator is appointed;
   and "the office-holder" means the administrator, the administrative receiver, the liquidator or the provisional liquidator, as the case may be.

(2) Where any person has in his possession or control any property, books, papers or records to which the company appears to be entitled, the court may require that person forthwith (or within such period as the court may direct) to pay, deliver, convey, surrender or transfer the property, books, papers or records to the office-holder.

(3) Where the office-holder—
   (a) seizes or disposes of any property which is not property of the company, and
   (b) at the time of seizure or disposal believes, and has reasonable grounds for believing, that he is entitled (whether in pursuance of an order of the court or otherwise) to seize or dispose of that property,
   the next subsection has effect.

(4) In that case the office-holder—
   (a) is not liable to any person in respect of any loss or damage resulting from the seizure or disposal except in so far as that loss or damage is caused by the office-holder's own negligence, and
   (b) has a lien on the property, or the proceeds of its sale, for such expenses as were incurred in connection with the seizure or disposal.

235 Duty to co-operate with office-holder

(1) This section applies as does section 234; and it also applies, in the case of a company in respect of which a winding-up order has been made by the court in England and Wales, as if references to the office-holder included the official receiver, whether or not he is the liquidator.

(2) Each of the persons mentioned in the next subsection shall—
   (a) give to the office-holder such information concerning the company and its promotion, formation, business, dealings, affairs or property as the office-holder may at any time after the effective date reasonably require, and
   (b) attend on the office-holder at such times as the latter may reasonably require.

(3) The persons referred to above are—
   (a) those who are or have at any time been officers of the company,
   (b) those who have taken part in the formation of the company at any time within one year before the effective date,
   (c) those who are in the employment of the company, or have been in its employment (including employment under a contract for services) within that year, and are in the office-holder's opinion capable of giving information which he requires,
   (d) those who are, or have within that year been, officers of, or in the employment (including employment under a contract for services) of, another company which is, or within that year was, an officer of the company in question, and
   (e) in the case of a company being wound up by the court, any person who has acted as administrator, administrative receiver or liquidator of the company.

(4) For the purposes of subsections (2) and (3), "the effective date" is whichever is applicable of the following dates—
   (a) the date on which the company entered administration,

      (b)   the date on which the administrative receiver was appointed or, if he was appointed in succession to another administrative receiver, the date on which the first of his predecessors was appointed,

      (c)   the date on which the provisional liquidator was appointed, and

      (d)   the date on which the company went into liquidation.

   (5)   If a person without reasonable excuse fails to comply with any obligation imposed by this section, he is liable to a fine and, for continued contravention, to a daily default fine.

236   Inquiry into company's dealings, etc

   (1)   This section applies as does section 234; and it also applies in the case of a company in respect of which a winding-up order has been made by the court in England and Wales as if references to the office-holder included the official receiver, whether or not he is the liquidator.

   (2)   The court may, on the application of the office-holder, summon to appear before it—

      (a)   any officer of the company,

      (b)   any person known or suspected to have in his possession any property of the company or supposed to be indebted to the company, or

      (c)   any person whom the court thinks capable of giving information concerning the promotion, formation, business, dealings, affairs or property of the company.

   (3)   The court may require any such person as is mentioned in subsection (2)(a) to (c) to submit an affidavit to the court containing an account of his dealings with the company or to produce any books, papers or other records in his possession or under his control relating to the company or the matters mentioned in paragraph (c) of the subsection.

   (4)   The following applies in a case where—

      (a)   a person without reasonable excuse fails to appear before the court when he is summoned to do so under this section, or

      (b)   there are reasonable grounds for believing that a person has absconded, or is about to abscond, with a view to avoiding his appearance before the court under this section.

   (5)   The court may, for the purpose of bringing that person and anything in his possession before the court, cause a warrant to be issued to a constable or prescribed officer of the court—

      (a)   for the arrest of that person, and

      (b)   for the seizure of any books, papers, records, money or goods in that person's possession.

   (6)   The court may authorise a person arrested under such a warrant to be kept in custody, and anything seized under such a warrant to be held, in accordance with the rules, until that person is brought before the court under the warrant or until such other time as the court may order.

237   Court's enforcement powers under s 236

   (1)   If it appears to the court, on consideration of any evidence obtained under section 236 or this section, that any person has in his possession any property of the company, the court may, on the application of the office-holder, order that person to deliver the whole or any part of the property to the office-holder at such time, in such manner and on such terms as the court thinks fit.

   (2)   If it appears to the court, on consideration of any evidence so obtained, that any person is indebted to the company, the court may, on the application of the office-holder, order that person to pay to the office-holder, at such time and in such manner as the court may direct, the whole or any part of the amount due, whether in full discharge of the debt or otherwise, as the court thinks fit.

   (3)   The court may, if it thinks fit, order that any person who if within the jurisdiction of the court would be liable to be summoned to appear before it under section 236 or this section shall be examined in any part of the United Kingdom where he may for the time being be, or in a place outside the United Kingdom.

(4) Any person who appears or is brought before the court under section 236 or this section may be examined on oath, either orally or ... by interrogatories, concerning the company or the matters mentioned in section 236(2)(c).

Adjustment of prior transactions (administration and liquidation)

238 Transactions at an undervalue (England and Wales)

(1) This section applies in the case of a company where—
    (a) the company enters administration, or
    (b) the company goes into liquidation;
and "the office-holder" means the administrator or the liquidator, as the case may be.

(2) Where the company has at a relevant time (defined in section 240) entered into a transaction with any person at an undervalue, the office-holder may apply to the court for an order under this section.

(3) Subject as follows, the court shall, on such an application, make such order as it thinks fit for restoring the position to what it would have been if the company had not entered into that transaction.

(4) For the purposes of this section and section 241, a company enters into a transaction with a person at an undervalue if—
    (a) the company makes a gift to that person or otherwise enters into a transaction with that person on terms that provide for the company to receive no consideration, or
    (b) the company enters into a transaction with that person for a consideration the value of which, in money or money's worth, is significantly less than the value, in money or money's worth, of the consideration provided by the company.

(5) The court shall not make an order under this section in respect of a transaction at an undervalue if it is satisfied—
    (a) that the company which entered into the transaction did so in good faith and for the purpose of carrying on its business, and
    (b) that at the time it did so there were reasonable grounds for believing that the transaction would benefit the company.

239 Preferences (England and Wales)

(1) This section applies as does section 238.

(2) Where the company has at a relevant time (defined in the next section, given a preference to any person, the office-holder may apply to the court for an order under this section.

(3) Subject as follows, the court shall, on such an application, make such order as it thinks fit for restoring the position to what it would have been if the company had not given that preference.

(4) For the purposes of this section and section 241, a company gives a preference to a person if—
    (a) that person is one of the company's creditors or a surety or guarantor for any of the company's debts or other liabilities, and
    (b) the company does anything or suffers anything to be done which (in either case) has the effect of putting that person into a position which, in the event of the company going into insolvent liquidation, will be better than the position he would have been in if that thing had not been done.

(5) The court shall not make an order under this section in respect of a preference given to any person unless the company which gave the preference was influenced in deciding to give it by a desire to produce in relation to that person the effect mentioned in subsection (4)(b).

(6) A company which has given a preference to a person connected with the company (otherwise than by reason only of being its employee) at the time the preference was given is presumed, unless the contrary is shown, to have been influenced in deciding to give it by such a desire as is mentioned in subsection (5).

(7) The fact that something has been done in pursuance of the order of a court does not, without more, prevent the doing or suffering of that thing from constituting the giving of a preference

240 "Relevant time" under ss 238, 239

(1) Subject to the next subsection, the time at which a company enters into a transaction at an undervalue or gives a preference is a relevant time if the transaction is entered into, or the preference given—

(a) in the case of a transaction at an undervalue or of a preference which is given to a person who is connected with the company (otherwise than by reason only of being its employee), at a time in the period of 2 years ending with the onset of insolvency (which expression is defined below),

(b) in the case of a preference which is not such a transaction and is not so given, at a time in the period of 6 months ending with the onset of insolvency,

(c) in either case, at a time between the making of an administration application in respect of the company and the making of an administration order on that application, and

(d) in either case, at a time between the filing with the court of a copy of notice of Intention to appoint an administrator under paragraph 14 or 22 of Schedule B1 and the making of an appointment under that paragraph.

(2) Where a company enters into a transaction at an undervalue or gives a preference at a time mentioned in subsection (1)(a) or (b), that time is not a relevant time for the purpose of section 238 or 239 unless the company—

(a) is at that time unable to pay its debts within the meaning of section 123 in Chapter VI of Part IV, or

(b) becomes unable to pay its debts within the meaning of that section in consequence of the transaction or preference;

but the requirements of this subsection are presumed to be satisfied, unless the contrary is shown, in relation to any transaction at an undervalue which is entered into by a company with a person who is connected with the company.

(3) For the purposes of subsection (1), the onset of insolvency is—

(a) in a case where section 238 or 239 applies by reason of an administrator of a company being appointed by administration order, the date on which the administration application is made,

(b) in a case where section 238 or 239 applies by reason of an administrator of a company being appointed under paragraph 14 or 22 of Schedule B1 following filing with the court of a copy of a notice of intention to appoint under that paragraph, the date on which the copy of the notice is filed,

(c) in a case where section 238 or 239 applies by reason of an administrator of a company being appointed otherwise than as mentioned in paragraph (a) or (b), the date on which the appointment takes effect,

(d) in a case where section 238 or 239 applies by reason of a company going into liquidation either following conversion of administration into winding up by virtue of Article 37 of the EC Regulation or at the time when the appointment of an administrator ceases to have effect, the date on which the company entered administration (or, if relevant, the date on which the application for the administration order was made or a copy of the notice of intention to appoint was filed), and

(e) in a case where section 238 or 239 applies by reason of a company going into liquidation at any other time, the date of the commencement of the winding up.

241 Orders under ss 238, 239

(1) Without prejudice to the generality of sections 238(3) and 239(3), an order under either of those sections with respect to a transaction or preference entered into or given by a company may (subject to the next subsection)—

(a) require any property transferred as part of the transaction, or in connection with the giving of the preference, to be vested in the company,

(b) require any property to be so vested if it represents in any person's hands the application either of the proceeds of sale of property so transferred or of money so transferred,

(c) release or discharge (in whole or in part) any security given by the company,

(d)   require any person to pay, in respect of benefits received by him from the company, such sums to the office-holder as the court may direct,

(e)   provide for any surety or guarantor whose obligations to any person were released or discharged (in whole or in part) under the transaction, or by the giving of the preference, to be under such new or revived obligations to that person as the court thinks appropriate,

(f)   provide for security to be provided for the discharge of any obligation imposed by or arising under the order, for such an obligation to be charged on any property and for the security or charge to have the same priority as a security or charge released or discharged (in whole or in part) under the transaction or by the giving of the preference, and

(g)   provide for the extent to which any person whose property is vested by the order in the company, or on whom obligations are imposed by the order, is to be able to prove in the winding up of the company for debts or other liabilities which arose from, or were released or discharged (in whole or in part) under or by, the transaction or the giving of the preference.

(2)   An order under section 238 or 239 may affect the property of, or impose any obligation on, any person whether or not he is the person with whom the company in question entered into the transaction or (as the case may be) the person to whom the preference was given; but such an order—

(a)   shall not prejudice any interest in property which was acquired from a person other than the company and was acquired in good faith and for value, or prejudice any interest deriving from such an interest, and

(b)   shall not require a person who received a benefit from the transaction or preference in good faith and for value to pay a sum to the office-holder, except where that person was a party to the transaction or the payment is to be in respect of a preference given to that person at a time when he was a creditor of the company.

(2A) Where a person has acquired an interest in property from a person other than the company in question, or has received a benefit from the transaction or preference, and at the time of that acquisition or receipt—

(a)   he had notice of the relevant surrounding circumstances and of the relevant proceedings, or

(b)   he was connected with, or was an associate of, either the company in question or the person with whom that company entered into the transaction or to whom that company gave the preference,

then, unless the contrary is shown, it shall be presumed for the purposes of paragraph (a) or (as the case may be) paragraph (b) of subsection (2) that the interest was acquired or the benefit was received otherwise than in good faith.

(3)   For the purposes of subsection (2A)(a), the relevant surrounding circumstances are (as the case may require)—

(a)   the fact that the company in question entered into the transaction at an undervalue; or

(b)   the circumstances which amounted to the giving of the preference by the company in question;

and subsections (3A) to (3C) have effect to determine whether, for those purposes, a person has notice of the relevant proceedings.

(3A) Where section 238 or 239 applies by reason of a company's entering administration, a person has notice of the relevant proceedings if he has notice that—

(a)   an administration application has been made,

(b)   an administration order has been made,

(c)   a copy of a notice of intention to appoint an administrator under paragraph 14 or 22 of Schedule B1 has been filed, or

(d)   notice of the appointment of an administrator has been filed under paragraph 18 or 29 of that Schedule.

(3B) Where section 238 or 239 applies by reason of a company's going into liquidation at the time when the appointment of an administrator of the company ceases to have effect, a person has notice of the relevant proceedings if he has notice that—

    (a)   an administration application has been made,

    (b)   an administration order has been made,

    (c)   a copy of a notice of intention to appoint an administrator under paragraph 14 or 22 of Schedule B1 has been filed,

    (d)   notice of the appointment of an administrator has been filed under paragraph 18 or 29 of that Schedule, or

    (e)   the company has gone into liquidation.

(3C) In a case where section 238 or 239 applies by reason of the company in question going into liquidation at any other time, a person has notice of the relevant proceedings if he has notice—

    (a)   where the company goes into liquidation on the making of a winding-up order, of the fact that the petition on which the winding-up order is made has been presented or of the fact that the company has gone into liquidation;

    (b)   in any other case, of the fact that the company has gone into liquidation.

(4)   The provisions of sections 238 to 241 apply without prejudice to the availability of any other remedy, even in relation to a transaction or preference which the company had no power to enter into or give.

...

244   Extortionate credit transactions

(1)   This section applies as does section 238, and where the company is, or has been, a party to a transaction for, or involving, the provision of credit to the company.

(2)   The court may, on the application of the office-holder, make an order with respect to the transaction if the transaction is or was extortionate and was entered into in the period of 3 years ending with [the day on which the company entered administration or went into liquidation.

(3)   For the purposes of this section a transaction is extortionate if, having regard to the risk accepted by the person providing the credit—

    (a)   the terms of it are or were such as to require grossly exorbitant payments to be made (whether unconditionally or in certain contingencies) in respect of the provision of the credit, or

    (b)   it otherwise grossly contravened ordinary principles of fair dealing;

    and it shall be presumed, unless the contrary is proved, that a transaction with respect to which an application is made under this section is or, as the case may be, was extortionate.

(4)   An order under this section with respect to any transaction may contain such one or more of the following as the court thinks fit, that is to say—

    (a)   provision setting aside the whole or part of any obligation created by the transaction,

    (b)   provision otherwise varying the terms of the transaction or varying the terms on which any security for the purposes of the transaction is held,

    (c)   provision requiring any person who is or was a party to the transaction to pay to the office-holder any sums paid to that person, by virtue of the transaction, by the company,

    (d)   provision requiring any person to surrender to the office-holder any property held by him as security for the purposes of the transaction,

    (e)   provision directing accounts to be taken between any persons.

(5)   The powers conferred by this section are exercisable in relation to any transaction concurrently with any powers exercisable in relation to that transaction as a transaction at an undervalue or under section 242 (gratuitous alienations in Scotland).

245   Avoidance of certain floating charges

(1)   This section applies as does section 238 ... to England and Wales.

(2) Subject as follows, a floating charge on the company's undertaking or property created at a relevant time is invalid except to the extent of the aggregate of—

    (a) the value of so much of the consideration for the creation of the charge as consists of money paid, or goods or services supplied, to the company at the same time as, or after, the creation of the charge,

    (b) the value of so much of that consideration as consists of the discharge or reduction, at the same time as, or after, the creation of the charge, of any debt of the company, and

    (c) the amount of such interest (if any) as is payable on the amount falling within paragraph (a) or (b) in pursuance of any agreement under which the money was so paid, the goods or services were so supplied or the debt was so discharged or reduced.

(3) Subject to the next subsection, the time at which a floating charge is created by a company is a relevant time for the purposes of this section if the charge is created—

    (a) in the case of a charge which is created in favour of a person who is connected with the company, at a time in the period of 2 years ending with the onset of insolvency,

    (b) in the case of a charge which is created in favour of any other person, at a time in the period of 12 months ending with the onset of insolvency,

    (c) in either case, at a time between the making of an administration application in respect of the company and the making of an administration order on that application, or

    (d) in either case, at a time between the filing with the court of a copy of notice of intention to appoint an administrator under paragraph 14 or 22 of Schedule B1 and the making of an appointment under that paragraph.

(4) Where a company creates a floating charge at a time mentioned in subsection (3)(b) and the person in favour of whom the charge is created is not connected with the company, that time is not a relevant time for the purposes of this section unless the company—

    (a) is at that time unable to pay its debts within the meaning of section 123 in Chapter VI of Part IV, or

    (b) becomes unable to pay its debts within the meaning of that section in consequence of the transaction under which the charge is created.

(5) For the purposes of subsection (3), the onset of insolvency is—

    (a) in a case where this section applies by reason of an administrator of a company being appointed by administration order, the date on which the administration application is made,

    (b) in a case where this section applies by reason of an administrator of a company being appointed under paragraph 14 or 22 of Schedule B1 following filing with the court of a copy of notice of intention to appoint under that paragraph, the date on which the copy of the notice is filed,

    (c) in a case where this section applies by reason of an administrator of a company being appointed otherwise than as mentioned in paragraph (a) or (b), the date on which the appointment takes effect, and

    (d) in a case where this section applies by reason of a company going into liquidation, the date of the commencement of the winding up.

(6) For the purposes of subsection (2)(a) the value of any goods or services supplied by way of consideration for a floating charge is the amount in money which at the time they were supplied could reasonably have been expected to be obtained for supplying the goods or services in the ordinary course of business and on the same terms (apart from the consideration) as those on which they were supplied to the company.

246 Unenforceability of liens on books, etc

(1) This section applies in the case of a company where—

    (a) the company enters administration, or

    (b) the company goes into liquidation, or

    (c) a provisional liquidator is appointed;

and "the office-holder" means the administrator, the liquidator or the provisional liquidator, as the case may be.

(2) Subject as follows, a lien or other right to retain possession of any of the books, papers or other records of the company is unenforceable to the extent that its enforcement would deny possession of any books, papers or other records to the office-holder.

(3) This does not apply to a lien on documents which give a title to property and are held as such.

PART VII
INTERPRETATION FOR FIRST GROUP OF PARTS

247 "Insolvency" and "go into liquidation"

(1) In this Group of Parts, except in so far as the context otherwise requires, "insolvency", in relation to a company, includes the approval of a voluntary arrangement under Part I, or the appointment of an administrator or administrative receiver.

(2) For the purposes of any provision in this Group of Parts, a company goes into liquidation if it passes a resolution for voluntary winding up or an order for its winding up is made by the court at a time when it has not already gone into liquidation by passing such a resolution.

(3) The reference to a resolution for voluntary winding up in subsection (2) includes a reference to a resolution which is deemed to occur by virtue of—

(a) paragraph 83(6)(b) of Schedule B1, or

(b) an order made following conversion of administration or a voluntary arrangement into winding up by virtue of Article 37 of the EC Regulation.

248 "Secured creditor", etc

In this Group of Parts, except in so far as the context otherwise requires—

(a) "secured creditor", in relation to a company, means a creditor of the company who holds in respect of his debt a security over property of the company, and "unsecured creditor" is to be read accordingly; and

(b) "security" means—

(i) in relation to England and Wales, any mortgage, charge, lien or other security, and

...

249 "Connected" with a company

For the purposes of any provision in this Group of Parts, a person is connected with a company if—

(a) he is a director or shadow director of the company or an associate of such a director or shadow director, or

(b) he is an associate of the company;

and "associate" has the meaning given by section 435 in Part XVIII of this Act.

250 "Member" of a company

For the purposes of any provision in this Group of Parts, a person who is not a member of a company but to whom shares in the company have been transferred, or transmitted by operation of law, is to be regarded as a member of the company, and references to a member or members are to be read accordingly.

251 Expressions used generally

In this Group of Parts, except in so far as the context otherwise requires—

"administrative receiver" means —

(a) an administrative receiver as defined by section 29(2) in Chapter I of Part III, or

(b) a receiver appointed under section 51 in Chapter II of that Part in a case where the whole (or substantially the whole) of the company's property is attached by the floating charge;

"business day" means any day other than a Saturday, a Sunday, Christmas Day, Good Friday or a day which is a bank holiday in any part of Great Britain;

"chattel leasing agreement" means an agreement for the bailment or, in Scotland, the hiring of goods which is capable of subsisting for more than 3 months;

"contributory" has the meaning given by section 79;

"director" includes any person occupying the position of director, by whatever name called;

"floating charge" means a charge which, as created, was a floating charge and includes a floating charge within section 462 of the Companies Act (Scottish floating charges);

"office copy", in relation to Scotland, means a copy certified by the clerk of court;

"the official rate", in relation to interest, means the rate payable under section 189(4);

"prescribed" means prescribed by the rules;

"receiver", in the expression "receiver or manager", does not include a receiver appointed under section 51 in Chapter II of Part III;

"retention of title agreement" means an agreement for the sale of goods to a company, being an agreement—

(a)   which does not constitute a charge on the goods, but

(b)   under which, if the seller is not paid and the company is wound up, the seller will have priority over all other creditors of the company as respects the goods or any property representing the goods;

"the rules" means rules under section 411 in Part XV; and

"shadow director", in relation to a company, means a person in accordance with whose directions or instructions the directors of the company are accustomed to act (but so that a person is not deemed a shadow director by reason only that the directors act on advice given by him in a professional capacity);

Any expression (other than one defined above in this section)—

(a)   for whose interpretation provision is made by Part 26 of the Companies Act, or

(b)   that is defined for the purposes of the Companies Acts,

has the same meaning in this Group of Parts.

PART VIII

INDIVIDUAL VOLUNTARY ARRANGEMENTS

Moratorium for insolvent debtor

252   Interim order of court

(1)   In the circumstances specified below, the court may in the case of a debtor (being an individual) make an interim order under this section.

(2)   An interim order has the effect that, during the period for which it is in force—

(a)   no bankruptcy petition relating to the debtor may be presented or proceeded with,

(aa)   no landlord or other person to whom rent is payable may exercise any right of forfeiture by peaceable re-entry in relation to premises let to the debtor in respect of a failure by the debtor to comply with any term or condition of his tenancy of such premises, except with the leave of the court, and

(b)   no other proceedings, and no execution or other legal process, may be commenced or continued and no distress may be levied against the debtor or his property except with the leave of the court.

253   Application for interim order

(1)   Application to the court for an interim order may be made where the debtor intends to make a proposal under this Part, that is, a proposal to his creditors for a composition in satisfaction of his debts or a scheme of arrangement of his affairs (from here on referred to, in either case, as a "voluntary arrangement").

(2)   The proposal must provide for some person ("the nominee") to act in relation to the voluntary arrangement either as trustee or otherwise for the purpose of supervising its implementation and the nominee must be a person who is qualified to act as an insolvency practitioner, or authorised to act as nominee, in relation to the voluntary arrangement.

(3)   Subject as follows, the application may be made—

(a)   if the debtor is an undischarged bankrupt, by the debtor, the trustee of his estate, or the official receiver, and

(b)   in any other case, by the debtor.

(4)   An application shall not be made under subsection (3)(a) unless the debtor has given notice of the proposal to the official receiver and, if there is one, the trustee of his estate.

(5)   An application shall not be made while a bankruptcy petition presented by the debtor is pending, if the court has, under section 273 below, appointed an insolvency practitioner to inquire into the debtor's affairs and report.

254   Effect of application

(1)   At any time when an application under section 253 for an interim order is pending,
   (a)   no landlord or other person to whom rent is payable may exercise any right of forfeiture by peaceable re-entry in relation to premises let to the debtor in respect of a failure by the debtor to comply with any term or condition of his tenancy of such premises, except with the leave of the court, and
   (b)   the court may forbid the levying of any distress on the debtor's property or its subsequent sale, or both, and stay any action, execution or other legal process against the property or person of the debtor.

(2)   Any court in which proceedings are pending against an individual may, on proof that an application under that section has been made in respect of that individual, either stay the proceedings or allow them to continue on such terms as it thinks fit.

255   Cases in which interim order can be made

(1)   The court shall not make an interim order on an application under section 253 unless it is satisfied—
   (a)   that the debtor intends to make a proposal under this Part;
   (b)   that on the day of the making of the application the debtor was an undischarged bankrupt or was able to petition for his own bankruptcy;
   (c)   that no previous application has been made by the debtor for an interim order in the period of 12 months ending with that day; and
   (d)   that the nominee under the debtor's proposal ... is willing to act in relation to the proposal.

(2)   The court may make an order if it thinks that it would be appropriate to do so for the purpose of facilitating the consideration and implementation of the debtor's proposal.

(3)   Where the debtor is an undischarged bankrupt, the interim order may contain provision as to the conduct of the bankruptcy, and the administration of the bankrupt's estate, during the period for which the order is in force.

(4)   Subject as follows, the provision contained in an interim order by virtue of subsection (3) may include provision staying proceedings in the bankruptcy or modifying any provision in this Group of Parts, and any provision of the rules in their application to the debtor's bankruptcy.

(5)   An interim order shall not, in relation to a bankrupt, make provision relaxing or removing any of the requirements of provisions in this Group of Parts, or of the rules, unless the court is satisfied that that provision is unlikely to result in any significant diminution in, or in the value of, the debtor's estate for the purposes of the bankruptcy.

(6)   Subject to the following provisions of this Part, an interim order made on an application under section 253 ceases to have effect at the end of the period of 14 days beginning with the day after the making of the order.

256   Nominee's report on debtor's proposal

(1)   Where an interim order has been made on an application under section 253, the nominee shall, before the order ceases to have effect, submit a report to the court stating—
   (a)   whether, in his opinion, the voluntary arrangement which the debtor is proposing has a reasonable prospect of being approved and implemented,
   (aa)   whether, in his opinion, a meeting of the debtor's creditors should be summoned to consider the debtor's proposal, and
   (b)   if in his opinion such a meeting should be summoned, the date on which, and time and place at which, he proposes the meeting should be held.

(2)   For the purpose of enabling the nominee to prepare his report the debtor shall submit to the nominee—

(a) a document setting out the terms of the voluntary arrangement which the debtor is proposing, and

(b) a statement of his affairs containing—

    (i) such particulars of his creditors and of his debts and other liabilities and of his assets as may be prescribed, and

    (ii) such other information as may be prescribed.

(3) The court may—

(a) on an application made by the debtor in a case where the nominee has failed to submit the report required by this section or has died, or

(b) on an application made by the debtor or the nominee in a case where it is impracticable or inappropriate for the nominee to continue to act as such,

direct that the nominee shall be replaced as such by another person qualified to act as an insolvency practitioner, or authorised to act as nominee, in relation to the voluntary arrangement.

(3A) The court may, on an application made by the debtor in a case where the nominee has failed to submit the report required by this section, direct that the interim order shall continue, or (if it has ceased to have effect) be renewed, for such further period as the court may specify in the direction.

(4) The court may, on the application of the nominee, extend the period for which the interim order has effect so as to enable the nominee to have more time to prepare his report.

(5) If the court is satisfied on receiving the nominee's report that a meeting of the debtor's creditors should be summoned to consider the debtor's proposal, the court shall direct that the period for which the interim order has effect shall be extended, for such further period as it may specify in the direction, for the purpose of enabling the debtor's proposal to be considered by his creditors in accordance with the following provisions of this Part.

(6) The court may discharge the interim order if it is satisfied, on the application of the nominee—

(a) that the debtor has failed to comply with his obligations under subsection (2), or

(b) that for any other reason it would be inappropriate for a meeting of the debtor's creditors to be summoned to consider the debtor's proposal.

256A Debtor's proposal and nominee's report

(1) This section applies where a debtor (being an individual)—

(a) intends to make a proposal under this Part (but an interim order has not been made in relation to the proposal and no application for such an order is pending), and

(b) if he is an undischarged bankrupt, has given notice of the proposal to the official receiver and, if there is one, the trustee of his estate,

unless a bankruptcy petition presented by the debtor is pending and the court has, under section 273, appointed an insolvency practitioner to inquire into the debtor's affairs and report.

(2) For the purpose of enabling the nominee to prepare a report to the court, the debtor shall submit to the nominee—

(a) a document setting out the terms of the voluntary arrangement which the debtor is proposing, and

(b) a statement of his affairs containing—

    (i) such particulars of his creditors and of his debts and other liabilities and of his assets as may be prescribed, and

    (ii) such other information as may be prescribed.

(3) If the nominee is of the opinion that the debtor is an undischarged bankrupt, or is able to petition for his own bankruptcy, the nominee shall, within 14 days (or such longer period as the court may allow) after receiving the document and statement mentioned in subsection (2), submit a report to the court stating—

(a) whether, in his opinion, the voluntary arrangement which the debtor is proposing has a reasonable prospect of being approved and implemented,

(b)   whether, in his opinion, a meeting of the debtor's creditors should be summoned to consider the debtor's proposal, and

(c)   if in his opinion such a meeting should be summoned, the date on which, and time and place at which, he proposes the meeting should be held.

(4)   The court may—

(a)   on an application made by the debtor in a case where the nominee has failed to submit the report required by this section or has died, or

(b)   on an application made by the debtor or the nominee in a case where it is impracticable or inappropriate for the nominee to continue to act as such,

direct that the nominee shall be replaced as such by another person qualified to act as an insolvency practitioner, or authorised to act as nominee, in relation to the voluntary arrangement.

(5)   The court may, on an application made by the nominee, extend the period within which the nominee is to submit his report.

Creditors' meeting

257   Summoning of creditors' meeting

(1)   Where it has been reported to the court under section 256 or 256A that a meeting of the debtor's creditors should be summoned, the nominee (or his replacement under section 256(3) or 256A(4)) shall, unless the court otherwise directs, summon that meeting for the time, date and place proposed in his report.

(2)   The persons to be summoned to the meeting are every creditor of the debtor of whose claim and address the person summoning the meeting is aware.

(3)   For this purpose the creditors of a debtor who is an undischarged bankrupt include—

(a)   every person who is a creditor of the bankrupt in respect of a bankruptcy debt, and

(b)   every person who would be such a creditor if the bankruptcy had commenced on the day on which notice of the meeting is given.

Consideration and implementation of debtor's proposal

258   Decisions of creditors' meeting

(1)   A creditors' meeting summoned under section 257 shall decide whether to approve the proposed voluntary arrangement.

(2)   The meeting may approve the proposed voluntary arrangement with modifications, but shall not do so unless the debtor consents to each modification.

(3)   The modifications subject to which the proposed voluntary arrangement may be approved may include one conferring the functions proposed to be conferred on the nominee on another person qualified to act as an insolvency practitioner or authorised to act as nominee, in relation to the voluntary arrangement.

But they shall not include any modification by virtue of which the proposal ceases to be a proposal under this Part.

(4)   The meeting shall not approve any proposal or modification which affects the right of a secured creditor of the debtor to enforce his security, except with the concurrence of the creditor concerned.

(5)   Subject as follows, the meeting shall not approve any proposal or modification under which—

(a)   any preferential debt of the debtor is to be paid otherwise than in priority to such of his debts as are not preferential debts, or

(b)   a preferential creditor of the debtor is to be paid an amount in respect of a preferential debt that bears to that debt a smaller proportion than is borne to another preferential debt by the amount that is to be paid in respect of that other debt.

However, the meeting may approve such a proposal or modification with the concurrence of the preferential creditor concerned.

(6)   Subject as above, the meeting shall be conducted in accordance with the rules.

(7) In this section "preferential debt" has the meaning given by section 386 in Part XII; and "preferential creditor" is to be construed accordingly.

259 Report of decisions to court

(1) After the conclusion in accordance with the rules of the meeting summoned under section 257, the chairman of the meeting shall report the result of it to the court and, immediately after so reporting, shall give notice of the result of the meeting to such persons as may be prescribed.

(2) If the report is that the meeting has declined (with or without modifications) to approve the debtor's proposal, the court may discharge any interim order which is in force in relation to the debtor.

260 Effect of approval

(1) This section has effect where the meeting summoned under section 257 approves the proposed voluntary arrangement (with or without modifications).

(2) The approved arrangement—
    (a) takes effect as if made by the debtor at the meeting, and
    (b) binds every person who in accordance with the rules—
        (i) was entitled to vote at the meeting (whether or not he was present or represented at it), or
        (ii) would have been so entitled if he had had notice of it,
    as if he were a party to the arrangement.

(2A) If—
    (a) when the arrangement ceases to have effect any amount payable under the arrangement to a person bound by virtue of subsection (2)(b)(ii) has not been paid, and
    (b) the arrangement did not come to an end prematurely,
the debtor shall at that time become liable to pay to that person the amount payable under the arrangement.

(3) The Deeds of Arrangement Act 1914 does not apply to the approved voluntary arrangement.

(4) Any interim order in force in relation to the debtor immediately before the end of the period of 28 days beginning with the day on which the report with respect to the creditors' meeting was made to the court under section 259 ceases to have effect at the end of that period.
This subsection applies except to such extent as the court may direct for the purposes of any application under section 262 below.

(5) Where proceedings on a bankruptcy petition have been stayed by an interim order which ceases to have effect under subsection (4), that petition is deemed, unless the court otherwise orders, to have been dismissed.

261 Additional effect on undischarged bankrupt

(1) This section applies where—
    (a) the creditors' meeting summoned under section 257 approves the proposed voluntary arrangement (with or without modifications), and
    (b) the debtor is an undischarged bankrupt.

(2) Where this section applies the court shall annul the bankruptcy order on an application made—
    (a) by the bankrupt, or
    (b) where the bankrupt has not made an application within the prescribed period, by the official receiver.

(3) An application under subsection (2) may not be made—
    (a) during the period specified in section 262(3)(a) during which the decision of the creditors' meeting can be challenged by application under section 262,
    (b) while an application under that section is pending, or
    (c) while an appeal in respect of an application under that section is pending or may be brought.

(4) Where this section applies the court may give such directions about the conduct of the bankruptcy and the administration of the bankrupt's estate as it thinks appropriate for facilitating the implementation of the approved voluntary arrangement.

262   Challenge of meeting's decision

(1) Subject to this section, an application to the court may be made, by any of the persons specified below, on one or both of the following grounds, namely—

   (a) that a voluntary arrangement approved by a creditors' meeting summoned under section 257 unfairly prejudices the interests of a creditor of the debtor;

   (b) that there has been some material irregularity at or in relation to such a meeting.

(2) The persons who may apply under this section are—

   (a) the debtor;

   (b) a person who—

      (i)   was entitled, in accordance with the rules, to vote at the creditors' meeting, or

      (ii) would have been so entitled if he had had notice of it;

   (c) the nominee (or his replacement under section 256(3), 256A(4) or 258(3)); and

   (d) if the debtor is an undischarged bankrupt, the trustee of his estate or the official receiver.

(3) An application under this section shall not be made—

   (a) after the end of the period of 28 days beginning with the day on which the report of the creditors' meeting was made to the court under section 259; or

   (b) in the case of a person who was not given notice of the creditors' meeting, after the end of the period of 28 days beginning with the day on which he became aware that the meeting had taken place,

   but (subject to that) an application made by a person within subsection (2)(b)(ii) on the ground that the arrangement prejudices his interests may be made after the arrangement has ceased to have effect, unless it has come to an end prematurely.

(4) Where on an application under this section the court is satisfied as to either of the grounds mentioned in subsection (1), it may do one or both of the following, namely—

   (a) revoke or suspend any approval given by the meeting;

   (b) give a direction to any person for the summoning of a further meeting of the debtor's creditors to consider any revised proposal he may make or, in a case falling within subsection (1)(b), to reconsider his original proposal.

(5) Where at any time after giving a direction under subsection (4)(b) for the summoning of a meeting to consider a revised proposal the court is satisfied that the debtor does not intend to submit such a proposal, the court shall revoke the direction and revoke or suspend any approval given at the previous meeting.

(6) Where the court gives a direction under subsection (4)(b), it may also give a direction continuing or, as the case may require, renewing, for such period as may be specified in the direction, the effect in relation to the debtor of any interim order.

(7) In any case where the court, on an application made under this section with respect to a creditors' meeting, gives a direction under subsection (4)(b) or revokes or suspends an approval under subsection (4)(a) or (5), the court may give such supplemental directions as it thinks fit and, in particular, directions with respect to—

   (a) things done since the meeting under any voluntary arrangement approved by the meeting, and

   (b) such things done since the meeting as could not have been done if an interim order had been in force in relation to the debtor when they were done.

(8) Except in pursuance of the preceding provisions of this section, an approval given at a creditors' meeting summoned under section 257 is not invalidated by any irregularity at or in relation to the meeting.

262A   False representations etc

(1) If for the purpose of obtaining the approval of his creditors to a proposal for a voluntary arrangement, the debtor—

    (a)   makes any false representation, or
    (b)   fraudulently does, or omits to do, anything,
    he commits an offence.
(2)   Subsection (1) applies even if the proposal is not approved.
(3)   A person guilty of an offence under this section is liable to imprisonment or a fine, or both.

262B   Prosecution of delinquent debtors

(1)   This section applies where a voluntary arrangement approved by a creditors' meeting
       summoned under section 257 has taken effect.
(2)   If it appears to the nominee or supervisor that the debtor has been guilty of any offence in
       connection with the arrangement for which he is criminally liable, he shall forthwith—
       (a)   report the matter to the Secretary of State, and
       (b)   provide the Secretary of State with such information and give the Secretary of State
              such access to and facilities for inspecting and taking copies of documents (being
              information or documents in his possession or under his control and relating to the
              matter in question) as the Secretary of State requires.
(3)   Where a prosecuting authority institutes criminal proceedings following any report under
       subsection (2), the nominee or, as the case may be, supervisor shall give the authority all
       assistance in connection with the prosecution which he is reasonably able to give.
       For this purpose, "prosecuting authority" means the Director of Public Prosecutions or the
       Secretary of State.
(4)   The court may, on the application of the prosecuting authority, direct a nominee or
       supervisor to comply with subsection (3) if he has failed to do so.

262C   Arrangements coming to an end prematurely

For the purposes of this Part, a voluntary arrangement approved by a creditors' meeting
summoned under section 257 comes to an end prematurely if, when it ceases to have effect, it has
not been fully implemented in respect of all persons bound by the arrangement by virtue of
section 260(2)(b)(i).

263   Implementation and supervision of approved voluntary arrangement

(1)   This section applies where a voluntary arrangement approved by a creditors' meeting
       summoned under section 257 has taken effect.
(2)   The person who is for the time being carrying out, in relation to the voluntary arrangement,
       the functions conferred by virtue of the approval on the nominee (or his replacement under
       section 256(3), 256A(4) or 258(3)) shall be known as the supervisor of the voluntary
       arrangement.
(3)   If the debtor, any of his creditors or any other person is dissatisfied by any act, omission or
       decision of the supervisor, he may apply to the court; and on such an application the court
       may—
       (a)   confirm, reverse or modify any act or decision of the supervisor,
       (b)   give him directions, or
       (c)   make such other order as it thinks fit.
(4)   The supervisor may apply to the court for directions in relation to any particular matter
       arising under the voluntary arrangement.
(5)   The court may, whenever—
       (a)   it is expedient to appoint a person to carry out the functions of the supervisor, and
       (b)   it is inexpedient, difficult or impracticable for an appointment to be made without the
              assistance of the court,
       make an order appointing a person who is qualified to act as an insolvency practitioner or
       authorised to act as supervisor, in relation to the voluntary arrangement , either in
       substitution for the existing supervisor or to fill a vacancy.

       ...

Fast-track voluntary arrangement

263A Availability

Section 263B applies where an individual debtor intends to make a proposal to his creditors for a voluntary arrangement and—

(a) the debtor is an undischarged bankrupt,

(b) the official receiver is specified in the proposal as the nominee in relation to the voluntary arrangement, and

(c) no interim order is applied for under section 253.

263B Decision

(1) The debtor may submit to the official receiver—

    (a) a document setting out the terms of the voluntary arrangement which the debtor is proposing, and

    (b) a statement of his affairs containing such particulars as may be prescribed of his creditors, debts, other liabilities and assets and such other information as may be prescribed.

(2) If the official receiver thinks that the voluntary arrangement proposed has a reasonable prospect of being approved and implemented, he may make arrangements for inviting creditors to decide whether to approve it.

(3) For the purposes of subsection (2) a person is a "creditor" only if—

    (a) he is a creditor of the debtor in respect of a bankruptcy debt, and

    (b) the official receiver is aware of his claim and his address.

(4) Arrangements made under subsection (2)—

    (a) must include the provision to each creditor of a copy of the proposed voluntary arrangement,

    (b) must include the provision to each creditor of information about the criteria by reference to which the official receiver will determine whether the creditors approve or reject the proposed voluntary arrangement, and

    (c) may not include an opportunity for modifications to the proposed voluntary arrangement to be suggested or made.

(5) Where a debtor submits documents to the official receiver under subsection (1) no application under section 253 for an interim order may be made in respect of the debtor until the official receiver has—

    (a) made arrangements as described in subsection (2), or

    (b) informed the debtor that he does not intend to make arrangements (whether because he does not think the voluntary arrangement has a reasonable prospect of being approved and implemented or because he declines to act).

263C Result

As soon as is reasonably practicable after the implementation of arrangements under section 263B(2) the official receiver shall report to the court whether the proposed voluntary arrangement has been approved or rejected.

263D Approval of voluntary arrangement

(1) This section applies where the official receiver reports to the court under section 263C that a proposed voluntary arrangement has been approved.

(2) The voluntary arrangement—

    (a) takes effect,

    (b) binds the debtor, and

    (c) binds every person who was entitled to participate in the arrangements made under section 263B(2).

(3) The court shall annul the bankruptcy order in respect of the debtor on an application made by the official receiver.

(4) An application under subsection (3) may not be made—

(a) during the period specified in section 263F(3) during which the voluntary arrangement can be challenged by application under section 263F(2),

(b) while an application under that section is pending, or

(c) while an appeal in respect of an application under that section is pending or may be brought.

(5) The court may give such directions about the conduct of the bankruptcy and the administration of the bankrupt's estate as it thinks appropriate for facilitating the implementation of the approved voluntary arrangement.

...

(7) A reference in this Act or another enactment to a voluntary arrangement approved under this Part includes a reference to a voluntary arrangement which has effect by virtue of this section.

263E Implementation

Section 263 shall apply to a voluntary arrangement which has effect by virtue of section 263D(2) as it applies to a voluntary arrangement approved by a creditors' meeting.

263F Revocation

(1) The court may make an order revoking a voluntary arrangement which has effect by virtue of section 263D(2) on the ground—

(a) that it unfairly prejudices the interests of a creditor of the debtor, or

(b) that a material irregularity occurred in relation to the arrangements made under section 263B(2).

(2) An order under subsection (1) may be made only on the application of—

(a) the debtor,

(b) a person who was entitled to participate in the arrangements made under section 263B(2),

(c) the trustee of the bankrupt's estate, or

(d) the official receiver.

(3) An application under subsection (2) may not be made after the end of the period of 28 days beginning with the date on which the official receiver makes his report to the court under section 263C.

(4) But a creditor who was not made aware of the arrangements under section 263B(2) at the time when they were made may make an application under subsection (2) during the period of 28 days beginning with the date on which he becomes aware of the voluntary arrangement.

...

PART IX
BANKRUPTCY

CHAPTER I
BANKRUPTCY PETITIONS; BANKRUPTCY ORDERS

Preliminary

264 Who may present a bankruptcy petition

(1) A petition for a bankruptcy order to be made against an individual may be presented to the court in accordance with the following provisions of this Part—

(a) by one of the individual's creditors or jointly by more than one of them,

(b) by the individual himself,

(ba) by a temporary administrator (within the meaning of Article 38 of the EC Regulation),

(bb) by a liquidator (within the meaning of Article 2(b) of the EC Regulation) appointed in proceedings by virtue of Article 3(1) of the EC Regulation,

(c) by the supervisor of, or any person (other than the individual) who is for the time being bound by, a voluntary arrangement proposed by the individual and approved under Part VIII, or

      (d)   where a criminal bankruptcy order has been made against the individual, by the Official Petitioner or by any person specified in the order in pursuance of section 39(3)(b) of the Powers of Criminal Courts Act 1973.

(2)   Subject to those provisions, the court may make a bankruptcy order on any such petition.

265   Conditions to be satisfied in respect of debtor

(1)   A bankruptcy petition shall not be presented to the court under section 264(1)(a) or (b) unless the debtor—

    (a)   is domiciled in England and Wales,

    (b)   is personally present in England and Wales on the day on which the petition is presented, or

    (c)   at any time in the period of 3 years ending with that day—

        (i)   has been ordinarily resident, or has had a place of residence, in England and Wales, or

        (ii)   has carried on business in England and Wales.

(2)   The reference in subsection (1)(c) to an individual carrying on business includes—

    (a)   the carrying on of business by a firm or partnership of which the individual is a member, and

    (b)   the carrying on of business by an agent or manager for the individual or for such a firm or partnership.

(3)   This section is subject to Article 3 of the EC Regulation.

266   Other preliminary conditions

(1)   Where a bankruptcy petition relating to an individual is presented by a person who is entitled to present a petition under two or more paragraphs of section 264(1), the petition is to be treated for the purposes of this Part as a petition under such one of those paragraphs as may be specified in the petition.

(2)   A bankruptcy petition shall not be withdrawn without the leave of the court.

(3)   The court has a general power, if it appears to it appropriate to do so on the grounds that there has been a contravention of the rules or for any other reason, to dismiss a bankruptcy petition or to stay proceedings on such a petition; and, where it stays proceedings on a petition, it may do so on such terms and conditions as it thinks fit.

(4)   Without prejudice to subsection (3), where a petition under section 264(1)(a), (b) or (c) in respect of an individual is pending at a time when a criminal bankruptcy order is made against him, or is presented after such an order has been so made, the court may on the application of the Official Petitioner dismiss the petition if it appears to it appropriate to do so.

Creditor's petition

267   Grounds of creditor's petition

(1)   A creditor's petition must be in respect of one or more debts owed by the debtor, and the petitioning creditor or each of the petitioning creditors must be a person to whom the debt or (as the case may be) at least one of the debts is owed.

(2)   Subject to the next three sections, a creditor's petition may be presented to the court in respect of a debt or debts only if, at the time the petition is presented—

    (a)   the amount of the debt, or the aggregate amount of the debts, is equal to or exceeds the bankruptcy level,

    (b)   the debt, or each of the debts, is for a liquidated sum payable to the petitioning creditor, or one or more of the petitioning creditors, either immediately or at some certain, future time, and is unsecured,

    (c)   the debt, or each of the debts, is a debt which the debtor appears either to be unable to pay or to have no reasonable prospect of being able to pay, and

    (d)   there is no outstanding application to set aside a statutory demand served (under section 268 below) in respect of the debt or any of the debts.

(3) A debt is not to be regarded for the purposes of subsection (2) as a debt for a liquidated sum by reason only that the amount of the debt is specified in a criminal bankruptcy order.

(4) "The bankruptcy level" is £750; but the Secretary of State may by order in a statutory instrument substitute any amount specified in the order for that amount or (as the case may be) for the amount which by virtue of such an order is for the time being the amount of the bankruptcy level.

(5) An order shall not be made under subsection (4) unless a draft of it has been laid before, and approved by a resolution of, each House of Parliament.

268 Definition of "inability to pay", etc; the statutory demand

(1) For the purposes of section 267(2)(c), the debtor appears to be unable to pay a debt if, but only if, the debt is payable immediately and either—

    (a) the petitioning creditor to whom the debt is owed has served on the debtor a demand (known as "the statutory demand") in the prescribed form requiring him to pay the debt or to secure or compound for it to the satisfaction of the creditor, at least 3 weeks have elapsed since the demand was served and the demand has been neither complied with nor set aside in accordance with the rules, or

    (b) execution or other process issued in respect of the debt on a judgment or order of any court in favour of the petitioning creditor, or one or more of the petitioning creditors to whom the debt is owed, has been returned unsatisfied in whole or in part.

(2) For the purposes of section 267(2)(c) the debtor appears to have no reasonable prospect of being able to pay a debt if, but only if, the debt is not immediately payable and—

    (a) the petitioning creditor to whom it is owed has served on the debtor a demand (also known as "the statutory demand") in the prescribed form requiring him to establish to the satisfaction of the creditor that there is a reasonable prospect that the debtor will be able to pay the debt when it falls due,

    (b) at least 3 weeks have elapsed since the demand was served, and

    (c) the demand has been neither complied with nor set aside in accordance with the rules.

269 Creditor with security

(1) A debt which is the debt, or one of the debts, in respect of which a creditor's petition is presented need not be unsecured if either—

    (a) the petition contains a statement by the person having the right to enforce the security that he is willing, in the event of a bankruptcy order being made, to give up his security for the benefit of all the bankrupt's creditors, or

    (b) the petition is expressed not to be made in respect of the secured part of the debt and contains a statement by that person of the estimated value at the date of the petition of the security for the secured part of the debt.

(2) In a case falling within subsection (1)(b) the secured and unsecured parts of the debt are to be treated for the purposes of sections 267 to 270 as separate debts.

270 Expedited petition

In the case of a creditor's petition presented wholly or partly in respect of a debt which is the subject of a statutory demand under section 268, the petition may be presented before the end of the 3-week period there mentioned if there is a serious possibility that the debtor's property or the value of any of his property will be significantly diminished during that period and the petition contains a statement to that effect.

271 Proceedings on creditor's petition

(1) The court shall not make a bankruptcy order on a creditor's petition unless it is satisfied that the debt, or one of the debts, in respect of which the petition was presented is either—

    (a) a debt which, having been payable at the date of the petition or having since become payable, has been neither paid nor secured or compounded for, or

    (b) a debt which the debtor has no reasonable prospect of being able to pay when it falls due.

(2)   In a case in which the petition contains such a statement as is required by section 270, the court shall not make a bankruptcy order until at least 3 weeks have elapsed since the service of any statutory demand under section 268.

(3)   The court may dismiss the petition if it is satisfied that the debtor is able to pay all his debts or is satisfied—

    (a)   that the debtor has made an offer to secure or compound for a debt in respect of which the petition is presented,

    (b)   that the acceptance of that offer would have required the dismissal of the petition, and

    (c)   that the offer has been unreasonably refused;

and, in determining for the purposes of this subsection whether the debtor is able to pay all his debts, the court shall take into account his contingent and prospective liabilities.

(4)   In determining for the purposes of this section what constitutes a reasonable prospect that a debtor will be able to pay a debt when it falls due, it is to be assumed that the prospect given by the facts and other matters known to the creditor at the time he entered into the transaction resulting in the debt was a reasonable prospect.

(5)   Nothing in sections 267 to 271 prejudices the power of the court, in accordance with the rules, to authorise a creditor's petition to be amended by the omission of any creditor or debt and to be proceeded with as if things done for the purposes of those sections had been done only by or in relation to the remaining creditors or debts.

Debtor's petition

272   Grounds of debtor's petition

(1)   A debtor's petition may be presented to the court only on the grounds that the debtor is unable to pay his debts.

(2)   The petition shall be accompanied by a statement of the debtor's affairs containing—

    (a)   such particulars of the debtor's creditors and of his debts and other liabilities and of his assets as may be prescribed, and

    (b)   such other information as may be prescribed.

273   Appointment of insolvency practitioner by the court

(1)   Subject to the next section, on the hearing of a debtor's petition the court shall not make a bankruptcy order if it appears to the court—

    (a)   that if a bankruptcy order were made the aggregate amount of the bankruptcy debts, so far as unsecured, would be less than the small bankruptcies level,

    (b)   that if a bankruptcy order were made, the value of the bankrupt's estate would be equal to or more than the minimum amount,

    (c)   that within the period of 5 years ending with the presentation of the petition the debtor has neither been adjudged bankrupt nor made a composition with his creditors in satisfaction of his debts or a scheme of arrangement of his affairs, and

    (d)   that it would be appropriate to appoint a person to prepare a report under section 274.

"The minimum amount" and "the small bankruptcies level" mean such amounts as may for the time being be prescribed for the purposes of this section.

(2)   Where on the hearing of the petition, it appears to the court as mentioned in subsection (1), the court shall appoint a person who is qualified to act as an insolvency practitioner in relation to the debtor—

    (a)   to prepare a report under the next section, and

    (b)   subject to section 258(3) in Part VIII, to act in relation to any voluntary arrangement to which the report relates either as trustee or otherwise for the purpose of supervising its implementation.

274   Action on report of insolvency practitioner

(1)   A person appointed under section 273 shall inquire into the debtor's affairs and, within such period as the court may direct, shall submit a report to the court stating whether the debtor is willing, for the purposes of Part VIII, to make a proposal for a voluntary arrangement.

(2)   A report which states that the debtor is willing as above mentioned shall also state—

(a) whether, in the opinion of the person making the report, a meeting of the debtor's creditors should be summoned to consider the proposal, and

(b) if in that person's opinion such a meeting should be summoned, the date on which, and time and place at which, he proposes the meeting should be held.

(3) On considering a report under this section the court may—

(a) without any application, make an interim order under section 252, if it thinks that it is appropriate to do so for the purpose of facilitating the consideration and implementation of the debtor's proposal, or

(b) if it thinks it would be inappropriate to make such an order, make a bankruptcy order.

(4) An interim order made by virtue of this section ceases to have effect at the end of such period as the court may specify for the purpose of enabling the debtor's proposal to be considered by his creditors in accordance with the applicable provisions of Part VIII.

(5) Where it has been reported to the court under this section that a meeting of the debtor's creditors should be summoned, the person making the report shall, unless the court otherwise directs, summon that meeting for the time, date and place proposed in his report. The meeting is then deemed to have been summoned under section 257 in Part VIII, and subsections (2) and (3)of that section, and sections 258 to 263 apply accordingly.

275 ...

Other cases for special consideration

276 Default in connection with voluntary arrangement

(1) The court shall not make a bankruptcy order on a petition under section 264(1)(c) (supervisor of, or person bound by, voluntary arrangement proposed and approved) unless it is satisfied—

(a) that the debtor has failed to comply with his obligations under the voluntary arrangement, or

(b) that information which was false or misleading in any material particular or which contained material omissions—

(i) was contained in any statement of affairs or other document supplied by the debtor under Part VIII to any person, or

(ii) was otherwise made available by the debtor to his creditors at or in connection with a meeting summoned under that Part, or

(c) that the debtor has failed to do all such things as may for the purposes of the voluntary arrangement have been reasonably required of him by the supervisor of the arrangement.

(2) Where a bankruptcy order is made on a petition under section 264(1)(c), any expenses properly incurred as expenses of the administration of the voluntary arrangement in question shall be a first charge on the bankrupt's estate.

...

Commencement and duration of bankruptcy; discharge

278 Commencement and continuance

The bankruptcy of an individual against whom a bankruptcy order has been made—

(a) commences with the day on which the order is made, and

(b) continues until the individual is discharged under the following provisions of this Chapter.

279 Duration

(1) A bankrupt is discharged from bankruptcy at the end of the period of one year beginning with the date on which the bankruptcy commences.

(2) If before the end of that period the official receiver files with the court a notice stating that investigation of the conduct and affairs of the bankrupt under section 289 is unnecessary or concluded, the bankrupt is discharged when the notice is filed.

(3) On the application of the official receiver or the trustee of a bankrupt's estate, the court may order that the period specified in subsection (1) shall cease to run until—

(a)   the end of a specified period, or

(b)   the fulfilment of a specified condition.

(4)   The court may make an order under subsection (3) only if satisfied that the bankrupt has failed or is failing to comply with an obligation under this Part.

(5)   In subsection (3)(b) "condition" includes a condition requiring that the court be satisfied of something.

(6)   In the case of an individual who is adjudged bankrupt on a petition under section 264(1)(d)—

(a)   subsections (1) to (5) shall not apply, and

(b)   the bankrupt is discharged from bankruptcy by an order of the court under section 280.

(7)   This section is without prejudice to any power of the court to annul a bankruptcy order.

280   Discharge by order of the court

(1)   An application for an order of the court discharging an individual from bankruptcy in a case falling within section 279(6) may be made by the bankrupt at any time after the end of the period of 5 years beginning with the date on which the bankruptcy commences.

(2)   On an application under this section the court may—

(a)   refuse to discharge the bankrupt from bankruptcy,

(b)   make an order discharging him absolutely, or

(c)   make an order discharging him subject to such conditions with respect to any income which may subsequently become due to him, or with respect to property devolving upon him, or acquired by him, after his discharge, as may be specified in the order.

(3)   The court may provide for an order falling within subsection (2)(b) or (c) to have immediate effect or to have its effect suspended for such period, or until the fulfilment of such conditions (including a condition requiring the court to be satisfied as to any matter), as may be specified in the order.

281   Effect of discharge

(1)   Subject as follows, where a bankrupt is discharged, the discharge releases him from all the bankruptcy debts, but has no effect—

(a)   on the functions (so far as they remain to be carried out) of the trustee of his estate, or

(b)   on the operation, for the purposes of the carrying out of those functions, of the provisions of this Part;

and, in particular, discharge does not affect the right of any creditor of the bankrupt to prove in the bankruptcy for any debt from which the bankrupt is released.

(2)   Discharge does not affect the right of any secured creditor of the bankrupt to enforce his security for the payment of a debt from which the bankrupt is released.

(3)   Discharge does not release the bankrupt from any bankruptcy debt which he incurred in respect of, or forbearance in respect of which was secured by means of, any fraud or fraudulent breach of trust to which he was a party.

(4)   Discharge does not release the bankrupt from any liability in respect of a fine imposed for an offence or from any liability under a recognisance except, in the case of a penalty imposed for an offence under an enactment relating to the public revenue or of a recognisance, with the consent of the Treasury.

(4A) In subsection (4) the reference to a fine includes a reference to a confiscation order under Part 2, 3 or 4 of the Proceeds of Crime Act 2002.

(5)   Discharge does not, except to such extent and on such conditions as the court may direct, release the bankrupt from any bankruptcy debt which—

(a)   consists in a liability to pay damages for negligence, nuisance or breach of a statutory, contractual or other duty, or to pay damages by virtue of Part I of the Consumer Protection Act 1987, being in either case damages in respect of personal injuries to any person, or

(b)   arises under any order made in family proceedings or under a maintenance calculation made under the Child Support Act 1991.

(6)   Discharge does not release the bankrupt from such other bankruptcy debts, not being debts provable in his bankruptcy, as are prescribed.

(7)   Discharge does not release any person other than the bankrupt from any liability (whether as partner or co-trustee of the bankrupt or otherwise) from which the bankrupt is released by the discharge, or from any liability as surety for the bankrupt or as a person in the nature of such a surety.

(8)   In this section—

"family proceedings" means —

(a)   family proceedings within the meaning of the Magistrates' Courts Act 1980 and any proceedings which would be such proceedings but for section 65(1)(ii) of that Act (proceedings for variation of order for periodical payments); and

(b)   family proceedings within the meaning of Part V of the Matrimonial and Family Proceedings Act 1984.

"fine" means the same as in the Magistrates' Courts Act 1980; and

"personal injuries" includes death and any disease or other impairment of a person's physical or mental condition.

281A   Post-discharge restrictions

Schedule 4A to this Act (bankruptcy restrictions order and bankruptcy restrictions undertaking) shall have effect.

282   Court's power to annul bankruptcy order

(1)   The court may annul a bankruptcy order if it at any time appears to the court—

(a)   that, on any grounds existing at the time the order was made, the order ought not to have been made, or

(b)   that, to the extent required by the rules, the bankruptcy debts and the expenses of the bankruptcy have all, since the making of the order, been either paid or secured for to the satisfaction of the court.

(2)   The court may annul a bankruptcy order made against an individual on a petition under paragraph (a), (b) or (c) of section 264(1) if it at any time appears to the court, on an application by the Official Petitioner—

(a)   that the petition was pending at a time when a criminal bankruptcy order was made against the individual or was presented after such an order was so made, and

(b)   no appeal is pending (within the meaning of section 277) against the individual's conviction of any offence by virtue of which the criminal bankruptcy order was made;

and the court shall annul a bankruptcy order made on a petition under section 264(1)(d) if it at any time appears to the court that the criminal bankruptcy order on which the petition was based has been rescinded in consequence of an appeal.

(3)   The court may annul a bankruptcy order whether or not the bankrupt has been discharged from the bankruptcy.

(4)   Where the court annuls a bankruptcy order (whether under this section or under section 261 or 263D in Part VIII)—

(a)   any sale or other disposition of property, payment made or other thing duly done, under any provision in this Group of Parts, by or under the authority of the official receiver or a trustee of the bankrupt's estate or by the court is valid, but

(b)   if any of the bankrupt's estate is then vested, under any such provision, in such a trustee, it shall vest in such person as the court may appoint or, in default of any such appointment, revert to the bankrupt on such terms (if any) as the court may direct;

and the court may include in its order such supplemental provisions as may be authorised by the rules.

CHAPTER II

PROTECTION OF BANKRUPT'S ESTATE AND INVESTIGATION OF HIS AFFAIRS

283   Definition of bankrupt's estate

(1)   Subject as follows, a bankrupt's estate for the purposes of any of this Group of Parts comprises—

     (a)   all property belonging to or vested in the bankrupt at the commencement of the bankruptcy, and

     (b)   any property which by virtue of any of the following provisions of this Part is comprised in that estate or is treated as falling within the preceding paragraph.

(2)   Subsection (1) does not apply to—

     (a)   such tools, books, vehicles and other items of equipment as are necessary to the bankrupt for use personally by him in his employment, business or vocation;

     (b)   such clothing, bedding, furniture, household equipment and provisions as are necessary for satisfying the basic domestic needs of the bankrupt and his family.

This subsection is subject to section 308 in Chapter IV (certain excluded property reclaimable by trustee).

(3)   Subsection (1) does not apply to—

     (a)   property held by the bankrupt on trust for any other person, or

     (b)   the right of nomination to a vacant ecclesiastical benefice.

...

(4)   References in any of this Group of Parts to property, in relation to a bankrupt, include references to any power exercisable by him over or in respect of property except in so far as the power is exercisable over or in respect of property not for the time being comprised in the bankrupt's estate and—

     (a)   is so exercisable at a time after either the official receiver has had his release in respect of that estate under section 299(2) in Chapter III or a meeting summoned by the trustee of that estate under section 331 in Chapter IV has been held, or

     (b)   cannot be so exercised for the benefit of the bankrupt;

and a power exercisable over or in respect of property is deemed for the purposes of any of this Group of Parts to vest in the person entitled to exercise it at the time of the transaction or event by virtue of which it is exercisable by that person (whether or not it becomes so exercisable at that time).

(5)   For the purposes of any such provision in this Group of Parts, property comprised in a bankrupt's estate is so comprised subject to the rights of any person other than the bankrupt (whether as a secured creditor of the bankrupt or otherwise) in relation thereto, but disregarding—

     (a)   any rights in relation to which a statement such as is required by section 269(1)(a) was made in the petition on which the bankrupt was adjudged bankrupt, and

     (b)   any rights which have been otherwise given up in accordance with the rules.

(6)   This section has effect subject to the provisions of any enactment not contained in this Act under which any property is to be excluded from a bankrupt's estate.

283A Bankrupt's home ceasing to form part of estate

(1)   This section applies where property comprised in the bankrupt's estate consists of an interest in a dwelling-house which at the date of the bankruptcy was the sole or principal residence of—

     (a)   the bankrupt,

     (b)   the bankrupt's spouse or civil partner, or

     (c)   a former spouse or former civil partner of the bankrupt.

(2)   At the end of the period of three years beginning with the date of the bankruptcy the interest mentioned in subsection (1) shall—

     (a)   cease to be comprised in the bankrupt's estate, and

     (b)   vest in the bankrupt (without conveyance, assignment or transfer).

(3)   Subsection (2) shall not apply if during the period mentioned in that subsection—

     (a)   the trustee realises the interest mentioned in subsection (1),

     (b)   the trustee applies for an order for sale in respect of the dwelling-house,

     (c)   the trustee applies for an order for possession of the dwelling-house,

     (d)   the trustee applies for an order under section 313 in Chapter IV in respect of that interest, or

(e) the trustee and the bankrupt agree that the bankrupt shall incur a specified liability to his estate (with or without the addition of interest from the date of the agreement) in consideration of which the interest mentioned in subsection (1) shall cease to form part of the estate.

(4) Where an application of a kind described in subsection (3)(b) to (d) is made during the period mentioned in subsection (2) and is dismissed, unless the court orders otherwise the interest to which the application relates shall on the dismissal of the application—

(a) cease to be comprised in the bankrupt's estate, and

(b) vest in the bankrupt (without conveyance, assignment or transfer).

(5) If the bankrupt does not inform the trustee or the official receiver of his interest in a property before the end of the period of three months beginning with the date of the bankruptcy, the period of three years mentioned in subsection (2)—

(a) shall not begin with the date of the bankruptcy, but

(b) shall begin with the date on which the trustee or official receiver becomes aware of the bankrupt's interest.

(6) The court may substitute for the period of three years mentioned in subsection (2) a longer period—

(a) in prescribed circumstances, and

(b) in such other circumstances as the court thinks appropriate.

(7) The rules may make provision for this section to have effect with the substitution of a shorter period for the period of three years mentioned in subsection (2) in specified circumstances (which may be described by reference to action to be taken by a trustee in bankruptcy).

(8) The rules may also, in particular, make provision—

(a) requiring or enabling the trustee of a bankrupt's estate to give notice that this section applies or does not apply;

(b) about the effect of a notice under paragraph (a);

(c) requiring the trustee of a bankrupt's estate to make an application to the Chief Land Registrar.

(9) Rules under subsection (8)(b) may, in particular—

(a) disapply this section;

(b) enable a court to disapply this section;

(c) make provision in consequence of a disapplication of this section;

(d) enable a court to make provision in consequence of a disapplication of this section;

(e) make provision (which may include provision conferring jurisdiction on a court or tribunal) about compensation.

284 Restrictions on dispositions of property

(1) Where a person is adjudged bankrupt, any disposition of property made by that person in the period to which this section applies is void except to the extent that it is or was made with the consent of the court, or is or was subsequently ratified by the court.

(2) Subsection (1) applies to a payment (whether in cash or otherwise) as it applies to a disposition of property and, accordingly, where any payment is void by virtue of that subsection, the person paid shall hold the sum paid for the bankrupt as part of his estate.

(3) This section applies to the period beginning with the day of the presentation of the petition for the bankruptcy order and ending with the vesting, under Chapter IV of this Part, of the bankrupt's estate in a trustee.

(4) The preceding provisions of this section do not give a remedy against any person—

(a) in respect of any property or payment which he received before the commencement of the bankruptcy in good faith, for value and without notice that the petition had been presented, or

(b) in respect of any interest in property which derives from an interest in respect of which there is, by virtue of this subsection, no remedy.

(5) Where after the commencement of his bankruptcy the bankrupt has incurred a debt to a banker or other person by reason of the making of a payment which is void under this

section, that debt is deemed for the purposes of any of this Group of Parts to have been incurred before the commencement of the bankruptcy unless—

(a)   that banker or person had notice of the bankruptcy before the debt was incurred, or

(b)   it is not reasonably practicable for the amount of the payment to be recovered from the person to whom it was made.

(6)   A disposition of property is void under this section notwithstanding that the property is not or, as the case may be, would not be comprised in the bankrupt's estate; but nothing in this section affects any disposition made by a person of property held by him on trust for any other person.

285   Restriction on proceedings and remedies

(1)   At any time when proceedings on a bankruptcy petition are pending or an individual has been adjudged bankrupt the court may stay any action, execution or other legal process against the property or person of the debtor or, as the case may be, of the bankrupt.

(2)   Any court in which proceedings are pending against any individual may, on proof that a bankruptcy petition has been presented in respect of that individual or that he is an undischarged bankrupt, either stay the proceedings or allow them to continue on such terms as it thinks fit.

(3)   After the making of a bankruptcy order no person who is a creditor of the bankrupt in respect of a debt provable in the bankruptcy shall—

(a)   have any remedy against the property or person of the bankrupt in respect of that debt, or

(b)   before the discharge of the bankrupt, commence any action or other legal proceedings against the bankrupt except with the leave of the court and on such terms as the court may impose.

This is subject to section 346 (enforcement procedures) and 347 (limited right to distress).

(4)   Subject as follows, subsection (3) does not affect the right of a secured creditor of the bankrupt to enforce his security.

(5)   Where any goods of an undischarged bankrupt are held by any person by way of pledge, pawn or other security, the official receiver may, after giving notice in writing of his intention to do so, inspect the goods.

Where such a notice has been given to any person, that person is not entitled, without leave of the court, to realise his security unless he has given the trustee of the bankrupt's estate a reasonable opportunity of inspecting the goods and of exercising the bankrupt's right of redemption.

(6)   References in this section to the property or goods of the bankrupt are to any of his property or goods, whether or not comprised in his estate.

286   Power to appoint interim receiver

(1)   The court may, if it is shown to be necessary for the protection of the debtor's property, at any time after the presentation of a bankruptcy petition and before making a bankruptcy order, appoint the official receiver to be interim receiver of the debtor's property.

(2)   Where the court has, on a debtor's petition, appointed an insolvency practitioner under section 273 and it is shown to the court as mentioned in subsection (1) of this section, the court may, without making a bankruptcy order, appoint that practitioner, instead of the official receiver, to be interim receiver of the debtor's property.

(3)   The court may by an order appointing any person to be an interim receiver direct that his powers shall be limited or restricted in any respect; but, save as so directed, an interim receiver has, in relation to the debtor's property, all the rights, powers, duties and immunities of a receiver and manager under the next section.

(4)   An order of the court appointing any person to be an interim receiver shall require that person to take immediate possession of the debtor's property or, as the case may be, the part of it to which his powers as interim receiver are limited.

(5)   Where an interim receiver has been appointed, the debtor shall give him such inventory of his property and such other information, and shall attend on the interim receiver at such

times, as the latter may for the purpose of carrying out his functions under this section reasonably require.

(6) Where an interim receiver is appointed, section 285(3) applies for the period between the appointment and the making of a bankruptcy order on the petition, or the dismissal of the petition, as if the appointment were the making of such an order.

(7) A person ceases to be interim receiver of a debtor's property if the bankruptcy petition relating to the debtor is dismissed, if a bankruptcy order is made on the petition or if the court by order otherwise terminates the appointment.

(8) References in this section to the debtor's property are to all his property, whether or not it would be comprised in his estate if he were adjudged bankrupt.

287 Receivership pending appointment of trustee

(1) Between the making of a bankruptcy order and the time at which the bankrupt's estate vests in a trustee under Chapter IV of this Part, the official receiver is the receiver and (subject to section 370 (special manager)) the manager of the bankrupt's estate and is under a duty to act as such.

(2) The function of the official receiver while acting as receiver or manager of the bankrupt's estate under this section is to protect the estate; and for this purpose—

(a) he has the same powers as if he were a receiver or manager appointed by the High Court, and

(b) he is entitled to sell or otherwise dispose of any perishable goods comprised in the estate and any other goods so comprised the value of which is likely to diminish if they are not disposed of.

(3) The official receiver while acting as receiver or manager of the estate under this section—

(a) shall take all such steps as he thinks fit for protecting any property which may be claimed for the estate by the trustee of that estate,

(b) is not, except in pursuance of directions given by the Secretary of State, required to do anything that involves his incurring expenditure,

(c) may, if he thinks fit (and shall, if so directed by the court) at any time summon a general meeting of the bankrupt's creditors.

(4) Where—

(a) the official receiver acting as receiver or manager of the estate under this section seizes or disposes of any property which is not comprised in the estate, and

(b) at the time of the seizure or disposal the official receiver believes, and has reasonable grounds for believing, that he is entitled (whether in pursuance of an order of the court or otherwise) to seize or dispose of that property,

the official receiver is not to be liable to any person in respect of any loss or damage resulting from the seizure or disposal except in so far as that loss or damage is caused by his negligence; and he has a *lien* on the property, or the proceeds of its sale, for such of the expenses of the bankruptcy as were incurred in connection with the seizure or disposal.

(5) This section does not apply where by virtue of section 297 (appointment of trustee; special cases) the bankrupt's estate vests in a trustee immediately on the making of the bankruptcy order.

288 Statement of affairs

(1) Where a bankruptcy order has been made otherwise than on a debtor's petition, the bankrupt shall submit a statement of his affairs to the official receiver before the end of the period of 21 days beginning with the commencement of the bankruptcy.

(2) The statement of affairs shall contain—

(a) such particulars of the bankrupt's creditors and of his debts and other liabilities and of his assets as may be prescribed, and

(b) such other information as may be prescribed.

(3) The official receiver may, if he thinks fit—

(a) release the bankrupt from his duty under subsection (1), or

(b) extend the period specified in that subsection;

and where the official receiver has refused to exercise a power conferred by this section, the court, if it thinks fit, may exercise it.

(4)   A bankrupt who—
  (a)   without reasonable excuse fails to comply with the obligation imposed by this section, or
  (b)   without reasonable excuse submits a statement of affairs that does not comply with the prescribed requirements,
  is guilty of a contempt of court and liable to be punished accordingly (in addition to any other punishment to which he may be subject).

289   Investigatory duties of official receiver

(1)   The official receiver shall—
  (a)   investigate the conduct and affairs of each bankrupt (including his conduct and affairs before the making of the bankruptcy order), and
  (b)   make such report (if any) to the court as the official receiver thinks fit.
(2)   Subsection (1) shall not apply to a case in which the official receiver thinks an investigation under that subsection unnecessary.
(3)   Where a bankrupt makes an application for discharge under section 280—
  (a)   the official receiver shall make a report to the court about such matters as may be prescribed, and
  (b)   the court shall consider the report before determining the application.
(4)   A report by the official receiver under this section shall in any proceedings be *prima facie* evidence of the facts stated in it.

290   Public examination of bankrupt

(1)   Where a bankruptcy order has been made, the official receiver may at any time before the discharge of the bankrupt apply to the court for the public examination of the bankrupt.
(2)   Unless the court otherwise orders, the official receiver shall make an application under subsection (1) if notice requiring him to do so is given to him, in accordance with the rules, by one of the bankrupt's creditors with the concurrence of not less than one-half, in value, of those creditors (including the creditor giving notice).
(3)   On an application under subsection (1), the court shall direct that a public examination of the bankrupt shall be held on a day appointed by the court; and the bankrupt shall attend on that day and be publicly examined as to his affairs, dealings and property.
(4)   The following may take part in the public examination of the bankrupt and may question him concerning his affairs, dealings and property and the causes of his failure, namely—
  (a)   the official receiver and, in the case of an individual adjudged bankrupt on a petition under section 264(1)(d), the Official Petitioner,
  (b)   the trustee of the bankrupt's estate, if his appointment has taken effect,
  (c)   any person who has been appointed as special manager of the bankrupt's estate or business,
  (d)   any creditor of the bankrupt who has tendered a proof in the bankruptcy.
(5)   If a bankrupt without reasonable excuse fails at any time to attend his public examination under this section he is guilty of a contempt of court and liable to be punished accordingly (in addition to any other punishment to which he may be subject).

291   Duties of bankrupt in relation to official receiver

(1)   Where a bankruptcy order has been made, the bankrupt is under a duty—
  (a)   to deliver possession of his estate to the official receiver, and
  (b)   to deliver up to the official receiver all books, papers and other records of which he has possession or control and which relate to his estate and affairs (including any which would be privileged from disclosure in any proceedings).
(2)   In the case of any part of the bankrupt's estate which consists of things possession of which cannot be delivered to the official receiver, and in the case of any property that may be claimed for the bankrupt's estate by the trustee, it is the bankrupt's duty to do all such things

as may reasonably be required by the official receiver for the protection of those things or that property.

(3) Subsections (1) and (2) do not apply where by virtue of section 297 below the bankrupt's estate vests in a trustee immediately on the making of the bankruptcy order.

(4) The bankrupt shall give the official receiver such inventory of his estate and such other information, and shall attend on the official receiver at such times, as the official receiver may reasonably require—

    (a) for a purpose of this Chapter, or

    (b) in connection with the making of a bankruptcy restrictions order.

(5) Subsection (4) applies to a bankrupt after his discharge.

(6) If the bankrupt without reasonable excuse fails to comply with any obligation imposed by this section, he is guilty of a contempt of court and liable to be punished accordingly (in addition to any other punishment to which he may be subject).

CHAPTER III

TRUSTEES IN BANKRUPTCY

Tenure of office as trustee

292 Power to make appointments

(1) The power to appoint a person as trustee of a bankrupt's estate (whether the first such trustee or a trustee appointed to fill any vacancy) is exercisable—

    (a) by a general meeting of the bankrupt's creditors;

    (b) under section 295(2), 296(2) or 300(6) below in this Chapter, by the Secretary of State; or

    (c) under section 297, by the court.

(2) No person may be appointed as trustee of a bankrupt's estate unless he is, at the time of the appointment, qualified to act as an insolvency practitioner in relation to the bankrupt.

(3) Any power to appoint a person as trustee of a bankrupt's estate includes power to appoint two or more persons as joint trustees; but such an appointment must make provision as to the circumstances in which the trustees must act together and the circumstances in which one or more of them may act for the others.

(4) The appointment of any person as trustee takes effect only if that person accepts the appointment in accordance with the rules. Subject to this, the appointment of any person as trustee takes effect at the time specified in his certificate of appointment.

(5) This section is without prejudice to the provisions of this Chapter under which the official receiver is, in certain circumstances, to be trustee of the estate.

293 Summoning of meeting to appoint first trustee

(1) Where a bankruptcy order has been made it is the duty of the official receiver, as soon as practicable in the period of 12 weeks beginning with the day on which the order was made, to decide whether to summon a general meeting of the bankrupt's creditors for the purpose of appointing a trustee of the bankrupt's estate.

This section does not apply where the bankruptcy order was made on a petition under section 264(1)(d) (criminal bankruptcy); and it is subject to the provision made in sections 294(3) and 297(6) below.

(2) Subject to the next section, if the official receiver decides not to summon such a meeting, he shall, before the end of the period of 12 weeks above mentioned, give notice of his decision to the court and to every creditor of the bankrupt who is known to the official receiver or is identified in the bankrupt's statement of affairs.

(3) As from the giving to the court of a notice under subsection (2), the official receiver is the trustee of the bankrupt's estate.

294 Power of creditors to requisition meeting

(1) Where in the case of any bankruptcy—

    (a) the official receiver has not yet summoned, or has decided not to summon, a general meeting of the bankrupt's creditors for the purpose of appointing the trustee,

(b)   ...
any creditor of the bankrupt may request the official receiver to summon such a meeting for that purpose.

(2)   If such a request appears to the official receiver to be made with the concurrence of not less than one-quarter, in value, of the bankrupt's creditors (including the creditor making the request), it is the duty of the official receiver to summon the requested meeting.

(3)   Accordingly, where the duty imposed by subsection (2) has arisen, the official receiver is required neither to reach a decision for the purposes of section 293(1) nor (if he has reached one) to serve any notice under section 293(2).

295   Failure of meeting to appoint trustee

(1)   If a meeting summoned under section 293 or 294 is held but no appointment of a person as trustee is made, it is the duty of the official receiver to decide whether to refer the need for an appointment to the Secretary of State.

(2)   On a reference made in pursuance of that decision, the Secretary of State shall either make an appointment or decline to make one.

(3)   If—
(a)   the official receiver decides not to refer the need for an appointment to the Secretary of State, or
(b)   on such a reference the Secretary of State declines to make an appointment,
the official receiver shall give notice of his decision or, as the case may be, of the Secretary of State's decision to the court.

(4)   As from the giving of notice under subsection (3) in a case in which no notice has been given under section 293(2), the official receiver shall be trustee of the bankrupt's estate.

296   Appointment of trustee by Secretary of State

(1)   At any time when the official receiver is the trustee of a bankrupt's estate by virtue of any provision of this Chapter (other than section 297(1) below) he may apply to the Secretary of State for the appointment of a person as trustee instead of the official receiver.

(2)   On an application under subsection (1) the Secretary of State shall either make an appointment or decline to make one.

(3)   Such an application may be made notwithstanding that the Secretary of State has declined to make an appointment either on a previous application under subsection (1) or on a reference under section 295 or under section 300(4) below.

(4)   Where the trustee of a bankrupt's estate has been appointed by the Secretary of State (whether under this section or otherwise), the trustee shall give notice to the bankrupt's creditors of his appointment or, if the court so allows, shall advertise his appointment in accordance with the court's directions.

(5)   In that notice or advertisement the trustee shall—
(a)   state whether he proposes to summon a general meeting of the bankrupt's creditors for the purpose of establishing a creditors' committee under section 301, and
(b)   if he does not propose to summon such a meeting, set out the power of the creditors under this Part to require him to summon one.

297   Special cases

(1)   Where a bankruptcy order is made on a petition under section 264(1)(d) (criminal bankruptcy), the official receiver shall be trustee of the bankrupt's estate.

(2)   ...

(3)   ...

(4)   Where a bankruptcy order is made in a case in which an insolvency practitioner's report has been submitted to the court under section 274 ..., the court, if it thinks fit, may on making the order appoint the person who made the report as trustee.

(5)   Where a bankruptcy order is made (whether or not on a petition under section 264(1)(c)) at a time when there is a supervisor of a voluntary arrangement approved in relation to the bankrupt under Part VIII, the court, if it thinks fit, may on making the order appoint the supervisor of the arrangement as trustee.

(6) Where an appointment is made under subsection (4) or (5) of this section, the official receiver is not under the duty imposed by section 293(1) (to decide whether or not to summon a meeting of creditors).

(7) Where the trustee of a bankrupt's estate has been appointed by the court, the trustee shall give notice to the bankrupt's creditors of his appointment or, if the court so allows, shall advertise his appointment in accordance with the directions of the court.

(8) In that notice or advertisement he shall—

  (a) state whether he proposes to summon a general meeting of the bankrupt's creditors for the purpose of establishing a creditors' committee under section 301 below, and

  (b) if he does not propose to summon such a meeting, set out the power of the creditors under this Part to require him to summon one.

298 Removal of trustee; vacation of office

(1) Subject as follows, the trustee of a bankrupt's estate may be removed from office only by an order of the court or by a general meeting of the bankrupt's creditors summoned specially for that purpose in accordance with the rules.

(2) Where the official receiver is trustee by virtue of section 297(1), he shall not be removed from office under this section.

(3) ...

(4) Where the official receiver is trustee by virtue of section 293(3) or 295(4) or a trustee is appointed by the Secretary of State or (otherwise than under section 297(5)) by the court, a general meeting of the bankrupt's creditors shall be summoned for the purpose of replacing the trustee only if—

  (a) the trustee thinks fit, or

  (b) the court so directs, or

  (c) the meeting is requested by one of the bankrupt's creditors with the concurrence of not less than one-quarter, in value, of the creditors (including the creditor making the request).

(5) If the trustee was appointed by the Secretary of State, he may be removed by a direction of the Secretary of State.

(6) The trustee (not being the official receiver) shall vacate office if he ceases to be a person who is for the time being qualified to act as an insolvency practitioner in relation to the bankrupt.

(7) The trustee may, in the prescribed circumstances, resign his office by giving notice of his resignation to the court.

(8) The trustee shall vacate office on giving notice to the court that a final meeting has been held under section 331 in Chapter IV and of the decision (if any) of that meeting.

(9) The trustee shall vacate office if the bankruptcy order is annulled.

299 Release of trustee

(1) Where the official receiver has ceased to be the trustee of a bankrupt's estate and a person is appointed in his stead, the official receiver shall have his release with effect from the following time, that is to say—

  (a) where that person is appointed by a general meeting of the bankrupt's creditors or by the Secretary of State, the time at which the official receiver gives notice to the court that he has been replaced, and

  (b) where that person is appointed by the court, such time as the court may determine.

(2) If the official receiver while he is the trustee gives notice to the Secretary of State that the administration of the bankrupt's estate in accordance with Chapter IV of this Part is for practical purposes complete, he shall have his release with effect from such time as the Secretary of State may determine.

(3) A person other than the official receiver who has ceased to be the trustee shall have his release with effect from the following time, that is to say—

  (a) in the case of a person who has been removed from office by a general meeting of the bankrupt's creditors that has not resolved against his release or who has died, the time at which notice is given to the court in accordance with the rules that that person has ceased to hold office;

(b)   in the case of a person who has been removed from office by a general meeting of the bankrupt's creditors that has resolved against his release, or by the court, or by the Secretary of State, or who has vacated office under section 298(6), such time as the Secretary of State may, on an application by that person, determine;

(c)   in the case of a person who has resigned, such time as may be prescribed;

(d)   in the case of a person who has vacated office under section 298(8)—

    (i)   if the final meeting referred to in that subsection has resolved against that person's release, such time as the Secretary of State may, on an application by that person, determine; and

    (ii)   if that meeting has not so resolved, the time at which the person vacated office.

(4)   Where a bankruptcy order is annulled, the trustee at the time of the annulment has his release with effect from such time as the court may determine.

(5)   Where the official receiver or the trustee has his release under this section, he shall, with effect from the time specified in the preceding provisions of this section, be discharged from all liability both in respect of acts or omissions of his in the administration of the estate and otherwise in relation to his conduct as trustee.

But nothing in this section prevents the exercise, in relation to a person who has had his release under this section, of the court's powers under section 304.

300   Vacancy in office of trustee

(1)   This section applies where the appointment of any person as trustee of a bankrupt's estate fails to take effect or, such an appointment having taken effect, there is otherwise a vacancy in the office of trustee.

(2)   The official receiver shall be trustee until the vacancy is filled.

(3)   The official receiver may summon a general meeting of the bankrupt's creditors for the purpose of filling the vacancy and shall summon such a meeting if required to do so in pursuance of section 314(7) (creditors' requisition).

(4)   If at the end of the period of 28 days beginning with the day on which the vacancy first came to the official receiver's attention he has not summoned, and is not proposing to summon, a general meeting of creditors for the purpose of filling the vacancy, he shall refer the need for an appointment to the Secretary of State.

(5)   ...

(6)   On a reference to the Secretary of State under subsection (4) the Secretary of State shall either make an appointment or decline to make one.

(7)   If on a reference under subsection (4) no appointment is made, the official receiver shall continue to be trustee of the bankrupt's estate, but without prejudice to his power to make a further reference.

(8)   References in this section to a vacancy include a case where it is necessary, in relation to any property which is or may be comprised in a bankrupt's estate, to revive the trusteeship of that estate after the holding of a final meeting summoned under section 331 or the giving by the official receiver of notice under section 299(2).

Control of trustee

301   Creditors' committee

(1)   Subject as follows, a general meeting of a bankrupt's creditors (whether summoned under the preceding provisions of this Chapter or otherwise) may, in accordance with the rules, establish a committee (known as "the creditors' committee") to exercise the functions conferred on it by or under this Act.

(2)   A general meeting of the bankrupt's creditors shall not establish such a committee, or confer any functions on such a committee, at any time when the official receiver is the trustee of the bankrupt's estate, except in connection with an appointment made by that meeting of a person to be trustee instead of the official receiver.

302   Exercise by Secretary of State of functions of creditors' committee

(1)   The creditors' committee is not to be able or required to carry out its functions at any time when the official receiver is trustee of the bankrupt's estate; but at any such time the functions of the committee under this Act shall be vested in the Secretary of State, except to the extent that the rules otherwise provide.

(2)   Where in the case of any bankruptcy there is for the time being no creditors' committee and the trustee of the bankrupt's estate is a person other than the official receiver, the functions of such a committee shall be vested in the Secretary of State, except to the extent that the rules otherwise provide.

303   General control of trustee by the court

(1)   If a bankrupt or any of his creditors or any other person is dissatisfied by any act, omission or decision of a trustee of the bankrupt's estate, he may apply to the court; and on such an application the court may confirm, reverse or modify any act or decision of the trustee, may give him directions or may make such other order as it thinks fit.

(2)   The trustee of a bankrupt's estate may apply to the court for directions in relation to any particular matter arising under the bankruptcy.

(2A)   Where at any time after a bankruptcy petition has been presented to the court against any person, whether under the provisions of the Insolvent Partnerships Order 1994 or not, the attention of the court is drawn to the fact that the person in question is a member of an insolvent partnership, the court may make an order as to the future conduct of the insolvency proceedings and any such order may apply any provisions of that Order with any necessary modifications.

(2B)   Where a bankruptcy petition has been presented against more than one individual in the circumstances mentioned in subsection (2A) above, the court may give such directions for consolidating the proceedings, or any of them, as it thinks just.

(2C)   Any order or directions under subsection (2A) or (2B) may be made or given on the application of the official receiver, any responsible insolvency practitioner, the trustee of the partnership or any other interested person and may include provisions as to the administration of the joint estate of the partnership, and in particular how it and the separate estate of any member are to be administered.

304   Liability of trustee

(1)   Where on an application under this section the court is satisfied—

(a)   that the trustee of a bankrupt's estate has misapplied or retained, or become accountable for, any money or other property comprised in the bankrupt's estate, or

(b)   that a bankrupt's estate has suffered any loss in consequence of any misfeasance or breach of fiduciary or other duty by a trustee of the estate in the carrying out of his functions,

the court may order the trustee, for the benefit of the estate, to repay, restore or account for money or other property (together with interest at such rate as the court thinks just) or, as the case may require, to pay such sum by way of compensation in respect of the misfeasance or breach of fiduciary or other duty as the court thinks just.

This is without prejudice to any liability arising apart from this section.

(2)   An application under this section may be made by the official receiver, the Secretary of State, a creditor of the bankrupt or (whether or not there is, or is likely to be, a surplus for the purposes of section 330(5) (final distribution)) the bankrupt himself.

But the leave of the court is required for the making of an application if it is to be made by the bankrupt or if it is to be made after the trustee has had his release under section 299.

(3)   Where—

(a)   the trustee seizes or disposes of any property which is not comprised in the bankrupt's estate, and

(b)   at the time of the seizure or disposal the trustee believes, and has reasonable grounds for believing, that he is entitled (whether in pursuance of an order of the court or otherwise) to seize or dispose of that property, the trustee is not liable to any person (whether under this section or otherwise) in respect of any loss or damage resulting from the seizure or disposal except in so far as that loss or damage is caused by the negligence of the trustee; and he has a lien on the property, or the proceeds of its sale, for such of the expenses of the bankruptcy as were incurred in connection with the seizure or disposal.

CHAPTER IV
ADMINISTRATION BY TRUSTEE

Preliminary

305 General functions of trustee

(1) This Chapter applies in relation to any bankruptcy where either—
  (a) the appointment of a person as trustee of a bankrupt's estate takes effect, or
  (b) the official receiver becomes trustee of a bankrupt's estate.
(2) The function of the trustee is to get in, realise and distribute the bankrupt's estate in accordance with the following provisions of this Chapter; and in the carrying out of that function and in the management of the bankrupt's estate the trustee is entitled, subject to those provisions, to use his own discretion.
(3) It is the duty of the trustee, if he is not the official receiver—
  (a) to furnish the official receiver with such information,
  (b) to produce to the official receiver, and permit inspection by the official receiver of, such books, papers and other records, and
  (c) to give the official receiver such other assistance,
  as the official receiver may reasonably require for the purpose of enabling him to carry out his functions in relation to the bankruptcy.
(4) The official name of the trustee shall be "the trustee of the estate of, a bankrupt" (inserting the name of the bankrupt); but he may be referred to as "the trustee in bankruptcy" of the particular bankrupt.

Acquisition, control and realisation of bankrupt's estate

306 Vesting of bankrupt's estate in trustee

(1) The bankrupt's estate shall vest in the trustee immediately on his appointment taking effect or, in the case of the official receiver, on his becoming trustee.
(2) Where any property which is, or is to be, comprised in the bankrupt's estate vests in the trustee (whether under this section or under any other provision of this Part), it shall so vest without any conveyance, assignment or transfer.

...

306B Property in respect of which receivership or administration order made

(1) This section applies where—
  (a) property is excluded from the bankrupt's estate by virtue of section 417(2)(b),
  (c) or (d) of the Proceeds of Crime Act 2002 (property in respect of which an order for the appointment of a receiver or administrator under certain provisions of that Act is in force),
  (b) a confiscation order is made under section 6 92 or 156 of that Act,
  (c) the amount payable under the confiscation order is fully paid, and
  (d) any of the property remains in the hands of the receiver or administrator (as the case may be).
(2) The property vests in the trustee as part of the bankrupt's estate.

...

307 After-acquired property

(1) Subject to this section and section 309, the trustee may by notice in writing claim for the bankrupt's estate any property which has been acquired by, or has devolved upon, the bankrupt since the commencement of the bankruptcy.

(2) A notice under this section shall not be served in respect of—
- (a) any property falling within subsection (2) or (3) of section 283 in Chapter II,
- (aa) any property vesting in the bankrupt by virtue of section 283A in Chapter II,
- (b) any property which by virtue of any other enactment is excluded from the bankrupt's estate, or
- (c) without prejudice to section 280(2)(c) (order of court on application for discharge), any property which is acquired by, or devolves upon, the bankrupt after his discharge.

(3) Subject to the next subsection, upon the service on the bankrupt of a notice under this section the property to which the notice relates shall vest in the trustee as part of the bankrupt's estate; and the trustee's title to that property has relation back to the time at which the property was acquired by, or devolved upon, the bankrupt.

(4) Where, whether before or after service of a notice under this section—
- (a) a person acquires property in good faith, for value and without notice of the bankruptcy, or
- (b) a banker enters into a transaction in good faith and without such notice,

the trustee is not in respect of that property or transaction entitled by virtue of this section to any remedy against that person or banker, or any person whose title to any property derives from that person or banker.

(5) References in this section to property do not include any property which, as part of the bankrupt's income, may be the subject of an income payments order under section 310.

308 Vesting in trustee of certain items of excess value

(1) Subject to section 309 , where—
- (a) property is excluded by virtue of section 283(2) (tools of trade, household effects, etc.) from the bankrupt's estate, and
- (b) it appears to the trustee that the realisable value of the whole or any part of that property exceeds the cost of a reasonable replacement for that property or that part of it,

the trustee may by notice in writing claim that property or, as the case may be, that part of it for the bankrupt's estate.

(2) Upon the service on the bankrupt of a notice under this section, the property to which the notice relates vests in the trustee as part of the bankrupt's estate; and, except against a purchaser in good faith, for value and without notice of the bankruptcy, the trustee's title to that property has relation back to the commencement of the bankruptcy.

(3) The trustee shall apply funds comprised in the estate to the purchase by or on behalf of the bankrupt of a reasonable replacement for any property vested in the trustee under this section; and the duty imposed by this subsection has priority over the obligation of the trustee to distribute the estate.

(4) For the purposes of this section property is a reasonable replacement for other property if it is reasonably adequate for meeting the needs met by the other property.

...

310 Income payments orders

(1) The court may make an order ("an income payments order") claiming for the bankrupt's estate so much of the income of the bankrupt during the period for which the order is in force as may be specified in the order.

(1A) An income payments order may be made only on an application instituted—
- (a) by the trustee, and
- (b) before the discharge of the bankrupt.

(2) The court shall not make an income payments order the effect of which would be to reduce the income of the bankrupt when taken together with any payments to which subsection (8) applies below what appears to the court to be necessary for meeting the reasonable domestic needs of the bankrupt and his family.

(3) An income payments order shall, in respect of any payment of income to which it is to apply, either—

(a) require the bankrupt to pay the trustee an amount equal to so much of that payment as is claimed by the order, or

(b) require the person making the payment to pay so much of it as is so claimed to the trustee, instead of to the bankrupt.

(4) Where the court makes an income payments order it may, if it thinks fit, discharge or vary any attachment of earnings order that is for the time being in force to secure payments by the bankrupt.

(5) Sums received by the trustee under an income payments order form part of the bankrupt's estate.

(6) An income payments order must specify the period during which it is to have effect; and that period—

(a) may end after the discharge of the bankrupt, but

(b) may not end after the period of three years beginning with the date on which the order is made.

(6A) An income payments order may (subject to subsection (6)(b)) be varied on the application of the trustee or the bankrupt (whether before or after discharge).

(7) For the purposes of this section the income of the bankrupt comprises every payment in the nature of income which is from time to time made to him or to which he from time to time becomes entitled, including any payment in respect of the carrying on of any business or in respect of any office or employment and (despite anything in section 11 or 12 of the Welfare Reform and Pensions Act 1999) any payment under a pension scheme but excluding any payment to which subsection (8) applies.

(8) This subsection applies to—

(a) payments by way of guaranteed minimum pension; and

(b) payments giving effect to the bankrupt's protected rights as a member of a pension scheme."

(9) In this section, "guaranteed minimum pension" and "protected rights" have the same meaning as in the Pension Schemes Act 1993.

310A Income payments agreement

(1) In this section "income payments agreement" means a written agreement between a bankrupt and his trustee or between a bankrupt and the official receiver which provides—

(a) that the bankrupt is to pay to the trustee or the official receiver an amount equal to a specified part or proportion of the bankrupt's income for a specified period, or

(b) that a third person is to pay to the trustee or the official receiver a specified proportion of money due to the bankrupt by way of income for a specified period.

(2) A provision of an income payments agreement of a kind specified in subsection (1)(a) or (b) may be enforced as if it were a provision of an income payments order.

(3) While an income payments agreement is in force the court may, on the application of the bankrupt, his trustee or the official receiver, discharge or vary an attachment of earnings order that is for the time being in force to secure payments by the bankrupt.

(4) The following provisions of section 310 shall apply to an income payments agreement as they apply to an income payments order—

(a) subsection (5) (receipts to form part of estate), and

(b) subsections (7) to (9) (meaning of income).

(5) An income payments agreement must specify the period during which it is to have effect; and that period—

(a) may end after the discharge of the bankrupt, but

(b) may not end after the period of three years beginning with the date on which the agreement is made.

(6) An income payments agreement may (subject to subsection (5)(b)) be varied—

(a) by written agreement between the parties, or

(b) by the court on an application made by the bankrupt, the trustee or the official receiver.

(7) The court—

(a) may not vary an income payments agreement so as to include provision of a kind which could not be included in an income payments order, and

(b) shall grant an application to vary an income payments agreement if and to the extent that the court thinks variation necessary to avoid the effect mentioned in section 310(2).

311 Acquisition by trustee of control

(1) The trustee shall take possession of all books, papers and other records which relate to the bankrupt's estate or affairs and which belong to him or are in his possession or under his control (including any which would be privileged from disclosure in any proceedings).

(2) In relation to, and for the purpose of acquiring or retaining possession of, the bankrupt's estate, the trustee is in the same position as if he were a receiver of property appointed by the High Court; and the court may, on his application, enforce such acquisition or retention accordingly.

(3) Where any part of the bankrupt's estate consists of stock or shares in a company, shares in a ship or any other property transferable in the books of a company, office or person, the trustee may exercise the right to transfer the property to the same extent as the bankrupt might have exercised it if he had not become bankrupt.

(4) Where any part of the estate consists of things in action, they are deemed to have been assigned to the trustee; but notice of the deemed assignment need not be given except in so far as it is necessary, in a case where the deemed assignment is from the bankrupt himself, for protecting the priority of the trustee.

(5) Where any goods comprised in the estate are held by any person by way of pledge, pawn or other security and no notice has been served in respect of those goods by the official receiver under subsection (5) of section 285 (restriction on realising security), the trustee may serve such a notice in respect of the goods; and whether or not a notice has been served under this subsection or that subsection, the trustee may, if he thinks fit, exercise the bankrupt's right of redemption in respect of any such goods.

(6) A notice served by the trustee under subsection (5) has the same effect as a notice served by the official receiver under section 285(5).

312 Obligation to surrender control to trustee

(1) The bankrupt shall deliver up to the trustee possession of any property, books, papers or other records of which he has possession or control and of which the trustee is required to take possession.

This is without prejudice to the general duties of the bankrupt under section 333 in this Chapter.

(2) If any of the following is in possession of any property, books, papers or other records of which the trustee is required to take possession, namely—

(a) the official receiver,

(b) a person who has ceased to be trustee of the bankrupt's estate, or

(c) a person who has been the supervisor of a voluntary arrangement approved in relation to the bankrupt under Part VIII,

the official receiver or, as the case may be, that person shall deliver up possession of the property, books, papers or records to the trustee.

(3) Any banker or agent of the bankrupt or any other person who holds any property to the account of, or for, the bankrupt shall pay or deliver to the trustee all property in his possession or under his control which forms part of the bankrupt's estate and which he is not by law entitled to retain as against the bankrupt or trustee.

(4) If any person without reasonable excuse fails to comply with any obligation imposed by this section, he is guilty of a contempt of court and liable to be punished accordingly (in addition to any other punishment to which he may be subject).

313 Charge on bankrupt's home

(1) Where any property consisting of an interest in a dwelling house which is occupied by the bankrupt or by his spouse or former spouse or by his civil partner or former civil partner is

comprised in the bankrupt's estate and the trustee is, for any reason, unable for the time being to realise that property, the trustee may apply to the court for an order imposing a charge on the property for the benefit of the bankrupt's estate.

(2) If on an application under this section the court imposes a charge on any property, the benefit of that charge shall be comprised in the bankrupt's estate and is enforceable, up to the charged value from time to time, for the payment of any amount which is payable otherwise than to the bankrupt out of the estate and of interest on that amount at the prescribed rate.

(2A) In subsection (2) the charged value means—

    (a) the amount specified in the charging order as the value of the bankrupt's interest in the property at the date of the order, plus

    (b) interest on that amount from the date of the charging order at the prescribed rate.

(2B) In determining the value of an interest for the purposes of this section the court shall disregard any matter which it is required to disregard by the rules.

(3) An order under this section made in respect of property vested in the trustee shall provide, in accordance with the rules, for the property to cease to be comprised in the bankrupt's estate and, subject to the charge (and any prior charge), to vest in the bankrupt.

...

313A Low value home: application for sale, possession or charge

(1) This section applies where—

    (a) property comprised in the bankrupt's estate consists of an interest in a dwelling-house which at the date of the bankruptcy was the sole or principal residence of—

        (i) the bankrupt,

        (ii) the bankrupt's spouse or civil partner, or

        (iii) a former spouse of the bankrupt or former civil partner, and

    (b) the trustee applies for an order for the sale of the property, for an order for possession of the property or for an order under section 313 in respect of the property.

(2) The court shall dismiss the application if the value of the interest is below the amount prescribed for the purposes of this subsection.

(3) In determining the value of an interest for the purposes of this section the court shall disregard any matter which it is required to disregard by the order which prescribes the amount for the purposes of subsection (2).

314 Powers of trustee

(1) The trustee may—

    (a) with the permission of the creditors' committee or the court, exercise any of the powers specified in Part I of Schedule 5 to this Act, and

    (b) without that permission, exercise any of the general powers specified in Part II of that Schedule.

(2) With the permission of the creditors' committee or the court, the trustee may appoint the bankrupt—

    (a) to superintend the management of his estate or any part of it,

    (b) to carry on his business (if any) for the benefit of his creditors, or

    (c) in any other respect to assist in administering the estate in such manner and on such terms as the trustee may direct.

(3) A permission given for the purposes of subsection (1)(a) or (2) shall not be a general permission but shall relate to a particular proposed exercise of the power in question; and a person dealing with the trustee in good faith and for value is not to be concerned to enquire whether any permission required in either case has been given.

(4) Where the trustee has done anything without the permission required by subsection (1)(a) or (2), the court or the creditors' committee may, for the purpose of enabling him to meet his expenses out of the bankrupt's estate, ratify what the trustee has done.

But the committee shall not do so unless it is satisfied that the trustee has acted in a case of urgency and has sought its ratification without undue delay.

(5) Part III of Schedule 5 to this Act has effect with respect to the things which the trustee is able to do for the purposes of, or in connection with, the exercise of any of his powers under any of this Group of Parts.

(6) Where the trustee (not being the official receiver) in exercise of the powers conferred on him by any provision in this Group of Parts—

    (a) disposes of any property comprised in the bankrupt's estate to an associate of the bankrupt, or

    (b) employs a solicitor,

he shall, if there is for the time being a creditors' committee, give notice to the committee of that exercise of his powers.

(7) Without prejudice to the generality of subsection (5) and Part III of Schedule 5, the trustee may, if he thinks fit, at any time summon a general meeting of the bankrupt's creditors.

Subject to the preceding provisions in this Group of Parts, he shall summon such a meeting if he is requested to do so by a creditor of the bankrupt and the request is made with the concurrence of not less than one-tenth, in value, of the bankrupt's creditors (including the creditor making the request).

(8) Nothing in this Act is to be construed as restricting the capacity of the trustee to exercise any of his powers outside England and Wales.

Disclaimer of onerous property

315 Disclaimer (general power)

(1) Subject as follows, the trustee may, by the giving of the prescribed notice, disclaim any onerous property and may do so notwithstanding that he has taken possession of it, endeavoured to sell it or otherwise exercised rights of ownership in relation to it.

(2) The following is onerous property for the purposes of this section, that is to say—

    (a) any unprofitable contract, and

    (b) any other property comprised in the bankrupt's estate which is unsaleable or not readily saleable, or is such that it may give rise to a liability to pay money or perform any other onerous act.

(3) A disclaimer under this section—

    (a) operates so as to determine, as from the date of the disclaimer, the rights, interests and liabilities of the bankrupt and his estate in or in respect of the property disclaimed, and

    (b) discharges the trustee from all personal liability in respect of that property as from the commencement of his trusteeship,

but does not, except so far as is necessary for the purpose of releasing the bankrupt, the bankrupt's estate and the trustee from any liability, affect the rights or liabilities of any other person.

(4) A notice of disclaimer shall not be given under this section in respect of any property that has been claimed for the estate under section 307 (after-acquired property) or 308 (personal property of bankrupt exceeding reasonable replacement value) or 308A, except with the leave of the court.

(5) Any person sustaining loss or damage in consequence of the operation of a disclaimer under this section is deemed to be a creditor of the bankrupt to the extent of the loss or damage and accordingly may prove for the loss or damage as a bankruptcy debt.

316 Notice requiring trustee's decision

(1) Notice of disclaimer shall not be given under section 315 in respect of any property if—

    (a) a person interested in the property has applied in writing to the trustee or one of his predecessors as trustee requiring the trustee or that predecessor to decide whether he will disclaim or not, and

    (b) the period of 28 days beginning with the day on which that application was made has expired without a notice of disclaimer having been given under section 315 in respect of that property.

(2) The trustee is deemed to have adopted any contract which by virtue of this section he is not entitled to disclaim.

317   Disclaimer of leaseholds

(1)   The disclaimer of any property of a leasehold nature does not take effect unless a copy of the disclaimer has been served (so far as the trustee is aware of their addresses) on every person claiming under the bankrupt as underlessee or mortgagee and either—

(a)   no application under section 320 below is made with respect to the property before the end of the period of 14 days beginning with the day on which the last notice served under this subsection was served, or

(b)   where such an application has been made, the court directs that the disclaimer is to take effect.

(2)   Where the court gives a direction under subsection (1)(b) it may also, instead of or in addition to any order it makes under section 320, make such orders with respect to fixtures, tenant's improvements and other matters arising out of the lease as it thinks fit.

318   Disclaimer of dwelling house

Without prejudice to section 317, the disclaimer of any property in a dwelling house does not take effect unless a copy of the disclaimer has been served (so far as the trustee is aware of their addresses) on every person in occupation of or claiming a right to occupy the dwelling house and either—

(a)   no application under section 320 is made with respect to the property before the end of the period of 14 days beginning with the day on which the last notice served under this section was served, or

(b)   where such an application has been made, the court directs that the disclaimer is to take effect.

...

320   Court order vesting disclaimed property

(1)   This section and the next apply where the trustee has disclaimed property under section 315.

(2)   An application may be made to the court under this section by—

(a)   any person who claims an interest in the disclaimed property,

(b)   any person who is under any liability in respect of the disclaimed property, not being a liability discharged by the disclaimer, or

(c)   where the disclaimed property is property in a dwelling house, any person who at the time when the bankruptcy petition was presented was in occupation of or entitled to occupy the dwelling house.

(3)   Subject as follows in this section and the next, the court may, on an application under this section, make an order on such terms as it thinks fit for the vesting of the disclaimed property in, or for its delivery to—

(a)   a person entitled to it or a trustee for such a person,

(b)   a person subject to such a liability as is mentioned in subsection (2)(b) or a trustee for such a person, or

(c)   where the disclaimed property is property in a dwelling house, any person who at the time when the bankruptcy petition was presented was in occupation of or entitled to occupy the dwelling house.

(4)   The court shall not make an order by virtue of subsection (3)(b) except where it appears to the court that it would be just to do so for the purpose of compensating the person subject to the liability in respect of the disclaimer.

(5)   The effect of any order under this section shall be taken into account in assessing for the purposes of section 315(5) the extent of any loss or damage sustained by any person in consequence of the disclaimer.

(6)   An order under this section vesting property in any person need not be completed by any conveyance, assignment or transfer.

321   Order under s 320 in respect of leaseholds

(1)   The court shall not make an order under section 320 vesting property of a leasehold nature in any person, except on terms making that person—

(a) subject to the same liabilities and obligations as the bankrupt was subject to under the lease on the day the bankruptcy petition was presented, or

(b) if the court thinks fit, subject to the same liabilities and obligations as that person would be subject to if the lease had been assigned to him on that day.

(2) For the purposes of an order under section 320 relating to only part of any property comprised in a lease, the requirements of subsection (1) apply as if the lease comprised only the property to which the order relates.

(3) Where subsection (1) applies and no person is willing to accept an order under section 320 on the terms required by that subsection, the court may (by order under section 320) vest the estate or interest of the bankrupt in the property in any person who is liable (whether personally or in a representative capacity and whether alone or jointly with the bankrupt) to perform the lessee's covenants in the lease.

The court may by virtue of this subsection vest that estate and interest in such a person freed and discharged from all estates, incumbrances and interests created by the bankrupt.

(4) Where subsection (1) applies and a person declines to accept any order under section 320, that person shall be excluded from all interest in the property.

Distribution of bankrupt's estate

322   Proof of debts

(1) Subject to this section and the next, the proof of any bankruptcy debt by a secured or unsecured creditor of the bankrupt and the admission or rejection of any proof shall take place in accordance with the rules.

(2) Where a bankruptcy debt bears interest, that interest is provable as part of the debt except in so far as it is payable in respect of any period after the commencement of the bankruptcy.

(3) The trustee shall estimate the value of any bankruptcy debt which, by reason of its being subject to any contingency or contingencies or for any other reason, does not bear a certain value.

(4) Where the value of a bankruptcy debt is estimated by the trustee under subsection (3) or, by virtue of section 303 in Chapter III, by the court, the amount provable in the bankruptcy in respect of the debt is the amount of the estimate.

323   Mutual credit and set-off

(1) This section applies where before the commencement of the bankruptcy there have been mutual credits, mutual debts or other mutual dealings between the bankrupt and any creditor of the bankrupt proving or claiming to prove for a bankruptcy debt.

(2) An account shall be taken of what is due from each party to the other in respect of the mutual dealings and the sums due from one party shall be set off against the sums due from the other.

(3) Sums due from the bankrupt to another party shall not be included in the account taken under subsection (2) if that other party had notice at the time they became due that a bankruptcy petition relating to the bankrupt was pending.

(4) Only the balance (if any) of the account taken under subsection (2) is provable as a bankruptcy debt or, as the case may be, to be paid to the trustee as part of the bankrupt's estate.

324   Distribution by means of dividend

(1) Whenever the trustee has sufficient funds in hand for the purpose he shall, subject to the retention of such sums as may be necessary for the expenses of the bankruptcy, declare and distribute dividends among the creditors in respect of the bankruptcy debts which they have respectively proved.

(2) The trustee shall give notice of his intention to declare and distribute a dividend.

(3) Where the trustee has declared a dividend, he shall give notice of the dividend and of how it is proposed to distribute it; and a notice given under this subsection shall contain the prescribed particulars of the bankrupt's estate.

(4) In the calculation and distribution of a dividend the trustee shall make provision—

(a)   for any bankruptcy debts which appear to him to be due to persons who, by reason of the distance of their place of residence, may not have had sufficient time to tender and establish their proofs,

(b)   for any bankruptcy debts which are the subject of claims which have not yet been determined, and

(c)   for disputed proofs and claims.

325   Claims by unsatisfied creditors

(1)   A creditor who has not proved his debt before the declaration of any dividend is not entitled to disturb, by reason that he has not participated in it, the distribution of that dividend or any other dividend declared before his debt was proved, but—

(a)   when he has proved that debt he is entitled to be paid, out of any money for the time being available for the payment of any further dividend, any dividend or dividends which he has failed to receive; and

(b)   any dividend or dividends payable under paragraph (a) shall be paid before that money is applied to the payment of any such further dividend.

...

326   Distribution of property in specie

(1)   Without prejudice to sections 315 to 319 (disclaimer), the trustee may, with the permission of the creditors' committee, divide in its existing form amongst the bankrupt's creditors, according to its estimated value, any property which from its peculiar nature or other special circumstances cannot be readily or advantageously sold.

(2)   A permission given for the purposes of subsection (1) shall not be a general permission but shall relate to a particular proposed exercise of the power in question; and a person dealing with the trustee in good faith and for value is not to be concerned to enquire whether any permission required by subsection (1) has been given.

(3)   Where the trustee has done anything without the permission required by subsection (1), the court or the creditors' committee may, for the purpose of enabling him to meet his expenses out of the bankrupt's estate, ratify what the trustee has done.

But the committee shall not do so unless it is satisfied that the trustee acted in a case of urgency and has sought its ratification without undue delay.

...

328   Priority of debts

(1)   In the distribution of the bankrupt's estate, his preferential debts (within the meaning given by section 386 in Part XII) shall be paid in priority to other debts.

(2)   Preferential debts rank equally between themselves after the expenses of the bankruptcy and shall be paid in full unless the bankrupt's estate is insufficient for meeting them, in which case they abate in equal proportions between themselves.

(3)   Debts which are neither preferential debts nor debts to which the next section applies also rank equally between themselves and, after the preferential debts, shall be paid in full unless the bankrupt's estate is insufficient for meeting them, in which case they abate in equal proportions between themselves.

(4)   Any surplus remaining after the payment of the debts that are preferential or rank equally under subsection (3) shall be applied in paying interest on those debts in respect of the periods during which they have been outstanding since the commencement of the bankruptcy; and interest on preferential debts ranks equally with interest on debts other than preferential debts.

(5)   The rate of interest payable under subsection (4) in respect of any debt is whichever is the greater of the following—

(a)   the rate specified in section 17 of the Judgments Act 1838 at the commencement of the bankruptcy, and

(b)   the rate applicable to that debt apart from the bankruptcy.

(6) This section and the next are without prejudice to any provision of this Act or any other Act under which the payment of any debt or the making of any other payment is, in the event of bankruptcy, to have a particular priority or to be postponed.

329 Debts to spouse

(1) This section applies to bankruptcy debts owed in respect of credit provided by a person who (whether or not the bankrupt's spouse or civil partner at the time the credit was provided) was the bankrupt's spouse or civil partner at the commencement of the bankruptcy.

(2) Such debts—

    (a) rank in priority after the debts and interest required to be paid in pursuance of section 328(3) and (4), and

    (b) are payable with interest at the rate specified in section 328(5) in respect of the period during which they have been outstanding since the commencement of the bankruptcy;

and the interest payable under paragraph (b) has the same priority as the debts on which it is payable.

330 Final distribution

(1) When the trustee has realised all the bankrupt's estate or so much of it as can, in the trustee's opinion, be realised without needlessly protracting the trusteeship, he shall give notice in the prescribed manner either—

    (a) of his intention to declare a final dividend, or

    (b) that no dividend, or further dividend, will be declared.

(2) The notice under subsection (1) shall contain the prescribed particulars and shall require claims against the bankrupt's estate to be established by a date ("the final date") specified in the notice.

(3) The court may, on the application of any person, postpone the final date.

(4) After the final date, the trustee shall—

    (a) defray any outstanding expenses of the bankruptcy out of the bankrupt's estate, and

    (b) if he intends to declare a final dividend, declare and distribute that dividend without regard to the claim of any person in respect of a debt not already proved in the bankruptcy.

(5) If a surplus remains after payment in full and with interest of all the bankrupt's creditors and the payment of the expenses of the bankruptcy, the bankrupt is entitled to the surplus.

(6) Subsection (5) is subject to Article 35 of the EC Regulation (surplus in secondary proceedings to be transferred to main proceedings).

331 Final meeting

(1) Subject as follows in this section and the next, this section applies where—

    (a) it appears to the trustee that the administration of the bankrupt's estate in accordance with this Chapter is for practical purposes complete, and

    (b) the trustee is not the official receiver.

(2) The trustee shall summon a final general meeting of the bankrupt's creditors which—

    (a) shall receive the trustee's report of his administration of the bankrupt's estate, and

    (b) shall determine whether the trustee should have his release under section 299 in Chapter III.

(3) The trustee may, if he thinks fit, give the notice summoning the final general meeting at the same time as giving notice under section 330(1); but, if summoned for an earlier date, that meeting shall be adjourned (and, if necessary, further adjourned) until a date on which the trustee is able to report to the meeting that the administration of the bankrupt's estate is for practical purposes complete.

(4) In the administration of the estate it is the trustee's duty to retain sufficient sums from the estate to cover the expenses of summoning and holding the meeting required by this section.

332 Saving for bankrupt's home

(1) This section applies where—

(a)   there is comprised in the bankrupt's estate property consisting of an interest in a
       dwelling house which is occupied by the bankrupt or by his spouse or former spouse
       or by his civil partner or former civil partner, and
(b)   the trustee has been unable for any reason to realise that property.

(2)   The trustee shall not summon a meeting under section 331 unless either—
       (a)   the court has made an order under section 313 imposing a charge on that property for
              the benefit of the bankrupt's estate, or
       (b)   the court has declined, on an application under that section, to make such an order, or
       (c)   the Secretary of State has issued a certificate to the trustee stating that it would be
              inappropriate or inexpedient for such an application to be made in the case in question.

Supplemental

333   Duties of bankrupt in relation to trustee

(1)   The bankrupt shall—
       (a)   give to the trustee such information as to his affairs,
       (b)   attend on the trustee at such times, and
       (c)   do all such other things,
       as the trustee may for the purposes of carrying out his functions under any of this Group of
       Parts reasonably require.

(2)   Where at any time after the commencement of the bankruptcy any property is acquired by,
       or devolves upon, the bankrupt or there is an increase of the bankrupt's income, the
       bankrupt shall, within the prescribed period, give the trustee notice of the property or, as the
       case may be, of the increase.

(3)   Subsection (1) applies to a bankrupt after his discharge.

(4)   If the bankrupt without reasonable excuse fails to comply with any obligation imposed by
       this section, he is guilty of a contempt of court and liable to be punished accordingly (in
       addition to any other punishment to which he may be subject).

334   Stay of distribution in case of second bankruptcy

(1)   This section and the next apply where a bankruptcy order is made against an undischarged
       bankrupt; and in both sections—
       (a)   "the later bankruptcy" means the bankruptcy arising from that order,
       (b)   "the earlier bankruptcy" means the bankruptcy (or, as the case may be, most recent
              bankruptcy) from which the bankrupt has not been discharged at the commencement
              of the later bankruptcy, and
       (c)   "the existing trustee" means the trustee (if any) of the bankrupt's estate for the
              purposes of the earlier bankruptcy.

(2)   Where the existing trustee has been given the prescribed notice of the presentation of the
       petition for the later bankruptcy, any distribution or other disposition by him of anything to
       which the next subsection applies, if made after the giving of the notice, is void except to the
       extent that it was made with the consent of the court or is or was subsequently ratified by the
       court.
       This is without prejudice to section 284 (restrictions on dispositions of property following
       bankruptcy order).

(3)   This subsection applies to—
       (a)   any property which is vested in the existing trustee under section 307(3) (after-
              acquired property);
       (b)   any money paid to the existing trustee in pursuance of an income payments order
              under section 310; and
       (c)   any property or money which is, or in the hands of the existing trustee represents, the
              proceeds of sale or application of property or money falling within paragraph (a) or (b)
              of this subsection.

335   Adjustment between earlier and later bankruptcy estates

(1)   With effect from the commencement of the later bankruptcy anything to which section 334(3) applies which, immediately before the commencement of that bankruptcy, is comprised in the bankrupt's estate for the purposes of the earlier bankruptcy is to be treated as comprised in the bankrupt's estate for the purposes of the later bankruptcy and, until there is a trustee of that estate, is to be dealt with by the existing trustee in accordance with the rules.

(2)   Any sums which in pursuance of an income payments order under section 310 are payable after the commencement of the later bankruptcy to the existing trustee shall form part of the bankrupt's estate for the purposes of the later bankruptcy; and the court may give such consequential directions for the modification of the order as it thinks fit.

(3)   Anything comprised in a bankrupt's estate by virtue of subsection (1) or (2) is so comprised subject to a first charge in favour of the existing trustee for any bankruptcy expenses incurred by him in relation thereto.

(4)   Except as provided above and in section 334, property which is, or by virtue of section 308 (personal property of bankrupt exceeding reasonable replacement value) or section 308A (vesting in trustee of certain tenancies) is capable of being, comprised in the bankrupt's estate for the purposes of the earlier bankruptcy, or of any bankruptcy prior to it, shall not be comprised in his estate for the purposes of the later bankruptcy.

(5)   The creditors of the bankrupt in the earlier bankruptcy and the creditors of the bankrupt in any bankruptcy prior to the earlier one, are not to be creditors of his in the later bankruptcy in respect of the same debts; but the existing trustee may prove in the later bankruptcy for—

(a)   the unsatisfied balance of the debts (including any debt under this subsection) provable against the bankrupt's estate in the earlier bankruptcy;

(b)   any interest payable on that balance; and

(c)   any unpaid expenses of the earlier bankruptcy.

(6)   Any amount provable under subsection (5) ranks in priority after all the other debts provable in the later bankruptcy and after interest on those debts and, accordingly, shall not be paid unless those debts and that interest have first been paid in full.

CHAPTER V

EFFECT OF BANKRUPTCY ON CERTAIN RIGHTS, TRANSACTIONS, ETC

Rights under trusts of land

335A   Rights under trusts of land

(1)   Any application by a trustee of a bankrupt's estate under section 14 of the Trusts of Land and Appointment of Trustees Act 1996 powers of court in relation to trusts of land for an order under that section for the sale of land shall be made to the court having jurisdiction in relation to the bankruptcy.

(2)   On such an application the court shall make such order as it thinks just and reasonable having regard to—

(a)   the interests of the bankrupt's creditors,

(b)   where the application is made in respect of land which includes a dwelling house which is or has been the home of the bankrupt or the bankrupt's spouse or civil partner or former spouse or former civil partner—

(i)   the conduct of the spouse, civil partner, former spouse or former civil partner, so far as contributing to the bankruptcy,

(ii)   the needs and financial resources of the spouse, civil partner, former spouse or former civil partner, and

(iii)   the needs of any children; and

(c)   all the circumstances of the case other than the needs of the bankrupt.

(3)   Where such an application is made after the end of the period of one year beginning with the first vesting under Chapter IV of this Part of the bankrupt's estate in a trustee, the court shall assume, unless the circumstances of the case are exceptional, that the interests of the bankrupt's creditors outweigh all other considerations.

(4)   The powers conferred on the court by this section are exercisable on an application whether it is made before or after the commencement of this section.

Rights of occupation

336   Rights of occupation etc of bankrupt's spouse or civil partner

(1)   Nothing occurring in the initial period of the bankruptcy (that is to say, the period beginning with the day of the presentation of the petition for the bankruptcy order and ending with the vesting of the bankrupt's estate in a trustee) is to be taken as having given rise to any home rights under Part IV of the Family Law Act 1996 in relation to a dwelling house comprised in the bankrupt's estate.

(2)   Where a spouse's or civil partner's home rights under the Act of 1996 are a charge on the estate or interest of the other spouse or civil partner, or of trustees for the other spouse or civil partner, and the other spouse is adjudged bankrupt—

    (a)   the charge continues to subsist notwithstanding the bankruptcy and, subject to the provisions of that Act, binds the trustee of the bankrupt's estate and persons deriving title under that trustee, and

    (b)   any application for an order under section 33 of that Act shall be made to the court having jurisdiction in relation to the bankruptcy.

(4)   On such an application as is mentioned in subsection (2) the court shall make such order under section 33 of the Act of 1996 as it thinks just and reasonable having regard to—

    (a)   the interests of the bankrupt's creditors,

    (b)   the conduct of the spouse or former spouse or civil partner or former civil partner , so far as contributing to the bankruptcy,

    (c)   the needs and financial resources of the spouse or former spouse or civil partner or former civil partner,

    (d)   the needs of any children, and

    (e)   all the circumstances of the case other than the needs of the bankrupt.

(5)   Where such an application is made after the end of the period of one year beginning with the first vesting under Chapter IV of this Part of the bankrupt's estate in a trustee, the court shall assume, unless the circumstances of the case are exceptional, that the interests of the bankrupt's creditors outweigh all other considerations.

337   Rights of occupation of bankrupt

(1)   This section applies where—

    (a)   a person who is entitled to occupy a dwelling house by virtue of a beneficial estate or interest is adjudged bankrupt, and

    (b)   any persons under the age of 18 with whom that person had at some time occupied that dwelling house had their home with that person at the time when the bankruptcy petition was presented and at the commencement of the bankruptcy.

(2)   Whether or not the bankrupt's spouse or civil partner (if any) has home rights under Part IV of the Family Law Act 1996—

    (a)   the bankrupt has the following rights as against the trustee of his estate—

        (i)   if in occupation, a right not to be evicted or excluded from the dwelling house or any part of it, except with the leave of the court,

        (ii)   if not in occupation, a right with the leave of the court to enter into and occupy the dwelling house, and

    (b)   the bankrupt's rights are a charge, having the like priority as an equitable interest created immediately before the commencement of the bankruptcy, on so much of his estate or interest in the dwelling house as vests in the trustee.

(3)   The Act of 1996 has effect, with the necessary modification, as if—

    (a)   the rights conferred by paragraph (a) of subsection (2) were home rights under that Act.

    (b)   any application for such leave as is mentioned in that paragraph were an application for an order under section 33 of that Act and

(c)   any charge under paragraph (b) of that subsection on the estate or interest of the trustee were a charge under that Act on the estate or interest of a spouse[or civil partner.

(4)   Any application for leave such as is mentioned in subsection (2)(a) or otherwise by virtue of this section for an order under section 33 of the Act of 1996 shall be made to the court having jurisdiction in relation to the bankruptcy.

(5)   On such an application the court shall make such order under section 33 of the Act of 1996 as it thinks just and reasonable having regard to the interests of the creditors, to the bankrupt's financial resources, to the needs of the children and to all the circumstances of the case other than the needs of the bankrupt.

(6)   Where such an application is made after the end of the period of one year beginning with the first vesting (under Chapter IV of this Part) of the bankrupt's estate in a trustee, the court shall assume, unless the circumstances of the case are exceptional, that the interests of the bankrupt's creditors outweigh all other considerations.

338 Payments in respect of premises occupied by bankrupt

Where any premises comprised in a bankrupt's estate are occupied by him (whether by virtue of the preceding section or otherwise) on condition that he makes payments towards satisfying any liability arising under a mortgage of the premises or otherwise towards the outgoings of the premises, the bankrupt does not, by virtue of those payments, acquire any interest in the premises.

Adjustment of prior transactions, etc

339 Transactions at an undervalue

(1)   Subject as follows in this section and sections 341 and 342, where an individual is adjudged bankrupt and he has at a relevant time (defined in section 341) entered into a transaction with any person at an undervalue, the trustee of the bankrupt's estate may apply to the court for an order under this section.

(2)   The court shall, on such an application, make such order as it thinks fit for restoring the position to what it would have been if that individual had not entered into that transaction.

(3)   For the purposes of this section and sections 341 and 342, an individual enters into a transaction with a person at an undervalue if—

(a)   he makes a gift to that person or he otherwise enters into a transaction with that person on terms that provide for him to receive no consideration,

(b)   he enters into a transaction with that person in consideration of marriage or the formation of a civil partnership, or

(c)   he enters into a transaction with that person for a consideration the value of which, in money or money's worth, is significantly less than the value, in money or money's worth, of the consideration provided by the individual.

340 Preferences

(1)   Subject as follows in this and the next two sections, where an individual is adjudged bankrupt and he has at a relevant time (defined in section 341) given a preference to any person, the trustee of the bankrupt's estate may apply to the court for an order under this section.

(2)   The court shall, on such an application, make such order as it thinks fit for restoring the position to what it would have been if that individual had not given that preference.

(3)   For the purposes of this and the next two sections, an individual gives a preference to a person if—

(a)   that person is one of the individual's creditors or a surety or guarantor for any of his debts or other liabilities, and

(b)   the individual does anything or suffers anything to be done which (in either case) has the effect of putting that person into a position which, in the event of the individual's bankruptcy, will be better than the position he would have been in if that thing had not been done.

(4)   The court shall not make an order under this section in respect of a preference given to any person unless the individual who gave the preference was influenced in deciding to give it

by a desire to produce in relation to that person the effect mentioned in subsection (3)(b) above.

(5) An individual who has given a preference to a person who, at the time the preference was given, was an associate of his (otherwise than by reason only of being his employee) is presumed, unless the contrary is shown, to have been influenced in deciding to give it by such a desire as is mentioned in subsection (4).

(6) The fact that something has been done in pursuance of the order of a court does not, without more, prevent the doing or suffering of that thing from constituting the giving of a preference.

341 "Relevant time" under ss 339, 340

(1) Subject as follows, the time at which an individual enters into a transaction at an undervalue or gives a preference is a relevant time if the transaction is entered into or the preference given—

(a) in the case of a transaction at an undervalue, at a time in the period of 5 years ending with the day of the presentation of the bankruptcy petition on which the individual is adjudged bankrupt,

(b) in the case of a preference which is not a transaction at an undervalue and is given to a person who is an associate of the individual (otherwise than by reason only of being his employee), at a time in the period of 2 years ending with that day, and

(c) in any other case of a preference which is not a transaction at an undervalue, at a time in the period of 6 months ending with that day.

(2) Where an individual enters into a transaction at an undervalue or gives a preference at a time mentioned in paragraph (a), (b) or (c) of subsection (1) (not being, in the case of a transaction at an undervalue, a time less than 2 years before the end of the period mentioned in paragraph (a), that time is not a relevant time for the purposes of sections 339 and 340 unless the individual—

(a) is insolvent at that time, or

(b) becomes insolvent in consequence of the transaction or preference;

but the requirements of this subsection are presumed to be satisfied, unless the contrary is shown, in relation to any transaction at an undervalue which is entered into by an individual with a person who is an associate of his (otherwise than by reason only of being his employee).

(3) For the purposes of subsection (2), an individual is insolvent if—

(a) he is unable to pay his debts as they fall due, or

(b) the value of his assets is less than the amount of his liabilities, taking into account his contingent and prospective liabilities.

…

(5) No order shall be made under section 339 or 340 by virtue of subsection (4) of this section where an appeal is pending (within the meaning of section 277) against the individual's conviction of any offence by virtue of which the criminal bankruptcy order was made.

342 Orders under ss 339, 340

(1) Without prejudice to the generality of section 339(2) or 340(2), an order under either of those sections with respect to a transaction or preference entered into or given by an individual who is subsequently adjudged bankrupt may (subject as follows)—

(a) require any property transferred as part of the transaction, or in connection with the giving of the preference, to be vested in the trustee of the bankrupt's estate as part of that estate;

(b) require any property to be so vested if it represents in any person's hands the application either of the proceeds of sale of property so transferred or of money so transferred;

(c) release or discharge (in whole or in part) any security given by the individual;

(d) require any person to pay, in respect of benefits received by him from the individual, such sums to the trustee of his estate as the court may direct;

(e)   provide for any surety or guarantor whose obligations to any person were released or discharged (in whole or in part) under the transaction or by the giving of the preference to be under such new or revived obligations to that person as the court thinks appropriate;

(f)   provide for security to be provided for the discharge of any obligation imposed by or arising under the order, for such an obligation to be charged on any property and for the security or charge to have the same priority as a security or charge released or discharged (in whole or in part) under the transaction or by the giving of the preference; and

(g)   provide for the extent to which any person whose property is vested by the order in the trustee of the bankrupt's estate, or on whom obligations are imposed by the order, is to be able to prove in the bankruptcy for debts or other liabilities which arose from, or were released or discharged (in whole or in part) under or by, the transaction or the giving of the preference.

(2)   An order under section 339 or 340 may affect the property of, or impose any obligation on, any person whether or not he is the person with whom the individual in question entered into the transaction or, as the case may be, the person to whom the preference was given; but such an order—

(a)   shall not prejudice any interest in property which was acquired from a person other than that individual and was acquired in good faith and for value, or prejudice any interest deriving from such an interest, and

(b)   shall not require a person who received a benefit from the transaction or preference in good faith and for value to pay a sum to the trustee of the bankrupt's estate, except where he was a party to the transaction or the payment is to be in respect of a preference given to that person at a time when he was a creditor of that individual.

(2A) Where a person has acquired an interest in property from a person other than the individual in question, or has received a benefit from the transaction or preference, and at the time of that acquisition or receipt—

(a)   he had notice of the relevant surrounding circumstances and of the relevant proceedings, or

(b)   he was an associate of, or was connected with, either the individual in question or the person with whom that individual entered into the transaction or to whom that individual gave the preference,

then, unless the contrary is shown, it shall be presumed for the purposes of paragraph (a) or (as the case may be) paragraph (b) of subsection (2) that the interest was acquired or the benefit was received otherwise than in good faith.

(3)   Any sums required to be paid to the trustee in accordance with an order under section 339 or 340 shall be comprised in the bankrupt's estate.

(4)   For the purposes of subsection (2A)(a), the relevant surrounding circumstances are (as the case may require)—

(a)   the fact that the individual in question entered into the transaction at an undervalue; or

(b)   the circumstances which amounted to the giving of the preference by the individual in question.

(5)   For the purposes of subsection (2A)(a), a person has notice of the relevant proceedings if he has notice—

(a)   of the fact that the petition on which the individual in question is adjudged bankrupt has been presented; or

(b)   of the fact that the individual in question has been adjudged bankrupt.

(6)   Section 249 in Part VII of this Act shall apply for the purposes of subsection (2A)(b) as it applies for the purposes of the first Group of Parts.

342A Recovery of excessive pension contributions

(1)   Where an individual who is adjudged bankrupt—

(a)   has rights under an approved pension arrangement, or

(b)   has excluded rights under an unapproved pension arrangement, the trustee of the bankrupt's estate may apply to the court for an order under this section.

(2) If the court is satisfied—

    (a) that the rights under the arrangement are to any extent, and whether directly or indirectly, the fruits of relevant contributions, and

    (b) that the making of any of the relevant contributions ("the excessive contributions") has unfairly prejudiced the individual's creditors,

the court may make such order as it thinks fit for restoring the position to what it would have been had the excessive contributions not been made.

(3) Subsection (4) applies where the court is satisfied that the value of the rights under the arrangement is, as a result of rights of the individual under the arrangement or any other pension arrangement having at any time become subject to a debit under section 29(1)(a) of the Welfare Reform and Pensions Act 1999 (debits giving effect to pension-sharing), less than it would otherwise have been.

(4) Where this subsection applies—

    (a) any relevant contributions which were represented by the rights which became subject to the debit shall, for the purposes of subsection (2), be taken to be contributions of which the rights under the arrangement are the fruits, and

    (b) where the relevant contributions represented by the rights under the arrangement (including those so represented by virtue of paragraph (a)) are not all excessive contributions, relevant contributions which are represented by the rights under the arrangement otherwise than by virtue of paragraph (a) shall be treated as excessive contributions before any which are so represented by virtue of that paragraph.

(5) In subsections (2) to (4) "relevant contributions" means contributions to the arrangement or any other pension arrangement—

    (a) which the individual has at any time made on his own behalf, or

    (b) which have at any time been made on his behalf.

(6) The court shall, in determining whether it is satisfied under subsection (2)(b), consider in particular—

    (a) whether any of the contributions were made for the purpose of putting assets beyond the reach of the individual's creditors or any of them, and

    (b) whether the total amount of any contributions—

        (i) made by or on behalf of the individual to pension arrangements, and

        (ii) represented (whether directly or indirectly) by rights under approved pension arrangements or excluded rights under unapproved pension arrangements,

is an amount which is excessive in view of the individual's circumstances when those contributions were made.

(7) For the purposes of this section and sections 342B and 342C ("the recovery provisions"), rights of an individual under an unapproved pension arrangement are excluded rights if they are rights which are excluded from his estate by virtue of regulations under section 12 of the Welfare Reform and Pensions Act 1999.

(8) In the recovery provisions—

"approved pension arrangement" has the same meaning as in section 11 of the Welfare Reform and Pensions Act 1999;

"unapproved pension arrangement" has the same meaning as in section 12 of that Act.

342B Orders under section 342A

(1) Without prejudice to the generality of section 342A(2), an order under section 342A may include provision—

    (a) requiring the person responsible for the arrangement to pay an amount to the individual's trustee in bankruptcy,

    (b) adjusting the liabilities of the arrangement in respect of the individual,

    (c) adjusting any liabilities of the arrangement in respect of any other person that derive, directly or indirectly, from rights of the individual under the arrangement,

    (d) for the recovery by the person responsible for the arrangement (whether by deduction from any amount which that person is ordered to pay or otherwise) of costs incurred by that person in complying in the bankrupt's case with any requirement under section 342C(1) or in giving effect to the order.

(2) In subsection (1), references to adjusting the liabilities of the arrangement in respect of a person include (in particular) reducing the amount of any benefit or future benefit to which that person is entitled under the arrangement.

(3) In subsection (1)(c), the reference to liabilities of the arrangement does not include liabilities in respect of a person which result from giving effect to an order or provision falling within section 28(1) of the Welfare Reform and Pensions Act 1999 (pension sharing orders and agreements).

(4) The maximum amount which the person responsible for an arrangement may be required to pay by an order under section 342A is the lesser of—
   (a) the amount of the excessive contributions, and
   (b) the value of the individual's rights under the arrangement (if the arrangement is an approved pension arrangement) or of his excluded rights under the arrangement (if the arrangement is an unapproved pension arrangement).

(5) An order under section 342A which requires the person responsible for an arrangement to pay an amount ("the restoration amount") to the individual's trustee in bankruptcy must provide for the liabilities of the arrangement to be correspondingly reduced.

(6) For the purposes of subsection (5), liabilities are correspondingly reduced if the difference between—
   (a) the amount of the liabilities immediately before the reduction, and
   (b) the amount of the liabilities immediately after the reduction,
   is equal to the restoration amount.

(7) An order under section 342A in respect of an arrangement—
   (a) shall be binding on the person responsible for the arrangement, and
   (b) overrides provisions of the arrangement to the extent that they conflict with the provisions of the order.

...

343 Extortionate credit transactions

(1) This section applies where a person is adjudged bankrupt who is or has been a party to a transaction for, or involving, the provision to him of credit.

(2) The court may, on the application of the trustee of the bankrupt's estate, make an order with respect to the transaction if the transaction is or was extortionate and was not entered into more than 3 years before the commencement of the bankruptcy.

(3) For the purposes of this section a transaction is extortionate if, having regard to the risk accepted by the person providing the credit—
   (a) the terms of it are or were such as to require grossly exorbitant payments to be made (whether unconditionally or in certain contingencies) in respect of the provision of the credit, or
   (b) it otherwise grossly contravened ordinary principles of fair dealing;
   and it shall be presumed, unless the contrary is proved, that a transaction with respect to which an application is made under this section is or, as the case may be, was extortionate.

(4) An order under this section with respect to any transaction may contain such one or more of the following as the court thinks, fit, that is to say—
   (a) provision setting aside the whole or part of any obligation created by the transaction;
   (b) provision otherwise varying the terms of the transaction or varying the terms on which any security for the purposes of the transaction is held;
   (c) provision requiring any person who is or was party to the transaction to pay to the trustee any sums paid to that person, by virtue of the transaction, by the bankrupt;
   (d) provision requiring any person to surrender to the trustee any property held by him as security for the purposes of the transaction;
   (e) provision directing accounts to be taken between any persons.

(5)   Any sums or property required to be paid or surrendered to the trustee in accordance with an order under this section shall be comprised in the bankrupt's estate.

(6)   ...

But the powers conferred by this section are exercisable in relation to any transaction concurrently with any powers exercisable under this Act in relation to that transaction as a transaction at an undervalue.

344   Avoidance of general assignment of book debts

(1)   The following applies where a person engaged in any business makes a general assignment to another person of his existing or future book debts, or any class of them, and is subsequently adjudged bankrupt.

(2)   The assignment is void against the trustee of the bankrupt's estate as regards book debts which were not paid before the presentation of the bankruptcy petition, unless the assignment has been registered under the Bills of Sale Act 1878.

(3)   For the purposes of subsections (1) and (2)—

(a)   "assignment" includes an assignment by way of security or charge on book debts, and

(b)   "general assignment" does not include—

(i)   an assignment of book debts due at the date of the assignment from specified debtors or of debts becoming due under specified contracts, or

(ii)   an assignment of book debts included either in a transfer of a business made in good faith and for value or in an assignment of assets for the benefit of creditors generally.

(4)   For the purposes of registration under the Act of 1878 an assignment of book debts is to be treated as if it were a bill of sale given otherwise than by way of security for the payment of a sum of money; and the provisions of that Act with respect to the registration of bills of sale apply accordingly with such necessary modifications as may be made by rules under that Act.

345   Contracts to which bankrupt is a party

(1)   The following applies where a contract has been made with a person who is subsequently adjudged bankrupt.

(2)   The court may, on the application of any other party to the contract, make an order discharging obligations under the contract on such terms as to payment by the applicant or the bankrupt of damages for non-performance or otherwise as appear to the court to be equitable.

(3)   Any damages payable by the bankrupt by virtue of an order of the court under this section are provable as a bankruptcy debt.

...

346   Enforcement procedures

(1)   Subject to section 285 in Chapter II (restrictions on proceedings and remedies) and to the following provisions of this section, where the creditor of any person who is adjudged bankrupt has, before the commencement of the bankruptcy—

(a)   issued execution against the goods or land of that person, or

(b)   attached a debt due to that person from another person,

that creditor is not entitled, as against the official receiver or trustee of the bankrupt's estate, to retain the benefit of the execution or attachment, or any sums paid to avoid it, unless the execution or attachment was completed, or the sums were paid, before the commencement of the bankruptcy.

(2)   Subject as follows, where any goods of a person have been taken in execution, then, if before the completion of the execution notice is given to the enforcement officer or other officer charged with the execution that that person has been adjudged bankrupt—

(a)   the enforcement officer or other officer shall on request deliver to the official receiver or trustee of the bankrupt's estate the goods and any money seized or recovered in part satisfaction of the execution, but

       (b)   the costs of the execution are a first charge on the goods or money so delivered and the official receiver or trustee may sell the goods or a sufficient part of them for the purpose of satisfying the charge.

(3)   Subject to subsection (6) below, where—

       (a)   under an execution in respect of a judgment for a sum exceeding such sum as may be prescribed for the purposes of this subsection, the goods of any person are sold or money is paid in order to avoid a sale, and

       (b)   before the end of the period of 14 days beginning with the day of the sale or payment the enforcement officer or other officer charged with the execution is given notice that a bankruptcy petition has been presented in relation to that person, and

       (c)   a bankruptcy order is or has been made on that petition,

the balance of the proceeds of sale or money paid, after deducting the costs of execution, shall (in priority to the claim of the execution creditor) be comprised in the bankrupt's estate.

(4)   Accordingly, in the case of an execution in respect of a judgment for a sum exceeding the sum prescribed for the purposes of subsection (3), the enforcement officer or other officer charged with the execution—

       (a)   shall not dispose of the balance mentioned in subsection (3) at any time within the period of 14 days so mentioned or while there is pending a bankruptcy petition of which he has been given notice under that subsection, and

       (b)   shall pay that balance, where by virtue of that subsection it is comprised in the bankrupt's estate, to the official receiver or (if there is one) to the trustee of that estate.

(5)   For the purposes of this section—

       (a)   an execution against goods is completed by seizure and sale or by the making of a charging order under section 1 of the Charging Orders Act 1979;

       (b)   an execution against land is completed by seizure, by the appointment of a receiver or by the making of a charging order under that section;

       (c)   an attachment of a debt is completed by the receipt of the debt.

(6)   The rights conferred by subsections (1) to (3) on the official receiver or the trustee may, to such extent and on such terms as it thinks fit, be set aside by the court in favour of the creditor who has issued the execution or attached the debt.

(7)   Nothing in this section entitles the trustee of a bankrupt's estate to claim goods from a person who has acquired them in good faith under a sale by an enforcement officer or other officer charged with an execution.

(8)   Neither subsection (2) nor subsection (3) applies in relation to any execution against property which has been acquired by or has devolved upon the bankrupt since the commencement of the bankruptcy, unless, at the time the execution is issued or before it is completed—

       (a)   the property has been or is claimed for the bankrupt's estate under section 307 (after-acquired property), and

       (b)   a copy of the notice given under that section has been or is served on the enforcement officer or other officer charged with the execution.

(9)   In this section "enforcement officer" means an individual who is authorised to act as an enforcement officer under the Courts Act 2003.

347   Distress, etc

(1)   The right of any landlord or other person to whom rent is payable to distrain upon the goods and effects of an undischarged bankrupt for rent due to him from the bankrupt is available (subject to sections 252(2)(b) and 254(1) above and subsection (5) below) against goods and effects comprised in the bankrupt's estate, but only for 6 months' rent accrued due before the commencement of the bankruptcy.

(2)   Where a landlord or other person to whom rent is payable has distrained for rent upon the goods and effects of an individual to whom a bankruptcy petition relates and a bankruptcy order is subsequently made on that petition, any amount recovered by way of that distress which—

(a)   is in excess of the amount which by virtue of subsection (1) would have been recoverable after the commencement of the bankruptcy, or

(b)   is in respect of rent for a period or part of a period after the distress was levied,

shall be held for the bankrupt as part of his estate.

(3)   Where any person (whether or not a landlord or person entitled to rent) has distrained upon the goods or effects of an individual who is adjudged bankrupt before the end of the period of 3 months beginning with the distraint, so much of those goods or effects, or of the proceeds of their sale, as is not held for the bankrupt under subsection (2) shall be charged for the benefit of the bankrupt's estate with the preferential debts of the bankrupt to the extent that the bankrupt's estate is for the time being insufficient for meeting those debts.

(4)   Where by virtue of any charge under subsection (3) any person surrenders any goods or effects to the trustee of a bankrupt's estate or makes a payment to such a trustee, that person ranks, in respect of the amount of the proceeds of the sale of those goods or effects by the trustee or, as the case may be, the amount of the payment, as a preferential creditor of the bankrupt, except as against so much of the bankrupt's estate as is available for the payment of preferential creditors by virtue of the surrender or payment.

(5)   A landlord or other person to whom rent is payable is not at any time after the discharge of a bankrupt entitled to distrain upon any goods or effects comprised in the bankrupt's estate.

(6)   Where in the case of any execution—

(a)   a landlord is (apart from this section) entitled under section 1 of the Landlord and Tenant Act 1709 or section 102 of the County Courts Act 1984 (claims for rent where goods seized in execution) to claim for an amount not exceeding one year's rent, and

(b)   the person against whom the execution is levied is adjudged bankrupt before the notice of claim is served on the enforcement officer, or other officer charged with the execution,

the right of the landlord to claim under that section is restricted to a right to claim for an amount not exceeding 6 months' rent and does not extend to any rent payable in respect of a period after the notice of claim is so served.

(7)   Nothing in subsection (6) imposes any liability on [an enforcement officer]1 or other officer charged with an execution to account to the official receiver or the trustee of a bankrupt's estate for any sums paid by him to a landlord at any time before the enforcement officer or other officer was served with notice of the bankruptcy order in question.

But this subsection is without prejudice to the liability of the landlord.

(8)   Subject to sections 252(2)(b) and 254(1) above. Nothing in this Group of Parts affects any right to distrain otherwise than for rent; and any such right is at any time exercisable without restriction against property comprised in a bankrupt's estate, even if that right is expressed by any enactment to be exercisable in like manner as a right to distrain for rent.

(9)   Any right to distrain against property comprised in a bankrupt's estate is exercisable notwithstanding that the property has vested in the trustee.

(10) The provisions of this section are without prejudice to a landlord's right in a bankruptcy to prove for any bankruptcy debt in respect of rent.

(11) In this section "enforcement officer" means an individual who is authorised to act as an enforcement officer under the Courts Act 2003.

348   Apprenticeships, etc

(1)   This section applies where—

(a)   a bankruptcy order is made in respect of an individual to whom another individual was an apprentice or articled clerk at the time when the petition on which the order was made was presented, and

(b)   the bankrupt or the apprentice or clerk gives notice to the trustee terminating the apprenticeship or articles.

(2)   Subject to subsection (6) below, the indenture of apprenticeship or, as the case may be, the articles of agreement shall be discharged with effect from the commencement of the bankruptcy.

(3) If any money has been paid by or on behalf of the apprentice or clerk to the bankrupt as a fee, the trustee may, on an application made by or on behalf of the apprentice or clerk, pay such sum to the apprentice or clerk as the trustee thinks reasonable, having regard to—

    (a) the amount of the fee,

    (b) the proportion of the period in respect of which the fee was paid that has been served by the apprentice or clerk before the commencement of the bankruptcy, and

    (c) the other circumstances of the case.

(4) The power of the trustee to make a payment under subsection (3) has priority over his obligation to distribute the bankrupt's estate.

(5) Instead of making a payment under subsection (3), the trustee may, if it appears to him expedient to do so on an application made by or on behalf of the apprentice or clerk, transfer the indenture or articles to a person other than the bankrupt.

(6) Where a transfer is made under subsection (5),subsection (2) has effect only as between the apprentice or clerk and the bankrupt.

349 Unenforceability of liens on books, etc

(1) Subject as follows, a lien or other right to retain possession of any of the books, papers or other records of a bankrupt is unenforceable to the extent that its enforcement would deny possession of any books, papers or other records to the official receiver or the trustee of the bankrupt's estate.

(2) Subsection (1) does not apply to a lien on documents which give a title to property and are held as such.

349A Arbitration agreements to which bankrupt is party

(1) This section applies where a bankrupt had become party to a contract containing an arbitration agreement before the commencement of his bankruptcy.

(2) If the trustee in bankruptcy adopts the contract, the arbitration agreement is enforceable by or against the trustee in relation to matters arising from or connected with the contract.

(3) If the trustee in bankruptcy does not adopt the contract and a matter to which the arbitration agreement applies requires to be determined in connection with or for the purposes of the bankruptcy proceedings—

    (a) the trustee with the consent of the creditors' committee, or

    (b) any other party to the agreement,

may apply to the court which may, if it thinks fit in all the circumstances of the case, order that the matter be referred to arbitration in accordance with the arbitration agreement.

(4) In this section—

"arbitration agreement" has the same meaning as in Part I of the Arbitration Act 1996; and "the court" means the court which has jurisdiction in the bankruptcy proceedings.

CHAPTER VI

BANKRUPTCY OFFENCES

Preliminary

350 Scheme of this Chapter

(1) Subject to section 360(3) below, this Chapter applies where the court has made a bankruptcy order on a bankruptcy petition.

(2) This Chapter applies whether or not the bankruptcy order is annulled, but proceedings for an offence under this Chapter shall not be instituted after the annulment.

(3) Without prejudice to his liability in respect of a subsequent bankruptcy, the bankrupt is not guilty of an offence under this Chapter in respect of anything done after his discharge; but nothing in this Group of Parts prevents the institution of proceedings against a discharged bankrupt for an offence committed before his discharge.

(3A) Subsection (3) is without prejudice to any provision of this Chapter which applies to a person in respect of whom a bankruptcy restrictions order is in force.

(4) It is not a defence in proceedings for an offence under this Chapter that anything relied on, in whole or in part, as constituting that offence was done outside England and Wales.

(5) Proceedings for an offence under this Chapter or under the rules shall not be instituted except by the Secretary of State or by or with the consent of the Director of Public Prosecutions.

(6) A person guilty of any offence under this Chapter is liable to imprisonment or a fine, or both.

351   Definitions

In the following provisions of this Chapter—

(a) references to property comprised in the bankrupt's estate or to property possession of which is required to be delivered up to the official receiver or the trustee of the bankrupt's estate include any property which would be such property if a notice in respect of it were given under section 307 (after-acquired property), section 308 (personal property and effects of bankrupt having more than replacement value) or section 308A (vesting in trustee of certain tenancies);

(b) "the initial period" means the period between the presentation of the bankruptcy petition and the commencement of the bankruptcy; and

(c) a reference to a number of months or years before petition is to that period ending with the presentation of the bankruptcy petition

352   Defence of innocent intention

Where in the case of an offence under any provision of this Chapter it is stated that this section applies, a person is not guilty of the offence if he proves that, at the time of the conduct constituting the offence, he had no intent to defraud or to conceal the state of his affairs.

Wrongdoing by the bankrupt before and after bankruptcy

353   Non-disclosure

(1) The bankrupt is guilty of an offence if—

(a) he does not to the best of his knowledge and belief disclose all the property comprised in his estate to the official receiver or the trustee, or

(b) he does not inform the official receiver or the trustee of any disposal of any property which but for the disposal would be so comprised, stating how, when, to whom and for what consideration the property was disposed of.

(2) Subsection (1)(b) does not apply to any disposal in the ordinary course of a business carried on by the bankrupt or to any payment of the ordinary expenses of the bankrupt or his family.

(3) Section 352 applies to this offence.

354   Concealment of property

(1) The bankrupt is guilty of an offence if—

(a) he does not deliver up possession to the official receiver or trustee, or as the official receiver or trustee may direct, of such part of the property comprised in his estate as is in his possession or under his control and possession of which he is required by law so to deliver up,

(b) he conceals any debt due to or from him or conceals any property the value of which is not less than the prescribed amount and possession of which he is required to deliver up to the official receiver or trustee, or

(c) in the 12 months before petition, or in the initial period, he did anything which would have been an offence under paragraph (b) above if the bankruptcy order had been made immediately before he did it.

Section 352 applies to this offence.

(2) The bankrupt is guilty of an offence if he removes, or in the initial period removed, any property the value of which was not less than the prescribed amount and possession of which he has or would have been required to deliver up to the official receiver or the trustee. Section 352 applies to this offence.

(3) The bankrupt is guilty of an offence if he without reasonable excuse fails, on being required to do so by the official receiver, the trustee or the court—

(a)   to account for the loss of any substantial part of his property incurred in the 12 months before petition or in the initial period, or

(b)   to give a satisfactory explanation of the manner in which such a loss was incurred.

355   Concealment of books and papers; falsification

(1)   The bankrupt is guilty of an offence if he does not deliver up possession to the official receiver or the trustee, or as the official receiver or trustee may direct, of all books, papers and other records of which he has possession or control and which relate to his estate or his affairs.

Section 352 applies to this offence.

(2)   The bankrupt is guilty of an offence if—

(a)   he prevents, or in the initial period prevented, the production of any books, papers or records relating to his estate or affairs;

(b)   he conceals, destroys, mutilates or falsifies, or causes or permits the concealment, destruction, mutilation or falsification of, any books, papers or other records relating to his estate or affairs;

(c)   he makes, or causes or permits the making of, any false entries in any book, document or record relating to his estate or affairs; or

(d)   in the 12 months before petition, or in the initial period, he did anything which would have been an offence under paragraph (b) or (c) above if the bankruptcy order had been made before he did it.

Section 352 applies to this offence.

(3)   The bankrupt is guilty of an offence if—

(a)   he disposes of, or alters or makes any omission in, or causes or permits the disposal, altering or making of any omission in, any book, document or record relating to his estate or affairs, or

(b)   in the 12 months before petition, or in the initial period, he did anything which would have been an offence under paragraph (a) if the bankruptcy order had been made before he did it.

Section 352 applies to this offence.

(4)   In their application to a trading record subsections (2)(d) and (3)(b) shall have effect as if the reference to 12 months were a reference to two years.

(5)   In subsection (4) "trading record" means a book, document or record which shows or explains the transactions or financial position of a person's business, including—

(a)   a periodic record of cash paid and received,

(b)   a statement of periodic stock-taking, and

(c)   except in the case of goods sold by way of retail trade, a record of goods sold and purchased which identifies the buyer and seller or enables them to be identified.

356   False statements

(1)   The bankrupt is guilty of an offence if he makes or has made any material omission in any statement made under any provision in this Group of Parts and relating to his affairs.

Section 352 applies to this offence.

(2)   The bankrupt is guilty of an offence if—

(a)   knowing or believing that a false debt has been proved by any person under the bankruptcy, he fails to inform the trustee as soon as practicable; or

(b)   he attempts to account for any part of his property by fictitious losses or expenses; or

(c)   at any meeting of his creditors in the 12 months before petition or (whether or not at such a meeting) at any time in the initial period, he did anything which would have been an offence under paragraph (b) if the bankruptcy order had been made before he did it; or

(d)   he is, or at any time has been, guilty of any false representation or other fraud for the purpose of obtaining the consent of his creditors, or any of them, to an agreement with reference to his affairs or to his bankruptcy.

357   Fraudulent disposal of property.

(1)   The bankrupt is guilty of an offence if he makes or causes to be made, or has in the period of 5 years ending with the commencement of the bankruptcy made or caused to be made, any gift or transfer of, or any charge on, his property.
Section 352 applies to this offence.

(2)   The reference to making a transfer of or charge on any property includes causing or conniving at the levying of any execution against that property.

(3)   The bankrupt is guilty of an offence if he conceals or removes, or has at any time before the commencement of the bankruptcy concealed or removed, any part of his property after, or within 2 months before, the date on which a judgment or order for the payment of money has been obtained against him, being a judgment or order which was not satisfied before the commencement of the bankruptcy.
Section 352 applies to this offence.

358   Absconding

The bankrupt is guilty of an offence if—

(a)   he leaves, or attempts or makes preparations to leave, England and Wales with any property the value of which is not less than the prescribed amount and possession of which he is required to deliver up to the official receiver or the trustee, or

(b)   in the 6 months before petition, or in the initial period, he did anything which would have been an offence under paragraph (a) if the bankruptcy order had been made immediately before he did it.

Section 352 applies to this offence.

359   Fraudulent dealing with property obtained on credit

(1)   The bankrupt is guilty of an offence if, in the 12 months before petition, or in the initial period, he disposed of any property which he had obtained on credit and, at the time he disposed of it, had not paid for.
Section 352 applies to this offence.

(2)   A person is guilty of an offence if, in the 12 months before petition or in the initial period, he acquired or received property from the bankrupt knowing or believing—

(a)   that the bankrupt owed money in respect of the property, and

(b)   that the bankrupt did not intend, or was unlikely to be able, to pay the money he so owed.

(3)   A person is not guilty of an offence under subsection (1) or (2) if the disposal, acquisition or receipt of the property was in the ordinary course of a business carried on by the bankrupt at the time of the disposal, acquisition or receipt.

(4)   In determining for the purpose of this section whether any property is disposed of, acquired or received in the ordinary course of a business carried on by the bankrupt, regard may be had, in particular, to the price paid for the property.

(5)   In this section references to disposing of property include pawning or pledging it; and references to acquiring or receiving property shall be read accordingly.

360   Obtaining credit; engaging in business

(1)   The bankrupt is guilty of an offence if—

(a)   either alone or jointly with any other person, he obtains credit to the extent of the prescribed amount or more without giving the person from whom he obtains it the relevant information about his status; or

(b)   he engages (whether directly or indirectly) in any business under a name other than that in which he was adjudged bankrupt without disclosing to all persons with whom he enters into any business transaction the name in which he was so adjudged.

(2)   The reference to the bankrupt obtaining credit includes the following cases—

(a)   where goods are bailed to him under a hire-purchase agreement, or agreed to be sold to him under a conditional sale agreement, and

(b)   where he is paid in advance (whether in money or otherwise) for the supply of goods or services.

...

(5) This section applies to the bankrupt after discharge while a bankruptcy restrictions order is in force in respect of him.

(6) For the purposes of subsection (1)(a) as it applies by virtue of subsection (5), the relevant information about the status of the person in question is the information that a bankruptcy restrictions order is in force in respect of him.

...

CHAPTER VII

POWERS OF COURT IN BANKRUPTCY

363   General control of court

(1) Every bankruptcy is under the general control of the court and, subject to the provisions in this Group of Parts, the court has full power to decide all questions of priorities and all other questions, whether of law or fact, arising in any bankruptcy.

(2) Without prejudice to any other provision in this Group of Parts, an undischarged bankrupt or a discharged bankrupt whose estate is still being administered under Chapter IV of this Part shall do all such things as he may be directed to do by the court for the purposes of his bankruptcy or, as the case may be, the administration of that estate.

(3) The official receiver or the trustee of a bankrupt's estate may at any time apply to the court for a direction under subsection (2).

(4) If any person without reasonable excuse fails to comply with any obligation imposed on him by subsection (2), he is guilty of a contempt of court and liable to be punished accordingly (in addition to any other punishment to which he may be subject).

364   Power of arrest

(1) In the cases specified in the next subsection the court may cause a warrant to be issued to a constable or prescribed officer of the court—

    (a)   for the arrest of a debtor to whom a bankruptcy petition relates or of an undischarged bankrupt, or of a discharged bankrupt whose estate is still being administered under Chapter IV of this Part, and

    (b)   for the seizure of any books, papers, records, money or goods in the possession of a person arrested under the warrant,

and may authorise a person arrested under such a warrant to be kept in custody, and anything seized under such a warrant to be held, in accordance with the rules, until such time as the court may order.

(2) The powers conferred by subsection (1) are exercisable in relation to a debtor or undischarged or discharged bankrupt if, at any time after the presentation of the bankruptcy petition relating to him or the making of the bankruptcy order against him, it appears to the court—

    (a)   that there are reasonable grounds for believing that he has absconded, or is about to abscond, with a view to avoiding or delaying the payment of any of his debts or his appearance to a bankruptcy petition or to avoiding, delaying or disrupting any proceedings in bankruptcy against him or any examination of his affairs, or

    (b)   that he is about to remove his goods with a view to preventing or delaying possession being taken of them by the official receiver or the trustee of his estate, or

    (c)   that there are reasonable grounds for believing that he has concealed or destroyed, or is about to conceal or destroy, any of his goods or any books, papers or records which might be of use to his creditors in the course of his bankruptcy or in connection with the administration of his estate, or

    (d)   that he has, without the leave of the official receiver or the trustee of his estate, removed any goods in his possession which exceed in value such sum as may be prescribed for the purposes of this paragraph, or

    (e)   that he has failed, without reasonable excuse, to attend any examination ordered by the court.

365 Seizure of bankrupt's property

(1) At any time after a bankruptcy order has been made, the court may, on the application of the official receiver or the trustee of the bankrupt's estate, issue a warrant authorising the person to whom it is directed to seize any property comprised in the bankrupt's estate which is, or any books, papers or records relating to the bankrupt's estate or affairs which are, in the possession or under the control of the bankrupt or any other person who is required to deliver the property, books, papers or records to the official receiver or trustee.

(2) Any person executing a warrant under this section may, for the purpose of seizing any property comprised in the bankrupt's estate or any books, papers or records relating to the bankrupt's estate or affairs, break open any premises where the bankrupt or anything that may be seized under the warrant is or is believed to be and any receptacle of the bankrupt which contains or is believed to contain anything that may be so seized.

(3) If, after a bankruptcy order has been made, the court is satisfied that any property comprised in the bankrupt's estate is, or any books, papers or records relating to the bankrupt's estate or affairs are, concealed in any premises not belonging to him, it may issue a warrant authorising any constable or prescribed officer of the court to search those premises for the property, books, papers or records.

(4) A warrant under subsection (3) shall not be executed except in the prescribed manner and in accordance with its terms.

366 Inquiry into bankrupt's dealings and property

(1) At any time after a bankruptcy order has been made the court may, on the application of the official receiver or the trustee of the bankrupt's estate, summon to appear before it—

(a) the bankrupt or the bankrupt's spouse or former spouse or civil partner or former civil partner,

(b) any person known or believed to have any property comprised in the bankrupt's estate in his possession or to be indebted to the bankrupt,

(c) any person appearing to the court to be able to give information concerning the bankrupt or the bankrupt's dealings, affairs or property.

The court may require any such person as is mentioned in paragraph (b) or (c) to submit an affidavit to the court containing an account of his dealings with the bankrupt or to produce any documents in his possession or under his control relating to the bankrupt or the bankrupt's dealings, affairs or property.

(2) Without prejudice to section 364, the following applies in a case where—

(a) a person without reasonable excuse fails to appear before the court when he is summoned to do so under this section, or

(b) there are reasonable grounds for believing that a person has absconded, or is about to abscond, with a view to avoiding his appearance before the court under this section.

(3) The court may, for the purpose of bringing that person and anything in his possession before the court, cause a warrant to be issued to a constable or prescribed officer of the court—

(a) for the arrest of that person, and

(b) for the seizure of any books, papers, records, money or goods in that person's possession.

(4) The court may authorise a person arrested under such a warrant to be kept in custody, and anything seized under such a warrant to be held, in accordance with the rules, until that person is brought before the court under the warrant or until such other time as the court may order.

367 Court's enforcement powers under s 366

(1) If it appears to the court, on consideration of any evidence obtained under section 366 or this section, that any person has in his possession any property comprised in the bankrupt's estate, the court may, on the application of the official receiver or the trustee of the bankrupt's estate, order that person to deliver the whole or any part of the property to the official receiver or the trustee at such time, in such manner and on such terms as the court thinks fit.

(2)   If it appears to the court, on consideration of any evidence obtained under section 366 or this section, that any person is indebted to the bankrupt, the court may, on the application of the official receiver or the trustee of the bankrupt's estate, order that person to pay to the official receiver or trustee, at such time and in such manner as the court may direct, the whole or part of the amount due, whether in full discharge of the debt or otherwise as the court thinks fit.

(3)   The court may, if it thinks fit, order that any person who if within the jurisdiction of the court would be liable to be summoned to appear before it under section 366 shall be examined in any part of the United Kingdom where he may be for the time being, or in any place outside the United Kingdom.

(4)   Any person who appears or is brought before the court under section 366 or this section may be examined on oath, either orally or by interrogatories, concerning the bankrupt or the bankrupt's dealings, affairs and property.

...

369   Order for production of documents by Inland Revenue

(1)   For the purpose of an examination under section 290 (public examination of bankrupt) or proceedings under section 366 to 368, the court may, on the application of the official receiver or the trustee of the bankrupt's estate, order an inland revenue official to produce to the court—

(a)   any return, account or accounts submitted (whether before or after the commencement of the bankruptcy) by the bankrupt to any inland revenue official,

(b)   any assessment or determination made (whether before or after the commencement of the bankruptcy) in relation to the bankrupt by any inland revenue official, or

(c)   any correspondence (whether before or after the commencement of the bankruptcy) between the bankrupt and any inland revenue official.

(2)   Where the court has made an order under subsection (1) for the purposes of any examination or proceedings, the court may, at any time after the document to which the order relates is produced to it, by order authorise the disclosure of the document, or of any part of its contents, to the official receiver, the trustee of the bankrupt's estate or the bankrupt's creditors.

(3)   The court shall not address an order under subsection (1) to an inland revenue official unless it is satisfied that that official is dealing, or has dealt, with the affairs of the bankrupt.

...

370   Power to appoint special manager

(1)   The court may, on an application under this section, appoint any person to be the special manager—

(a)   of a bankrupt's estate, or

(b)   of the business of an undischarged bankrupt, or

(c)   of the property or business of a debtor in whose case the official receiver has been appointed interim receiver under section 286.

(2)   An application under this section may be made by the official receiver or the trustee of the bankrupt's estate in any case where it appears to the official receiver or trustee that the nature of the estate, property or business, or the interests of the creditors generally, require the appointment of another person to manage the estate, property or business.

(3)   A special manager appointed under this section has such powers as may be entrusted to him by the court.

(4)   The power of the court under subsection (3) to entrust powers to a special manager includes power to direct that any provision in this Group of Parts that has effect in relation to the official receiver, interim receiver or trustee shall have the like effect in relation to the special manager for the purposes of the carrying out by the special manager of any of the functions of the official receiver, interim receiver or trustee.

(5)   A special manager appointed under this section shall—

(a)   give such security as may be prescribed,

(b)   prepare and keep such accounts as may be prescribed, and

(c)   produce those accounts in accordance with the rules to the Secretary of State or to such other persons as may be prescribed.

371   Re-direction of bankrupt's letters, etc

(1)   Where a bankruptcy order has been made, the court may from time to time, on the application of the official receiver or the trustee of the bankrupt's estate, order a postal operator (within the meaning of the Postal Services Act 2000) to re-direct and send or deliver to the official receiver or trustee or otherwise any postal packet (within the meaning of that Act) which would otherwise be sent or delivered by the operator concerned to the bankrupt at such place or places as may be specified in the order.

(2)   An order under this section has effect for such period, not exceeding 3 months, as may be specified in the order.

PART X
INDIVIDUAL INSOLVENCY: GENERAL PROVISIONS

372   Supplies of gas, water, electricity, etc

(1)   This section applies where on any day ("the relevant day")—

(a)   a bankruptcy order is made against an individual or an interim receiver of an individual's property is appointed, or

(b)   a voluntary arrangement proposed by an individual is approved under Part VIII, or

(c)   a deed of arrangement is made for the benefit of an individual's creditors;

and in this section "the office-holder" means the official receiver, the trustee in bankruptcy, the interim receiver, the supervisor of the voluntary arrangement or the trustee under the deed of arrangement, as the case may be.

(2)   If a request falling within the next subsection is made for the giving after the relevant day of any of the supplies mentioned in subsection (4), the supplier—

(a)   may make it a condition of the giving of the supply that the office-holder personally guarantees the payment of any charges in respect of the supply, but

(b)   shall not make it a condition of the giving of the supply, or do anything which has the effect of making it a condition of the giving of the supply, that any outstanding charges in respect of a supply given to the individual before the relevant day are paid.

(3)   A request falls within this subsection if it is made—

(a)   by or with the concurrence of the office-holder, and

(b)   for the purposes of any business which is or has been carried on by the individual, by a firm or partnership of which the individual is or was a member, or by an agent or manager for the individual or for such a firm or partnership.

(4)   The supplies referred to in subsection (2) are—

(a)   a supply of gas by a gas supplier within the meaning of Part I of the Gas Act 1986;

(b)   a supply of electricity by an electricity supplier within the meaning of Part I of the Electricity Act 1989,

(c)   a supply of water by a water undertaker,

(d)   a supply of communications services by a provider of a public electronic communications service.

...

373   Jurisdiction in relation to insolvent individuals

(1)   The High Court and the county courts have jurisdiction throughout England and Wales for the purposes of the Parts in this Group.

(2)   For the purposes of those Parts, a county court has, in addition to its ordinary jurisdiction, all the powers and jurisdiction of the High Court; and the orders of the court may be enforced accordingly in the prescribed manner.

(3)   Jurisdiction for the purposes of those Parts is exercised—

(a)   by the High Court in relation to the proceedings which, in accordance with the rules, are allocated to the London insolvency district, and

(b)   by each county court in relation to the proceedings which are so allocated to the insolvency district of that court.

(4)   Subsection (3) is without prejudice to the transfer of proceedings from one court to another in the manner prescribed by the rules; and nothing in that subsection invalidates any proceedings on the grounds that they were initiated or continued in the wrong court.

374   Insolvency districts

(1)   The Lord Chancellor may, with the concurrence of the Lord Chief Justice, by order designate the areas which are for the time being to be comprised, for the purposes of the Parts in this Group, in the London insolvency district and the insolvency district of each county court; and an order under this section may—

(a)   exclude any county court from having jurisdiction for the purposes of those Parts, or

(b)   confer jurisdiction for those purposes on any county court which has not previously had that jurisdiction.

(2)   An order under this section may contain such incidental, supplemental and transitional provisions as may appear to the Lord Chancellor and the Lord Chief Justice necessary or expedient.

(3)   An order under this section shall be made by statutory instrument and, after being made, shall be laid before each House of Parliament.

(4)   Subject to any order under this section—

(a)   the district which, immediately before the appointed day, is the London bankruptcy district becomes, on that day, the London insolvency district;

(b)   any district which immediately before that day is the bankruptcy district of a county court becomes, on that day, the insolvency district of that court, and

(c)   any county court which immediately before that day is excluded from having jurisdiction in bankruptcy is excluded, on and after that day, from having jurisdiction for the purposes of the Parts in this Group.

...

375   Appeals etc from courts exercising insolvency jurisdiction

(1)   Every court having jurisdiction for the purposes of the Parts in this Group may review, rescind or vary any order made by it in the exercise of that jurisdiction.

(2)   An appeal from a decision made in the exercise of jurisdiction for the purposes of those Parts by a county court or by a registrar in bankruptcy of the High Court lies to a single judge of the High Court; and an appeal from a decision of that judge on such an appeal lies to the Court of Appeal.

(3)   A county court is not, in the exercise of its jurisdiction for the purposes of those Parts, to be subject to be restrained by the order of any other court, and no appeal lies from its decision in the exercise of that jurisdiction except as provided by this section.

376   Time-limits

Where by any provision in this Group of Parts or by the rules the time for doing anything is limited, the court may extend the time, either before or after it has expired, on such terms, if any, as it thinks fit.

377   Formal defects

The acts of a person as the trustee of a bankrupt's estate or as a special manager, and the acts of the creditors' committee established for any bankruptcy, are valid notwithstanding any defect in the appointment, election or qualifications of the trustee or manager or, as the case may be, of any member of the committee.

378   Exemption from stamp duty

Stamp duty shall not be charged on—

(a)   any document, being a deed, conveyance, assignment, surrender, admission or other assurance relating solely to property which is comprised in a bankrupt's estate and which, after the execution of that document, is or remains at law or in equity the property of the bankrupt or of the trustee of that estate.

(b)   any writ, order, certificate or other instrument relating solely to the property of a bankrupt or to any bankruptcy proceedings.

...

PART XI

INTERPRETATION FOR SECOND GROUP OF PARTS

380   Introductory

The next five sections have effect for the interpretation of the provisions of this Act which are comprised in this Group of Parts; and where a definition is provided for a particular expression, it applies except so far as the context otherwise requires.

381   "Bankrupt" and associated terminology

(1)   "Bankrupt" means an individual who has been adjudged bankrupt and, in relation to a bankruptcy order, it means the individual adjudged bankrupt by that order.

(2)   "Bankruptcy order" means an order adjudging an individual bankrupt.

(3)   "Bankruptcy petition" means a petition to the court for a bankruptcy order.

382   "Bankruptcy debt", etc

(1)   "Bankruptcy debt", in relation to a bankrupt, means (subject to the next subsection) any of the following—

(a)   any debt or liability to which he is subject at the commencement of the bankruptcy,

(b)   any debt or liability to which he may become subject after the commencement of the bankruptcy (including after his discharge from bankruptcy) by reason of any obligation incurred before the commencement of the bankruptcy,

(c)   any amount specified in pursuance of section 39(3)(c) of the Powers of Criminal Courts Act 1973 in any criminal bankruptcy order made against him before the commencement of the bankruptcy, and

(d)   any interest provable as mentioned in section 322(2) in Chapter IV of Part IX.

(2)   In determining for the purposes of any provision in this Group of Parts whether any liability in tort is a bankruptcy debt, the bankrupt is deemed to become subject to that liability by reason of an obligation incurred at the time when the cause of action accrued.

(3)   For the purposes of references in this Group of Parts to a debt or liability, it is immaterial whether the debt or liability is present or future, whether it is certain or contingent or whether its amount is fixed or liquidated, or is capable of being ascertained by fixed rules or as a matter of opinion; and references in this Group of Parts to owing a debt are to be read accordingly.

(4)   In this Group of Parts, except in so far as the context otherwise requires, "liability" means (subject to subsection (3) above) a liability to pay money or money's worth, including any liability under an enactment, any liability for breach of trust, any liability in contract, tort or bailment and any liability arising out of an obligation to make restitution.

383   "Creditor", "security", etc

(1)   "Creditor"—

(a)   in relation to a bankrupt, means a person to whom any of the bankruptcy debts is owed (being, in the case of an amount falling within paragraph (c) of the definition in section 382(1) of "bankruptcy debt", the person in respect of whom that amount is specified in the criminal bankruptcy order in question), and

(b)   in relation to an individual to whom a bankruptcy petition relates, means a person who would be a creditor in the bankruptcy if a bankruptcy order were made on that petition.

(2)   Subject to the next two subsections and any provision of the rules requiring a creditor to give up his security for the purposes of proving a debt, a debt is secured for the purposes of this Group of Parts to the extent that the person to whom the debt is owed holds any security for the debt (whether a mortgage, charge, lien or other security) over any property of the person by whom the debt is owed.

(3)   Where a statement such as is mentioned in section 269(1)(a) in Chapter I of Part IX has been made by a secured creditor for the purposes of any bankruptcy petition and a bankruptcy order is subsequently made on that petition, the creditor is deemed for the purposes of the Parts in this Group to have given up the security specified in the statement.

(4)   In subsection (2) the reference to a security does not include a lien on books, papers or other records, except to the extent that they consist of documents which give a title to property and are held as such.

...

385   Miscellaneous definitions

(1)   The following definitions have effect—

"the court", in relation to any matter, means the court to which, in accordance with section 373 in Part X and the rules, proceedings with respect to that matter are allocated or transferred;

"creditor's petition" means a bankruptcy petition under section 264(1)(a);

"criminal bankruptcy order" means an order under section 39(1) of the Powers of Criminal Courts Act 1973;

"debt" is to be construed in accordance with section 382(3);

"the debtor"—

(a)   in relation to a proposal for the purposes of Part VIII, means the individual making or intending to make that proposal, and

(b)   in relation to a bankruptcy petition, means the individual to whom the petition relates;

"debtor's petition" means a bankruptcy petition presented by the debtor himself under section 264(1)(b);

"dwelling house" includes any building or part of a building which is occupied as a dwelling and any yard, garden, garage or outhouse belonging to the dwelling house and occupied with it;

"estate", in relation to a bankrupt is to be construed in accordance with section 283 in Chapter II of Part IX;

"family", in relation to a bankrupt, means the persons (if any) who are living with him and are dependent on him;

"secured" and related expressions are to be construed in accordance with section 383; and

"the trustee", in relation to a bankruptcy and the bankrupt, means the trustee of the bankrupt's estate.

"insolvency administration order" means an order for the administration in bankruptcy of the insolvent estate of a deceased debtor (being an individual at the date of his death);

"insolvency administration petition" means a petition for an insolvency administration order; and

"the Rules" means the Insolvency Rules 1986.

(2)   References in this Group of Parts to a person's affairs include his business, if any.

PART XII
PREFERENTIAL DEBTS IN COMPANY AND INDIVIDUAL INSOLVENCY

386   Categories of preferential debts

(1)   A reference in this Act to the preferential debts of a company or an individual is to the debts listed in Schedule 6 to this Act (contributions to occupational pension schemes; remuneration, &c. of employees; levies on coal and steel production) ; and references to preferential creditors are to be read accordingly.

(2)   In that Schedule "the debtor" means the company or the individual concerned.

(3)   Schedule 6 is to be read with Schedule 4 to the Pension Schemes Act 1993 (occupational pension scheme contributions).

387   "The relevant date"

(1)   This section explains references in Schedule 6 to the relevant date (being the date which determines the existence and amount of a preferential debt).

(2)   For the purposes of section 4 in Part I (meetings to consider company voluntary arrangement), the relevant date in relation to a company which is not being wound up is—
  (a)   if the company is in administration, the date on which it entered administration, and
  (b)   if the company is not in administration, the date on which the voluntary arrangement takes effect.

(2A) For the purposes of paragraph 31 of Schedule A1 (meetings to consider company voluntary arrangement where a moratorium under section 1A is in force), the relevant date in relation to a company is the date of filing.

(3)   In relation to a company which is being wound up, the following applies—
  (a)   if the winding up is by the court, and the winding-up order was made immediately upon the discharge of an administration order, the relevant date is the date on which the company entered administration;
  (aa) if the winding up is by the court and the winding-up order was made following conversion of administration into winding up by virtue of Article 37 of the EC Regulation, the relevant date is the date on which the company entered administration;
  (ab) if the company is deemed to have passed a resolution for voluntary winding up by virtue of an order following conversion of administration into winding up under Article 37 of the EC Regulation, the relevant date is the date on which the company entered administration;
  (b)   if the case does not fall within paragraph (a), (aa) or (ab) and the company—
    (i)   is being wound up by the court, and
    (ii) had not commenced to be wound up voluntarily before the date of the making of the winding-up order,
  the relevant date is the date of the appointment (or first appointment) of a provisional liquidator or, if no such appointment has been made, the date of the winding-up order;
  (ba) if the case does not fall within paragraph (a), (aa), (ab) or (b) and the company is being wound up following administration pursuant to paragraph 83 of Schedule B1, the relevant date is the date on which the company entered administration;
  (c)   if the case does not fall within paragraph (a), (aa), (ab), (b) or (ba), the relevant date is the date of the passing of the resolution for the winding up of the company.

(3A) In relation to a company which is in administration (and to which no other provision of this section applies) the relevant date is the date on which the company enters administration.

(4)   In relation to a company in receivership (where section 40 or, as the case may be, section 59 applies), the relevant date is—
  (a)   in England and Wales, the date of the appointment of the receiver by debenture-holders, and
    …

(5)   For the purposes of section 258 in Part VIII (individual voluntary arrangements), the relevant date is, in relation to a debtor who is not an undischarged bankrupt
  (a)   where an interim order has been made under section 252 with respect to his proposal, the date of that order, and
  (b)   in any other case, the date on which the voluntary arrangement takes effect.

(6)   In relation to a bankrupt, the following applies—
  (a)   where at the time the bankruptcy order was made there was an interim receiver appointed under section 286, the relevant date is the date on which the interim receiver was first appointed after the presentation of the bankruptcy petition;
  (b)   otherwise, the relevant date is the date of the making of the bankruptcy order.

PART XIII
INSOLVENCY PRACTITIONERS AND THEIR QUALIFICATION

Restrictions on unqualified persons acting as liquidator, trustee in bankruptcy, etc

388   Meaning of "act as insolvency practitioner"

(1)   A person acts as an insolvency practitioner in relation to a company by acting—
  (a)   as its liquidator, provisional liquidator, administrator or administrative receiver, or

      (b)   where a voluntary arrangement in relation to the company is proposed or approved under Part I, as nominee or supervisor

(2)   A person acts as an insolvency practitioner in relation to an individual by acting—

      (a)   as his trustee in bankruptcy or interim receiver of his property or as permanent or interim trustee in the sequestration of his estate; or

      (b)   as trustee under a deed which is a deed of arrangement made for the benefit of his creditors ... or

      (c)   where a voluntary arrangement in relation to the individual is proposed or approved under Part VIII, as nominee or supervisor

      (d)   in the case of a deceased individual to the administration of whose estate this section applies by virtue of an order under section 421 (application of provisions of this Act to insolvent estates of deceased persons), as administrator of that estate.

(2A) A person acts as an insolvency practitioner in relation to an insolvent partnership by acting—

      (a)   as its liquidator, provisional liquidator or administrator, or

      (b)   as trustee of the partnership under article 11 of the Insolvent Partnerships Order 1994, or

      (c)   as supervisor of a voluntary arrangement approved in relation to it under Part I of this Act.

(2B) In relation to a voluntary arrangement proposed under Part I or VIII, a person acts as nominee if he performs any of the functions conferred on nominees under the Part in question.

...

(4)   In this section—

"administrative receiver" has the meaning given by section 251 in Part VII;

"company" means a company within the meaning given by section 735(1) of the 1985 Act, a company which may be wound up under Part XXI of that Act or a building society within the meaning of the Building Societies Act 1986; and

...

(5)   Nothing in this section applies to anything done by—

      (a)   the official receiver; or

...

(6)   Nothing in this section applies to anything done (whether in the United Kingdom or elsewhere) in relation to insolvency proceedings under the EC Regulation in a member State other than the United Kingdom.

389   Acting without qualification an offence

(1)   A person who acts as an insolvency practitioner in relation to a company or an individual at a time when he is not qualified to do so is liable to imprisonment or a fine, or to both.

(1A) This section is subject to section 389A.

...

389A   Authorisation of nominees and supervisors

(1)   Section 389 does not apply to a person acting, in relation to a voluntary arrangement proposed or approved under Part I or Part VIII, as nominee or supervisor if he is authorised so to act.

(2)   For the purposes of subsection (1) and those Parts, an individual to whom subsection

(3)   does not apply is authorised to act as nominee or supervisor in relation to such an arrangement if—

      (a)   he is a member of a body recognised for the purpose by the Secretary of State, and

      (b)   there is in force security ... for the proper performance of his functions and that security or caution meets the prescribed requirements with respect to his so acting in relation to the arrangement.

(3)   This subsection applies to a person if—

(a)   he has been adjudged bankrupt or sequestration of his estate has been awarded and (in either case) he has not been discharged,

(b)   he is subject to a disqualification order made or a disqualification undertaking accepted under the Company Directors Disqualification Act 1986 or to a disqualification order made under Part II of the Companies (Northern Ireland) Order 1989,

...

(d)   he lacks capacity (within the meaning of the Mental Capacity Act 2005) to act as nominee or supervisor.

(4)   The Secretary of State may by order declare a body which appears to him to fall within subsection (5) to be a recognised body for the purposes of subsection (2)(a).

(5)   A body may be recognised if it maintains and enforces rules for securing that its members—

(a)   are fit and proper persons to act as nominees or supervisors, and

(b)   meet acceptable requirements as to education and practical training and experience.

(6)   For the purposes of this section, a person is a member of a body only if he is subject to its rules when acting as nominee or supervisor (whether or not he is in fact a member of the body).

(7)   An order made under subsection (4) in relation to a body may be revoked by a further order if it appears to the Secretary of State that the body no longer falls within subsection (5).

(8)   An order of the Secretary of State under this section has effect from such date as is specified in the order; and any such order revoking a previous order may make provision for members of the body in question to continue to be treated as members of a recognised body for a specified period after the revocation takes effect.

389B Official receiver as nominee or supervisor

(1)   The official receiver is authorised to act as nominee or supervisor in relation to a voluntary arrangement approved under Part VIII provided that the debtor is an undischarged bankrupt when the arrangement is proposed.

(2)   The Secretary of State may by order repeal the proviso in subsection (1).

(3)   An order under subsection (2)—

(a)   must be made by statutory instrument, and

(b)   shall be subject to annulment in pursuance of a resolution of either House of Parliament.

The requisite qualification, and the means of obtaining it

390 Persons not qualified to act as insolvency practitioners

(1)   A person who is not an individual is not qualified to act as an insolvency practitioner.

(2)   A person is not qualified to act as an insolvency practitioner at any time unless at that time—

(a)   he is authorised so to act by virtue of membership of a professional body recognised under section 391 below, being permitted so to act by or under the rules of that body, or

(b)   he holds an authorisation granted by a competent authority under section 393.

(3)   A person is not qualified to act as an insolvency practitioner in relation to another person at any time unless—

(a)   there is in force at that time security ..., and

(b)   that security or caution meets the prescribed requirements with respect to his so acting in relation to that other person.

(4)   A person is not qualified to act as an insolvency practitioner at any time if at that time—

(a)   he has been adjudged bankrupt or sequestration of his estate has been awarded and (in either case) he has not been discharged,

(b)   he is subject to a disqualification order made or a disqualification undertaking accepted under the Company Directors Disqualification Act 1986 or to a disqualification order made under Part II of the Companies (Northern Ireland) Order 1989,

...
(d) he lacks capacity (within the meaning of the Mental Capacity Act 2005) to act as an insolvency practitioner.

(5) A person is not qualified to act as an insolvency practitioner while a bankruptcy restrictions order is in force in respect of him.

391 Recognised professional bodies

(1) The Secretary of State may by order declare a body which appears to him to fall within subsection (2) below to be a recognised professional body for the purposes of this section.

(2) A body may be recognised if it regulates the practice of a profession and maintains and enforces rules for securing that such of its members as are permitted by or under the rules to act as insolvency practitioners—
    (a) are fit and proper persons so to act, and
    (b) meet acceptable requirements as to education and practical training and experience.

(3) References to members of a recognised professional body are to persons who, whether members of that body or not, are subject to its rules in the practice of the profession in question.
    The reference in section 390(2) above to membership of a professional body recognised under this section is to be read accordingly.

(4) An order made under subsection (1) in relation to a professional body may be revoked by a further order if it appears to the Secretary of State that the body no longer falls within subsection (2).

(5) An order of the Secretary of State under this section has effect from such date as is specified in the order; and any such order revoking a previous order may make provision whereby members of the body in question continue to be treated as authorised to act as insolvency practitioners for a specified period after the revocation takes effect.

392 Authorisation by competent authority

(1) Application may be made to a competent authority for authorisation to act as an insolvency practitioner.

(2) The competent authorities for this purpose are—
    (a) in relation to a case of any description specified in directions given by the Secretary of State, the body or person so specified in relation to cases of that description, and
    (b) in relation to a case not falling within paragraph (a), the Secretary of State.

(3) The application—
    (a) shall be made in such manner as the competent authority may direct,
    (b) shall contain or be accompanied by such information as that authority may reasonably require for the purpose of determining the application, and
    (c) shall be accompanied by the prescribed fee;
    and the authority may direct that notice of the making of the application shall be published in such manner as may be specified in the direction.

(4) At any time after receiving the application and before determining it the authority may require the applicant to furnish additional information.

(5) Directions and requirements given or imposed under subsection (3) or (4) may differ as between different applications.

(6) Any information to be furnished to the competent authority under this section shall, if it so requires, be in such form or verified in such manner as it may specify.

(7) An application may be withdrawn before it is granted or refused.

(8) Any sums received under this section by a competent authority other than the Secretary of State may be retained by the authority; and any sums so received by the Secretary of State shall be paid into the Consolidated Fund.

(9) Subsection (3)(c) shall not have effect in respect of an application made to the Secretary of State (but this subsection is without prejudice to section 415A).

393   Grant, refusal and withdrawal of authorisation

(1)   The competent authority may, on an application duly made in accordance with section 392 and after being furnished with all such information as it may require under that section, grant or refuse the application.

(2)   The authority shall grant the application if it appears to it from the information furnished by the applicant and having regard to such other information, if any, as it may have—

(a)   that the applicant is a fit and proper person to act as an insolvency practitioner, and

(b)   that the applicant meets the prescribed requirements with respect to education and practical training and experience.

(3)   An authorisation granted under this section, if not previously withdrawn, continues in force for such period not exceeding the prescribed maximum as may be specified in the authorisation.

(4)   An authorisation so granted may be withdrawn by the competent authority if it appears to it—

(a)   that the holder of the authorisation is no longer a fit and proper person to act as an insolvency practitioner, or

(b)   without prejudice to paragraph (a), that the holder—

(i)   has failed to comply with any provision of this Part or of any regulations made under this Part or Part XV, or

(ii)   in purported compliance with any such provision, has furnished the competent authority with false, inaccurate or misleading information.

(5)   An authorisation granted under this section may be withdrawn by the competent authority at the request or with the consent of the holder of the authorisation.

394   Notices

(1)   Where a competent authority grants an authorisation under section 393, it shall give written notice of that fact to the applicant, specifying the date on which the authorisation takes effect.

(2)   Where the authority proposes to refuse an application, or to withdraw an authorisation under section 393(4), it shall give the applicant or holder of the authorisation written notice of its intention to do so, setting out particulars of the grounds on which it proposes to act.

(3)   In the case of a proposed withdrawal the notice shall state the date on which it is proposed that the withdrawal should take effect.

(4)   A notice under subsection (2) shall give particulars of the rights exercisable under the next two sections by a person on whom the notice is served.

395   Right to make representations

(1)   A person on whom a notice is served under section 394(2) may within 14 days after the date of service make written representations to the competent authority.

(2)   The competent authority shall have regard to any representations so made in determining whether to refuse the application or withdraw the authorisation, as the case may be.

396   Reference to Tribunal

(1)   The Insolvency Practitioners Tribunal ("the Tribunal") continues in being; and the provisions of Schedule 7 apply to it.

(2)   Where a person is served with a notice under section 394(2), he may—

(a)   at any time within 28 days after the date of service of the notice, or

(b)   at any time after the making by him of representations under section 395 and before the end of the period of 28 days after the date of the service on him of a notice by the competent authority that the authority does not propose to alter its decision in consequence of the representations,

give written notice to the authority requiring the case to be referred to the Tribunal.

(3)   Where a requirement is made under subsection (2), then, unless the competent authority—

(a)   has decided or decides to grant the application or, as the case may be, not to withdraw the authorisation, and

(b)   within 7 days after the date of the making of the requirement, gives written notice of
        that decision to the person by whom the requirement was made,
it shall refer the case to the Tribunal.

397   Action of Tribunal on reference

(1)   On a reference under section 396 the Tribunal shall—
      (a)   investigate the case, and
      (b)   make a report to the competent authority stating what would in their opinion be the
            appropriate decision in the matter and the reasons for that opinion,
      and it is the duty of the competent authority to decide the matter accordingly.
(2)   The Tribunal shall send a copy of the report to the applicant or, as the case may be, the
      holder of the authorisation; and the competent authority shall serve him with a written
      notice of the decision made by it in accordance with the report.
(3)   The competent authority may, if he thinks fit, publish the report of the Tribunal.

398   Refusal or withdrawal without reference to Tribunal

Where in the case of any proposed refusal or withdrawal of an authorisation either—
(a)   the period mentioned in section 396(2)(a) has expired without the making of any
      requirement under that subsection or of any representations under section 395, or
(b)   the competent authority has given a notice such as is mentioned in section 396(2)(b) and the
      period so mentioned has expired without the making of any such requirement,
the competent authority may give written notice of the refusal or withdrawal to the person
concerned in accordance with the proposal in the notice given under section 394(2).

PART XIV
PUBLIC ADMINISTRATION (ENGLAND AND WALES)

Official Receivers

399   Appointment, etc of official receivers

(1)   For the purposes of this Act the official receiver, in relation to any bankruptcy, winding up
      or individual voluntary arrangement, is any person who by virtue of the following
      provisions of this section or section 401 below is authorised to act as the official receiver in
      relation to that bankruptcy, winding up or individual voluntary arrangement.
(2)   The Secretary of State may (subject to the approval of the Treasury as to numbers) appoint
      persons to the office of official receiver, and a person appointed to that office (whether
      under this section or section 70 of the Bankruptcy Act 1914)—
      (a)   shall be paid out of money provided by Parliament such salary as the Secretary of
            State may with the concurrence of the Treasury direct,
      (b)   shall hold office on such other terms and conditions as the Secretary of State may with
            the concurrence of the Treasury direct, and
      (c)   may be removed from office by a direction of the Secretary of State.
(3)   Where a person holds the office of official receiver, the Secretary of State shall from time to
      time attach him either to the High Court or to a county court having jurisdiction for the
      purposes of the second Group of Parts of this Act.
(4)   Subject to any directions under subsection (6) below, an official receiver attached to a
      particular court is the person authorised to act as the official receiver in relation to every
      bankruptcy, winding up or individual voluntary arrangement falling within the jurisdiction
      of that court.
(5)   The Secretary of State shall ensure that there is, at all times, at least one official receiver
      attached to the High Court and at least one attached to each county court having jurisdiction
      for the purposes of the second Group of Parts; but he may attach the same official receiver
      to two or more different courts.
(6)   The Secretary of State may give directions with respect to the disposal of the business of
      official receivers, and such directions may, in particular—

(a)   authorise an official receiver attached to one court to act as the official receiver in relation to any case or description of cases falling within the jurisdiction of another court;

(b)   provide, where there is more than one official receiver authorised to act as the official receiver in relation to cases falling within the jurisdiction of any court, for the distribution of their business between or among themselves.

(7)   A person who at the coming into force of section 222 of the Insolvency Act 1985 (replaced by this section) is an official receiver attached to a court shall continue in office after the coming into force of that section as an official receiver attached to that court under this section.

400   Functions and status of official receivers

(1)   In addition to any functions conferred on him by this Act, a person holding the office of official receiver shall carry out such other functions as may from time to time be conferred on him by the Secretary of State.

(2)   In the exercise of the functions of his office a person holding the office of official receiver shall act under the general directions of the Secretary of State and shall also be an officer of the court in relation to which he exercises those functions.

(3)   Any property vested in his official capacity in a person holding the office of official receiver shall, on his dying, ceasing to hold office or being otherwise succeeded in relation to the bankruptcy or winding up in question by another official receiver, vest in his successor without any conveyance, assignment or transfer.

401   Deputy official receivers and staff

(1)   The Secretary of State may, if he thinks it expedient to do so in order to facilitate the disposal of the business of the official receiver attached to any court, appoint an officer of his department to act as deputy to that official receiver.

(2)   Subject to any directions given by the Secretary of State under section 399 or 400, a person appointed to act as deputy to an official receiver has, on such conditions and for such period as may be specified in the terms of his appointment, the same status and functions as the official receiver to whom he is appointed deputy.
Accordingly, references in this Act (except section 399(1) to (5)) to an official receiver include a person appointed to act as his deputy.

(3)   An appointment made under subsection (1) may be terminated at any time by the Secretary of State.

(4)   The Secretary of State may, subject to the approval of the Treasury as to numbers and remuneration and as to the other terms and conditions of the appointments, appoint officers of his department to assist official receivers in the carrying out of their functions.

The Official Petitioner

402   Official Petitioner

(1)   There continues to be an officer known as the Official Petitioner for the purpose of discharging, in relation to cases in which a criminal bankruptcy order is made, the functions assigned to him by or under this Act; and the Director of Public Prosecutions continues, by virtue of his office, to be the Official Petitioner.

(2)   The functions of the Official Petitioner include the following—

(a)   to consider whether, in a case in which a criminal bankruptcy order is made, it is in the public interest that he should himself present a petition under section 264(1)(d) of this Act;

(b)   to present such a petition in any case where he determines that it is in the public interest for him to do so;

(c)   to make payments, in such cases as he may determine, towards expenses incurred by other persons in connection with proceedings in pursuance of such a petition; and

(d)   to exercise, so far as he considers it in the public interest to do so, any of the powers conferred on him by or under this Act.

(3)   Any functions of the Official Petitioner may be discharged on his behalf by any person acting with his authority.

(4)   Neither the Official Petitioner nor any person acting with his authority is liable to any action or proceeding in respect of anything done or omitted to be done in the discharge, or purported discharge, of the functions of the Official Petitioner.

...

Insolvency Service finance, accounting and investment

403 Insolvency Services Account

(1)   All money received by the Secretary of State in respect of proceedings under this Act as it applies to England and Wales shall be paid into the Insolvency Services Account kept by the Secretary of State with the Bank of England; and all payments out of money standing to the credit of the Secretary of State in that account shall be made by the Bank of England in such manner as he may direct.

(2)   Whenever the cash balance standing to the credit of the Insolvency Services Account is in excess of the amount which in the opinion of the Secretary of State is required for the time being to answer demands in respect of bankrupts' estates or companies' estates, the Secretary of State shall—

(a)   notify the excess to the National Debt Commissioners, and

(b)   pay into the Insolvency Services Investment Account ("the Investment Account") kept by the Commissioners with the Bank of England the whole or any part of the excess as the Commissioners may require for investment in accordance with the following provisions of this Part.

(3)   Whenever any part of the money so invested is, in the opinion of the Secretary of State, required to answer any demand in respect of bankrupt's estates or companies' estates, he shall notify to the National Debt Commissioners the amount so required and the Commissioners—

(a)   shall thereupon repay to the Secretary of State such sum as may be required to the credit of the Insolvency Services Account, and

(b)   for that purpose may direct the sale of such part of the securities in which the money has been invested as may be necessary.

404 Investment Account

Any money standing to the credit of the Investment Account (including any money received by the National Debt Commissioners by way of interest on or proceeds of any investment under this section) may be invested by the Commissioners, in accordance with such directions as may be given by the Treasury, in any manner for the time being specified in Part II of Schedule 1 to the Trustee Investments Act 1961.

...

406 Interest on money received by liquidators or trustees in bankruptcy and invested

Where under rules made by virtue of paragraph 16 of Schedule 8 to this Act (investment of money received by company liquidators) [or paragraph 21 of Schedule 9 to this Act (investment of money received by trustee in bankruptcy) a company or a bankrupt's estate]1 has become entitled to any sum by way of interest, the Secretary of State shall certify that sum and the amount of tax payable on it to the National Debt Commissioners; and the Commissioners shall pay, out of the Investment Account—

(a)   into the Insolvency Services Account, the sum so certified less the amount of tax so certified, and

(b)   to the Commissioners of Inland Revenue, the amount of tax so certified.

407 Unclaimed dividends and undistributed balances

(1)   The Secretary of State shall from time to time pay into the Consolidated Fund out of the Insolvency Services Account so much of the sums standing to the credit of that Account as represents—

(a) dividends which were declared before such date as the Treasury may from time to time determine and have not been claimed, and

(b) balances ascertained before that date which are too small to be divided among the persons entitled to them.

(2) For the purposes of this section the sums standing to the credit of the Insolvency Services Account are deemed to include any sums paid out of that Account and represented by any sums or securities standing to the credit of the Investment Account.

(3) The Secretary of State may require the National Debt Commissioners to pay out of the Investment Account into the Insolvency Services Account the whole or part of any sum which he is required to pay out of that account under subsection (1); and the Commissioners may direct the sale of such securities standing to the credit of the Investment Account as may be necessary for that purpose.

...

Supplementary

410 Extent of this Part

This part of this Act extends to England and Wales only.

PART XV
SUBORDINATE LEGISLATION

General insolvency rules

411 Company insolvency rules

(1) Rules may be made—

(a) in relation to England and Wales, by the Lord Chancellor with the concurrence of the Secretary of State and, in the case of rules that affect court procedure, with the concurrence of the Lord Chief Justice, or

...

for the purpose of giving effect to Parts I to VII of this Act or the EC Regulation.

(2) Without prejudice to the generality of subsection (1), or to any provision of those Parts by virtue of which rules under this section may be made with respect to any matter, rules under this section may contain—

(a) any such provision as is specified in Schedule 8 to this Act or corresponds to provision contained immediately before the coming into force of section 106 of the Insolvency Act 1985 in rules made, or having effect as if made, under section 663(1) or (2) (old winding-up rules), and

(b) such incidental, supplemental and transitional provisions as may appear to the Lord Chancellor or, as the case may be, the Secretary of State necessary or expedient.

(2A) For the purposes of subsection (2), a reference in Schedule 8 to this Act to doing anything under or for the purposes of a provision of this Act includes a reference to doing anything under or for the purposes of the EC Regulation (in so far as the provision of this Act relates to a matter to which the EC Regulation applies).

(2B) Rules under this section for the purpose of giving effect to the EC Regulation may not create an offence of a kind referred to in paragraph 1(1)(d) of Schedule 2 to the European Communities Act 1972.

(3) In Schedule 8 to this Act "liquidator" includes a provisional liquidator; and references above in this section to Parts I to VII of this Act are to be read as including the Companies Acts so far as relating to, and to matters connected with or arising out of, the insolvency or winding up of companies.

(4) Rules under this section shall be made by statutory instrument subject to annulment in pursuance of a resolution of either House of Parliament.

(5) Regulations made by the Secretary of State under a power conferred by rules under this section shall be made by statutory instrument and, after being made, shall be laid before each House of Parliament.

(6) Nothing in this section prejudices any power to make rules of court.

(7) The Lord Chief Justice may nominate a judicial office holder (as defined in section 109(4) of the Constitutional Reform Act 2005) to exercise his functions under this section.

412 Individual insolvency rules (England and Wales)

(1) The Lord Chancellor may, with the concurrence of the Secretary of State and, in the case of rules that affect court procedure, with the concurrence of the Lord Chief Justice, make rules for the purpose of giving effect to Parts VIII to XI of this Act or the EC Regulation.

(2) Without prejudice to the generality of subsection (1), or to any provision of those Parts by virtue of which rules under this section may be made with respect to any matter, rules under this section may contain—

    (a) any such provision as is specified in Schedule 9 to this Act or corresponds to provision contained immediately before the appointed day in rules made under section 132 of the Bankruptcy Act 1914; and

    (b) such incidental, supplemental and transitional provisions as may appear to the Lord Chancellor necessary or expedient.

(2A) For the purposes of subsection (2), a reference in Schedule 9 to this Act to doing anything under or for the purposes of a provision of this Act includes a reference to doing anything under or for the purposes of the EC Regulation (in so far as the provision of this Act relates to a matter to which the EC Regulation applies).

(2B) Rules under this section for the purpose of giving effect to the EC Regulation may not create an offence of a kind referred to in paragraph 1(1)(d) of Schedule 2 to the European Communities Act 1972.

(3) Rules under this section shall be made by statutory instrument subject to annulment in pursuance of a resolution of either House of Parliament.

(4) Regulations made by the Secretary of State under a power conferred by rules under this section shall be made by statutory instrument and, after being made, shall be laid before each House of Parliament.

(5) Nothing in this section prejudices any power to make rules of court.

...

413 Insolvency Rules Committee

(1) The committee established under section 10 of the Insolvency Act 1976 (advisory committee on bankruptcy and winding-up rules) continues to exist for the purpose of being consulted under this section.

(2) The Lord Chancellor shall consult the committee before making any rules under section 411 or 412 other than rules which contain a statement that the only provision made by the rules is provision applying rules made under section 411, with or without modifications, for the purposes of provision made by any of sections 23 to 26 of the Water Industry Act 1991 or Schedule 3 to that Act or by any of sections 59 to 65 of, or Schedule 6 or 7 to, the Railways Act 1993.

(3) Subject to the next subsection, the committee shall consist of—

    (a) a judge of the High Court attached to the Chancery Division;

    (b) a circuit judge;

    (c) a registrar in bankruptcy of the High Court;

    (d) the registrar of a county court;

    (e) a practising barrister;

    (f) a practising solicitor; and

    (g) a practising accountant;

and the appointment of any person as a member of the committee shall be made in accordance with subsection (3A) or (3B).

(3A) The Lord Chief Justice must appoint the persons referred to in paragraphs (a) to (d) of subsection (3), after consulting the Lord Chancellor.

(3B) The Lord Chancellor must appoint the persons referred to in paragraphs (e) to (g) of subsection (3), after consulting the Lord Chief Justice.

(4) The Lord Chancellor may appoint as additional members of the committee any persons appearing to him to have qualifications or experience that would be of value to the committee in considering any matter with which it is concerned.

(5) The Lord Chief Justice may nominate a judicial office holder (as defined in section 109(4) of the Constitutional Reform Act 2005) to exercise his functions under this section.

Fees orders

...

417   Money sum in s 222

The Secretary of State may by regulations in a statutory instrument increase or reduce the money sum for the time being specified in section 222(1) (minimum debt for service of demand on unregistered company by unpaid creditor); but such regulations shall not be made unless a draft of the statutory instrument containing them has been approved by resolution of each House of Parliament.

417A   Money sums (company moratorium)

(1) The Secretary of State may by order increase or reduce any of the money sums for the time being specified in the following provisions of Schedule A1 to this Act—
paragraph 17(1) (maximum amount of credit which company may obtain without disclosure of moratorium);
paragraph 41(4) (minimum value of company property concealed or fraudulently removed, affecting criminal liability of company's officer).

(2) An order under this section may contain such transitional provisions as may appear to the Secretary of State necessary or expedient.

(3) An order under this section shall be made by statutory instrument subject to annulment in pursuance of a resolution of either House of Parliament.

418   Monetary limits (bankruptcy)

(1) The Secretary of State may by order prescribe amounts for the purposes of the following provisions in the second Group of Parts—
section 273 (minimum value of debtor's estate determining whether immediate bankruptcy order should be made; small bankruptcies level);
section 313A (value of property below which application for sale, possession or charge to be dismissed);
section 346(3) (minimum amount of judgment, determining whether amount recovered on sale of debtor's goods is to be treated as part of his estate in bankruptcy);
section 354(1) and (2) (minimum amount of concealed debt, or value of property concealed or removed, determining criminal liability under the section);
section 358 (minimum value of property taken by a bankrupt out of England and Wales, determining his criminal liability);
section 360(1) (maximum amount of credit which bankrupt may obtain without disclosure of his status);
section 361(2) (exemption of bankrupt from criminal liability for failure to keep proper accounts, if unsecured debts not more than the prescribed minimum);
section 364(2)(d) (minimum value of goods removed by the bankrupt, determining his liability to arrest);
and references in the second Group of Parts to the amount prescribed for the purposes of any of those provisions, and references in those provisions to the prescribed amount, are to be construed accordingly.

(2) An order under this section may contain such transitional provisions as may appear to the Secretary of State necessary or expedient.

(3) An order under this section shall be made by statutory instrument subject to annulment in pursuance of a resolution of either House of Parliament.

Insolvency practice

419 Regulations for purposes of Part XIII

(1) The Secretary of State may make regulations for the purpose of giving effect to Part XIII of this Act; and "prescribed" in that Part means prescribed by regulations made by the Secretary of State.

(2) Without prejudice to the generality of subsection (1) or to any provision of that Part by virtue of which regulations may be made with respect to any matter, regulations under this section may contain—

    (a) provision as to the matters to be taken into account in determining whether a person is a fit and proper person to act as an insolvency practitioner;

    (b) provision prohibiting a person from so acting in prescribed cases, being cases in which a conflict of interest will or may arise;

    (c) provision imposing requirements with respect to—

        (i) the preparation and keeping by a person who acts as an insolvency practitioner of prescribed books, accounts and other records, and

        (ii) the production of those books, accounts and records to prescribed persons;

    (d) provision conferring power on prescribed persons—

        (i) to require any person who acts or has acted as an insolvency practitioner to answer any inquiry in relation to a case in which he is so acting or has so acted, and

        (ii) to apply to a court to examine such a person or any other person on oath concerning such a case;

    (e) provision making non-compliance with any of the regulations a criminal offence; and

    (f) such incidental, supplemental and transitional provisions as may appear to the Secretary of State necessary or expedient.

(3) Any power conferred by Part XIII or this Part to make regulations, rules or orders is exercisable by statutory instrument subject to annulment by resolution of either House of Parliament.

(4) Any rule or regulation under Part XIII or this Part may make different provision with respect to different cases or descriptions of cases, including different provision for different areas.

Other order-making powers

420 Insolvent partnerships

(1) The Lord Chancellor may, by order made with the concurrence of the Secretary of State and the Lord Chief Justice, provide that such provisions of this Act as may be specified in the order shall apply in relation to insolvent partnerships with such modifications as may be so specified.

(1A) An order under this section may make provision in relation to the EC Regulation.

(1B) But provision made by virtue of this section in relation to the EC Regulation may not create an offence of a kind referred to in paragraph 1(1)(d) of Schedule 2 to the European Communities Act 1972.

(2) An order under this section may make different provision for different cases and may contain such incidental, supplemental and transitional provisions as may appear to the Lord Chancellor and the Lord Chief Justice necessary or expedient.

(3) An order under this section shall be made by statutory instrument subject to annulment in pursuance of a resolution of either House of Parliament.

(4) The Lord Chief Justice may nominate a judicial office holder (as defined in section 109(4) of the Constitutional Reform Act 2005) to exercise his functions under this section.

421 Insolvent estates of deceased persons

(1) The Lord Chancellor may, by order made with the concurrence of the Secretary of State and the Lord Chief Justice, provide that such provisions of this Act as may be specified in the

order shall apply in relation to the administration of the insolvent estates of deceased persons with such modifications as may be so specified.

(1A) An order under this section may make provision in relation to the EC Regulation.

(1B) But provision made by virtue of this section in relation to the EC Regulation may not create an offence of a kind referred to in paragraph 1(1)(d) of Schedule 2 to the European Communities Act 1972.

(2) An order under this section may make different provision for different cases and may contain such incidental, supplemental and transitional provisions as may appear to the Lord Chancellor and the Lord Chief Justice necessary or expedient.

(3) An order under this section shall be made by statutory instrument subject to annulment in pursuance of a resolution of either House of Parliament.

(4) For the purposes of this section the estate of a deceased person is insolvent if, when realised, it will be insufficient to meet in full all the debts and other liabilities to which it is subject.

(5) The Lord Chief Justice may nominate a judicial office holder (as defined in section 109(4) of the Constitutional Reform Act 2005) to exercise his functions under this section.

421A   Insolvent estates: joint tenancies

(1) This section applies where—

    (a) an insolvency administration order has been made in respect of the insolvent estate of a deceased person,

    (b) the petition for the order was presented after the commencement of this section and within the period of five years beginning with the day on which he died, and

    (c) immediately before his death he was beneficially entitled to an interest in any property as joint tenant.

(2) For the purpose of securing that debts and other liabilities to which the estate is subject are met, the court may, on an application by the trustee appointed pursuant to the insolvency administration order, make an order under this section requiring the survivor to pay to the trustee an amount not exceeding the value lost to the estate.

(3) In determining whether to make an order under this section, and the terms of such an order, the court must have regard to all the circumstances of the case, including the interests of the deceased's creditors and of the survivor; but, unless the circumstances are exceptional, the court must assume that the interests of the deceased's creditors outweigh all other considerations.

(4) The order may be made on such terms and conditions as the court thinks fit.

(5) Any sums required to be paid to the trustee in accordance with an order under this section shall be comprised in the estate.

(6) The modifications of this Act which may be made by an order under section 421 include any modifications which are necessary or expedient in consequence of this section.

(7) In this section, "survivor" means the person who, immediately before the death, was beneficially entitled as joint tenant with the deceased or, if the person who was so entitled dies after the making of the insolvency administration order, his personal representatives.

(8) If there is more than one survivor—

    (a) an order under this section may be made against all or any of them, but

    (b) no survivor shall be required to pay more than so much of the value lost to the estate as is properly attributable to him.

(9) In this section—

"insolvency administration order" has the same meaning as in any order under section 421 having effect for the time being,

"value lost to the estate" means the amount which, if paid to the trustee, would in the court's opinion restore the position to what it would have been if the deceased had been adjudged bankrupt immediately before his death.

...

Part XVI

PROVISIONS AGAINST DEBT AVOIDANCE (ENGLAND AND WALES ONLY)

423 Transactions defrauding creditors

(1) This section relates to transactions entered into at an undervalue; and a person enters into such a transaction with another person if—

    (a) he makes a gift to the other person or he otherwise enters into a transaction with the other on terms that provide for him to receive no consideration;

    (b) he enters into a transaction with the other in consideration of marriage or the formation of a civil partnership; or

    (c) he enters into a transaction with the other for a consideration the value of which, in money or money's worth, is significantly less than the value, in money or money's worth, of the consideration provided by himself.

(2) Where a person has entered into such a transaction, the court may, if satisfied under the next subsection, make such order as it thinks fit for—

    (a) restoring the position to what it would have been if the transaction had not been entered into, and

    (b) protecting the interests of persons who are victims of the transaction.

(3) In the case of a person entering into such a transaction, an order shall only be made if the court is satisfied that it was entered into by him for the purpose—

    (a) of putting assets beyond the reach of a person who is making, or may at some time make, a claim against him, or

    (b) of otherwise prejudicing the interests of such a person in relation to the claim which he is making or may make.

(4) In this section "the court" means the High Court or—

    (a) if the person entering into the transaction is an individual, any other court which would have jurisdiction in relation to a bankruptcy petition relating to him;

    (b) if that person is a body capable of being wound up under Part IV or V of this Act, any other court having jurisdiction to wind it up.

(5) In relation to a transaction at an undervalue, references here and below to a victim of the transaction are to a person who is, or is capable of being, prejudiced by it; and in the following two sections the person entering into the transaction is referred to as "the debtor".

424 Those who may apply for an order under s 423

(1) An application for an order under section 423 shall not be made in relation to a transaction except—

    (a) in a case where the debtor has been adjudged bankrupt or is a body corporate which is being wound up or [is in administration , by the official receiver, by the trustee of the bankrupt's estate or the liquidator or administrator of the body corporate or (with the leave of the court) by a victim of the transaction;

    (b) in a case where a victim of the transaction is bound by a voluntary arrangement approved under Part I or Part VIII of this Act, by the supervisor of the voluntary arrangement or by any person who (whether or not so bound) is such a victim; or

    (c) in any other case, by a victim of the transaction.

(2) An application made under any of the paragraphs of subsection (1) is to be treated as made on behalf of every victim of the transaction.

425 Provision which may be made by order under s 423

(1) Without prejudice to the generality of section 423, an order made under that section with respect to a transaction may (subject as follows)—

    (a) require any property transferred as part of the transaction to be vested in any person, either absolutely or for the benefit of all the persons on whose behalf the application for the order is treated as made;

    (b) require any property to be so vested if it represents, in any person's hands, the application either of the proceeds of sale of property so transferred or of money so transferred;

(c)   release or discharge (in whole or in part) any security given by the debtor;

(d)   require any person to pay to any other person in respect of benefits received from the debtor such sums as the court may direct;

(e)   provide for any surety or guarantor whose obligations to any person were released or discharged (in whole or in part) under the transaction to be under such new or revived obligations as the court thinks appropriate;

(f)   provide for security to be provided for the discharge of any obligation imposed by or arising under the order, for such an obligation to be charged on any property and for such security or charge to have the same priority as a security or charge released or discharged (in whole or in part) under the transaction.

(2)   An order under section 423 may affect the property of, or impose any obligation on, any person whether or not he is the person with whom the debtor entered into the transaction; but such an order—

(a)   shall not prejudice any interest in property which was acquired from a person other than the debtor and was acquired in good faith, for value and without notice of the relevant circumstances, or prejudice any interest deriving from such an interest, and

(b)   shall not require a person who received a benefit from the transaction in good faith, for value and without notice of the relevant circumstances to pay any sum unless he was a party to the transaction.

(3)   For the purposes of this section the relevant circumstances in relation to a transaction are the circumstances by virtue of which an order under section 423 may be made in respect of the transaction.

(4)   In this section "security" means any mortgage, charge, lien or other security.

PART XVII
MISCELLANEOUS AND GENERAL

426   Co-operation between courts exercising jurisdiction in relation to insolvency

(1)   An order made by a court in any part of the United Kingdom in the exercise of jurisdiction in relation to insolvency law shall be enforced in any other part of the United Kingdom as if it were made by a court exercising the corresponding jurisdiction in that other part.

…

426A   Disqualification from Parliament (England and Wales)

(1)   A person in respect of whom a bankruptcy restrictions order has effect shall be disqualified—

(a)   from membership of the House of Commons,

(b)   from sitting or voting in the House of Lords, and

(c)   from sitting or voting in a committee of the House of Lords or a joint committee of both Houses.

(2)   If a member of the House of Commons becomes disqualified under this section, his seat shall be vacated.

(3)   If a person who is disqualified under this section is returned as a member of the House of Commons, his return shall be void.

(4)   No writ of summons shall be issued to a member of the House of Lords who is disqualified under this section.

(5)   If a court makes a bankruptcy restrictions order or interim order in respect of a member of the House of Commons or the House of Lords the court shall notify the Speaker of that House.

(6)   If the Secretary of State accepts a bankruptcy restrictions undertaking made by a member of the House of Commons or the House of Lords, the Secretary of State shall notify the Speaker of that House.

426B   Devolution

(1)   If a court makes a bankruptcy restrictions order or interim order in respect of a member of the Scottish Parliament, the Northern Ireland Assembly or the National Assembly for Wales, the court shall notify the presiding officer of that body.

(2)   If the Secretary of State accepts a bankruptcy restrictions undertaking made by a member of the Scottish Parliament, the Northern Ireland Assembly or the National Assembly for Wales, the Secretary of State shall notify the presiding officer of that body.

...

427   Parliamentary disqualification

(1)   Where a court in Northern Ireland adjudges an individual bankrupt or a court in Scotland awards sequestration of an individual's estate, the individual is disqualified—

(a)   for sitting or voting in the House of Lords,

(b)   for being elected to, or sitting or voting in, the House of Commons, and

(c)   for sitting or voting in a committee of either House.

(2)   Where an individual is disqualified under this section, the disqualification ceases—

(a)   except where the adjudication is annulled or the award recalled or reduced without the individual having been first discharged, on the discharge of the individual, and

(b)   in the excepted case, on the annulment, recall or reduction, as the case may be.

(3)   No writ of summons shall be issued to any lord of Parliament who is for the time being disqualified under this section for sitting and voting in the House of Lords.

(4)   Where a member of the House of Commons who is disqualified under this section continues to be so disqualified until the end of the period of 6 months beginning with the day of the adjudication or award, his seat shall be vacated at the end of that period.

(5)   A court which makes an adjudication or award such as is mentioned in subsection (1) in relation to any lord of Parliament or member of the House of Commons shall forthwith certify the adjudication or award to the Speaker of the House of Lords or, as the case may be, to the Speaker of the House of Commons.

(6)   Where a court has certified an adjudication or award to the Speaker of the House of Commons under subsection (5), then immediately after it becomes apparent which of the following certificates is applicable, the court shall certify to the Speaker of the House of Commons—

(a)   that the period of 6 months beginning with the day of the adjudication or award has expired without the adjudication or award having been annulled, recalled or reduced, or

(b)   that the adjudication or award has been annulled, recalled or reduced before the end of that period.

...

429   Disabilities on revocation of administration order against an individual

(1)   The following applies where a person fails to make any payment which he is required to make by virtue of an administration order under Part VI of the County Courts Act 1984.

(2)   The court which is administering that person's estate under the order may, if it thinks fit—

(a)   revoke the administration order, and

(b)   make an order directing that this section and section 12 of the Company Directors Disqualification Act 1986 shall apply to the person for such period, not exceeding one year , as may be specified in the order.

(3)   A person to whom this section so applies shall not—

(a)   either alone or jointly with another person, obtain credit to the extent of the amount prescribed for the purposes of section 360(1)(a) or more, or

(b)   enter into any transaction in the course of or for the purposes of any business in which he is directly or indirectly engaged,

without disclosing to the person from whom he obtains the credit, or (as the case may be) with whom the transaction is entered into, the fact that this section applies to him.

(4)   The reference in subsection (3) to a person obtaining credit includes—

(a)   a case where goods are bailed or hired to him under a hire-purchase agreement or agreed to be sold to him under a conditional sale agreement, and

(b)   a case where he is paid in advance (whether in money or otherwise) for the supply of goods or services.

(5)   A person who contravenes this section is guilty of an offence and liable to imprisonment or a fine, or both.

...

433   Admissibility in evidence of statements of affairs, etc

(1)   In any proceedings (whether or not under this Act)—

(a)   a statement of affairs prepared for the purposes of any provision of this Act which is derived from the Insolvency Act 1985, and

(b)   any other statement made in pursuance of a requirement imposed by or under any such provision or by or under rules made under this Act,

may be used in evidence against any person making or concurring in making the statement.

(2)   However, in criminal proceedings in which any such person is charged with an offence to which this subsection applies—

(a)   no evidence relating to the statement may be adduced, and

(b)   no question relating to it may be asked,

by or on behalf of the prosecution, unless evidence relating to it is adduced, or a question relating to it is asked, in the proceedings by or on behalf of that person.

...

...

PART XVIII
INTERPRETATION

435   Meaning of "associate"

(1)   For the purposes of this Act any question whether a person is an associate of another person is to be determined in accordance with the following provisions of this section (any provision that a person is an associate of another person being taken to mean that they are associates of each other).

(2)   A person is an associate of an individual if that person is—

(a)   the individual's husband or wife or civil partner,

(b)   a relative of—

(i)   the individual, or

(ii)   the individual's husband or wife or civil partner, or

(c)   the husband or wife or civil partner of a relative of—

(i)   the individual, or

(ii)   the individual's husband or wife or civil partner.

(3)   A person is an associate of any person with whom he is in partnership, and of the husband or wife or civil partner or a relative of any individual with whom he is in partnership; ...

(4)   A person is an associate of any person whom he employs or by whom he is employed.

(5)   A person in his capacity as trustee of a trust other than—

(a)   a trust arising under any of the second Group of Parts

(b)   a pension scheme or an employees' share scheme (within the meaning of the Companies Act),

is an associate of another person if the beneficiaries of the trust include, or the terms of the trust confer a power that may be exercised for the benefit of, that other person or an associate of that other person.

(6)   A company is an associate of another company—

(a)   if the same person has control of both, or a person has control of one and persons who are his associates, or he and persons who are his associates, have control of the other, or

(b)   if a group of two or more persons has control of each company, and the groups either consist of the same persons or could be regarded as consisting of the same persons by treating (in one or more cases) a member of either group as replaced by a person of whom he is an associate.

(7) A company is an associate of another person if that person has control of it or if that person and persons who are his associates together have control of it.

(8) For the purposes of this section a person is a relative of an individual if he is that individual's brother, sister, uncle, aunt, nephew, niece, lineal ancestor or lineal descendant, treating—

  (a) any relationship of the half blood as a relationship of the whole blood and the stepchild or adopted child of any person as his child, and

  (b) an illegitimate child as the legitimate child of his mother and reputed father;

  and references in this section to a husband or wife include a former husband or wife and a reputed husband or wife and references to a civil partner include a former civil partner and a reputed civil partner.

(9) For the purposes of this section any director or other officer of a company is to be treated as employed by that company.

(10) For the purposes of this section a person is to be taken as having control of a company if—

  (a) the directors of the company or of another company which has control of it (or any of them) are accustomed to act in accordance with his directions or instructions, or

  (b) he is entitled to exercise, or control the exercise of, one third or more of the voting power at any general meeting of the company or of another company which has control of it;

  and where two or more persons together satisfy either of the above conditions, they are to be taken as having control of the company.

(11) In this section "company" includes any body corporate (whether incorporated in Great Britain or elsewhere); and references to directors and other officers of a company and to voting power at any general meeting of a company have effect with any necessary modifications.

436 Expressions used generally

In this Act, except in so far as the context otherwise requires (and subject to Parts VII and XI)—

"the appointed day" means the day on which this Act comes into force under section 443;

"associate" has the meaning given by section 435;

"business" includes a trade or profession;

"the Companies Act" means the Companies Act 1985;

"the Companies Acts" means the Companies Acts (as defined in section 2 of the Companies Act 2006) as they have effect in Great Britain;

"conditional sale agreement" and "hire-purchase agreement" have the same meanings as in the Consumer Credit Act 1974;

"the EC Regulation" means Council Regulation (EC) No. 1346/2000;

"EEA State" means a state that is a Contracting Party to the Agreement on the European Economic Area signed at Oporto on 2nd May 1992 as adjusted by the Protocol signed at Brussels on 17th March 1993;

"modifications" includes additions, alterations and omissions and cognate expressions shall be construed accordingly;

"property" includes money, goods, things in action, land and every description of property wherever situated and also obligations and every description of interest, whether present or future or vested or contingent, arising out of, or incidental to, property;

"records" includes computer records and other non-documentary records;

"subordinate legislation" has the same meaning as in the Interpretation Act 1978; and

"transaction" includes a gift, agreement or arrangement, and references to entering into a transaction shall be construed accordingly.

436A Proceedings under EC Regulation: modified definition of property

In the application of this Act to proceedings by virtue of Article 3 of the EC Regulation, a reference to property is a reference to property which may be dealt with in the proceedings.

...

SCHEDULE A1
MORATORIUM WHERE DIRECTORS PROPOSE VOLUNTARY ARRANGEMENT
PART 1
INTRODUCTORY

Eligible companies

2.— (1) A company is eligible for a moratorium if it meets the requirements of paragraph 3, unless—

   (a) it is excluded from being eligible by virtue of paragraph 4, or

   (b) it falls within sub-paragraph (2).

   (2) A company falls within this sub-paragraph if—

   (a) it effects or carries out contracts of insurance, but is not exempt from the general prohibition, within the meaning of section 19 of the Financial Services and Markets Act 2000, in relation to that activity,

   (b) it has permission under Part IV of that Act to accept deposits,

   (bb) it has a liability in respect of a deposit which it accepted in accordance with the Banking Act 1979 or 1987,

   (c) it is a party to a market contract or any of its property is subject to a market charge or a system-charge, or

   (d) it is a participant (within the meaning of the settlement finality regulations) or any of its property is subject to a collateral security charge (within the meaning of those regulations).

   ...

3.— (1) A company meets the requirements of this paragraph if the qualifying conditions are met—

   (a) in the year ending with the date of filing, or

   (b) in the financial year of the company which ended last before that date.

   (2) For the purposes of sub-paragraph (1)—

   (a) the qualifying conditions are met by a company in a period if, in that period, it satisfies two or more of the requirements for being a small company specified for the time being in section 247(3) of the Companies Act 1985, and

   (b) a company's financial year is to be determined in accordance with that Act.

   (3) Subsections (4), (5) and (6) of section 247 of that Act apply for the purposes of this paragraph as they apply for the purposes of that section.

   (4) A company does not meet the requirements of this paragraph if it is a holding company of a group of companies which does not qualify as a small group or a medium-sized group in respect of the financial year of the company which ended last before the date of filing.

   (5) For the purposes of sub-paragraph (4) "group" has the meaning given by section 262 of the Companies Act 1985 (definitions for Part VII) and a group qualifies as small or medium-sized if it qualifies as such under section 249 of the Companies Act 1985 (qualification of group as small or medium-sized).

4.— (1) A company is excluded from being eligible for a moratorium if, on the date of filing—

   (a) the company is in administration,

   (b) the company is being wound up,

   (c) there is an administrative receiver of the company,

   (d) a voluntary arrangement has effect in relation to the company,

   (e) there is a provisional liquidator of the company,

   (f) a moratorium has been in force for the company at any time during the period of 12 months ending with the date of filing and—

      (i) no voluntary arrangement had effect at the time at which the moratorium came to an end, or

      (ii) a voluntary arrangement which had effect at any time in that period has come to an end prematurely, (fa) an administrator appointed under paragraph 22 of Schedule B1 has held office in the period of 12 months ending with the date of filing, or

(g) a voluntary arrangement in relation to the company which had effect in pursuance of a proposal under section 1(3) has come to an end prematurely and, during the period of 12 months ending with the date of filing, an order under section 5(3)(a) has been made.

(2) Sub-paragraph (1)(b) does not apply to a company which, by reason of a winding-up order made after the date of filing, is treated as being wound up on that date.

Capital market arrangement

4A. A company is also excluded from being eligible for a moratorium if, on the date of filing, it is a party to an agreement which is or forms part of a capital market arrangement under which—

(i) a party has incurred, or when the agreement was entered into was expected to incur, a debt of at least £10 million under the arrangement, and

(ii) the arrangement involves the issue of a capital market investment.

Public Private Partnership

4B. A company is also excluded from being eligible for a moratorium if, on the date of filing, it is a project company of a project which—

(i) is a public-private partnership project, and

(ii) includes step-in rights.

Liability under an arrangement

4C.— (1) A company is also excluded from being eligible for a moratorium if, on the date of filing, it has incurred a liability under an agreement of £10 million or more.

(2) Where the liability in sub-paragraph (1) is a contingent liability under or by virtue of a guarantee or an indemnity or security provided on behalf of another person, the amount of that liability is the full amount of the liability in relation to which the guarantee, indemnity or security is provided.

(3) In this paragraph—

(a) the reference to "liability" includes a present or future liability whether, in either case, it is certain or contingent,

(b) the reference to "liability" includes a reference to a liability to be paid wholly or partly in foreign currency (in which case the sterling equivalent shall be calculated as at the time when the liability is incurred).

Interpretation of capital market arrangement

4D.— (1) For the purposes of paragraph 4A an arrangement is a capital market arrangement if—

(a) it involves a grant of security to a person holding it as trustee for a person who holds a capital market investment issued by a party to the arrangement, or

(b) at least one party guarantees the performance of obligations of another party, or

(c) at least one party provides security in respect of the performance of obligations of another party, or

(d) the arrangement involves an investment of a kind described in articles 83 to 85 of the Financial Services and Markets Act 2000 (Regulated Activities) Order 2001 (S.I. 2001/544) (options, futures and contracts for differences).

(2) For the purposes of sub-paragraph (1)—

(a) a reference to holding as trustee includes a reference to holding as nominee or agent,

(b) a reference to holding for a person who holds a capital market investment includes a reference to holding for a number of persons at least one of whom holds a capital market investment, and

(c) a person holds a capital market investment if he has a legal or beneficial interest in it.

(3) In paragraph 4A, 4C, 4J and this paragraph—

"agreement" includes an agreement or undertaking effected by—

(a) contract,

(b)   deed, or

(c)   any other instrument intended to have effect in accordance with the law of England and Wales, … or another jurisdiction, and

"party" to an arrangement includes a party to an agreement which—

(a)   forms part of the arrangement,

(b)   provides for the raising of finance as part of the arrangement, or

(c)   is necessary for the purposes of implementing the arrangement.

…

Debt

4G.   The debt of at least £10 million referred to in paragraph 4A—

(a)   may be incurred at any time during the life of the capital market arrangement, and

(b)   may be expressed wholly or partly in a foreign currency (in which case the sterling equivalent shall be calculated as at the time when the arrangement is entered into).

Interpretation of project company

4H.—   (1)   For the purposes of paragraph 4B a company is a "project company" of a project if—

(a)   it holds property for the purpose of the project,

(b)   it has sole or principal responsibility under an agreement for carrying out all or part of the project,

(c)   it is one of a number of companies which together carry out the project,

(d)   it has the purpose of supplying finance to enable the project to be carried out, or

(e)   it is the holding company of a company within any of paragraphs (a) to (d).

(2)   But a company is not a "project company" of a project if—

(a)   it performs a function within sub-paragraph (1)(a) to (d) or is within sub-paragraph (1)(e), but

(b)   it also performs a function which is not—

(i)   within sub-paragraph (1)(a) to (d),

(ii)   related to a function within sub-paragraph (1)(a) to (d), or

(iii)   related to the project.

(3)   For the purposes of this paragraph a company carries out all or part of a project whether or not it acts wholly or partly through agents.

Public-private partnership project

4I.—   (1)   In paragraph 4B "public-private partnership project" means a project—

(a)   the resources for which are provided partly by one or more public bodies and partly by one or more private persons, or

(b)   which is designed wholly or mainly for the purpose of assisting a public body to discharge a function.

(2)   In sub-paragraph (1) "resources" includes—

(a)   funds (including payment for the provision of services or facilities),

(b)   assets,

(c)   professional skill,

(d)   the grant of a concession or franchise, and

(e)   any other commercial resource.

(3)   In sub-paragraph (1) "public body" means—

(a)   a body which exercises public functions,

(b)   a body specified for the purposes of this paragraph by the Secretary of State, and

(c)   a body within a class specified for the purposes of this paragraph by the Secretary of State.

(4)   A specification under sub-paragraph (3) may be—

(a)   general, or

(b)   for the purpose of the application of paragraph 4B to a specified case.

…

Person

4K.   For the purposes of paragraphs 4A to 4J, a reference to a person includes a reference to a partnership or another unincorporated group of persons.

5.   The Secretary of State may by regulations modify the qualifications for eligibility of a company for a moratorium.

PART II
OBTAINING A MORATORIUM

Nominee's Statement

6.— (1)   Where the directors of a company wish to obtain a moratorium, they shall submit to the nominee—

    (a)   a document setting out the terms of the proposed voluntary arrangement,

    (b)   a statement of the company's affairs containing—

        (i)   such particulars of its creditors and of its debts and other liabilities and of its assets as may be prescribed, and

        (ii)   such other information as may be prescribed, and

    (c)   any other information necessary to enable the nominee to comply with sub-paragraph (2) which he requests from them.

(2)   The nominee shall submit to the directors a statement in the prescribed form indicating whether or not, in his opinion—

    (a)   the proposed voluntary arrangement has a reasonable prospect of being approved and implemented,

    (b)   the company is likely to have sufficient funds available to it during the proposed moratorium to enable it to carry on its business, and

    (c)   meetings of the company and its creditors should be summoned to consider the proposed voluntary arrangement.

(3)   In forming his opinion on the matters mentioned in sub-paragraph (2), the nominee is entitled to rely on the information submitted to him under sub-paragraph (1) unless he has reason to doubt its accuracy.

(4)   The reference in sub-paragraph (2)(b) to the company's business is to that business as the company proposes to carry it on during the moratorium.

Documents to be submitted to court

7.— (1)   To obtain a moratorium the directors of a company must file … with the court—

    (a)   a document setting out the terms of the proposed voluntary arrangement,

    (b)   a statement of the company's affairs containing—

        (i)   such particulars of its creditors and of its debts and other liabilities and of its assets as may be prescribed, and

        (ii)   such other information as may be prescribed,

    (c)   a statement that the company is eligible for a moratorium,

    (d)   a statement from the nominee that he has given his consent to act, and

    (e)   a statement from the nominee that, in his opinion—

        (i)   the proposed voluntary arrangement has a reasonable prospect of being approved and implemented,

        (ii)   the company is likely to have sufficient funds available to it during the proposed moratorium to enable it to carry on its business, and

        (iii)   meetings of the company and its creditors should be summoned to consider the proposed voluntary arrangement.

(2)   Each of the statements mentioned in sub-paragraph (1)(b) to (e), except so far as it contains the particulars referred to in paragraph (b)(i), must be in the prescribed form.

(3)   The reference in sub-paragraph (1)(e)(ii) to the company's business is to that business as the company proposes to carry it on during the moratorium.

(4)   The Secretary of State may by regulations modify the requirements of this paragraph as to the documents required to be filed … with the court in order to obtain a moratorium.

Duration of moratorium

8.— (1) A moratorium comes into force when the documents for the time being referred to in paragraph 7(1) are filed or lodged with the court and references in this Schedule to "the beginning of the moratorium" shall be construed accordingly.

(2) A moratorium ends at the end of the day on which the meetings summoned under paragraph 29(1) are first held (or, if the meetings are held on different days, the later of those days), unless it is extended under paragraph 32.

(3) If either of those meetings has not first met before the end of the period of 28 days beginning with the day on which the moratorium comes into force, the moratorium ends at the end of the day on which those meetings were to be held (or, if those meetings were summoned to be held on different days, the later of those days), unless it is extended under paragraph 32.

(4) If the nominee fails to summon either meeting within the period required by paragraph 29(1), the moratorium ends at the end of the last day of that period.

(5) If the moratorium is extended (or further extended) under paragraph 32, it ends at the end of the day to which it is extended (or further extended).

...

Notification of beginning of moratorium

9.— (1) When a moratorium comes into force, the directors shall notify the nominee of that fact forthwith.

(2) If the directors without reasonable excuse fail to comply with sub-paragraph (1), each of them is liable to imprisonment or a fine, or both.

10.— (1) When a moratorium comes into force, the nominee shall, in accordance with the rules—
     (a) advertise that fact forthwith, and
     (b) notify the registrar of companies, the company and any petitioning creditor of the company of whose claim he is aware of that fact.

(2) In sub-paragraph (1)(b), "petitioning creditor" means a creditor by whom a winding-up petition has been presented before the beginning of the moratorium, as long as the petition has not been dismissed or withdrawn.

(3) If the nominee without reasonable excuse fails to comply with sub-paragraph (1)(a) or (b), he is liable to a fine.

Notification of end of moratorium

11.— (1) When a moratorium comes to an end, the nominee shall, in accordance with the rules—
     (a) advertise that fact forthwith, and
     (b) notify the court, the registrar of companies, the company and any creditor of the company of whose claim he is aware of that fact.

(2) If the nominee without reasonable excuse fails to comply with sub-paragraph (1)(a) or (b), he is liable to a fine.

PART III
EFFECTS OF MORATORIUM

Effect on creditors, etc

12.— (1) During the period for which a moratorium is in force for a company—
     (a) no petition may be presented for the winding up of the company,
     (b) no meeting of the company may be called or requisitioned except with the consent of the nominee or the leave of the court and subject (where the court gives leave) to such terms as the court may impose,
     (c) no resolution may be passed or order made for the winding up of the company,
     (d) no administration application may be made in respect of the company,
     (da) no administrator of the company may be appointed under paragraph 14 or 22 of Schedule B1,
     (e) no administrative receiver of the company may be appointed,

    (f)   no landlord or other person to whom rent is payable may exercise any right of forfeiture by peaceable re-entry in relation to premises let to the company in respect of a failure by the company to comply with any term or condition of its tenancy of such premises, except with the leave of the court and subject to such terms as the court may impose,

    (g)   no other steps may be taken to enforce any security over the company's property, or to repossess goods in the company's possession under any hire-purchase agreement, except with the leave of the court and subject to such terms as the court may impose, and

    (h)   no other proceedings and no execution or other legal process may be commenced or continued, and no distress may be levied, against the company or its property except with the leave of the court and subject to such terms as the court may impose.

(2)   Where a petition, other than an excepted petition, for the winding up of the company has been presented before the beginning of the moratorium, section 127 shall not apply in relation to any disposition of property, transfer of shares or alteration in status made during the moratorium or at a time mentioned in paragraph 37(5)(a).

...

13.—   (1)   This paragraph applies where there is an uncrystallised floating charge on the property of a company for which a moratorium is in force.

    (2)   If the conditions for the holder of the charge to give a notice having the effect mentioned in sub-paragraph (4) are met at any time, the notice may not be given at that time but may instead be given as soon as practicable after the moratorium has come to an end.

    (3)   If any other event occurs at any time which (apart from this sub-paragraph) would have the effect mentioned in sub-paragraph (4), then—

        (a)   the event shall not have the effect in question at that time, but

        (b)   if notice of the event is given to the company by the holder of the charge as soon as is practicable after the moratorium has come to an end, the event is to be treated as if it had occurred when the notice was given.

    (4)   The effect referred to in sub-paragraphs (2) and (3) is—

        (a)   causing the crystallisation of the floating charge, or

        (b)   causing the imposition, by virtue of provision in the instrument creating the charge, of any restriction on the disposal of any property of the company.

    (5)   Application may not be made for leave under paragraph 12(1)(g) or (h) with a view to obtaining—

        (a)   the crystallisation of the floating charge, or

        (b)   the imposition, by virtue of provision in the instrument creating the charge, of any restriction on the disposal of any property of the company.

14.   Security granted by a company at a time when a moratorium is in force in relation to the company may only be enforced if, at that time, there were reasonable grounds for believing that it would benefit the company.

Effect on company

15.—   (1)   Paragraphs 16 to 23 apply in relation to a company for which a moratorium is in force.

    (2)   The fact that a company enters into a transaction in contravention of any of paragraphs 16 to 22 does not—

        (a)   make the transaction void, or

        (b)   make it to any extent unenforceable against the company.

Company invoices, etc

16.—   (1)   Every invoice, order for goods or business letter which—

        (a)   is issued by or on behalf of the company, and

        (b)   on or in which the company's name appears,

    shall also contain the nominee's name and a statement that the moratorium is in force for the company.

(2)   If default is made in complying with sub-paragraph (1), the company and (subject to sub-paragraph (3)) any officer of the company is liable to a fine.

(3)   An officer of the company is only liable under sub-paragraph (2) if, without reasonable excuse, he authorises or permits the default.

Obtaining credit during moratorium

17.—   (1)   The company may not obtain credit to the extent of £250 or more from a person who has not been informed that a moratorium is in force in relation to the company.

(2)   The reference to the company obtaining credit includes the following cases—

     (a)   where goods are bailed (in Scotland, hired) to the company under a hire-purchase agreement, or agreed to be sold to the company under a conditional sale agreement, and

     (b)   where the company is paid in advance (whether in money or otherwise) for the supply of goods or services.

(3)   Where the company obtains credit in contravention of sub-paragraph (1)—

     (a)   the company is liable to a fine, and

     (b)   if any officer of the company knowingly and willfully authorised or permitted the contravention, he is liable to imprisonment or a fine, or both.

(4)   The money sum specified in sub-paragraph (1) is subject to increase or reduction by order under section 417A in Part XV.

Disposals and payments

18.—   (1)   Subject to sub-paragraph (2), the company may only dispose of any of its property if—

     (a)   there are reasonable grounds for believing that the disposal will benefit the company, and

     (b)   the disposal is approved by the committee established under paragraph 35(1) or, where there is no such committee, by the nominee.

(2)   Sub-paragraph (1) does not apply to a disposal made in the ordinary way of the company's business.

(3)   If the company makes a disposal in contravention of sub-paragraph (1) otherwise than in pursuance of an order of the court—

     (a)   the company is liable to a fine, and

     (b)   if any officer of the company authorised or permitted the contravention, without reasonable excuse, he is liable to imprisonment or a fine, or both.

19.—   (1)   Subject to sub-paragraph (2), the company may only make any payment in respect of any debt or other liability of the company in existence before the beginning of the moratorium if—

     (a)   there are reasonable grounds for believing that the payment will benefit the company, and

     (b)   the payment is approved by the committee established under paragraph 35(1) or, where there is no such committee, by the nominee.

(2)   Sub-paragraph (1) does not apply to a payment required by paragraph 20(6).

(3)   If the company makes a payment in contravention of sub-paragraph (1) otherwise than in pursuance of an order of the court—

     (a)   the company is liable to a fine, and

     (b)   if any officer of the company authorised or permitted the contravention, without reasonable excuse, he is liable to imprisonment or a fine, or both.

Disposal of charged property, etc

20.—   (1)   This paragraph applies where—

     (a)   any property of the company is subject to a security, or

     (b)   any goods are in the possession of the company under a hire-purchase agreement.

(2)   If the holder of the security consents, or the court gives leave, the company may dispose of the property as if it were not subject to the security.

(3) If the owner of the goods consents, or the court gives leave, the company may dispose of the goods as if all rights of the owner under the hire-purchase agreement were vested in the company.

(4) Where property subject to a security which, as created, was a floating charge is disposed of under sub-paragraph (2), the holder of the security has the same priority in respect of any property of the company directly or indirectly representing the property disposed of as he would have had in respect of the property subject to the security.

(5) Sub-paragraph (6) applies to the disposal under sub-paragraph (2) or (as the case may be) sub-paragraph (3) of—

    (a) any property subject to a security other than a security which, as created, was a floating charge, or

    (b) any goods in the possession of the company under a hire-purchase agreement.

(6) It shall be a condition of any consent or leave under sub-paragraph (2) or (as the case may be) sub-paragraph (3) that—

    (a) the net proceeds of the disposal, and

    (b) where those proceeds are less than such amount as may be agreed, or determined by the court, to be the net amount which would be realised on a sale of the property or goods in the open market by a willing vendor, such sums as may be required to make good the deficiency,

shall be applied towards discharging the sums secured by the security or payable under the hire-purchase agreement.

(7) Where a condition imposed in pursuance of sub-paragraph (6) relates to two or more securities, that condition requires—

    (a) the net proceeds of the disposal, and

    (b) where paragraph (b) of sub-paragraph (6) applies, the sums mentioned in that paragraph,

to be applied towards discharging the sums secured by those securities in the order of their priorities.

(8) Where the court gives leave for a disposal under sub-paragraph (2) or (3), the directors shall, within 14 days after leave is given, send an office copy of the order giving leave to the registrar of companies.

(9) If the directors without reasonable excuse fail to comply with sub-paragraph (8), they are liable to a fine.

...

22.— (1) If the company—

    (a) without any consent or leave under paragraph 20, disposes of any of its property which is subject to a security otherwise than in accordance with the terms of the security,

    (b) without any consent or leave under paragraph 20, disposes of any goods in the possession of the company under a hire-purchase agreement otherwise than in accordance with the terms of the agreement, or

    (c) fails to comply with any requirement imposed by paragraph 20 or 21,

it is liable to a fine.

(2) If any officer of the company, without reasonable excuse, authorises or permits any such disposal or failure to comply, he is liable to imprisonment or a fine, or both.

Market contracts, etc

23.— (1) If the company enters into any transaction to which this paragraph applies—

    (a) the company is liable to a fine, and

    (b) if any officer of the company, without reasonable excuse, authorised or permitted the company to enter into the transaction, he is liable to imprisonment or a fine, or both.

(2) A company enters into a transaction to which this paragraph applies if it—

    (a) enters into a market contract,

    (b) gives a transfer order,

    (c) grants a market charge or a system-charge, or

        (d)   provides any collateral security.

(3)   The fact that a company enters into a transaction in contravention of this paragraph does not—

        (a)   make the transaction void, or

        (b)   make it to any extent unenforceable by or against the company.

...

PART IV
NOMINEES

Monitoring of company's activities

24.— (1) During a moratorium, the nominee shall monitor the company's affairs for the purpose of forming an opinion as to whether—

        (a)   the proposed voluntary arrangement or, if he has received notice of proposed modifications under paragraph 31(7), the proposed arrangement with those modifications has a reasonable prospect of being approved and implemented, and

        (b)   the company is likely to have sufficient funds available to it during the remainder of the moratorium to enable it to continue to carry on its business.

     (2) The directors shall submit to the nominee any information necessary to enable him to comply with sub-paragraph (1) which he requests from them.

     (3) In forming his opinion on the matters mentioned in sub-paragraph (1), the nominee is entitled to rely on the information submitted to him under sub-paragraph (2) unless he has reason to doubt its accuracy.

     (4) The reference in sub-paragraph (1)(b) to the company's business is to that business as the company proposes to carry it on during the remainder of the moratorium.

Withdrawal of consent to act

25.— (1) The nominee may only withdraw his consent to act in the circumstances mentioned in this paragraph.

     (2) The nominee must withdraw his consent to act if, at any time during a moratorium—

        (a)   he forms the opinion that—

            (i)   the proposed voluntary arrangement or, if he has received notice of proposed modifications under paragraph 31(7), the proposed arrangement with those modifications no longer has a reasonable prospect of being approved or implemented, or

          (ii)   the company will not have sufficient funds available to it during the remainder of the moratorium to enable it to continue to carry on its business,

        (b)   he becomes aware that, on the date of filing, the company was not eligible for a moratorium, or

        (c)   the directors fail to comply with their duty under paragraph 24(2).

     (3) The reference in sub-paragraph (2)(a)(ii) to the company's business is to that business as the company proposes to carry it on during the remainder of the moratorium.

     (4) If the nominee withdraws his consent to act, the moratorium comes to an end.

     (5) If the nominee withdraws his consent to act he must, in accordance with the rules, notify the court, the registrar of companies, the company and any creditor of the company of whose claim he is aware of his withdrawal and the reason for it.

     (6) If the nominee without reasonable excuse fails to comply with sub-paragraph (5), he is liable to a fine.

Challenge of nominee's actions, etc

26.— (1) If any creditor, director or member of the company, or any other person affected by a moratorium, is dissatisfied by any act, omission or decision of the nominee during the moratorium, he may apply to the court.

     (2) An application under sub-paragraph (1) may be made during the moratorium or after it has ended.

(3) On an application under sub-paragraph (1) the court may—

    (a) confirm, reverse or modify any act or decision of the nominee,

    (b) give him directions, or

    (c) make such other order as it thinks fit.

(4) An order under sub-paragraph (3) may (among other things) bring the moratorium to an end and make such consequential provision as the court thinks fit.

27.— (1) Where there are reasonable grounds for believing that—

    (a) as a result of any act, omission or decision of the nominee during the moratorium, the company has suffered loss, but

    (b) the company does not intend to pursue any claim it may have against the nominee,

any creditor of the company may apply to the court.

(2) An application under sub-paragraph (1) may be made during the moratorium or after it has ended.

(3) On an application under sub-paragraph (1) the court may—

    (a) order the company to pursue any claim against the nominee,

    (b) authorise any creditor to pursue such a claim in the name of the company, or

    (c) make such other order with respect to such a claim as it thinks fit,

unless the court is satisfied that the act, omission or decision of the nominee was in all the circumstances reasonable.

(4) An order under sub-paragraph (3) may (among other things)—

    (a) impose conditions on any authority given to pursue a claim,

    (b) direct the company to assist in the pursuit of a claim,

    (c) make directions with respect to the distribution of anything received as a result of the pursuit of a claim,

    (d) bring the moratorium to an end and make such consequential provision as the court thinks fit.

(5) On an application under sub-paragraph (1) the court shall have regard to the interests of the members and creditors of the company generally.

...

PART V
CONSIDERATION AND IMPLEMENTATION OF VOLUNTARY ARRANGEMENT

Summoning of meetings

29.— (1) Where a moratorium is in force, the nominee shall summon meetings of the company and its creditors for such a time, date (within the period for the time being specified in paragraph 8(3)) and place as he thinks fit.

(2) The persons to be summoned to a creditors' meeting under this paragraph are every creditor of the company of whose claim the nominee is aware.

Conduct of meetings

30.— (1) Subject to the provisions of paragraphs 31 to 35, the meetings summoned under paragraph 29 shall be conducted in accordance with the rules.

(2) A meeting so summoned may resolve that it be adjourned (or further adjourned).

(3) After the conclusion of either meeting in accordance with the rules, the chairman of the meeting shall report the result of the meeting to the court, and, immediately after reporting to the court, shall give notice of the result of the meeting to such persons as may be prescribed.

Approval of voluntary arrangement

31.— (1) The meetings summoned under paragraph 29 shall decide whether to approve the proposed voluntary arrangement (with or without modifications).

(2) The modifications may include one conferring the functions proposed to be conferred on the nominee on another person qualified to act as an insolvency practitioner, or authorised to act as nominee, in relation to the voluntary arrangement.

(3)   The modifications shall not include one by virtue of which the proposal ceases to be a proposal such as is mentioned in section 1.

(4)   A meeting summoned under paragraph 29 shall not approve any proposal or modification which affects the right of a secured creditor of the company to enforce his security, except with the concurrence of the creditor concerned.

(5)   Subject to sub-paragraph (6), a meeting so summoned shall not approve any proposal or modification under which—

(a)   any preferential debt of the company is to be paid otherwise than in priority to such of its debts as are not preferential debts, or

(b)   a preferential creditor of the company is to be paid an amount in respect of a preferential debt that bears to that debt a smaller proportion than is borne to another preferential debt by the amount that is to be paid in respect of that other debt.

(6)   The meeting may approve such a proposal or modification with the concurrence of the preferential creditor concerned.

(7)   The directors of the company may, before the beginning of the period of seven days which ends with the meetings (or either of them) summoned under paragraph 29 being held, give notice to the nominee of any modifications of the proposal for which the directors intend to seek the approval of those meetings.

(8)   References in this paragraph to preferential debts and preferential creditors are to be read in accordance with section 386 in Part XII of this Act.

Extension of moratorium

32.— (1)   Subject to sub-paragraph (2), a meeting summoned under paragraph 29 which resolves that it be adjourned (or further adjourned) may resolve that the moratorium be extended (or further extended), with or without conditions.

(2)   The moratorium may not be extended (or further extended) to a day later than the end of the period of two months which begins—

(a)   where both meetings summoned under paragraph 29 are first held on the same day, with that day,

(b)   in any other case, with the day on which the later of those meetings is first held.

(3)   At any meeting where it is proposed to extend (or further extend) the moratorium, before a decision is taken with respect to that proposal, the nominee shall inform the meeting—

(a)   of what he has done in order to comply with his duty under paragraph 24 and the cost of his actions for the company, and

(b)   of what he intends to do to continue to comply with that duty if the moratorium is extended (or further extended) and the expected cost of his actions for the company.

(4)   Where, in accordance with sub-paragraph (3)(b), the nominee informs a meeting of the expected cost of his intended actions, the meeting shall resolve whether or not to approve that expected cost.

(5)   If a decision not to approve the expected cost of the nominee's intended actions has effect under paragraph 36, the moratorium comes to an end.

(6)   A meeting may resolve that a moratorium which has been extended (or further extended) be brought to an end before the end of the period of the extension (or further extension).

(7)   The Secretary of State may by order increase or reduce the period for the time being specified in sub-paragraph (2).

...

Moratorium committee

35.— (1)   A meeting summoned under paragraph 29 which resolves that the moratorium be extended (or further extended) may, with the consent of the nominee, resolve that a committee be established to exercise the functions conferred on it by the meeting.

(2)   The meeting may not so resolve unless it has approved an estimate of the expenses to be incurred by the committee in the exercise of the proposed functions.

(3)   Any expenses, not exceeding the amount of the estimate, incurred by the committee in the exercise of its functions shall be reimbursed by the nominee.

(4) The committee shall cease to exist when the moratorium comes to an end.

Effectiveness of decisions

36.— (1) Sub-paragraph (2) applies to references to one of the following decisions having effect, that is, a decision, under paragraph 31, 32 or 35, with respect to—
  (a) the approval of a proposed voluntary arrangement,
  (b) the extension (or further extension) of a moratorium,
  (c) the bringing of a moratorium to an end,
  (d) the establishment of a committee, or
  (e) the approval of the expected cost of a nominee's intended actions.

(2) The decision has effect if, in accordance with the rules—
  (a) it has been taken by both meetings summoned under paragraph 29, or
  (b) (subject to any order made under sub-paragraph (5)) it has been taken by the creditors' meeting summoned under that paragraph.

(3) If a decision taken by the creditors' meeting under any of paragraphs 31, 32 or 35 with respect to any of the matters mentioned in sub-paragraph (1) differs from one so taken by the company meeting with respect to that matter, a member of the company may apply to the court.

(4) An application under sub-paragraph (3) shall not be made after the end of the period of 28 days beginning with—
  (a) the day on which the decision was taken by the creditors' meeting, or
  (b) where the decision of the company meeting was taken on a later day, that day.

(5) On an application under sub-paragraph (3), the court may—
  (a) order the decision of the company meeting to have effect instead of the decision of the creditors' meeting, or
  (b) make such other order as it thinks fit.

Effect of approval of voluntary arrangement

37.— (1) This paragraph applies where a decision approving a voluntary arrangement has effect under paragraph 36.

(2) The approved voluntary arrangement—
  (a) takes effect as if made by the company at the creditors' meeting, and
  (b) binds every person who in accordance with the rules—
    (i) was entitled to vote at that meeting (whether or not he was present or represented at it), or
    (ii) would have been so entitled if he had had notice of it,
  as if he were a party to the voluntary arrangement.

(3) If—
  (a) when the arrangement ceases to have effect any amount payable under the arrangement to a person bound by virtue of sub-paragraph (2)(b)(ii) has not been paid, and
  (b) the arrangement did not come to an end prematurely,
  the company shall at that time become liable to pay to that person the amount payable under the arrangement.

(4) Where a petition for the winding up of the company, other than an excepted petition within the meaning of paragraph 12, was presented before the beginning of the moratorium, the court shall dismiss the petition.

(5) The court shall not dismiss a petition under sub-paragraph (4)—
  (a) at any time before the end of the period of 28 days beginning with the first day on which each of the reports of the meetings required by paragraph 30(3) has been made to the court, or
  (b) at any time when an application under paragraph 38 or an appeal in respect of such an application is pending, or at any time in the period within which such an appeal may be brought.

Challenge of decisions

38.— (1) Subject to the following provisions of this paragraph, any of the persons mentioned in sub-paragraph (2) may apply to the court on one or both of the following grounds—

 (a) that a voluntary arrangement approved at one or both of the meetings summoned under paragraph 29 and which has taken effect unfairly prejudices the interests of a creditor, member or contributory of the company,

 (b) that there has been some material irregularity at or in relation to either of those meetings.

(2) The persons who may apply under this paragraph are—

 (a) a person entitled, in accordance with the rules, to vote at either of the meetings,

 (b) a person who would have been entitled, in accordance with the rules, to vote at the creditors' meeting if he had had notice of it, and

 (c) the nominee.

(3) An application under this paragraph shall not be made—

 (a) after the end of the period of 28 days beginning with the first day on which each of the reports required by paragraph 30(3) has been made to the court, or

 (b) in the case of a person who was not given notice of the creditors' meeting, after the end of the period of 28 days beginning with the day on which he became aware that the meeting had taken place,

but (subject to that) an application made by a person within sub-paragraph (2)(b) on the ground that the arrangement prejudices his interests may be made after the arrangement has ceased to have effect, unless it came to an end prematurely.

(4) Where on an application under this paragraph the court is satisfied as to either of the grounds mentioned in sub-paragraph (1), it may do any of the following—

 (a) revoke or suspend—

  (i) any decision approving the voluntary arrangement which has effect under paragraph 36, or

  (ii) in a case falling within sub-paragraph (1)(b), any decision taken by the meeting in question which has effect under that paragraph,

 (b) give a direction to any person—

  (i) for the summoning of further meetings to consider any revised proposal for a voluntary arrangement which the directors may make, or

  (ii) in a case falling within sub-paragraph (1)(b), for the summoning of a further company or (as the case may be) creditors' meeting to reconsider the original proposal.

(5) Where at any time after giving a direction under sub-paragraph (4)(b)(i) the court is satisfied that the directors do not intend to submit a revised proposal, the court shall revoke the direction and revoke or suspend any decision approving the voluntary arrangement which has effect under paragraph 36.

(6) Where the court gives a direction under sub-paragraph (4)(b), it may also give a direction continuing or, as the case may require, renewing, for such period as may be specified in the direction, the effect of the moratorium.

(7) Sub-paragraph (8) applies in a case where the court, on an application under this paragraph—

 (a) gives a direction under sub-paragraph (4)(b), or

 (b) revokes or suspends a decision under sub-paragraph (4)(a) or (5).

(8) In such a case, the court may give such supplemental directions as it thinks fit and, in particular, directions with respect to—

 (a) things done under the voluntary arrangement since it took effect, and

 (b) such things done since that time as could not have been done if a moratorium had been in force in relation to the company when they were done.

(9) Except in pursuance of the preceding provisions of this paragraph, a decision taken at a meeting summoned under paragraph 29 is not invalidated by any irregularity at or in relation to the meeting.

Implementation of voluntary arrangement

39.— (1) This paragraph applies where a voluntary arrangement approved by one or both of the meetings summoned under paragraph 29 has taken effect.

(2) The person who is for the time being carrying out in relation to the voluntary arrangement the functions conferred—

(a) by virtue of the approval of the arrangement, on the nominee, or

(b) by virtue of paragraph 31(2), on a person other than the nominee,

shall be known as the supervisor of the voluntary arrangement.

(3) If any of the company's creditors or any other person is dissatisfied by any act, omission or decision of the supervisor, he may apply to the court.

(4) On an application under sub-paragraph (3) the court may—

(a) confirm, reverse or modify any act or decision of the supervisor,

(b) give him directions, or

(c) make such other order as it thinks fit.

(5) The supervisor—

(a) may apply to the court for directions in relation to any particular matter arising under the voluntary arrangement, and

(b) is included among the persons who may apply to the court for the winding up of the company or for an administration order to be made in relation to it.

(6) The court may, whenever—

(a) it is expedient to appoint a person to carry out the functions of the supervisor, and

(b) it is inexpedient, difficult or impracticable for an appointment to be made without the assistance of the court,

make an order appointing a person who is qualified to act as an insolvency practitioner, or authorised to act as supervisor, in relation to the voluntary arrangement, either in substitution for the existing supervisor or to fill a vacancy.

(7) The power conferred by sub-paragraph (6) is exercisable so as to increase the number of persons exercising the functions of supervisor or, where there is more than one person exercising those functions, so as to replace one or more of those persons.

PART VI
MISCELLANEOUS

Challenge of director's actions

40.— (1) This paragraph applies in relation to acts or omissions of the directors of a company during a moratorium.

(2) A creditor or member of the company may apply to the court for an order under this paragraph on the ground—

(a) that the company's affairs, business and property are being or have been managed by the directors in a manner which is unfairly prejudicial to the interests of its creditors or members generally, or of some part of its creditors or members (including at least the petitioner), or

(b) that any actual or proposed act or omission of the directors is or would be so prejudicial.

(3) An application for an order under this paragraph may be made during or after the moratorium.

(4) On an application for an order under this paragraph the court may—

(a) make such order as it thinks fit for giving relief in respect of the matters complained of,

(b) adjourn the hearing conditionally or unconditionally, or

(c) make an interim order or any other order that it thinks fit.

(5) An order under this paragraph may in particular—

(a) regulate the management by the directors of the company's affairs, business and property during the remainder of the moratorium,

      (b)   require the directors to refrain from doing or continuing an act complained of by the petitioner, or to do an act which the petitioner has complained they have omitted to do,

      (c)   require the summoning of a meeting of creditors or members for the purpose of considering such matters as the court may direct,

      (d)   bring the moratorium to an end and make such consequential provision as the court thinks fit.

(6)   In making an order under this paragraph the court shall have regard to the need to safeguard the interests of persons who have dealt with the company in good faith and for value.

(7)   Sub-paragraph (8) applies where—

      (a)   the appointment of an administrator has effect in relation to the company and that appointment was in pursuance of—

          (i)   an administration application made, or

          (ii)   a notice of intention to appoint filed,

      before the moratorium came into force, or

      (b)   the company is being wound up in pursuance of a petition presented before the moratorium came into force.

(8)   No application for an order under this paragraph may be made by a creditor or member of the company; but such an application may be made instead by the administrator or (as the case may be) the liquidator.

Offences

41.—   (1)   This paragraph applies where a moratorium has been obtained for a company.

      (2)   If, within the period of 12 months ending with the day on which the moratorium came into force, a person who was at the time an officer of the company—

          (a)   did any of the things mentioned in paragraphs (a) to (f) of sub-paragraph (4), or

          (b)   was privy to the doing by others of any of the things mentioned in paragraphs (c), (d) and (e) of that sub-paragraph,

      he is to be treated as having committed an offence at that time.

      (3)   If, at any time during the moratorium, a person who is an officer of the company—

          (a)   does any of the things mentioned in paragraphs (a) to (f) of sub-paragraph (4), or

          (b)   is privy to the doing by others of any of the things mentioned in paragraphs (c), (d) and (e) of that sub-paragraph,

      he commits an offence.

      (4)   Those things are—

          (a)   concealing any part of the company's property to the value of £500 or more, or concealing any debt due to or from the company, or

          (b)   fraudulently removing any part of the company's property to the value of £500 or more, or

          (c)   concealing, destroying, mutilating or falsifying any book or paper affecting or relating to the company's property or affairs, or

          (d)   making any false entry in any book or paper affecting or relating to the company's property or affairs, or

          (e)   fraudulently parting with, altering or making any omission in any document affecting or relating to the company's property or affairs, or

          (f)   pawning, pledging or disposing of any property of the company which has been obtained on credit and has not been paid for (unless the pawning, pledging or disposal was in the ordinary way of the company's business).

      (5)   For the purposes of this paragraph, "officer" includes a shadow director.

      (6)   It is a defence—

          (a)   for a person charged under sub-paragraph (2) or (3) in respect of the things mentioned in paragraph (a) or (f) of sub-paragraph (4) to prove that he had no intent to defraud, and

(b)   for a person charged under sub-paragraph (2) or (3) in respect of the things mentioned in paragraph (c) or (d) of sub-paragraph (4) to prove that he had no intent to conceal the state of affairs of the company or to defeat the law.

(7)   Where a person pawns, pledges or disposes of any property of a company in circumstances which amount to an offence under sub-paragraph (2) or (3), every person who takes in pawn or pledge, or otherwise receives, the property knowing it to be pawned, pledged or disposed of in circumstances which—

   (a)   would, if a moratorium were obtained for the company within the period of 12 months beginning with the day on which the pawning, pledging or disposal took place, amount to an offence under sub-paragraph (2), or

   (b)   amount to an offence under sub-paragraph (3),

commits an offence.

(8)   A person guilty of an offence under this paragraph is liable to imprisonment or a fine, or both.

...

...

Void provisions in floating charge documents

43.—   (1)   A provision in an instrument creating a floating charge is void if it provides for—

   (a)   obtaining a moratorium, or

   (b)   anything done with a view to obtaining a moratorium (including any preliminary decision or investigation),

to be an event causing the floating charge to crystallise or causing restrictions which would not otherwise apply to be imposed on the disposal of property by the company or a ground for the appointment of a receiver.

(2)   In sub-paragraph (1), "receiver" includes a manager and a person who is appointed both receiver and manager.

...

SCHEDULE B1
ADMINISTRATION

NATURE OF ADMINISTRATION

Administration

1.—   (1)   For the purposes of this Act "administrator" of a company means a person appointed under this Schedule to manage the company's affairs, business and property.

(2)   For the purposes of this Act—

   (a)   a company is "in administration" while the appointment of an administrator of the company has effect,

   (b)   a company "enters administration" when the appointment of an administrator takes effect,

   (c)   a company ceases to be in administration when the appointment of an administrator of the company ceases to have effect in accordance with this Schedule, and

   (d)   a company does not cease to be in administration merely because an administrator vacates office (by reason of resignation, death or otherwise) or is removed from office.

2.—   A person may be appointed as administrator of a company—

   (a)   by administration order of the court under paragraph 10,

   (b)   by the holder of a floating charge under paragraph 14, or

   (c)   by the company or its directors under paragraph 22.

Purpose of administration

3.—   (1)   The administrator of a company must perform his functions with the objective of—

   (a)   rescuing the company as a going concern, or

   (b)   achieving a better result for the company's creditors as a whole than would be likely if the company were wound up (without first being in administration), or

(c)   realising property in order to make a distribution to one or more secured or preferential creditors.

(2)   Subject to sub-paragraph (4), the administrator of a company must perform his functions in the interests of the company's creditors as a whole.

(3)   The administrator must perform his functions with the objective specified in sub-paragraph (1)(a) unless he thinks either—

(a)   that it is not reasonably practicable to achieve that objective, or

(b)   that the objective specified in sub-paragraph (1)(b) would achieve a better result for the company's creditors as a whole.

(4)   The administrator may perform his functions with the objective specified in sub-paragraph (1)(c) only if—

(a)   he thinks that it is not reasonably practicable to achieve either of the objectives specified in sub-paragraph (1)(a) and (b), and

(b)   he does not unnecessarily harm the interests of the creditors of the company as a whole.

4.   The administrator of a company must perform his functions as quickly and efficiently as is reasonably practicable.

Status of administrator

5.   An administrator is an officer of the court (whether or not he is appointed by the court).

General restrictions

6.   A person may be appointed as administrator of a company only if he is qualified to act as an insolvency practitioner in relation to the company.

7.   A person may not be appointed as administrator of a company which is in administration (subject to the provisions of paragraphs 90 to 97 and 100 to 103 about replacement and additional administrators).

8.   (1)   A person may not be appointed as administrator of a company which is in liquidation by virtue of—

(a)   a resolution for voluntary winding up, or

(b)   a winding-up order.

(2)   Sub-paragraph (1)(a) is subject to paragraph 38.

(3)   Sub-paragraph (1)(b) is subject to paragraphs 37 and 38.

9.—   (1)   A person may not be appointed as administrator of a company which—

(a)   has a liability in respect of a deposit which it accepted in accordance with the Banking Act 1979 or 1987, but

(b)   is not an authorised deposit taker.

(2)   A person may not be appointed as administrator of a company which effects or carries out contracts of insurance.

(3)   But sub-paragraph (2) does not apply to a company which—

(a)   is exempt from the general prohibition in relation to effecting or carrying out contracts of insurance, or

(b)   is an authorised deposit taker effecting or carrying out contracts of insurance in the course of a banking business.

(4)   In this paragraph—

"authorised deposit taker" means a person with permission under Part IV of the Financial Services and Markets Act 2000 to accept deposits, and

"the general prohibition" has the meaning given by section 19 of that Act.

(5)   This paragraph shall be construed in accordance with—

(a)   section 22 of the Financial Services and Markets Act 2000 (classes of regulated activity and categories of investment),

(b)   any relevant order under that section, and

(c)   Schedule 2 to that Act (regulated activities).

APPOINTMENT OF ADMINISTRATOR BY COURT

Administration order

10. An administration order is an order appointing a person as the administrator of a company.

Conditions for making order

11. The court may make an administration order in relation to a company only if satisfied—
   (a) that the company is or is likely to become unable to pay its debts, and
   (b) that the administration order is reasonably likely to achieve the purpose of administration.

Administration application

12.— (1) An application to the court for an administration order in respect of a company (an "administration application") may be made only by—
   (a) the company,
   (b) the directors of the company,
   (c) one or more creditors of the company,
   (d) the designated officer for a magistrates' court in the exercise of the power conferred by section 87A of the Magistrates' Courts Act 1980 (c 43) (fine imposed on company), or
   (e) a combination of persons listed in paragraphs (a) to (d).
   (2) As soon as is reasonably practicable after the making of an administration application the applicant shall notify—
   (a) any person who has appointed an administrative receiver of the company,
   (b) any person who is or may be entitled to appoint an administrative receiver of the company,
   (c) any person who is or may be entitled to appoint an administrator of the company under paragraph 14, and
   (d) such other persons as may be prescribed.
   (3) An administration application may not be withdrawn without the permission of the court.
   (4) In sub-paragraph (1) "creditor" includes a contingent creditor and a prospective creditor.
   (5) Sub-paragraph (1) is without prejudice to section 7(4)(b).

Powers of court

13.— (1) On hearing an administration application the court may—
   (a) make the administration order sought;
   (b) dismiss the application;
   (c) adjourn the hearing conditionally or unconditionally;
   (d) make an interim order;
   (e) treat the application as a winding-up petition and make any order which the court could make under section 125;
   (f) make any other order which the court thinks appropriate.
   (2) An appointment of an administrator by administration order takes effect—
   (a) at a time appointed by the order, or
   (b) where no time is appointed by the order, when the order is made.
   (3) An interim order under sub-paragraph (1)(d) may, in particular—
   (a) restrict the exercise of a power of the directors or the company;
   (b) make provision conferring a discretion on the court or on a person qualified to act as an insolvency practitioner in relation to the company.
   (4) This paragraph is subject to paragraph 39.

APPOINTMENT OF ADMINISTRATOR BY HOLDER OF FLOATING CHARGE

Power to appoint

14.— (1) The holder of a qualifying floating charge in respect of a company's property may appoint an administrator of the company.

(2) For the purposes of sub-paragraph (1) a floating charge qualifies if created by an instrument which—

    (a) states that this paragraph applies to the floating charge,

    (b) purports to empower the holder of the floating charge to appoint an administrator of the company,

    (c) purports to empower the holder of the floating charge to make an appointment which would be the appointment of an administrative receiver within the meaning given by section 29(2), or

    (d) purports to empower the holder of a floating charge in Scotland to appoint a receiver who on appointment would be an administrative receiver.

(3) For the purposes of sub-paragraph (1) a person is the holder of a qualifying floating charge in respect of a company's property if he holds one or more debentures of the company secured—

    (a) by a qualifying floating charge which relates to the whole or substantially the whole of the company's property,

    (b) by a number of qualifying floating charges which together relate to the whole or substantially the whole of the company's property, or

    (c) by charges and other forms of security which together relate to the whole or substantially the whole of the company's property and at least one of which is a qualifying floating charge.

Restrictions on power to appoint

15.— (1) A person may not appoint an administrator under paragraph 14 unless—

    (a) he has given at least two business days' written notice to the holder of any prior floating charge which satisfies paragraph 14(2), or

    (b) the holder of any prior floating charge which satisfies paragraph 14(2) has consented in writing to the making of the appointment.

(2) One floating charge is prior to another for the purposes of this paragraph if—

    (a) it was created first, or

    (b) it is to be treated as having priority in accordance with an agreement to which the holder of each floating charge was party.

(3) Sub-paragraph (2) shall have effect in relation to Scotland as if the following were substituted for paragraph (a)—

    "(a) it has priority of ranking in accordance with section 464(4)(b) of the Companies Act 1985".

16. An administrator may not be appointed under paragraph 14 while a floating charge on which the appointment relies is not enforceable.

17. An administrator of a company may not be appointed under paragraph 14 if—

    (a) a provisional liquidator of the company has been appointed under section 135, or

    (b) an administrative receiver of the company is in office.

Notice of appointment

18.— (1) A person who appoints an administrator of a company under paragraph 14 shall file with the court—

    (a) a notice of appointment, and

    (b) such other documents as may be prescribed.

(2) The notice of appointment must include a statutory declaration by or on behalf of the person who makes the appointment—

    (a) that the person is the holder of a qualifying floating charge in respect of the company's property,

    (b) that each floating charge relied on in making the appointment is (or was) enforceable on the date of the appointment, and

    (c) that the appointment is in accordance with this Schedule.

(3) The notice of appointment must identify the administrator and must be accompanied by a statement by the administrator—

        (a)   that he consents to the appointment,

        (b)   that in his opinion the purpose of administration is reasonably likely to be achieved, and

        (c)   giving such other information and opinions as may be prescribed.

  (4)   For the purpose of a statement under sub-paragraph (3) an administrator may rely on information supplied by directors of the company (unless he has reason to doubt its accuracy).

  (5)   The notice of appointment and any document accompanying it must be in the prescribed form.

  (6)   A statutory declaration under sub-paragraph (2) must be made during the prescribed period.

  (7)   A person commits an offence if in a statutory declaration under sub-paragraph (2) he makes a statement—

        (a)   which is false, and

        (b)   which he does not reasonably believe to be true.

Commencement of appointment

19.   The appointment of an administrator under paragraph 14 takes effect when the requirements of paragraph 18 are satisfied.

...

21.— (1)   This paragraph applies where—

        (a)   a person purports to appoint an administrator under paragraph 14, and

        (b)   the appointment is discovered to be invalid.

  (2)   The court may order the person who purported to make the appointment to indemnify the person appointed against liability which arises solely by reason of the appointment's invalidity.

APPOINTMENT OF ADMINISTRATOR BY COMPANY OR DIRECTORS

Power to appoint

22.— (1)   A company may appoint an administrator.

  (2)   The directors of a company may appoint an administrator.

Restrictions on power to appoint

23.— (1)   This paragraph applies where an administrator of a company is appointed—

        (a)   under paragraph 22, or

        (b)   on an administration application made by the company or its directors.

  (2)   An administrator of the company may not be appointed under paragraph 22 during the period of 12 months beginning with the date on which the appointment referred to in sub-paragraph (1) ceases to have effect.

24.— (1)   If a moratorium for a company under Schedule A1 ends on a date when no voluntary arrangement is in force in respect of the company, this paragraph applies for the period of 12 months beginning with that date.

  (2)   This paragraph also applies for the period of 12 months beginning with the date on which a voluntary arrangement in respect of a company ends if—

        (a)   the arrangement was made during a moratorium for the company under Schedule A1, and

        (b)   the arrangement ends prematurely (within the meaning of section 7B).

  (3)   While this paragraph applies, an administrator of the company may not be appointed under paragraph 22.

25.   An administrator of a company may not be appointed under paragraph 22 if—

  (a)   a petition for the winding up of the company has been presented and is not yet disposed of,

  (b)   an administration application has been made and is not yet disposed of, or

  (c)   an administrative receiver of the company is in office.

Notice of intention to appoint

26.— (1)   A person who proposes to make an appointment under paragraph 22 shall give at least five business days' written notice to—
   (a)   any person who is or may be entitled to appoint an administrative receiver of the company, and
   (b)   any person who is or may be entitled to appoint an administrator of the company under paragraph 14.
(2)   A person who proposes to make an appointment under paragraph 22 shall also give such notice as may be prescribed to such other persons as may be prescribed.
(3)   A notice under this paragraph must—
   (a)   identify the proposed administrator, and
   (b)   be in the prescribed form.

...

Commencement of appointment

31.   The appointment of an administrator under paragraph 22 takes effect when the requirements of paragraph 29 are satisfied.

32.   A person who appoints an administrator under paragraph 22—
   (a)   shall notify the administrator and such other persons as may be prescribed as soon as is reasonably practicable after the requirements of paragraph 29 are satisfied, and
   (b)   commits an offence if he fails without reasonable excuse to comply with paragraph (a).

33.   If before the requirements of paragraph 29 are satisfied the company enters administration by virtue of an administration order or an appointment under paragraph 14—
   (a)   the appointment under paragraph 22 shall not take effect, and
   (b)   paragraph 32 shall not apply.

Invalid appointment: indemnity

34.— (1)   This paragraph applies where—
   (a)   a person purports to appoint an administrator under paragraph 22, and
   (b)   the appointment is discovered to be invalid.
(2)   The court may order the person who purported to make the appointment to indemnify the person appointed against liability which arises solely by reason of the appointment's invalidity.

ADMINISTRATION APPLICATION—SPECIAL CASES

Application by holder of floating charge

35.— (1)   This paragraph applies where an administration application in respect of a company—
   (a)   is made by the holder of a qualifying floating charge in respect of the company's property, and
   (b)   includes a statement that the application is made in reliance on this paragraph.
(2)   The court may make an administration order—
   (a)   whether or not satisfied that the company is or is likely to become unable to pay its debts, but
   (b)   only if satisfied that the applicant could appoint an administrator under paragraph 14.

Intervention by holder of floating charge

36.— (1)   This paragraph applies where—
   (a)   an administration application in respect of a company is made by a person who is not the holder of a qualifying floating charge in respect of the company's property, and
   (b)   the holder of a qualifying floating charge in respect of the company's property applies to the court to have a specified person appointed as administrator (and not the person specified by the administration applicant).
(2)   The court shall grant an application under sub-paragraph (1)(b) unless the court thinks it right to refuse the application because of the particular circumstances of the case.

Application where company in liquidation

37.— (1) This paragraph applies where the holder of a qualifying floating charge in respect of a company's property could appoint an administrator under paragraph 14 but for paragraph 8(1)(b).

(2) The holder of the qualifying floating charge may make an administration application.

(3) If the court makes an administration order on hearing an application made by virtue of sub-paragraph (2)—

    (a) the court shall discharge the winding-up order,

    (b) the court shall make provision for such matters as may be prescribed,

    (c) the court may make other consequential provision,

    (d) the court shall specify which of the powers under this Schedule are to be exercisable by the administrator, and

    (e) this Schedule shall have effect with such modifications as the court may specify.

38.— (1) The liquidator of a company may make an administration application.

(2) If the court makes an administration order on hearing an application made by virtue of sub-paragraph (1)—

    (a) the court shall discharge any winding-up order in respect of the company,

    (b) the court shall make provision for such matters as may be prescribed,

    (c) the court may make other consequential provision,

    (d) the court shall specify which of the powers under this Schedule are to be exercisable by the administrator, and

    (e) this Schedule shall have effect with such modifications as the court may specify.

Effect of administrative receivership

39.— (1) Where there is an administrative receiver of a company the court must dismiss an administration application in respect of the company unless—

    (a) the person by or on behalf of whom the receiver was appointed consents to the making of the administration order,

    (b) the court thinks that the security by virtue of which the receiver was appointed would be liable to be released or discharged under sections 238 to 240 (transaction at undervalue and preference) if an administration order were made,

    (c) the court thinks that the security by virtue of which the receiver was appointed would be avoided under section 245 (avoidance of floating charge) if an administration order were made, or

    (d) the court thinks that the security by virtue of which the receiver was appointed would be challengeable under section 242 (gratuitous alienations) or 243 (unfair preferences) or under any rule of law in Scotland.

(2) Sub-paragraph (1) applies whether the administrative receiver is appointed before or after the making of the administration application.

EFFECT OF ADMINISTRATION

Dismissal of pending winding-up petition

40.— (1) A petition for the winding up of a company—

    (a) shall be dismissed on the making of an administration order in respect of the company, and

    (b) shall be suspended while the company is in administration following an appointment under paragraph 14.

    ...

(3) Where an administrator becomes aware that a petition was presented under a provision referred to in sub-paragraph (2) before his appointment, he shall apply to the court for directions under paragraph 63.

Dismissal of administrative or other receiver

41.— (1) When an administration order takes effect in respect of a company any administrative receiver of the company shall vacate office.

(2) Where a company is in administration, any receiver of part of the company's property shall vacate office if the administrator requires him to.

(3) Where an administrative receiver or receiver vacates office under sub-paragraph (1) or (2)—

    (a) his remuneration shall be charged on and paid out of any property of the company which was in his custody or under his control immediately before he vacated office, and

    (b) he need not take any further steps under section 40 or 59.

(4) In the application of sub-paragraph (3)(a)—

    (a) "remuneration" includes expenses properly incurred and any indemnity to which the administrative receiver or receiver is entitled out of the assets of the company,

    (b) the charge imposed takes priority over security held by the person by whom or on whose behalf the administrative receiver or receiver was appointed, and

    (c) the provision for payment is subject to paragraph 43.

Moratorium on insolvency proceedings

42.— (1) This paragraph applies to a company in administration.

(2) No resolution may be passed for the winding up of the company.

(3) No order may be made for the winding up of the company.

…

Moratorium on other legal process

43.— (1) This paragraph applies to a company in administration.

(2) No step may be taken to enforce security over the company's property except—

    (a) with the consent of the administrator, or

    (b) with the permission of the court.

(3) No step may be taken to repossess goods in the company's possession under a hire-purchase agreement except—

    (a) with the consent of the administrator, or

    (b) with the permission of the court.

(4) A landlord may not exercise a right of forfeiture by peaceable re-entry in relation to premises let to the company except—

    (a) with the consent of the administrator, or

    (b) with the permission of the court.

…

(6) No legal process (including legal proceedings, execution, distress and diligence) may be instituted or continued against the company or property of the company except—

    (a) with the consent of the administrator, or

    (b) with the permission of the court.

(6A) An administrative receiver of the company may not be appointed.

(7) Where the court gives permission for a transaction under this paragraph it may impose a condition on or a requirement in connection with the transaction.

(8) In this paragraph "landlord" includes a person to whom rent is payable.

Interim moratorium

44.— (1) This paragraph applies where an administration application in respect of a company has been made and—

    (a) the application has not yet been granted or dismissed, or

    (b) the application has been granted but the administration order has not yet taken effect.

(2) This paragraph also applies from the time when a copy of notice of intention to appoint an administrator under paragraph 14 is filed with the court until—

      (a)   the appointment of the administrator takes effect, or

      (b)   the period of five business days beginning with the date of filing expires without an administrator having been appointed.

(3)   Sub-paragraph (2) has effect in relation to a notice of intention to appoint only if it is in the prescribed form.

(4)   This paragraph also applies from the time when a copy of notice of intention to appoint an administrator is filed with the court under paragraph 27(1) until—

      (a)   the appointment of the administrator takes effect, or

      (b)   the period specified in paragraph 28(2) expires without an administrator having been appointed.

(5)   The provisions of paragraphs 42 and 43 shall apply (ignoring any reference to the consent of the administrator).

(6)   If there is an administrative receiver of the company when the administration application is made, the provisions of paragraphs 42 and 43 shall not begin to apply by virtue of this paragraph until the person by or on behalf of whom the receiver was appointed consents to the making of the administration order.

(7)   This paragraph does not prevent or require the permission of the court for—

      (a)   the presentation of a petition for the winding up of the company under a provision mentioned in paragraph 42(4),

      (b)   the appointment of an administrator under paragraph 14,

      (c)   the appointment of an administrative receiver of the company, or

      (d)   the carrying out by an administrative receiver (whenever appointed) of his functions.

Publicity

45.— (1)   While a company is in administration every business document issued by or on behalf of the company or the administrator must state—

      (a)   the name of the administrator, and

      (b)   that the affairs, business and property of the company are being managed by him.

(2)   Any of the following commits an offence if without reasonable excuse he authorises or permits a contravention of sub-paragraph (1)—

      (a)   the administrator,

      (b)   an officer of the company, and

      (c)   the company.

(3)   In sub-paragraph (1) "business document" means—

      (a)   an invoice,

      (b)   an order for goods or services, and

      (c)   a business letter.

PROCESS OF ADMINISTRATION

Announcement of administrator's appointment

46.— (1)   This paragraph applies where a person becomes the administrator of a company.

(2)   As soon as is reasonably practicable the administrator shall—

      (a)   send a notice of his appointment to the company, and

      (b)   publish a notice of his appointment in the prescribed manner.

(3)   As soon as is reasonably practicable the administrator shall—

      (a)   obtain a list of the company's creditors, and

      (b)   send a notice of his appointment to each creditor of whose claim and address he is aware.

(4)   The administrator shall send a notice of his appointment to the registrar of companies before the end of the period of 7 days beginning with the date specified in sub-paragraph (6).

(5)   The administrator shall send a notice of his appointment to such persons as may be prescribed before the end of the prescribed period beginning with the date specified in sub-paragraph (6).

(6)   The date for the purpose of sub-paragraphs (4) and (5) is—

(a)   in the case of an administrator appointed by administration order, the date of the order,
(b)   in the case of an administrator appointed under paragraph 14, the date on which he receives notice under paragraph 20, and
(c)   in the case of an administrator appointed under paragraph 22, the date on which he receives notice under paragraph 32.

(7)   The court may direct that sub-paragraph (3)(b) or (5)—
(a)   shall not apply, or
(b)   shall apply with the substitution of a different period.

(8)   A notice under this paragraph must—
(a)   contain the prescribed information, and
(b)   be in the prescribed form.

(9)   An administrator commits an offence if he fails without reasonable excuse to comply with a requirement of this paragraph.

Statement of company's affairs

47.—   (1)   As soon as is reasonably practicable after appointment the administrator of a company shall by notice in the prescribed form require one or more relevant persons to provide the administrator with a statement of the affairs of the company.

(2)   The statement must—
(a)   be verified by a statement of truth in accordance with Civil Procedure Rules,
(b)   be in the prescribed form,
(c)   give particulars of the company's property, debts and liabilities,
(d)   give the names and addresses of the company's creditors,
(e)   specify the security held by each creditor,
(f)   give the date on which each security was granted, and
(g)   contain such other information as may be prescribed.

(3)   In sub-paragraph (1) "relevant person" means—
(a)   a person who is or has been an officer of the company,
(b)   a person who took part in the formation of the company during the period of one year ending with the date on which the company enters administration,
(c)   a person employed by the company during that period, and
(d)   a person who is or has been during that period an officer or employee of a company which is or has been during that year an officer of the company.

(4)   For the purpose of sub-paragraph (3) a reference to employment is a reference to employment through a contract of employment or a contract for services.

...

Administrator's proposals

49.—   (1)   The administrator of a company shall make a statement setting out proposals for achieving the purpose of administration.

(2)   A statement under sub-paragraph (1) must, in particular—
(a)   deal with such matters as may be prescribed, and
(b)   where applicable, explain why the administrator thinks that the objective mentioned in paragraph 3(1)(a) or (b) cannot be achieved.

(3)   Proposals under this paragraph may include—
(a)   a proposal for a voluntary arrangement under Part I of this Act (although this paragraph is without prejudice to section 4(3));
(b)   a proposal for a compromise or arrangement to be sanctioned under section 425 of the Companies Act (compromise with creditors or members).

(4)   The administrator shall send a copy of the statement of his proposals—
(a)   to the registrar of companies,
(b)   to every creditor of the company of whose claim and address he is aware, and
(c)   to every member of the company of whose address he is aware.

(5)   The administrator shall comply with sub-paragraph (4)—
(a)   as soon as is reasonably practicable after the company enters administration, and

(b)   in any event, before the end of the period of eight weeks beginning with the day on which the company enters administration.

(6)   The administrator shall be taken to comply with sub-paragraph (4)(c) if he publishes in the prescribed manner a notice undertaking to provide a copy of the statement of proposals free of charge to any member of the company who applies in writing to a specified address.

(7)   An administrator commits an offence if he fails without reasonable excuse to comply with sub-paragraph (5).

(8)   A period specified in this paragraph may be varied in accordance with paragraph 107.

Creditors' meeting

50.—   (1)   In this Schedule "creditors' meeting" means a meeting of creditors of a company summoned by the administrator—

(a)   in the prescribed manner, and

(b)   giving the prescribed period of notice to every creditor of the company of whose claim and address he is aware.

(2)   A period prescribed under sub-paragraph (1)(b) may be varied in accordance with paragraph 107.

(3)   A creditors' meeting shall be conducted in accordance with the rules.

Requirement for initial creditors' meeting

51.—   (1)   Each copy of an administrator's statement of proposals sent to a creditor under paragraph 49(4)(b) must be accompanied by an invitation to a creditors' meeting (an "initial creditors' meeting").

(2)   The date set for an initial creditors' meeting must be—

(a)   as soon as is reasonably practicable after the company enters administration, and

(b)   in any event, within the period of ten weeks beginning with the date on which the company enters administration.

(3)   An administrator shall present a copy of his statement of proposals to an initial creditors' meeting.

(4)   A period specified in this paragraph may be varied in accordance with paragraph 107.

(5)   An administrator commits an offence if he fails without reasonable excuse to comply with a requirement of this paragraph.

52.—   (1)   Paragraph 51(1) shall not apply where the statement of proposals states that the administrator thinks—

(a)   that the company has sufficient property to enable each creditor of the company to be paid in full,

(b)   that the company has insufficient property to enable a distribution to be made to unsecured creditors other than by virtue of section 176A(2)(a), or

(c)   that neither of the objectives specified in paragraph 3(1)(a) and (b) can be achieved.

(2)   But the administrator shall summon an initial creditors' meeting if it is requested—

(a)   by creditors of the company whose debts amount to at least 10% of the total debts of the company,

(b)   in the prescribed manner, and

(c)   in the prescribed period.

(3)   A meeting requested under sub-paragraph (2) must be summoned for a date in the prescribed period.

(4)   The period prescribed under sub-paragraph (3) may be varied in accordance with paragraph 107.

Business and result of initial creditors' meeting

53.—   (1)   An initial creditors' meeting to which an administrator's proposals are presented shall consider them and may—

(a)   approve them without modification, or

(b)   approve them with modification to which the administrator consents.

(2) After the conclusion of an initial creditors' meeting the administrator shall as soon as is reasonably practicable report any decision taken to—

 (a) the court,

 (b) the registrar of companies, and

 (c) such other persons as may be prescribed.

(3) An administrator commits an offence if he fails without reasonable excuse to comply with sub-paragraph (2).

Revision of administrator's proposals

54.— (1) This paragraph applies where—

 (a) an administrator's proposals have been approved (with or without modification) at an initial creditors' meeting,

 (b) the administrator proposes a revision to the proposals, and

 (c) the administrator thinks that the proposed revision is substantial.

 (2) The administrator shall—

 (a) summon a creditors' meeting,

 (b) send a statement in the prescribed form of the proposed revision with the notice of the meeting sent to each creditor,

 (c) send a copy of the statement, within the prescribed period, to each member of the company of whose address he is aware, and

 (d) present a copy of the statement to the meeting.

 (3) The administrator shall be taken to have complied with sub-paragraph (2)(c) if he publishes a notice undertaking to provide a copy of the statement free of charge to any member of the company who applies in writing to a specified address.

 (4) A notice under sub-paragraph (3) must be published—

 (a) in the prescribed manner, and

 (b) within the prescribed period.

 (5) A creditors' meeting to which a proposed revision is presented shall consider it and may—

 (a) approve it without modification, or

 (b) approve it with modification to which the administrator consents.

 (6) After the conclusion of a creditors' meeting the administrator shall as soon as is reasonably practicable report any decision taken to—

 (a) the court,

 (b) the registrar of companies, and

 (c) such other persons as may be prescribed.

 (7) An administrator commits an offence if he fails without reasonable excuse to comply with sub-paragraph (6).

Failure to obtain approval of administrator's proposals

55.— (1) This paragraph applies where an administrator reports to the court that—

 (a) an initial creditors' meeting has failed to approve the administrator's proposals presented to it, or

 (b) a creditors' meeting has failed to approve a revision of the administrator's proposals presented to it.

 (2) The court may—

 (a) provide that the appointment of an administrator shall cease to have effect from a specified time;

 (b) adjourn the hearing conditionally or unconditionally;

 (c) make an interim order;

 (d) make an order on a petition for winding up suspended by virtue of paragraph 40(1)(b);

 (e) make any other order (including an order making consequential provision) that the court thinks appropriate.

Further creditors' meetings

56.— (1) The administrator of a company shall summon a creditors' meeting if—

(a)   it is requested in the prescribed manner by creditors of the company whose debts amount to at least 10% of the total debts of the company, or

(b)   he is directed by the court to summon a creditors' meeting.

(2)   An administrator commits an offence if he fails without reasonable excuse to summon a creditors' meeting as required by this paragraph.

Creditors' committee

57.— (1)   A creditors' meeting may establish a creditors' committee.

(2)   A creditors' committee shall carry out functions conferred on it by or under this Act.

(3)   A creditors' committee may require the administrator—

(a)   to attend on the committee at any reasonable time of which he is given at least seven days' notice, and to provide the committee with information about the exercise of his functions.

...

FUNCTIONS OF ADMINISTRATOR

General powers

59.— (1)   The administrator of a company may do anything necessary or expedient for the management of the affairs, business and property of the company.

(2)   A provision of this Schedule which expressly permits the administrator to do a specified thing is without prejudice to the generality of sub-paragraph (1).

(3)   A person who deals with the administrator of a company in good faith and for value need not inquire whether the administrator is acting within his powers.

60.   The administrator of a company has the powers specified in Schedule 1 to this Act.

61.   The administrator of a company—

(a)   may remove a director of the company, and

(b)   may appoint a director of the company (whether or not to fill a vacancy).

62.   The administrator of a company may call a meeting of members or creditors of the company.

63.   The administrator of a company may apply to the court for directions in connection with his functions.

64.— (1)   A company in administration or an officer of a company in administration may not exercise a management power without the consent of the administrator.

(2)   For the purpose of sub-paragraph (1)—

(a)   "management power" means a power which could be exercised so as to interfere with the exercise of the administrator's powers,

(b)   it is immaterial whether the power is conferred by an enactment or an instrument, and

(c)   consent may be general or specific.

Distribution

65.— (1)   The administrator of a company may make a distribution to a creditor of the company.

(2)   Section 175 shall apply in relation to a distribution under this paragraph as it applies in relation to a winding up.

(3)   A payment may not be made by way of distribution under this paragraph to a creditor of the company who is neither secured nor preferential unless the court gives permission.

66.   The administrator of a company may make a payment otherwise than in accordance with paragraph 65 or paragraph 13 of Schedule 1 if he thinks it likely to assist achievement of the purpose of administration.

General duties

67.   The administrator of a company shall on his appointment take custody or control of all the property to which he thinks the company is entitled.

68.— (1)   Subject to sub-paragraph (2), the administrator of a company shall manage its affairs, business and property in accordance with—

(a)   any proposals approved under paragraph 53,

     (b)   any revision of those proposals which is made by him and which he does not consider substantial, and

     (c)   any revision of those proposals approved under paragraph 54.

  (2)   If the court gives directions to the administrator of a company in connection with any aspect of his management of the company's affairs, business or property, the administrator shall comply with the directions.

  (3)   The court may give directions under sub-paragraph (2) only if—

     (a)   no proposals have been approved under paragraph 53,

     (b)   the directions are consistent with any proposals or revision approved under paragraph 53 or 54,

     (c)   the court thinks the directions are required in order to reflect a change in circumstances since the approval of proposals or a revision under paragraph 53 or 54, or

     (d)   the court thinks the directions are desirable because of a misunderstanding about proposals or a revision approved under paragraph 53 or 54.

Administrator as agent of company

69.   In exercising his functions under this Schedule the administrator of a company acts as its agent.

Charged property: floating charge

70.— (1)   The administrator of a company may dispose of or take action relating to property which is subject to a floating charge as if it were not subject to the charge.

  (2)   Where property is disposed of in reliance on sub-paragraph (1) the holder of the floating charge shall have the same priority in respect of acquired property as he had in respect of the property disposed of.

  (3)   In sub-paragraph (2) "acquired property" means property of the company which directly or indirectly represents the property disposed of.

Charged property: non-floating charge

71.— (1)   The court may by order enable the administrator of a company to dispose of property which is subject to a security (other than a floating charge) as if it were not subject to the security.

  (2)   An order under sub-paragraph (1) may be made only—

     (a)   on the application of the administrator, and

     (b)   where the court thinks that disposal of the property would be likely to promote the purpose of administration in respect of the company.

  (3)   An order under this paragraph is subject to the condition that there be applied towards discharging the sums secured by the security—

     (a)   the net proceeds of disposal of the property, and

     (b)   any additional money required to be added to the net proceeds so as to produce the amount determined by the court as the net amount which would be realised on a sale of the property at market value.

  (4)   If an order under this paragraph relates to more than one security, application of money under sub-paragraph (3) shall be in the order of the priorities of the securities.

  (5)   An administrator who makes a successful application for an order under this paragraph shall send a copy of the order to the registrar of companies before the end of the period of 14 days starting with the date of the order.

  (6)   An administrator commits an offence if he fails to comply with sub-paragraph (5) without reasonable excuse.

Hire-purchase property

72.— (1)   The court may by order enable the administrator of a company to dispose of goods which are in the possession of the company under a hire-purchase agreement as if all the rights of the owner under the agreement were vested in the company.

  (2)   An order under sub-paragraph (1) may be made only—

     (a)   on the application of the administrator, and

(b) where the court thinks that disposal of the goods would be likely to promote the purpose of administration in respect of the company.

(3) An order under this paragraph is subject to the condition that there be applied towards discharging the sums payable under the hire-purchase agreement—

(a) the net proceeds of disposal of the goods, and

(b) any additional money required to be added to the net proceeds so as to produce the amount determined by the court as the net amount which would be realised on a sale of the goods at market value.

(4) An administrator who makes a successful application for an order under this paragraph shall send a copy of the order to the registrar of companies before the end of the period of 14 days starting with the date of the order.

(5) An administrator commits an offence if he fails without reasonable excuse to comply with sub-paragraph (4).

Protection for secured or preferential creditor

73.— (1) An administrator's statement of proposals under paragraph 49 may not include any action which—

(a) affects the right of a secured creditor of the company to enforce his security,

(b) would result in a preferential debt of the company being paid otherwise than in priority to its non-preferential debts, or

(c) would result in one preferential creditor of the company being paid a smaller proportion of his debt than another.

(2) Sub-paragraph (1) does not apply to—

(a) action to which the relevant creditor consents,

(b) a proposal for a voluntary arrangement under Part I of this Act (although this sub-paragraph is without prejudice to section 4(3)),

(c) a proposal for a compromise or arrangement to be sanctioned under section 425 of the Companies Act (compromise with creditors or members), or

(d) a proposal for a cross-border merger within the meaning of regulation 2 of the Companies (Cross-Border Mergers) Regulations 2007.

(3) The reference to a statement of proposals in sub-paragraph (1) includes a reference to a statement as revised or modified.

Challenge to administrator's conduct of company

74.— (1) A creditor or member of a company in administration may apply to the court claiming that—

(a) the administrator is acting or has acted so as unfairly to harm the interests of the applicant (whether alone or in common with some or all other members or creditors), or

(b) the administrator proposes to act in a way which would unfairly harm the interests of the applicant (whether alone or in common with some or all other members or creditors).

(2) A creditor or member of a company in administration may apply to the court claiming that the administrator is not performing his functions as quickly or as efficiently as is reasonably practicable.

(3) The court may—

(a) grant relief;

(b) dismiss the application;

(c) adjourn the hearing conditionally or unconditionally;

(d) make an interim order;

(e) make any other order it thinks appropriate.

(4) In particular, an order under this paragraph may—

(a) regulate the administrator's exercise of his functions;

(b) require the administrator to do or not do a specified thing;

(c) require a creditors' meeting to be held for a specified purpose;

(d) provide for the appointment of an administrator to cease to have effect;

(e) make consequential provision.

(5) An order may be made on a claim under sub-paragraph (1) whether or not the action complained of—

(a) is within the administrator's powers under this Schedule;

(b) was taken in reliance on an order under paragraph 71 or 72.

(6) An order may not be made under this paragraph if it would impede or prevent the implementation of—

(a) a voluntary arrangement approved under Part I,

(b) a compromise or arrangement sanctioned under section 425 of the Companies Act (compromise with creditors and members), ...

(ba) a cross-border merger within the meaning of regulation 2 of the Companies (Cross-Border Mergers) Regulations 2007, or

(c) proposals or a revision approved under paragraph 53 or 54 more than 28 days before the day on which the application for the order under this paragraph is made.

Misfeasance

75.— (1) The court may examine the conduct of a person who—

(a) is or purports to be the administrator of a company, or

(b) has been or has purported to be the administrator of a company.

(2) An examination under this paragraph may be held only on the application of—

(a) the official receiver,

(b) the administrator of the company,

(c) the liquidator of the company,

(d) a creditor of the company, or

(e) a contributory of the company.

(3) An application under sub-paragraph (2) must allege that the administrator—

(a) has misapplied or retained money or other property of the company,

(b) has become accountable for money or other property of the company,

(c) has breached a fiduciary or other duty in relation to the company, or

(d) has been guilty of misfeasance.

(4) On an examination under this paragraph into a person's conduct the court may order him—

(a) to repay, restore or account for money or property;

(b) to pay interest;

(c) to contribute a sum to the company's property by way of compensation for breach of duty or misfeasance.

(5) In sub-paragraph (3) "administrator" includes a person who purports or has purported to be a company's administrator.

(6) An application under sub-paragraph (2) may be made in respect of an administrator who has been discharged under paragraph 98 only with the permission of the court.

ENDING ADMINISTRATION

Automatic end of administration

76.— (1) The appointment of an administrator shall cease to have effect at the end of the period of one year beginning with the date on which it takes effect.

(2) But—

(a) on the application of an administrator the court may by order extend his term of office for a specified period, and

(b) an administrator's term of office may be extended for a specified period not exceeding six months by consent.

77.— (1) An order of the court under paragraph 76—

(a) may be made in respect of an administrator whose term of office has already been extended by order or by consent, but

(b) may not be made after the expiry of the administrator's term of office.

(2) Where an order is made under paragraph 76 the administrator shall as soon as is reasonably practicable notify the registrar of companies.

(3) An administrator who fails without reasonable excuse to comply with sub-paragraph (2) commits an offence.

...

Court ending administration on application of administrator

79.— (1) On the application of the administrator of a company the court may provide for the appointment of an administrator of the company to cease to have effect from a specified time.

(2) The administrator of a company shall make an application under this paragraph if—
   (a) he thinks the purpose of administration cannot be achieved in relation to the company,
   (b) he thinks the company should not have entered administration, or
   (c) a creditors' meeting requires him to make an application under this paragraph.

(3) The administrator of a company shall make an application under this paragraph if—
   (a) the administration is pursuant to an administration order, and
   (b) the administrator thinks that the purpose of administration has been sufficiently achieved in relation to the company.

(4) On an application under this paragraph the court may—
   (a) adjourn the hearing conditionally or unconditionally;
   (b) dismiss the application;
   (c) make an interim order;
   (d) make any order it thinks appropriate (whether in addition to, in consequence of or instead of the order applied for).

Termination of administration where objective achieved

80.— (1) This paragraph applies where an administrator of a company is appointed under paragraph 14 or 22.

(2) If the administrator thinks that the purpose of administration has been sufficiently achieved in relation to the company he may file a notice in the prescribed form—
   (a) with the court, and
   (b) with the registrar of companies.

(3) The administrator's appointment shall cease to have effect when the requirements of sub-paragraph (2) are satisfied.

(4) Where the administrator files a notice he shall within the prescribed period send a copy to every creditor of the company of whose claim and address he is aware.

(5) The rules may provide that the administrator is taken to have complied with sub-paragraph (4) if before the end of the prescribed period he publishes in the prescribed manner a notice undertaking to provide a copy of the notice under sub-paragraph (2) to any creditor of the company who applies in writing to a specified address.

(6) An administrator who fails without reasonable excuse to comply with sub-paragraph (4) commits an offence.

Court ending administration on application of creditor

81.— (1) On the application of a creditor of a company the court may provide for the appointment of an administrator of the company to cease to have effect at a specified time.

(2) An application under this paragraph must allege an improper motive—
   (a) in the case of an administrator appointed by administration order, on the part of the applicant for the order, or
   (b) in any other case, on the part of the person who appointed the administrator.

(3) On an application under this paragraph the court may—
   (a) adjourn the hearing conditionally or unconditionally;
   (b) dismiss the application;
   (c) make an interim order;

(d)   make any order it thinks appropriate (whether in addition to, in consequence of or instead of the order applied for).

Public interest winding-up

82.—   (1)   This paragraph applies where a winding-up order is made for the winding up of a company in administration on a petition presented under—

(a)   section 124A (public interest),

(aa)   section 124B (SEs), or

...

(2)   This paragraph also applies where a provisional liquidator of a company in administration is appointed following the presentation of a petition under any of the provisions listed in sub-paragraph (1).

(3)   The court shall order—

(a)   that the appointment of the administrator shall cease to have effect, or

(b)   that the appointment of the administrator shall continue to have effect.

(4)   If the court makes an order under sub-paragraph (3)(b) it may also—

(a)   specify which of the powers under this Schedule are to be exercisable by the administrator, and

(b)   order that this Schedule shall have effect in relation to the administrator with specified modifications.

Moving from administration to creditors' voluntary liquidation

83.—   (1)   This paragraph applies in England and Wales where the administrator of a company thinks—

(a)   that the total amount which each secured creditor of the company is likely to receive has been paid to him or set aside for him, and

(b)   that a distribution will be made to unsecured creditors of the company (if there are any).

...

(3)   The administrator may send to the registrar of companies a notice that this paragraph applies.

(4)   On receipt of a notice under sub-paragraph (3) the registrar shall register it.

(5)   If an administrator sends a notice under sub-paragraph (3) he shall as soon as is reasonably practicable—

(a)   file a copy of the notice with the court, and

(b)   send a copy of the notice to each creditor of whose claim and address he is aware.

(6)   On the registration of a notice under sub-paragraph (3)—

(a)   the appointment of an administrator in respect of the company shall cease to have effect, and

(b)   the company shall be wound up as if a resolution for voluntary winding up under section 84 were passed on the day on which the notice is registered.

(7)   The liquidator for the purposes of the winding up shall be—

(a)   a person nominated by the creditors of the company in the prescribed manner and within the prescribed period, or

(b)   if no person is nominated under paragraph (a), the administrator.

(8)   In the application of Part IV to a winding up by virtue of this paragraph—

(a)   section 85 shall not apply,

(b)   section 86 shall apply as if the reference to the time of the passing of the resolution for voluntary winding up were a reference to the beginning of the date of registration of the notice under sub-paragraph (3),

(c)   section 89 does not apply,

(d)   sections 98, 99 and 100 shall not apply,

(e)   section 129 shall apply as if the reference to the time of the passing of the resolution for voluntary winding up were a reference to the beginning of the date of registration of the notice under sub-paragraph (3), and (f)　any creditors' committee which is in existence immediately before the company ceases to be in administration shall continue in existence after that time as if appointed as a liquidation committee under section 101.

Moving from administration to dissolution

84.— (1)　If the administrator of a company thinks that the company has no property which might permit a distribution to its creditors, he shall send a notice to that effect to the registrar of companies.

(2)　The court may on the application of the administrator of a company disapply sub-paragraph (1) in respect of the company.

(3)　On receipt of a notice under sub-paragraph (1) the registrar shall register it.

(4)　On the registration of a notice in respect of a company under sub-paragraph (1) the appointment of an administrator of the company shall cease to have effect.

(5)　If an administrator sends a notice under sub-paragraph (1) he shall as soon as is reasonably practicable—

(a)　file a copy of the notice with the court, and

(b)　send a copy of the notice to each creditor of whose claim and address he is aware.

(6)　At the end of the period of three months beginning with the date of registration of a notice in respect of a company under sub-paragraph (1) the company is deemed to be dissolved.

(7)　On an application in respect of a company by the administrator or another interested person the court may—

(a)　extend the period specified in sub-paragraph (6),

(b)　suspend that period, or

(c)　disapply sub-paragraph (6).

(8)　Where an order is made under sub-paragraph (7) in respect of a company the administrator shall as soon as is reasonably practicable notify the registrar of companies.

(9)　An administrator commits an offence if he fails without reasonable excuse to comply with sub-paragraph (5).

Discharge of administration order where administration ends

85.— (1)　This paragraph applies where—

(a)　the court makes an order under this Schedule providing for the appointment of an administrator of a company to cease to have effect, and

(b)　the administrator was appointed by administration order.

(2)　The court shall discharge the administration order.

...

REPLACING ADMINISTRATOR

Resignation of administrator

87.— (1)　An administrator may resign only in prescribed circumstances.

(2)　Where an administrator may resign he may do so only—

(a)　in the case of an administrator appointed by administration order, by notice in writing to the court,

(b)　in the case of an administrator appointed under paragraph 14, by notice in writing to the [holder of the floating charge by virtue of which the appointment was made,

(c)　in the case of an administrator appointed under paragraph 22(1), by notice in writing to the company, or

(d)　in the case of an administrator appointed under paragraph 22(2), by notice in writing to the directors of the company.

Removal of administrator from office

88.　The court may by order remove an administrator from office.

Administrator ceasing to be qualified

89.— (1) The administrator of a company shall vacate office if he ceases to be qualified to act as an insolvency practitioner in relation to the company.

(2) Where an administrator vacates office by virtue of sub-paragraph (1) he shall give notice in writing—

(a) in the case of an administrator appointed by administration order, to the court,

(b) in the case of an administrator appointed under paragraph 14, to the holder of the floating charge by virtue of which the appointment was made,

(c) in the case of an administrator appointed under paragraph 22(1), to the company, or

(d) in the case of an administrator appointed under paragraph 22(2), to the directors of the company.

(3) An administrator who fails without reasonable excuse to comply with sub-paragraph (2) commits an offence.

Supplying vacancy in office of administrator

90. Paragraphs 91 to 95 apply where an administrator—

(a) dies,

(b) resigns,

(c) is removed from office under paragraph 88, or

(d) vacates office under paragraph 89.

91.— (1) Where the administrator was appointed by administration order, the court may replace the administrator on an application under this sub-paragraph made by—

(a) a creditors' committee of the company,

(b) the company,

(c) the directors of the company,

(d) one or more creditors of the company, or

(e) where more than one person was appointed to act jointly or concurrently as the administrator, any of those persons who remains in office.

(2) But an application may be made in reliance on sub-paragraph (1)(b) to (d) only where—

(a) there is no creditors' committee of the company,

(b) the court is satisfied that the creditors' committee or a remaining administrator is not taking reasonable steps to make a replacement, or

(c) the court is satisfied that for another reason it is right for the application to be made.

92. Where the administrator was appointed under paragraph 14 the holder of the floating charge by virtue of which the appointment was made may replace the administrator.

93.— (1) Where the administrator was appointed under paragraph 22(1) by the company it may replace the administrator.

(2) A replacement under this paragraph may be made only—

(a) with the consent of each person who is the holder of a qualifying floating charge in respect of the company's property, or

(b) where consent is withheld, with the permission of the court.

94.— (1) Where the administrator was appointed under paragraph 22(2) the directors of the company may replace the administrator.

(2) A replacement under this paragraph may be made only—

(a) with the consent of each person who is the holder of a qualifying floating charge in respect of the company's property, or

(b) where consent is withheld, with the permission of the court.

95. The court may replace an administrator on the application of a person listed in paragraph 91(1) if the court—

(a) is satisfied that a person who is entitled to replace the administrator under any of paragraphs 92 to 94 is not taking reasonable steps to make a replacement, or

(b) that for another reason it is right for the court to make the replacement.

SUBSTITUTION OF ADMINISTRATOR: COMPETING FLOATING CHARGE-HOLDER

96.— (1) This paragraph applies where an administrator of a company is appointed under paragraph 14 by the holder of a qualifying floating charge in respect of the company's property.

(2) The holder of a prior qualifying floating charge in respect of the company's property may apply to the court for the administrator to be replaced by an administrator nominated by the holder of the prior floating charge.

(3) One floating charge is prior to another for the purposes of this paragraph if—

(a) it was created first, or

(b) it is to be treated as having priority in accordance with an agreement to which the holder of each floating charge was party.

(4) Sub-paragraph (3) shall have effect in relation to Scotland as if the following were substituted for paragraph (a)—

"(a) it has priority of ranking in accordance with section 464(4)(b) of the Companies Act 1985,".

Substitution of administrator appointed by company or directors: creditors' meeting

97.— (1) This paragraph applies where—

(a) an administrator of a company is appointed by a company or directors under paragraph 22, and

(b) there is no holder of a qualifying floating charge in respect of the company's property.

(2) A creditors' meeting may replace the administrator.

(3) A creditors' meeting may act under sub-paragraph (2) only if the new administrator's written consent to act is presented to the meeting before the replacement is made.

Vacation of office: discharge from liability

98.— (1) Where a person ceases to be the administrator of a company (whether because he vacates office by reason of resignation, death or otherwise, because he is removed from office or because his appointment ceases to have effect) he is discharged from liability in respect of any action of his as administrator.

(2) The discharge provided by sub-paragraph (1) takes effect—

(a) in the case of an administrator who dies, on the filing with the court of notice of his death,

(b) in the case of an administrator appointed under paragraph 14 or 22, at a time appointed by resolution of the creditors' committee or, if there is no committee, by resolution of the creditors, or

(c) in any case, at a time specified by the court.

(3) For the purpose of the application of sub-paragraph (2)(b) in a case where the administrator has made a statement under paragraph 52(1)(b), a resolution shall be taken as passed if (and only if) passed with the approval of—

(a) each secured creditor of the company, or

(b) if the administrator has made a distribution to preferential creditors or thinks that a distribution may be made to preferential creditors—

(i) each secured creditor of the company, and

(ii) preferential creditors whose debts amount to more than 50% of the preferential debts of the company, disregarding debts of any creditor who does not respond to an invitation to give or withhold approval.

(4) Discharge—

(a) applies to liability accrued before the discharge takes effect, and

(b) does not prevent the exercise of the court's powers under paragraph 75.

Vacation of office: charges and liabilities

99.— (1) This paragraph applies where a person ceases to be the administrator of a company (whether because he vacates office by reason of resignation, death or otherwise, because he is removed from office or because his appointment ceases to have effect).

(2) In this paragraph—

"the former administrator" means the person referred to in sub-paragraph (1), and

"cessation" means the time when he ceases to be the company's administrator.

(3) The former administrator's remuneration and expenses shall be—

    (a) charged on and payable out of property of which he had custody or control immediately before cessation, and

    (b) payable in priority to any security to which paragraph 70 applies.

(4) A sum payable in respect of a debt or liability arising out of a contract entered into by the former administrator or a predecessor before cessation shall be—

    (a) charged on and payable out of property of which the former administrator had custody or control immediately before cessation, and

    (b) payable in priority to any charge arising under sub-paragraph (3).

(5) Sub-paragraph (4) shall apply to a liability arising under a contract of employment which was adopted by the former administrator or a predecessor before cessation; and for that purpose—

    (a) action taken within the period of 14 days after an administrator's appointment shall not be taken to amount or contribute to the adoption of a contract,

    (b) no account shall be taken of a liability which arises, or in so far as it arises, by reference to anything which is done or which occurs before the adoption of the contract of employment, and

    (c) no account shall be taken of a liability to make a payment other than wages or salary.

(6) In sub-paragraph (5)(c) "wages or salary" includes—

    (a) a sum payable in respect of a period of holiday (for which purpose the sum shall be treated as relating to the period by reference to which the entitlement to holiday accrued),

    (b) a sum payable in respect of a period of absence through illness or other good cause,

    (c) a sum payable in lieu of holiday,

    (d) in respect of a period, a sum which would be treated as earnings for that period for the purposes of an enactment about social security, and

    (e) a contribution to an occupational pension scheme.

GENERAL

Joint and concurrent administrators

100.— (1) In this Schedule—

    (a) a reference to the appointment of an administrator of a company includes a reference to the appointment of a number of persons to act jointly or concurrently as the administrator of a company, and

    (b) a reference to the appointment of a person as administrator of a company includes a reference to the appointment of a person as one of a number of persons to act jointly or concurrently as the administrator of a company.

(2) The appointment of a number of persons to act as administrator of a company must specify—

    (a) which functions (if any) are to be exercised by the persons appointed acting jointly, and

    (b) which functions (if any) are to be exercised by any or all of the persons appointed.

101.— (1) This paragraph applies where two or more persons are appointed to act jointly as the administrator of a company.

(2) A reference to the administrator of the company is a reference to those persons acting jointly.

(3) But a reference to the administrator of a company in paragraphs 87 to 99 of this Schedule is a reference to any or all of the persons appointed to act jointly.

(4) Where an offence of omission is committed by the administrator, each of the persons appointed to act jointly—

    (a) commits the offence, and

(b)   may be proceeded against and punished individually.

(5)   The reference in paragraph 45(1)(a) to the name of the administrator is a reference to the name of each of the persons appointed to act jointly.

(6)   Where persons are appointed to act jointly in respect of only some of the functions of the administrator of a company, this paragraph applies only in relation to those functions.

...

103.— (1)   Where a company is in administration, a person may be appointed to act as administrator jointly or concurrently with the person or persons acting as the administrator of the company.

(2)   Where a company entered administration by administration order, an appointment under sub-paragraph (1) must be made by the court on the application of—

(a)   a person or group listed in paragraph 12(1)(a) to (e), or

(b)   the person or persons acting as the administrator of the company.

(3)   Where a company entered administration by virtue of an appointment under paragraph 14, an appointment under sub-paragraph (1) must be made by—

(a)   the holder of the floating charge by virtue of which the appointment was made, or

(b)   the court on the application of the person or persons acting as the administrator of the company.

(4)   Where a company entered administration by virtue of an appointment under paragraph 22(1), an appointment under sub-paragraph (1) above must be made either by the court on the application of the person or persons acting as the administrator of the company or—

(a)   by the company, and

(b)   with the consent of each person who is the holder of a qualifying floating charge in respect of the company's property or, where consent is withheld, with the permission of the court.

(5)   Where a company entered administration by virtue of an appointment under paragraph 22(2), an appointment under sub-paragraph (1) must be made either by the court on the application of the person or persons acting as the administrator of the company or—

(a)   by the directors of the company, and

(b)   with the consent of each person who is the holder of a qualifying floating charge in respect of the company's property or, where consent is withheld, with the permission of the court.

(6)   An appointment under sub-paragraph (1) may be made only with the consent of the person or persons acting as the administrator of the company.

Presumption of validity

104.   An act of the administrator of a company is valid in spite of a defect in his appointment or qualification.

Majority decision of directors

105.   A reference in this Schedule to something done by the directors of a company includes a reference to the same thing done by a majority of the directors of a company.

...

Extension of time limit

107.— (1)   Where a provision of this Schedule provides that a period may be varied in accordance with this paragraph, the period may be varied in respect of a company—

(a)   by the court, and

(b)   on the application of the administrator.

(2)   A time period may be extended in respect of a company under this paragraph—

(a)   more than once, and

(b)   after expiry.

108.— (1)   A period specified in paragraph 49(5), 50(1)(b) or 51(2) may be varied in respect of a company by the administrator with consent.

(2)   In sub-paragraph (1) "consent" means consent of—

      (a)   each secured creditor of the company, and

      (b)   if the company has unsecured debts, creditors whose debts amount to more than 50% of the company's unsecured debts, disregarding debts of any creditor who does not respond to an invitation to give or withhold consent.

(3)   But where the administrator has made a statement under paragraph 52(1)(b) "consent" means—

      (a)   consent of each secured creditor of the company, or

      (b)   if the administrator thinks that a distribution may be made to preferential creditors, consent of—

           (i)   each secured creditor of the company, and

           (ii)   preferential creditors whose debts amount to more than 50% of the total preferential debts of the company, disregarding debts of any creditor who does not respond to an invitation to give or withhold consent.

(4)   Consent for the purposes of sub-paragraph (1) may be—

      (a)   written, or

      (b)   signified at a creditors' meeting.

(5)   The power to extend under sub-paragraph (1)—

      (a)   may be exercised in respect of a period only once,

      (b)   may not be used to extend a period by more than 28 days,

      (c)   may not be used to extend a period which has been extended by the court, and

      (d)   may not be used to extend a period after expiry.

109.   Where a period is extended under paragraph 107 or 108, a reference to the period shall be taken as a reference to the period as extended.

Amendment of provision about time

110.— (1)   The Secretary of State may by order amend a provision of this Schedule which—

      (a)   requires anything to be done within a specified period of time,

      (b)   prevents anything from being done after a specified time, or

      (c)   requires a specified minimum period of notice to be given.

(2)   An order under this paragraph—

      (a)   must be made by statutory instrument, and

      (b)   shall be subject to annulment in pursuance of a resolution of either House of Parliament.

Interpretation

111.— (1)   In this Schedule—

      "administrative receiver" has the meaning given by section 251,

      "administrator" has the meaning given by paragraph 1 and, where the context requires, includes a reference to a former administrator,

      "correspondence" includes correspondence by telephonic or other electronic means,

      "creditors' meeting" has the meaning given by paragraph 50,

      "enters administration" has the meaning given by paragraph 1,

      "floating charge" means a charge which is a floating charge on its creation,

      "in administration" has the meaning given by paragraph 1,

      "hire-purchase agreement" includes a conditional sale agreement, a chattel leasing agreement and a retention of title agreement,

      "holder of a qualifying floating charge" in respect of a company's property has the meaning given by paragraph 14,

      "market value" means the amount which would be realised on a sale of property in the open market by a willing vendor,

      "the purpose of administration" means an objective specified in paragraph 3, and

      "unable to pay its debts" has the meaning given by section 123.

(1A) In this Schedule, "company" means—

      (a)   a company within the meaning of section 735(1) of the Companies Act 1985,

      (b)   a company incorporated in an EEA State other than the United Kingdom, or

   (c) a company not incorporated in an EEA State but having its centre of main interests in a member State other than Denmark.

  (1B) In sub-paragraph (1A), in relation to a company, "centre of main interests" has the same meaning as in the EC Regulation and, in the absence of proof to the contrary, is presumed to be the place of its registered office (within the meaning of that Regulation).

  (2) A reference in this Schedule to a thing in writing includes a reference to a thing in electronic form.

  (3) In this Schedule a reference to action includes a reference to inaction.

...

SCHEDULE 1
POWERS OF ADMINISTRATOR OR ADMINISTRATIVE RECEIVER

1. Power to take possession of, collect and get in the property of the company and, for that purpose, to take such proceedings as may seem to him expedient.

2. Power to sell or otherwise dispose of the property of the company by public auction or private contract or, in Scotland, to sell, hire out or otherwise dispose of the property of the company by public group or private bargain.

3. Power to raise or borrow money and grant security therefor over the property of the company.

4. Power to appoint a solicitor or accountant or other professionally qualified person to assist him in the performance of his functions.

5. Power to bring or defend any action or other legal proceedings in the name and on behalf of the company.

6. Power to refer to arbitration any question affecting the company.

7. Power to effect and maintain insurances in respect of the business and property of the company.

8. Power to use the company's seal.

9. Power to do all acts and to execute in the name and on behalf of the company any deed, receipt or other document.

10. Power to draw, accept, make and endorse any bill of exchange or promissory note in the name and on behalf of the company.

11. Power to appoint any agent to do any business which he is unable to do himself or which can more conveniently be done by an agent and power to employ and dismiss employees.

12. Power to do all such things (including the carrying out of works) as may be necessary for the realisation of the property of the company.

13. Power to make any payment which is necessary or incidental to the performance of his functions.

14. Power to carry on the business of the company.

15. Power to establish subsidiaries of the company.

16. Power to transfer to subsidiaries of the company the whole or any part of the business and property of the company.

17. Power to grant or accept a surrender of a lease or tenancy of any of the property of the company, and to take a lease or tenancy of any property required or convenient for the business of the company.

18. Power to make any arrangement or compromise on behalf of the company.

19. Power to call up any uncalled capital of the company.

20. Power to rank and claim in the bankruptcy, insolvency, sequestration or liquidation of any person indebted to the company and to receive dividends, and to accede to trust deeds for the creditors of any such person.

21. Power to present or defend a petition for the winding up of the company.

22. Power to change the situation of the company's registered office.

23. Power to do all other things incidental to the exercise of the foregoing powers.

...

SCHEDULE 4
POWERS OF LIQUIDATOR IN A WINDING UP

PART I
POWERS EXERCISABLE WITH SANCTION

1.   Power to pay any class of creditors in full.
2.   Power to make any compromise or arrangement with creditors or persons claiming to be creditors, or having or alleging themselves to have any claim (present or future, certain or contingent, ascertained or sounding only in damages) against the company, or whereby the company may be rendered liable.
3.   Power to compromise, on such terms as may be agreed—
   (a)   all calls and liabilities to calls, all debts and liabilities capable of resulting in debts, and all claims (present or future, certain or contingent, ascertained or sounding only in damages) subsisting or supposed to subsist between the company and a contributory or alleged contributory or other debtor or person apprehending liability to the company, and
   (b)   all questions in any way relating to or affecting the assets or the winding up of the company, and take any security for the discharge of any such call, debt, liability or claim and give a complete discharge in respect of it.
3A.   Power to bring legal proceedings under section 213, 214, 238, 239, 242, 243 or 423.

PART II
POWERS EXERCISABLE WITHOUT SANCTION IN VOLUNTARY WINDING UP, WITH SANCTION IN WINDING UP BY THE COURT

4.   Power to bring or defend any action or other legal proceeding in the name and on behalf of the company.
5.   Power to carry on the business of the company so far as may be necessary for its beneficial winding up.

PART III
POWERS EXERCISABLE WITHOUT SANCTION IN ANY WINDING UP

6.   Power to sell any of the company's property by public auction or private contract with power to transfer the whole of it to any person or to sell the same in parcels.
7.   Power to do all acts and execute, in the name and on behalf of the company, all deeds, receipts and other documents and for that purpose to use, when necessary, the company's seal.
8.   Power to prove, rank and claim in the bankruptcy, insolvency or sequestration of any contributory for any balance against his estate, and to receive dividends in the bankruptcy, insolvency or sequestration in respect of that balance, as a separate debt due from the bankrupt or insolvent, and rateably with the other separate creditors.
9.   Power to draw, accept, make and indorse any bill of exchange or promissory note in the name and on behalf of the company, with the same effect with respect to the company's liability as if the bill or note had been drawn, accepted, made or indorsed by or on behalf of the company in the course of its business.
10.   Power to raise on the security of the assets of the company any money requisite.
11.   Power to take out in his official name letters of administration to any deceased contributory, and to do in his official name any other act necessary for obtaining payment of any money due from a contributory or his estate which cannot conveniently be done in the name of the company.
        In all such cases the money due is deemed, for the purpose of enabling the liquidator to take out the letters of administration or recover the money, to be due to the liquidator himself.
12.   Power to appoint an agent to do any business which the liquidator is unable to do himself.
13.   Power to do all such other things as may be necessary for winding up the company's affairs and distributing its assets.

SCHEDULE 4A
BANKRUPTCY RESTRICTIONS ORDER AND UNDERTAKING

Bankruptcy restrictions order

1.— (1) A bankruptcy restrictions order may be made by the court.

(2) An order may be made only on the application of—

    (a)   the Secretary of State, or

    (b)   the official receiver acting on a direction of the Secretary of State.

Grounds for making order

2.— (1) The court shall grant an application for a bankruptcy restrictions order if it thinks it appropriate having regard to the conduct of the bankrupt (whether before or after the making of the bankruptcy order).

(2) The court shall, in particular, take into account any of the following kinds of behaviour on the part of the bankrupt—

    (a)   failing to keep records which account for a loss of property by the bankrupt, or by a business carried on by him, where the loss occurred in the period beginning 2 years before petition and ending with the date of the application;

    (b)   failing to produce records of that kind on demand by the official receiver or the trustee;

    (c)   entering into a transaction at an undervalue;

    (d)   giving a preference;

    (e)   making an excessive pension contribution;

    (f)   a failure to supply goods or services which were wholly or partly paid for which gave rise to a claim provable in the bankruptcy;

    (g)   trading at a time before commencement of the bankruptcy when the bankrupt knew or ought to have known that he was himself to be unable to pay his debts;

    (h)   incurring, before commencement of the bankruptcy, a debt which the bankrupt had no reasonable expectation of being able to pay;

    (i)   failing to account satisfactorily to the court, the official receiver or the trustee for a loss of property or for an insufficiency of property to meet bankruptcy debts;

    (j)   carrying on any gambling, rash and hazardous speculation or unreasonable extravagance which may have materially contributed to or increased the extent of the bankruptcy or which took place between presentation of the petition and commencement of the bankruptcy;

    (k)   neglect of business affairs of a kind which may have materially contributed to or increased the extent of the bankruptcy;

    (l)   fraud or fraudulent breach of trust;

    (m) failing to cooperate with the official receiver or the trustee.

(3) The court shall also, in particular, consider whether the bankrupt was an undischarged bankrupt at some time during the period of six years ending with the date of the bankruptcy to which the application relates.

(4) For the purpose of sub-paragraph (2)—

"before petition" shall be construed in accordance with section 351(c),

"excessive pension contribution" shall be construed in accordance with section 342A,

"preference" shall be construed in accordance with section 340, and

"undervalue" shall be construed in accordance with section 339.

Timing of application for order

3.— (1) An application for a bankruptcy restrictions order in respect of a bankrupt must be made—

    (a)   before the end of the period of one year beginning with the date on which the bankruptcy commences, or

    (b)   with the permission of the court.

(2) The period specified in sub-paragraph (1)(a) shall cease to run in respect of a bankrupt while the period set for his discharge is suspended under section 279(3).

Duration of order

4.—   (1)   A bankruptcy restrictions order—
           (a)   shall come into force when it is made, and
           (b)   shall cease to have effect at the end of a date specified in the order.
      (2)   The date specified in a bankruptcy restrictions order under sub-paragraph (1)(b) must not
           be—
           (a)   before the end of the period of two years beginning with the date on which the order is
                 made, or
           (b)   after the end of the period of 15 years beginning with that date.

Interim bankruptcy restrictions order

...
6.—   (1)   This paragraph applies to a case in which both an interim bankruptcy restrictions order and
           a bankruptcy restrictions order are made.
      (2)   Paragraph 4(2) shall have effect in relation to the bankruptcy restrictions order as if a
           reference to the date of that order were a reference to the date of the interim order.

Bankruptcy restrictions undertaking

7.—   (1)   A bankrupt may offer a bankruptcy restrictions undertaking to the Secretary of State.
      (2)   In determining whether to accept a bankruptcy restrictions undertaking the Secretary of
           State shall have regard to the matters specified in paragraph 2(2) and (3).
8.   A reference in an enactment to a person in respect of whom a bankruptcy restrictions order has
           effect (or who is "the subject of" a bankruptcy restrictions order) includes a reference to a person
           in respect of whom a bankruptcy restrictions undertaking has effect.
9.—   (1)   A bankruptcy restrictions undertaking—
           (a)   shall come into force on being accepted by the Secretary of State, and
           (b)   shall cease to have effect at the end of a date specified in the undertaking.
      (2)   The date specified under sub-paragraph (1)(b) must not be—
           (a)   before the end of the period of two years beginning with the date on which the
                 undertaking is accepted, or
           (b)   after the end of the period of 15 years beginning with that date.
      (3)   On an application by the bankrupt the court may—
           (a)   annul a bankruptcy restrictions undertaking;
           (b)   provide for a bankruptcy restrictions undertaking to cease to have effect before the
                 date specified under sub-paragraph (1)(b).

Effect of annulment of bankruptcy order

10.   Where a bankruptcy order is annulled under section 282(1)(a) or (2)—
           (a)   any bankruptcy restrictions order, interim order or undertaking which is in force in respect
                 of the bankrupt shall be annulled,
           (b)   no new bankruptcy restrictions order or interim order may be made in respect of the
                 bankrupt, and
           (c)   no new bankruptcy restrictions undertaking by the bankrupt may be accepted.
11.   Where a bankruptcy order is annulled under section 261, 263D or 282(1)(b)—
           (a)   the annulment shall not affect any bankruptcy restrictions order, interim order or
                 undertaking in respect of the bankrupt,
           (b)   the court may make a bankruptcy restrictions order in relation to the bankrupt on an
                 application instituted before the annulment,
           (c)   the Secretary of State may accept a bankruptcy restrictions undertaking offered before the
                 annulment, and
           (d)   an application for a bankruptcy restrictions order or interim order in respect of the bankrupt
                 may not be instituted after the annulment.

Registration

12.   The Secretary of State shall maintain a register of—
(a)   bankruptcy restrictions orders,
(b)   interim bankruptcy restrictions orders, and
(c)   bankruptcy restrictions undertakings.

SCHEDULE 5
POWERS OF TRUSTEE IN BANKRUPTCY

PART I
POWERS EXERCISABLE WITH SANCTION

1.   Power to carry on any business of the bankrupt so far as may be necessary for winding it up beneficially and so far as the trustee is able to do so without contravening any requirement imposed by or under any enactment.

2.   Power to bring, institute or defend any action or legal proceedings relating to the property comprised in the bankrupt's estate.

2A.   Power to bring legal proceedings under section 339, 340 or 423.

3.   Power to accept as the consideration for the sale of any property comprised in the bankrupt's estate a sum of money payable at a future time subject to such stipulations as to security or otherwise as the creditors' committee or the court thinks fit.

4.   Power to mortgage or pledge any part of the property comprised in the bankrupt's estate for the purpose of raising money for the payment of his debts.

5.   Power, where any right, option or other power forms part of the bankrupt's estate, to make payments or incur liabilities with a view to obtaining, for the benefit of the creditors, any property which is the subject of the right, option or power.

6.   Power to refer to arbitration, or compromise on such terms as may be agreed on, any debts, claims or liabilities subsisting or supposed to subsist between the bankrupt and any person who may have incurred any liability to the bankrupt.

7.   Power to make such compromise or other arrangement as may be thought expedient with creditors, or persons claiming to be creditors, in respect of bankruptcy debts.

8.   Power to make such compromise or other arrangement as may be thought expedient with respect to any claim arising out of or incidental to the bankrupt's estate made or capable of being made on the trustee by any person or by the trustee on any person.

PART II
GENERAL POWERS

9.   Power to sell any part of the property for the time being comprised in the bankrupt's estate, including the goodwill and book debts of any business.

10.   Power to give receipts for any money received by him, being receipts which effectually discharge the person paying the money from all responsibility in respect of its application.

11.   Power to prove, rank, claim and draw a dividend in respect of such debts due to the bankrupt as are comprised in his estate.

12.   Power to exercise in relation to any property comprised in the bankrupt's estate any powers the capacity to exercise which is vested in him under Parts VIII to XI of this Act.

13.   Power to deal with any property comprised in the estate to which the bankrupt is beneficially entitled as tenant in tail in the same manner as the bankrupt might have dealt with it.

PART III
ANCILLARY POWERS

14.   For the purposes of, or in connection with, the exercise of any of his powers under Parts VIII to XI of this Act, the trustee may, by his official name—
(a)   hold property of every description,
(b)   make contracts,
(c)   sue and be sued,

(d)   enter into engagements binding on himself and, in respect of the bankrupt's estate, on his successors in office,

(e)   employ an agent,

(f)   execute any power of attorney, deed or other instrument;

and he may do any other act which is necessary or expedient for the purposes of or in connection with the exercise of those powers.

SCHEDULE 6
THE CATEGORIES OF PREFERENTIAL DEBTS

. . .

Category 4: Contributions to occupational pension schemes, etc

8.   Any sum which is owed by the debtor and is a sum to which Schedule 4 to the Pension Schemes Act 1993 applies (contributions to occupational pension schemes and state scheme premiums).

Category 5: Remuneration, etc, of employees

9.   So much of any amount which—

(a)   is owed by the debtor to a person who is or has been an employee of the debtor, and

(b)   is payable by way of remuneration in respect of the whole or any part of the period of 4 months next before the relevant date,

as does not exceed so much as may be prescribed by order made by the Secretary of State.

10.   An amount owed by way of accrued holiday remuneration, in respect of any period of employment before the relevant date, to a person whose employment by the debtor has been terminated, whether before, on or after that date.

11.   So much of any sum owed in respect of money advanced for the purpose as has been applied for the payment of a debt which, if it had not been paid, would have been a debt falling within paragraph 9 or 10.

12.   So much of any amount which—

(a)   is ordered (whether before or after the relevant date) to be paid by the debtor under the Reserve Forces (Safeguard of Employment) Act 1985, and

(b)   is so ordered in respect of a default made by the debtor before that date in the discharge of his obligations under that Act,

as does no exceed such amount as may be prescribed by order made by the Secretary of State.

. . .

Category 6: Levies on coal and steel production

15A.—   Any sums due at the relevant date from the debtor in respect of—

(a)   the levies on the production of coal and steel referred to in Articles 49 and 50 of the ECSC Treaty, or

(b)   any surcharge for delay provided for in Article 50(3) of that Treaty and Article 6 of Decision 3/52 of the High Authority of the Coal and Steel Community.

COMPANY DIRECTORS DISQUALIFICATION ACT 1986
(1986, c 46)

Preliminary

1   **Disqualification orders: general**

(1)   In the circumstances specified below in this Act a court may, and under sections 6 and 9A shall, make against a person a disqualification order, that is to say an order that for a period specified in the order—

(a)   he shall not be a director of a company, act as receiver of a company's property or in any way, whether directly or indirectly, be concerned or take part in the promotion, formation or management of a company unless (in each case) he has the leave of the court, and

(b)   he shall not act as an insolvency practitioner.

(2)   In each section of this Act which gives to a court power or, as the case may be, imposes on it the duty to make a disqualification order there is specified the maximum (and, in section 6, the minimum) period of disqualification which may or (as the case may be) must be imposed by means of the order and, unless the court otherwise orders, the period of disqualification so imposed shall begin at the end of the period of 21 days beginning with the date of the order.

(3)   Where a disqualification order is made against a person who is already subject to such an order or to a disqualification undertaking, the periods specified in those orders or, as the case may be, in the order and the undertaking shall run concurrently.

(4)   A disqualification order may be made on grounds which are or include matters other than criminal convictions, notwithstanding that the person in respect of whom it is to be made may be criminally liable in respect of those matters.

1A   Disqualification undertakings: general

(1)   In the circumstances specified in sections 7 and 8 the Secretary of State may accept a disqualification undertaking, that is to say an undertaking by any person that, for a period specified in the undertaking, the person—

(a)   will not be a director of a company, act as receiver of a company's property or in any way, whether directly or indirectly, be concerned or take part in the promotion, formation or management of a company unless (in each case) he has the leave of a court, and

(b)   will not act as an insolvency practitioner.

(2)   The maximum period which may be specified in a disqualification undertaking is 15 years; and the minimum period which may be specified in a disqualification undertaking under section 7 is two years.

(3)   Where a disqualification undertaking by a person who is already subject to such an undertaking or to a disqualification order is accepted, the periods specified in those undertakings or (as the case may be) the undertaking and the order shall run concurrently.

(4)   In determining whether to accept a disqualification undertaking by any person, the Secretary of State may take account of matters other than criminal convictions, notwithstanding that the person may be criminally liable in respect of those matters.

Disqualification for general misconduct in connection with companies

2   Disqualification on conviction of indictable offence

(1)   The court may make a disqualification order against a person where he is convicted of an indictable offence (whether on indictment or summarily) in connection with the promotion, formation, management, liquidation or striking off of a company, with the receivership of a company's property or with his being an administrative receiver of a company.

(2)   "The court" for this purpose means—

(a)   any court having jurisdiction to wind up the company in relation to which the offence was committed, or

(b)   the court by or before which the person is convicted of the offence, or

(c)   in the case of a summary conviction in England and Wales, any other magistrates' court acting in the same local justice area;

...

(3)   The maximum period of disqualification under this section is—

(a)   where the disqualification order is made by a court of summary jurisdiction, 5 years, and

(b)   in any other case, 15 years.

3   Disqualification for persistent breaches of companies legislation

(1)   The court may make a disqualification order against a person where it appears to it that he has been persistently in default in relation to provisions of the companies legislation

requiring any return, account or other document to be filed with, delivered or sent, or notice of any matter to be given, to the registrar of companies.

(2)　On an application to the court for an order to be made under this section, the fact that a person has been persistently in default in relation to such provisions as are mentioned above may (without prejudice to its proof in any other manner) be conclusively proved by showing that in the 5 years ending with the date of the application he has been adjudged guilty (whether or not on the same occasion) of three or more defaults in relation to those provisions.

(3)　A person is to be treated under subsection (2) as being adjudged guilty of a default in relation to any provision of that legislation if—

(a)　he is convicted (whether on indictment or summarily) of an offence consisting in a contravention of or failure to comply with that provision (whether on his own part or on the part of any company), or

(b)　a default order is made against him, that is to say an order under any of the following provisions—

(i)　section 242(4) of the Companies Act (order requiring delivery of company accounts),

(ia)　a section 245B of that Act (order requiring preparation of revised accounts),

(ii)　section 713 of that Act (enforcement of company's duty to make returns),

(iii)　section 41 of the Insolvency Act (enforcement of receiver's or manager's duty to make returns), or

(iv)　section 170 of that Act (corresponding provision for liquidator in winding up),

in respect of any such contravention of or failure to comply with that provision (whether on his own part or on the part of any company).

(4)　In this section "the court" means any court having jurisdiction to wind up any of the companies in relation to which the offence or other default has been or is alleged to have been committed.

(5)　The maximum period of disqualification under this section is 5 years.

4　Disqualification for fraud, etc, in winding up

(1)　The court may make a disqualification order against a person if, in the course of the winding up of a company, it appears that he—

(a)　has been guilty of an offence for which he is liable (whether he has been convicted or not) under section 993 of the Companies Act 2006 (fraudulent trading), or

(b)　has otherwise been guilty, while an officer or liquidator of the company receiver of the company's property or administrative receiver of the company, of any fraud in relation to the company or of any breach of his duty as such officer, liquidator, receiver or administrative receiver.

(2)　In this section "the court" means any court having jurisdiction to wind up any of the companies in relation to which the offence or other default has been or is alleged to have been committed; and "officer" includes a shadow director.

(3)　The maximum period of disqualification under this section is 15 years.

...

Disqualification for unfitness

6　Duty of court to disqualify unfit directors of insolvent companies

(1)　The court shall make a disqualification order against a person in any case where, on an application under this section, it is satisfied—

(a)　that he is or has been a director of a company which has at any time become insolvent (whether while he was a director or subsequently), and

(b)　that his conduct as a director of that company (either taken alone or taken together with his conduct as a director of any other company or companies) makes him unfit to be concerned in the management of a company.

(2)　For the purposes of this section and the next, a company becomes insolvent if—

(a)   the company goes into liquidation at a time when its assets are insufficient for the payment of its debts and other liabilities and the expenses of the winding up,

(b)   the company enters administration, or

(c)   an administrative receiver of the company is appointed;

and references to a person's conduct as a director of any company or companies include, where that company or any of those companies has become insolvent, that person's conduct in relation to any matter connected with or arising out of the insolvency of that company.

(3)   In this section and section 7(2), "the court" means—

(a)   where the company in question is being or has been wound up by the court, that court,

(b)   where the company in question is being or has been wound up voluntarily, any court which has or (as the case may be) had jurisdiction to wind it up,

(c)   where neither paragraph (a) nor (b) applies but an administrator or administrative receiver has at any time been appointed in respect of the company in question, any court which has jurisdiction to wind it up.

...

(3C)   In this section and section 7, "director" includes a shadow director.

(4)   Under this section the minimum period of disqualification is 2 years, and the maximum period is 15 years.

7   Disqualification order or undertaking; and reporting provisions

(1)   If it appears to the Secretary of State that it is expedient in the public interest that a disqualification order under section 6 should be made against any person, an application for the making of such an order against that person may be made—

(a)   by the Secretary of State, or

(b)   if the Secretary of State so directs in the case of a person who is or has been a director of a company which is being or has been wound up by the court in England and Wales, by the official receiver.

(2)   Except with the leave of the court, an application for the making under that section of a disqualification order against any person shall not be made after the end of the period of 2 years beginning with the day on which the company of which that person is or has been a director became insolvent.

(2A)   If it appears to the Secretary of State that the conditions mentioned in section 6(1) are satisfied as respects any person who has offered to give him a disqualification undertaking, he may accept the undertaking if it appears to him that it is expedient in the public interest that he should do so (instead of applying, or proceeding with an application, for a disqualification order).

(3)   If it appears to the office-holder responsible under this section, that is to say—

(a)   in the case of a company which is being wound up by the court in England and Wales, the official receiver,

(b)   in the case of a company which is being wound up otherwise, the liquidator,

(c)   in the case of a company which is in administration, the administrator, or

(d)   in the case of a company of which there is an administrative receiver, that receiver,

that the conditions mentioned in section 6(1) are satisfied as respects a person who is or has been a director of that company, the office-holder shall forthwith report the matter to the Secretary of State.

(4)   The Secretary of State or the official receiver may require the liquidator, administrator or administrative receiver of a company, or the former liquidator, administrator or administrative receiver of a company—

(a)   to furnish him with such information with respect to any person's conduct as a director of the company, and

(b)   to produce and permit inspection of such books, papers and other records relevant to that person's conduct as such a director,

as the Secretary of State or the official receiver may reasonably require for the purpose of determining whether to exercise, or of exercising, any function of his under this section.

8   Disqualification after investigation of company

(1) If it appears to the Secretary of State from investigative material that it is expedient in the public interest that a disqualification order should be made against a person who is, or has been, a director or shadow director of a company, he may apply to the court for such an order.

...

(2) The court may make a disqualification order against a person where, on an application under this section, it is satisfied that his conduct in relation to the company makes him unfit to be concerned in the management of a company.

(2A) Where it appears to the Secretary of State from such report, information or documents that, in the case of a person who has offered to give him a disqualification undertaking—

    (a) the conduct of the person in relation to a company of which the person is or has been a director or shadow director makes him unfit to be concerned in the management of a company, and

    (b) it is expedient in the public interest that he should accept the undertaking (instead of applying, or proceeding with an application, for a disqualification order),

he may accept the undertaking.

(3) In this section "the court" means the High Court ...

(4) The maximum period of disqualification under this section is 15 years.

8A   Variation etc of disqualification undertaking

(1) The court may, on the application of a person who is subject to a disqualification undertaking—

    (a) reduce the period for which the undertaking is to be in force, or

    (b) provide for it to cease to be in force.

(2) On the hearing of an application under subsection (1), the Secretary of State shall appear and call the attention of the court to any matters which seem to him to be relevant, and may himself give evidence or call witnesses.

...

(3) In this section "the court"—

    (a) in the case of an undertaking given under section 9B means the High Court;

    (b) in any other case has the same meaning as in section 7(2) or 8 (as the case may be).

9   Matters for determining unfitness of directors

(1) Where it falls to a court to determine whether a person's conduct as a director of any particular company or companies makes him unfit to be concerned in the management of a company, the court shall, as respects his conduct as a director of that company or, as the case may be, each of those companies, have regard in particular—

    (a) to the matters mentioned in Part I of Schedule 1 to this Act, and

    (b) where the company has become insolvent, to the matters mentioned in Part II of that Schedule;

and references in that Schedule to the director and the company are to be read accordingly.

(1A) In determining whether he may accept a disqualification undertaking from any person the Secretary of State shall, as respects the person's conduct as a director of any company concerned, have regard in particular—

    (a) to the matters mentioned in Part I of Schedule 1 to this Act, and

    (b) where the company has become insolvent, to the matters mentioned in Part II of that Schedule;

and references in that Schedule to the director and the company are to be read accordingly.

(2) Section 6(2) applies for the purposes of this section and Schedule 1 as it applies for the purposes of sections 6 and 7 and in this section and that Schedule "director" includes a shadow director.

(3) Subject to the next subsection, any reference in Schedule 1 to an enactment contained in the Companies Act or the Insolvency Act includes, in relation to any time before the coming into force of that enactment, the corresponding enactment in force at that time.

(4) The Secretary of State may by order modify any of the provisions of Schedule 1; and such an order may contain such transitional provisions as may appear to the Secretary of State necessary or expedient.

(5) The power to make orders under this section is exercisable by statutory instrument subject to annulment in pursuance of a resolution of either House of Parliament.

...

Other cases of disqualification

10   Participation in wrongful trading

(1) Where the court makes a declaration under section 213 or 214 of the Insolvency Act that a person is liable to make a contribution to a company's assets, then, whether or not an application for such an order is made by any person, the court may, if it thinks fit, also make a disqualification order against the person to whom the declaration relates.

(2) The maximum period of disqualification under this section is 15 years.

11   Undischarged bankrupts

(1) It is an offence for a person to act as director of a company or directly or indirectly to take part in or be concerned in the promotion, formation or management of a company, without the leave of the court, at a time when—
   (a) he is an undischarged bankrupt,
   (aa) a moratorium period under a debt relief order applies in relation to him, or
   (b) a bankruptcy restrictions order or a debt relief restrictions order is in force in respect of him.

(2) "The court" for this purpose is the court by which the person was adjudged bankrupt ...

(3) In England and Wales, the leave of the court shall not be given unless notice of intention to apply for it has been served on the official receiver; and it is the latter's duty, if he is of opinion that it is contrary to the public interest that the application should be granted, to attend on the hearing of the application and oppose it.

12   Failure to pay under county court administration order

(1) The following has effect where a court under section 429 of the Insolvency Act revokes an administration order under Part VI of the County Courts Act 1984.

(2) A person to whom that section applies by virtue of the order under section 429(2)(b) section 429 of the Insolvency Act applies by virtue of an order under subsection (2) of that section] shall not, except with the leave of the court which made the order, act as director or liquidator of, or directly or indirectly take part or be concerned in the promotion, formation or management of, a company.

...

Consequences of contravention

13   Criminal penalties

(1) If a person acts in contravention of a disqualification order or disqualification undertaking or in contravention of section 12(2), 12A or 12B, or is guilty of an offence under section 11, he is liable—
   (a) on conviction on indictment, to imprisonment for not more than 2 years or a fine, or both; and
   (b) on summary conviction, to imprisonment for not more than 6 months or a fine not exceeding the statutory maximum, or both.

14   Offences by body corporate

(1) Where a body corporate is guilty of an offence of acting in contravention of a disqualification order [or disqualification undertaking or in contravention of section 12A or 12B, and it is proved that the offence occurred with the consent or connivance of, or was attributable to any neglect on the part of any director, manager, secretary or other similar officer of the body corporate, or any person who was purporting to act in any such capacity

he, as well as the body corporate, is guilty of the offence and liable to be proceeded against and punished accordingly.

(2)   Where the affairs of a body corporate are managed by its members, subsection (1) applies in relation to the acts and defaults of a member in connection with his functions of management as if he were a director of the body corporate.

15   Personal liability for company's debts where person acts while disqualified

(1)   A person is personally responsible for all the relevant debts of a company if at any time—

    (a)   in contravention of a disqualification order or disqualification undertaking or in contravention of section 11, 12A or 12B of this Act he is involved in the management of the company, or

    ...

(2)   Where a person is personally responsible under this section for the relevant debts of a company, he is jointly and severally liable in respect of those debts with the company and any other person who, whether under this section or otherwise, is so liable.

(3)   For the purposes of this section the relevant debts of a company are—

    (a)   in relation to a person who is personally responsible under paragraph (a) of subsection (1), such debts and other liabilities of the company as are incurred at a time when that person was involved in the management of the company, and

    (b)   in relation to a person who is personally responsible under paragraph (b) of that subsection, such debts and other liabilities of the company as are incurred at a time when that person was acting or was willing to act on instructions given as mentioned in that paragraph.

(4)   For the purposes of this section, a person is involved in the management of a company if he is a director of the company or if he is concerned, whether directly or indirectly, or takes part, in the management of the company.

...

Supplementary provisions

16   Application for disqualification order

(1)   A person intending to apply for the making of a disqualification order by the court having jurisdiction to wind up a company shall give not less than 10 days' notice of his intention to the person against whom the order is sought; and on the hearing of the application the last-mentioned person may appear and himself give evidence or call witnesses.

(2)   An application to a court with jurisdiction to wind up companies for the making against any person of a disqualification order under any of sections 2 to 4 may be made by the Secretary of State or the official receiver, or by the liquidator or any past or present member or creditor of any company in relation to which that person has committed or is alleged to have committed an offence or other default.

(3)   On the hearing of any application under this Act made by a person falling within subsection (4), the applicant shall appear and call the attention of the court to any matters which seem to him to be relevant, and may himself give evidence or call witnesses.

(4)   The following fall within this subsection—

    (a)   the Secretary of State;

    (b)   the official receiver;

    (c)   the OFT;

    (d)   the liquidator;

    (e)   a specified regulator (within the meaning of section 9E).

17   Application for leave under an order or undertaking

(1)   Where a person is subject to a disqualification order made by a court having jurisdiction to wind up companies, any application for leave for the purposes of section 1(1)(a) shall be made to that court.

(2)   Where—

(a) a person is subject to a disqualification order made under section 2 by a court other than a court having jurisdiction to wind up companies, or

(b) a person is subject to a disqualification order made under section 5,

any application for leave for the purposes of section 1(1)(a) shall be made to any court which, when the order was made, had jurisdiction to wind up the company (or, if there is more than one such company, any of the companies) to which the offence (or any of the offences) in question related.

(3) Where a person is subject to a disqualification undertaking accepted at any time under section 7 or 8, any application for leave for the purposes of section 1A(1)(a) shall be made to any court to which, if the Secretary of State had applied for a disqualification order under the section in question at that time, his application could have been made.

...

18 Register of disqualification orders and undertakings

(1) The Secretary of State may make regulations requiring officers of courts to furnish him with such particulars as the regulations may specify of cases in which—

(a) a disqualification order is made, or

(b) any action is taken by a court in consequence of which such an order or a disqualification undertaking is varied or ceases to be in force, or

(c) leave is granted by a court for a person subject to such an order to do any thing which otherwise the order prohibits him from doing, or

(d) leave is granted by a court for a person subject to such an undertaking to do anything which otherwise the undertaking prohibits him from doing;

and the regulations may specify the time within which, and the form and manner in which, such particulars are to be furnished.

(2) The Secretary of State shall, from the particulars so furnished, continue to maintain the register of orders, and of cases in which leave has been granted as mentioned in subsection (1)(c), which was set up by him under section 29 of the Companies Act 1976 and continued under section 301 of the Companies Act 1985.

(2A) The Secretary of State must include in the register such particulars as he considers appropriate of—

(a) disqualification undertakings accepted by him under section 7 or 8;

...

(c) cases in which leave has been granted as mentioned in subsection (1)(d).

(3) When an order or undertaking of which entry is made in the register ceases to be in force, the Secretary of State shall delete the entry from the register and all particulars relating to it which have been furnished to him under this section or any previous corresponding provision and, in the case of a disqualification undertaking, any other particulars he has included in the register.

(4) The register shall be open to inspection on payment of such fee as may be specified by the Secretary of State in regulations.

...

(5) Regulations under this section shall be made by statutory instrument subject to annulment in pursuance of a resolution of either House of Parliament.

...

Miscellaneous and general

20 Admissibility in evidence of statements

(1) In any proceedings (whether or not under this Act), any statement made in pursuance of a requirement imposed by or under sections 6 to 10, 15 or 19(c) of, or Schedule 1 to, this Act, or by or under rules made for the purposes of this Act under the Insolvency Act, may be used in evidence against any person making or concurring in making the statement.

(2) However, in criminal proceedings in which any such person is charged with an offence to which this subsection applies—

        (a)   no evidence relating to the statement may be adduced, and

        (b)   no question relating to it may be asked,

        by or on behalf of the prosecution, unless evidence relating to it is adduced, or a question relating to it is asked, in the proceedings by or on behalf of that person.

(3)   Subsection (2) applies to any offence other than—

        (a)   an offence which is—

               (i)   created by rules made for the purposes of this Act under the Insolvency Act, and

               (ii)   designated for the purposes of this subsection by such rules or by regulations made by the Secretary of State;

        (b)   an offence which is—

               (i)   created by regulations made under any such rules, and

               (ii)   designated for the purposes of this subsection by such regulations;

        (c)   an offence under section 5 of the Perjury Act 1911 (false statements made otherwise than on oath); or

        …

(4)   Regulations under subsection (3)(a)(ii) shall be made by statutory instrument and, after being made, shall be laid before each House of Parliament.

…

22   Interpretation

    …

(4)   "Director" includes any person occupying the position of director, by whatever name called.

(5)   "Shadow director", in relation to a company, means a person in accordance with whose directions or instructions the directors of the company are accustomed to act (but so that a person is not deemed a shadow director by reason only that the directors act on advice given by him in a professional capacity).

    …

…

SCHEDULE 1

MATTERS FOR DETERMINING UNFITNESS OF DIRECTORS

PART I

MATTERS APPLICABLE IN ALL CASES

1.   Any misfeasance or breach of any fiduciary or other duty by the director in relation to the company.

2.   Any misapplication or retention by the director of, or any conduct by the director giving rise to an obligation to account for, any money or other property of the company.

3.   The extent of the director's responsibility for the company entering into any transaction liable to be set aside under Part XVI of the Insolvency Act (provisions against debt avoidance).

4.   The extent of the director's responsibility for any failure by the company to comply with any of the following provisions of the Companies Act, namely—

        (a)   section 221 (companies to keep accounting records);

        (b)   section 222 (where and for how long records to be kept);

        (c)   section 288 (register of directors and secretaries);

        (d)   section 352 (obligation to keep and enter up register of members);

        (e)   section 353 (location of register of members);

        (f)   section 363 (duty of company to make annual returns);

        (h)   sections 398 and 703D (duty of company to deliver particulars of charges on its property).

5.   The extent of the director's responsibility for any failure by the directors of the company to comply with—

        (a)   section 226 or 227 of the Companies Act (duty to prepare annual accounts), or

        (b)   section 233 of that Act (approval and signature of accounts).

    …

PART II
MATTERS APPLICABLE WHERE COMPANY HAS BECOME INSOLVENT

6. The extent of the director's responsibility for the causes of the company becoming insolvent.

7. The extent of the director's responsibility for any failure by the company to supply any goods or services which have been paid for (in whole or in part).

8. The extent of the director's responsibility for the company entering into any transaction or giving any preference, being a transaction or preference—
   (a) liable to be set aside under section 127 or sections 238 to 240 of the Insolvency Act, or
   (b) challengeable under section 242 or 243 of that Act.

9. The extent of the director's responsibility for any failure by the directors of the company to comply with section 98 of the Insolvency Act (duty to call creditors' meeting in creditors' voluntary winding up).

10. Any failure by the director to comply with any obligation imposed on him by or under any of the following provisions of the Insolvency Act—
    (a) paragraph 47 of Schedule B1 (company's statement of affairs in administration);
    (b) section 47 (statement of affairs to administrative receiver);
    ...
    (d) section 99 (directors' duty to attend meeting; statement of affairs in creditors' voluntary winding up);
    (e) section 131 (statement of affairs in winding up by the court);
    (f) section 234 (duty of any one with company property to deliver it up);
    (g) section 235 (duty to co-operate with liquidator, etc).

. . .

COMPANIES ACT 2006
(2006, c 46)

CHAPTER 2
GENERAL DUTIES OF DIRECTORS

172   Duty to promote the success of the company

(1) A director of a company must act in the way he considers, in good faith, would be most likely to promote the success of the company for the benefit of its members as a whole, and in doing so have regard (amongst other matters) to—
   (a) the likely consequences of any decision in the long term,
   (b) the interests of the company's employees,
   (c) the need to foster the company's business relationships with suppliers, customers and others,
   (d) the impact of the company's operations on the community and the environment,
   (e) the desirability of the company maintaining a reputation for high standards of business conduct, and
   (f) the need to act fairly as between members of the company.

(2) Where or to the extent that the purposes of the company consist of or include purposes other than the benefit of its members, subsection (1) has effect as if the reference to promoting the success of the company for the benefit of its members were to achieving those purposes.

(3) The duty imposed by this section has effect subject to any enactment or rule of law requiring directors, in certain circumstances, to consider or act in the interests of creditors of the company.

Companies subject to the small companies regime

381   Companies subject to the small companies regime

The small companies regime applies to a company for a financial year in relation to which the company—
   (a) qualifies as small (see sections 382 and 383), and

(b)   is not excluded from the regime (see section 384).

382   Companies qualifying as small: general

(1)   A company qualifies as small in relation to its first financial year if the qualifying conditions are met in that year.

(2)   A company qualifies as small in relation to a subsequent financial year—

    (a)   if the qualifying conditions are met in that year and the preceding financial year;

    (b)   if the qualifying conditions are met in that year and the company qualified as small in relation to the preceding financial year;

    (c)   if the qualifying conditions were met in the preceding financial year and the company qualified as small in relation to that year.

(3)   The qualifying conditions are met by a company in a year in which it satisfies two or more of the following requirements—

1 Turnover	Not more than £6.5 million
2 Balance sheet total	Not more than £3.26 million
3 Number of employees	Not more than 50

(4)   For a period that is a company's financial year but not in fact a year the maximum figures for turnover must be proportionately adjusted.

(5)   The balance sheet total means the aggregate of the amounts shown as assets in the company's balance sheet.

(6)   The number of employees means the average number of persons employed by the company in the year, determined as follows—

    (a)   find for each month in the financial year the number of persons employed under contracts of service by the company in that month (whether throughout the month or not),

    (b)   add together the monthly totals, and

    (c)   divide by the number of months in the financial year.

(7)   This section is subject to section 383 (companies qualifying as small: parent companies).

383   Companies qualifying as small: parent companies

(1)   A parent company qualifies as a small company in relation to a financial year only if the group headed by it qualifies as a small group.

(2)   A group qualifies as small in relation to the parent company's first financial year if the qualifying conditions are met in that year.

(3)   A group qualifies as small in relation to a subsequent financial year of the parent company—

    (a)   if the qualifying conditions are met in that year and the preceding financial year;

    (b)   if the qualifying conditions are met in that year and the group qualified as small in relation to the preceding financial year;

    (c)   if the qualifying conditions were met in the preceding financial year and the group qualified as small in relation to that year.

(4)   The qualifying conditions are met by a group in a year in which it satisfies two or more of the following requirements—

1 Aggregate turnover	Not more than £6.5 million net (or £7.8 million gross)
2 Aggregate balance sheet total	Not more than £3.26 million net (or £3.9 million gross)
3 Aggregate number of employees	Not more than 50

(5)   The aggregate figures are ascertained by aggregating the relevant figures determined in accordance with section 382 for each member of the group.

(6)   In relation to the aggregate figures for turnover and balance sheet total—

"net" means after any set-offs and other adjustments made to eliminate group transactions—

    (a)   in the case of Companies Act accounts, in accordance with regulations under section 404,

    (b)   in the case of IAS accounts, in accordance with international accounting standards; and

"gross" means without those set-offs and other adjustments.

A company may satisfy any relevant requirement on the basis of either the net or the gross figure.

(7)   The figures for each subsidiary undertaking shall be those included in its individual accounts for the relevant financial year, that is—

(a)   if its financial year ends with that of the parent company, that financial year, and

(b)   if not, its financial year ending last before the end of the financial year of the parent company.

If those figures cannot be obtained without disproportionate expense or undue delay, the latest available figures shall be taken.

384   Companies excluded from the small companies regime

(1)   The small companies regime does not apply to a company that is, or was at any time within the financial year to which the accounts relate—

(a)   a public company,

(b)   a company that—

(i)   is an authorised insurance company, a banking company, an e-money issuer, a MiFID investment firm or a UCITS management company, or

(ii)   carries on insurance market activity, or

(c)   a member of an ineligible group.

(2)   A group is ineligible if any of its members is—

(a)   a public company,

(b)   a body corporate (other than a company) whose shares are admitted to trading on a regulated market in an EEA State,

(c)   a person (other than a small company) who has permission under Part 4 of the Financial Services and Markets Act 2000 to carry on a regulated activity,

(d)   a small company that is an authorised insurance company, a banking company, an e-money issuer, a MiFID investment firm or a UCITS management company, or

(e)   a person who carries on insurance market activity.

(3)   A company is a small company for the purposes of subsection (2) if it qualified as small in relation to its last financial year ending on or before the end of the financial year to which the accounts relate.

PART 25
COMPANY CHARGES

CHAPTER 1
COMPANIES REGISTERED IN ENGLAND AND WALES OR IN NORTHERN IRELAND

The register of charges

869   Register of charges to be kept by registrar

(1)   The registrar shall keep, with respect to each company, a register of all the charges requiring registration under this Chapter.

(2)   In the case of a charge to the benefit of which holders of a series of debentures are entitled, the registrar shall enter in the register the required particulars specified in section 863(2).

...

(4)   In the case of any other charge, the registrar shall enter in the register the following particulars—

(a)   if it is a charge created by a company, the date of its creation and, if it is a charge which was existing on property acquired by the company, the date of the acquisition,

(b)   the amount secured by the charge,

(c)   short particulars of the property charged, and

(d)   the persons entitled to the charge.

(5)   The registrar shall give a certificate of the registration of any charge registered in pursuance of this Chapter, stating the amount secured by the charge.

(6)   The certificate—

(a)   shall be signed by the registrar or authenticated by the registrar's official seal, and

      (b)   is conclusive evidence that the requirements of this Chapter as to registration have been satisfied.

  (7) The register kept in pursuance of this section shall be open to inspection by any person.

PART 26
ARRANGEMENTS AND RECONSTRUCTIONS

Application of this Part

895   Application of this Part

  (1) The provisions of this Part apply where a compromise or arrangement is proposed between a company and—

      (a) its creditors, or any class of them, or

      (b) its members, or any class of them.

  (2) In this Part—

"arrangement" includes a reorganisation of the company's share capital by the consolidation of shares of different classes or by the division of shares into shares of different classes, or by both of those methods; and "company"—

      (a) in section 900 (powers of court to facilitate reconstruction or amalgamation) means a company within the meaning of this Act, and

      (b) elsewhere in this Part means any company liable to be wound up under the Insolvency Act 1986 or the Insolvency (Northern Ireland) Order 1989.

  (3) The provisions of this Part have effect subject to Part 27 (mergers and divisions of public companies) where that Part applies (see sections 902 and 903).

Meeting of creditors or members

896   Court order for holding of meeting

  (1) The court may, on an application under this section, order a meeting of the creditors or class of creditors, or of the members of the company or class of members (as the case may be), to be summoned in such manner as the court directs.

  (2) An application under this section may be made by—

      (a) the company,

      (b) any creditor or member of the company, or

      (c) if the company is being wound up or an administration order is in force in relation to it, the liquidator or administrator.

897   Statement to be circulated or made available

  (1) Where a meeting is summoned under section 896—

      (a) every notice summoning the meeting that is sent to a creditor or member must be accompanied by a statement complying with this section, and

      (b) every notice summoning the meeting that is given by advertisement must either—

         (i) include such a statement, or

         (ii) state where and how creditors or members entitled to attend the meeting may obtain copies of such a statement.

  (2) The statement must—

      (a) explain the effect of the compromise or arrangement, and

      (b) in particular, state—

         (i) any material interests of the directors of the company (whether as directors or as members or as creditors of the company or otherwise), and

        (ii) the effect on those interests of the compromise or arrangement, in so far as it is different from the effect on the like interests of other persons.

  (3) Where the compromise or arrangement affects the rights of debenture holders of the company, the statement must give the like explanation as respects the trustees of any deed for securing the issue of the debentures as it is required to give as respects the company's directors.

(4)   Where a notice given by advertisement states that copies of an explanatory statement can be obtained by creditors or members entitled to attend the meeting, every such creditor or member is entitled, on making application in the manner indicated by the notice, to be provided by the company with a copy of the statement free of charge.

(5)   If a company makes default in complying with any requirement of this section, an offence is committed by—

    (a)   the company, and

    (b)   every officer of the company who is in default.

    This is subject to subsection (7) below.

(6)   For this purpose the following are treated as officers of the company—

    (a)   a liquidator or administrator of the company, and

    (b)   a trustee of a deed for securing the issue of debentures of the company.

(7)   A person is not guilty of an offence under this section if he shows that the default was due to the refusal of a director or trustee for debenture holders to supply the necessary particulars of his interests.

(8)   A person guilty of an offence under this section is liable—

    (a)   on conviction on indictment, to a fine;

    (b)   on summary conviction, to a fine not exceeding the statutory maximum.

898   Duty of directors and trustees to provide information

(1)   It is the duty of—

    (a)   any director of the company, and

    (b)   any trustee for its debenture holders,

    to give notice to the company of such matters relating to himself as may be necessary for the purposes of section 897 (explanatory statement to be circulated or made available).

(2)   Any person who makes default in complying with this section commits an offence.

(3)   A person guilty of an offence under this section is liable on summary conviction to a fine not exceeding level 3 on the standard scale.

Court sanction for compromise or arrangement

899   Court sanction for compromise or arrangement

(1)   If a majority in number representing 75% in value of the creditors or class of creditors or members or class of members (as the case may be), present and voting either in person or by proxy at the meeting summoned under section 896, agree a compromise or arrangement, the court may, on an application under this section, sanction the compromise or arrangement.

(2)   An application under this section may be made by—

    (a)   the company,

    (b)   any creditor or member of the company, or

    (c)   if the company is being wound up or an administration order is in force in relation it, the liquidator or administrator.

(3)   A compromise or agreement sanctioned by the court is binding on—

    (a)   all creditors or the class of creditors or on the members or class of members (as the case may be), and

    (b)   the company or, in the case of a company in the course of being wound up, the liquidator and contributories of the company.

(4)   The court's order has no effect until a copy of it has been delivered to the registrar.

Reconstructions and amalgamations

900   Powers of court to facilitate reconstruction or amalgamation

(1)   This section applies where application is made to the court under section 899 to sanction a compromise or arrangement and it is shown that—

    (a)   the compromise or arrangement is proposed for the purposes of, or in connection with, a scheme for the reconstruction of any company or companies, or the amalgamation of any two or more companies, and

    (b)   under the scheme the whole or any part of the undertaking or the property of any company concerned in the scheme ("a transferor company") is to be transferred to another company ("the transferee company").

(2)   The court may, either by the order sanctioning the compromise or arrangement or by a subsequent order, make provision for all or any of the following matters—

    (a)   the transfer to the transferee company of the whole or any part of the undertaking and of the property or liabilities of any transferor company;

    (b)   the allotting or appropriation by the transferee company of any shares, debentures, policies or other like interests in that company which under the compromise or arrangement are to be allotted or appropriated by that company to or for any person;

    (c)   the continuation by or against the transferee company of any legal proceedings pending by or against any transferor company;

    (d)   the dissolution, without winding up, of any transferor company;

    (e)   the provision to be made for any persons who, within such time and in such manner as the court directs, dissent from the compromise or arrangement;

    (f)   such incidental, consequential and supplemental matters as are necessary to secure that the reconstruction or amalgamation is fully and effectively carried out.

(3)   If an order under this section provides for the transfer of property or liabilities—

    (a)   the property is by virtue of the order transferred to, and vests in, the transferee company, and

    (b)   the liabilities are, by virtue of the order, transferred to and become liabilities of that company.

(4)   The property (if the order so directs) vests freed from any charge that is by virtue of the compromise or arrangement to cease to have effect.

(5)   In this section—

"property" includes property, rights and powers of every description; and

"liabilities" includes duties.

(6)   Every company in relation to which an order is made under this section must cause a copy of the order to be delivered to the registrar within seven days after its making.

(7)   If default is made in complying with subsection (6) an offence is committed by—

    (a)   the company, and

    (b)   every officer of the company who is in default.

(8)   A person guilty of an offence under subsection (7) is liable on summary conviction to a fine not exceeding level 3 on the standard scale and, for continued contravention, a daily default fine not exceeding one-tenth of level 3 on the standard scale.

PART 31
DISSOLUTION AND RESTORATION TO THE REGISTER

CHAPTER 1
STRIKING OFF

Registrar's power to strike off defunct company

1000   Power to strike off company not carrying on business or in operation

(1)   If the registrar has reasonable cause to believe that a company is not carrying on business or in operation, the registrar may send to the company by post a letter inquiring whether the company is carrying on business or in operation.

(2)   If the registrar does not within one month of sending the letter receive any answer to it, the registrar must within 14 days after the expiration of that month send to the company by post a registered letter referring to the first letter, and stating—

    (a)   that no answer to it has been received, and

    (b)   that if an answer is not received to the second letter within one month from its date, a notice will be published in the Gazette with a view to striking the company's name off the register.

(3)   If the registrar—

    (a)   receives an answer to the effect that the company is not carrying on business or in operation, or

    (b)   does not within one month after sending the second letter receive any answer,

the registrar may publish in the Gazette, and send to the company by post, a notice that at the expiration of three months from the date of the notice the name of the company mentioned in it will, unless cause is shown to the contrary, be struck off the register and the company will be dissolved.

(4)   At the expiration of the time mentioned in the notice the registrar may, unless cause to the contrary is previously shown by the company, strike its name off the register.

(5)   The registrar must publish notice in the Gazette of the company's name having been struck off the register.

(6)   On the publication of the notice in the Gazette the company is dissolved.

(7)   However—

    (a)   the liability (if any) of every director, managing officer and member of the company continues and may be enforced as if the company had not been dissolved, and

    (b)   nothing in this section affects the power of the court to wind up a company the name of which has been struck off the register.

1001 Duty to act in case of company being wound up

(1)   If, in a case where a company is being wound up—

    (a)   the registrar has reasonable cause to believe—

        (i)   that no liquidator is acting, or

        (ii)   that the affairs of the company are fully wound up, and

    (b)   the returns required to be made by the liquidator have not been made for a period of six consecutive months,

the registrar must publish in the Gazette and send to the company or the liquidator (if any) a notice that at the expiration of three months from the date of the notice the name of the company mentioned in it will, unless cause is shown to the contrary, be struck off the register and the company will be dissolved.

(2)   At the expiration of the time mentioned in the notice the registrar may, unless cause to the contrary is previously shown by the company, strike its name off the register.

(3)   The registrar must publish notice in the Gazette of the company's name having been struck off the register.

(4)   On the publication of the notice in the Gazette the company is dissolved.

(5)   However—

    (a)   the liability (if any) of every director, managing officer and member of the company continues and may be enforced as if the company had not been dissolved, and

    (b)   nothing in this section affects the power of the court to wind up a company the name of which has been struck off the register.

TRIBUNALS, COURTS AND ENFORCEMENT ACT 2007
(2007, c 15)

PART 5
DEBT MANAGEMENT AND RELIEF

CHAPTER 1
ADMINISTRATION ORDERS

106 Administration orders

(1)   For Part 6 of the County Courts Act 1984 (administration orders) substitute—

"PART 6
ADMINISTRATION ORDERS

Administration orders

112A   Administration orders

An administration order is an order—

    (a)   to which certain debts are scheduled in accordance with section 112C, 112D or 112Y(3) or (4),

    (b)   which imposes the requirement specified in section 112E on the debtor, and

    (c)   which imposes the requirements specified in sections 112F to 112I on certain creditors.

112B   Power to make order

    (1)   A county court may make an administration order if the conditions in subsections (2) to (7) are met.

    (2)   The order must be made in respect of an individual who is a debtor under two or more qualifying debts.

    (3)   That individual ("the debtor") must not be a debtor under any business debts.

    (4)   The debtor must not be excluded under any of the following—

        (a)   the AO exclusion;

        (b)   the voluntary arrangement exclusion;

        (c)   the bankruptcy exclusion.

    (5)   The debtor must be unable to pay one or more of his qualifying debts.

    (6)   The total amount of the debtor's qualifying debts must be less than, or the same as, the prescribed maximum.

    (7)   The debtor's surplus income must be more than the prescribed minimum.

    (8)   Before making an administration order, the county court must have regard to any representations made—

        (a)   by any person about why the order should not be made, or

        (b)   by a creditor under a debt about why the debt should not be taken into account in calculating the total amount of the debtor's qualifying debts.

Scheduling debts

112C   Scheduling declared debts

    (1)   This section applies to a qualifying debt ("the declared debt") if—

        (a)   an administration order is made, and

        (b)   when the order is made, the debt is taken into account in calculating the total amount of the debtor's qualifying debts for the purposes of section 112B(6).

    (2)   If the declared debt is already due at the time the administration order is made, the proper county court must schedule the debt to the order when the order is made.

    (3)   If the declared debt becomes due after the administration order is made, the proper county court must schedule the debt to the order if the debtor, or the creditor under the debt, applies to the court for the debt to be scheduled.

    …

112D   Scheduling new debts

    (1)   This section applies to a qualifying debt ("the new debt") if the debt—

        (a)   arises after an administration order is made, and

        (b)   becomes due during the currency of the order.

(2) The proper county court may schedule the new debt to the administration order if these conditions are met—

    (a) the debtor, or the creditor under the new debt, applies to the court for the debt to be scheduled;

    (b) the total amount of the debtor's qualifying debts (including the new debt) is less than, or the same as, the prescribed maximum.

Requirements imposed by order

112E   Repayment requirement

(1) An administration order must, during the currency of the order, impose a repayment requirement on the debtor.

(2) A repayment requirement is a requirement for the debtor to repay the scheduled debts.

(3) The repayment requirement may provide for the debtor to repay a particular scheduled debt in full or to some other extent.

(4) The repayment requirement may provide for the debtor to repay different scheduled debts to different extents.

(5) In the case of a new debt scheduled to the order in accordance with section 112D, the repayment requirement may provide that no due repayment in respect of the new debt is to be made until the debtor has made all due repayments in respect of declared debts.

(6) The repayment requirement must provide that the due repayments are to be made by instalments.

(7) It is for the proper county court to decide when the instalments are to be made.

(8) But the proper county court is to determine the amount of the instalments in accordance with repayment regulations.

…

(10) The repayment requirement may provide that the due repayments are to be made by other means (including by one or more lump sums) in addition to the instalments required in accordance with subsection (6).

…

112F   Presentation of bankruptcy petition

(1) An administration order must, during the currency of the order, impose the following requirement.

(2) The requirement is that no qualifying creditor of the debtor is to present a bankruptcy petition against the debtor in respect of a qualifying debt, unless the creditor has the permission of the proper county court.

(3) The proper county court may give permission for the purposes of subsection (2) subject to such conditions as it thinks fit.

112G   Remedies other than bankruptcy

(1) An administration order must, during the currency of the order, impose the following requirement.

(2) The requirement is that no qualifying creditor of the debtor is to pursue any remedy for the recovery of a qualifying debt unless—

    (a) regulations under subsection (3) provide otherwise, or

    (b) the creditor has the permission of the proper county court.

(3) Regulations may specify classes of debt which are exempted (or exempted for specified purposes) from the restriction imposed by subsection (2).

(4) The proper county court may give permission for the purposes of subsection (2)(b) subject to such conditions as it thinks fit.

(5) This section does not have any effect in relation to bankruptcy proceedings.

112H   Charging of interest etc

(1)   An administration order must, during the currency of the order, impose the following requirement.

(2)   The requirement is that no creditor under a scheduled debt is to charge any sum by way of interest, fee or other charge in respect of that debt.

112I   Stopping supplies of gas or electricity

(1)   An administration order must, during the currency of the order, impose the requirement in subsection (3).

(2)   In relation to that requirement, a domestic utility creditor is any person who—

(a)   provides the debtor with a supply of mains gas or mains electricity for the debtor's own domestic purposes, and

(b)   is a creditor under a qualifying debt that relates to the provision of that supply.

(3)   The requirement is that no domestic utility creditor is to stop the supply of gas or electricity, or the supply of any associated services, except in the cases in subsections (4) to (6).

(4)   The first case is where the reason for stopping a supply relates to the non-payment by the debtor of charges incurred in connection with that supply after the making of the administration order.

(5)   The second case is where the reason for stopping a supply is unconnected with the non-payment by the debtor of any charges incurred in connection with—

(a)   that supply, or

(b)   any other supply of mains gas or mains electricity, or of associated services, that is provided by the domestic utility creditor.

(6)   The third case is where the proper county court gives permission to stop a supply.

(7)   The proper county court may give permission for the purposes of subsection (6) subject to such conditions as it thinks fit.

(8)   A supply of mains gas is a supply of the kind mentioned in section 5(1)(b) of the Gas Act 1986.

(9)   A supply of mains electricity is a supply of the kind mentioned in section 4(1)(c) of the Electricity Act 1989.

Making an order

112J   Application for an order

(1)   A county court may make an administration order only on the application of the debtor.

(2)   The debtor may make an application for an administration order whether or not a judgment has been obtained against him in respect of any of his debts.

112K   Duration

(1)   A county court may, at the time it makes an administration order, specify a day on which the order will cease to have effect.

(2)   The court may not specify a day which falls after the last day of the maximum permitted period.

(3)   If the court specifies a day under this section, the order ceases to have effect on that day.

(4)   If the court does not specify a day under this section, the order ceases to have effect at the end of the maximum permitted period.

(5)   The maximum permitted period is the period of five years beginning with the day on which the order is made.

(6)   This section is subject to—

    (a)   section 112S (variation of duration);

    (b)   section 112W (effect of revocation).

(7)   This section is also subject to the following (effect of enforcement restriction order or debt relief order on administration order)—

    (a)   section 117I of this Act;

    (b)   section 251F of the Insolvency Act 1986.

Effects of order

112L   Effect on other debt management arrangements

(1)   This section applies if—

    (a)   an administration order is made, and

    (b)   immediately before the order is made, other debt management arrangements are in force in respect of the debtor.

(2)   The other debt management arrangements cease to be in force when the administration order is made.

(3)   If the proper county court is aware of the other debt management arrangements, the court must give the relevant authority notice that the order has been made.

(4)   In a case where the proper county court is aware of other debt management arrangements at the time it makes the order, it must give the notice as soon as practicable after making the order.

(5)   In a case where the proper county court becomes aware of those arrangements after it makes the order, it must give the notice as soon as practicable after becoming aware of them.

(6)   "Other debt management arrangements" means any of the following—

    (a)   an enforcement restriction order under Part 6A of this Act;

    (b)   a debt relief order under Part 7A of the Insolvency Act 1986;

    (c)   a debt repayment plan arranged in accordance with a debt management scheme that is approved under Chapter 4 of Part 5 of the Tribunals, Courts and Enforcement Act 2007.

(7)   "The relevant authority" means—

    (a)   in relation to an enforcement restriction order: the proper county court (within the meaning of Part 6A);

    (b)   in relation to a debt relief order: the official receiver;

    (c)   in relation to a debt repayment plan: the operator of the debt management scheme in accordance with which the plan is arranged.

(8)   For the purposes of this section a debt relief order is "in force" if the moratorium applicable to the order under section 251H of the Insolvency Act 1986 has not yet ended.

112M   Duty to provide information

(1)   This section applies if, and for as long as, an administration order has effect in respect of a debtor.

(2)   The debtor must, at the prescribed times, provide the proper county court with particulars of his—

    (a)   earnings,

    (b)   income,

    (c)   assets, and

    (d)   outgoings.

(3)   The debtor must provide particulars of those matters—

    (a)   as the matters are at the time the particulars are provided, and

    (b)   as the debtor expects the matters to be at such times in the future as are prescribed.

(4)   If the debtor intends to dispose of any of his property he must, within the prescribed period, provide the proper county court with particulars of the following matters—

    (a)   the property he intends to dispose of;

    (b)   the consideration (if any) he expects will be given for the disposal;

    (c)   such other matters as may be prescribed;

    (d)   such other matters as the court may specify.

(5)   But subsection (4) does not apply if the disposal is of—

    (a)   goods that are exempt goods for the purposes of Schedule 12 to the Tribunals, Courts and Enforcement Act 2007,

    (b)   goods that are protected under any other enactment from being taken control of under that Schedule, or

    (c)   prescribed property.

(6)   The duty under subsection (4) to provide the proper county court with particulars of a proposed disposal of property applies whether the debtor is the sole owner, or one of several owners, of the property.

(7)   In any provision of this section "prescribed" means prescribed in regulations for the purposes of that provision.

112N   Offence if information not provided

(1)   A person commits an offence if he fails to comply with—

    (a)   section 112M(2) and (3), or

    (b)   section 112M(4).

(2)   A person who commits an offence under subsection (1) may be ordered by a judge of the proper county court to pay a fine of not more than £250 or to be imprisoned for not more than 14 days.

(3)   Where under subsection (2) a person is ordered to be imprisoned by a judge of the proper county court, the judge may at any time—

    (a)   revoke the order, and

    (b)   if the person is already in custody, order his discharge.

(4)   Section 129 of this Act (enforcement of fines) applies to payment of a fine imposed under subsection (2).

(5)   For the purposes of section 13 of the Administration of Justice Act 1960 (appeal in cases of contempt of court), subsection (2) is to be treated as an enactment enabling a county court to deal with an offence under subsection (1) as if it were a contempt of court.

(6)   A district judge or deputy district judge shall have the same powers under this section as a judge of a county court.

112O   Existing county court proceedings to be stayed

(1)   This section applies if these conditions are met—

    (a)   an administration order is made;

    (b)   proceedings in a county court (other than bankruptcy proceedings) are pending against the debtor in respect of a qualifying debt;

    (c)   by virtue of a requirement included in the order by virtue of section 112G, the creditor under the qualifying debt is not entitled to continue the proceedings in respect of the debt;

    (d)   the county court receives notice of the administration order.

(2)   The county court must stay the proceedings.

(3)   The court may allow costs already incurred by the creditor.

(4)   If the court allows such costs, it may on application or of its motion add them—

    (a)   to the debt, or

    (b)   if the debt is a scheduled debt, to the amount scheduled to the order in respect of the debt.

(5)   But the court may not add the costs under subsection (4)(b) if the court is under a duty under section 112U(6)(b) to revoke the order because the total amount of the debtor's qualifying debts (including the costs) is more than the prescribed maximum.

112P   Appropriation of money paid

(1)   Money paid into court under an administration order is to be appropriated—
  (a)   first in satisfaction of any relevant court fees, and
  (b)   then in liquidation of debts.

(2)   Relevant court fees are any fees under an order made under section 92 of the Courts Act 2003 which are payable by the debtor in respect of the administration order.

112Q   Discharge from debts

(1)   If the debtor repays a scheduled debt to the extent provided for by the administration order, the proper county court must—
  (a)   order that the debtor is discharged from the debt, and
  (b)   de-schedule the debt.

(2)   If the debtor repays all of the scheduled debts to the extent provided for by the administration order, the proper county court must revoke the order.

(3)   Subsections (1) and (2) apply to all scheduled debts, including any which, under the administration order, are to be repaid other than to their full extent.

Variation

112R   Variation

(1)   The proper county court may vary an administration order.

(2)   The power under this section is exercisable—
  (a)   on the application of the debtor;
  (b)   on the application of a qualifying creditor;
  (c)   of the court's own motion.

112S   Variation of duration

(1)   The power under section 112R includes power to vary an administration order so as to specify a day, or (if a day has already been specified under section 112K or this subsection) a different day, on which the order will cease to have effect.

(2)   But the new termination day must fall on or before the last day of the maximum permitted period.

(3)   If the proper county court varies an administration under subsection (1), the order ceases to have effect on the new termination day.

(4)   In this section—
  (a)   "new termination day" means the day on which the order will cease to have effect in accordance with the variation under subsection (1);
  (b)   "maximum permitted period" means the period of five years beginning with the day on which the order was originally made.

(5)   This section is subject to section 112W (effect of revocation).

112T   De-scheduling debts

(1)   The power under section 112R includes power to vary an administration order by de-scheduling a debt.

(2)   But the debt may be de-scheduled only if it appears to the proper county court that it is just and equitable to do so.

...

Interpretation

112AA Main definitions

(1) In this Part—

"administration order" has the meaning given by section 112A;

"debtor" has the meaning given by section 112B;

"prescribed maximum" means the amount prescribed in regulations for the purposes of section 112B(6);

"prescribed minimum" means the amount prescribed in regulations for the purposes of section 112B(7);

"qualifying creditor" means a creditor under a qualifying debt.

(2) References to the currency of an administration order are references to the period which—

(a) begins when the order first has effect, and

(b) ends when the order ceases to have effect.

(3) In relation to an administration order, references to the proper county court are references to the county court that made the order.

(4) But that is subject to rules of court as to the venue for, and transfer of, proceedings in county courts.

112AB Expressions relating to debts

(1) All debts are qualifying debts, except for the following—

(a) any debt secured against an asset;

(b) any debt of a description specified in regulations.

(2) A business debt is any debt (whether or not a qualifying debt) which is incurred by a person in the course of a business.

(3) Only debts that have already arisen are included in references to debts; and accordingly such references do not include any debt that will arise only on the happening of some future contingency.

112AC Inability to pay debts

(1) In a case where an individual is the debtor under a debt that is repayable by a single payment, the debtor is to be regarded as unable to pay the debt only if—

(a) the debt has become due,

(b) the debtor has failed to make the single payment, and

(c) the debtor is unable to make that payment.

(2) In a case where an individual is the debtor under a debt that is repayable by a number of payments, the debtor is to be regarded as unable to pay the debt only if—

(a) the debt has become due,

(b) the debtor has failed to make one or more of the payments, and

(c) the debtor is unable to make all of the missed payments.

112AD Calculating the debtor's qualifying debts

(1) The total amount of a debtor's qualifying debts is to be calculated in accordance with subsections (2) and (3).

(2) All of the debtor's qualifying debts which have arisen before the calculation must be taken into account (whether or not the debts are already due at the time of the calculation).

(3) Regulations must make further provision about how the total amount of a debtor's qualifying debts is to be calculated.

(4) Regulations may make provision about how the amount of any particular qualifying debt is to be calculated.

(5) That includes the calculation of the amount of a debt for these purposes—

(a) calculating the total amount of the debtor's qualifying debts;

(b)   scheduling the debt to an administration order.

112AE   Calculating the debtor's surplus income

(1)   The debtor's surplus income is to be calculated in accordance with regulations.

(2)   Regulations under this section must, in particular, make the following provision—

(a)   provision about what is surplus income;

(b)   provision about the period by reference to which the debtor's surplus income is to be calculated.

(3)   Regulations under this section may, in particular, provide for the debtor's assets to be taken account of when calculating his surplus income.

112AF   Debts becoming due

(1)   A debt that is repayable by a single payment becomes due when the time for making that payment is reached.

(2)   A debt that is repayable by a number of payments becomes due when the time for making the first of the payments is reached.

112AG   Scheduling and de-scheduling debts

(1)   A debt is scheduled to an administration order if the relevant information is included in a schedule to the order.

(2)   A debt is de-scheduled if the relevant information is removed from a schedule in which it was included as mentioned in subsection (1).

(3)   In relation to a debt, the relevant information is—

(a)   the amount of the debt, and

(b)   the name of the creditor under the debt.

(4)   A scheduled debt is a debt that is scheduled to an administration order.

(5)   The proper county court must not schedule a debt to an administration order unless the court has had regard to any representations made by any person about why the debt should not be scheduled.

(6)   But subsection (5) does not apply to any representations which are made by the debtor in relation to the scheduling of a debt under section 112Y.

(7)   The proper county court must not de-schedule a debt unless the court has had regard to any representations made by any person about why the debt should not be de-scheduled.

(8)   But subsection (7) does not apply in relation to the de-scheduling of a debt under section 112Q.

(9)   A court must not schedule a debt to an administration order, or de-schedule a debt, except in accordance with the provisions of this Part.

112AH   The AO, voluntary arrangement and bankruptcy exclusions

(1)   The debtor is excluded under the AO exclusion if—

(a)   an administration order currently has effect in respect of him, or

(b)   an administration order has previously had effect in respect of him, and the period of 12 months — beginning with the day when that order ceased to have effect — has yet to finish.

(2)   But in a case that falls within subsection (1)(b), the debtor is not excluded under the AO exclusion if the previous administration order—

(a)   ceased to have effect in accordance with any of the provisions listed in section 112K(7) (effect of enforcement restriction order or debt relief order on administration order), or

(b)   was revoked in accordance with section 112U(1)(b) (debtor no longer has any qualifying debts).

(3)   The debtor is excluded under the voluntary arrangement exclusion if—

(a)   an interim order under section 252 of the Insolvency Act 1986 has
        effect in respect of him (interim order where debtor intends to make
        proposal for voluntary arrangement), or

(b)   he is bound by a voluntary arrangement approved under Part 8 of the
        Insolvency Act 1986.

(4)   The debtor is excluded under the bankruptcy exclusion if—

(a)   a petition for a bankruptcy order to be made against him has been
        presented but not decided, or

(b)   he is an undischarged bankrupt.

...”

...

CHAPTER 3
DEBT RELIEF ORDERS

108   Debt relief orders and debt relief restrictions orders etc

(1)   In the Second Group of Parts of the Insolvency Act 1986 (insolvency of individuals), before
        Part 8 there is inserted, as Part 7A, the Part set out in Schedule 17.

(2)   After Schedule 4 to that Act there is inserted, as Schedules 4ZA and 4ZB, the Schedules set
        out in Schedules 18 and 19.

...

CHAPTER 4
DEBT MANAGEMENT SCHEMES

Introductory

109   Debt management schemes

(1)   A debt management scheme is a scheme that meets the conditions in this section.

(2)   The scheme must be open to some or all non-business debtors.

(3)   A scheme is open to a non-business debtor if it allows him to make a request to the scheme
        operator for a debt repayment plan to be arranged for him.

(4)   The scheme must provide that, if such a request is made—

(a)   a decision must be made about whether a debt repayment plan is to be arranged for the
        non-business debtor, and

(b)   such a plan must be arranged (if that is the decision made).

(5)   The scheme must be operated by a body of persons (whether a body corporate or not).

110   Debt repayment plans

(1)   A debt repayment plan is a plan that meets the conditions in this section.

(2)   The plan must specify all of the debtor's qualifying debts.

(3)   The plan must require the debtor to make payments in respect of each of the specified debts.

(4)   It does not matter if—

(a)   the plan requires payments of different amounts to be made in respect of a specified
        debt at different times;

(b)   the payments that the plan requires to be made in respect of a specified debt would, if
        all made, repay the debt only in part.

Approval of schemes

111   Approval by supervising authority

(1)   The supervising authority may approve one or more debt management schemes.

(2)   Regulations may make provision about any or all of the following—

(a)   conditions that must be met before the supervising authority may approve a debt
        management scheme;

(b)   considerations that the supervising authority must, or must not, take into account in
        deciding whether to approve a debt management scheme.

(3) Regulations under this section may, in particular, make provision about conditions or considerations that relate to any matter listed in Schedule 21.

(4) The supervising authority may approve a debt management scheme whether a body is—

    (a) operating the scheme at the time of the approval, or

    (b) proposing to operate the scheme from a time in the future.

112 Applications for approval

(1) Regulations may specify a procedure for making an application for approval of a debt management scheme.

(2) Regulations under this section may, in particular, specify a procedure that requires any or all of the following—

    (a) an application to be made in a particular form;

    (b) information to be supplied in support of an application;

    (c) a fee to be paid in respect of an application.

...

Effect of plans etc

114 Discharge from specified debts

(1) This section applies if—

    (a) a debt repayment plan is arranged for a non-business debtor in accordance with an approved scheme, and

    (b) the plan comes into effect.

(2) The debtor is discharged from the debts that are specified in the plan.

(3) The discharge from a particular specified debt takes effect at the time when all the required payments have been made.

(4) The required payments are the payments in respect of the debt that are required by the provision included in the plan in accordance with section 110(3).

115 Presentation of bankruptcy petition

(1) This section applies during the currency of a debt repayment plan arranged in accordance with an approved scheme.

(2) No qualifying creditor of the debtor is to present a bankruptcy petition against the debtor in respect of a qualifying debt, unless—

    (a) regulations provide otherwise, or

    (b) the creditor has the permission of a county court.

(3) A county court may give permission for the purposes of subsection (2)(b) subject to such conditions as it thinks fit.

(4) The reference to the currency of a debt repayment plan is a reference to the period which—

    (a) begins when the plan first has effect, and

    (b) ends when the plan ceases to have effect.

116 Remedies other than bankruptcy

(1) This section applies in relation to a non-business debtor during a period of protection.

(2) No qualifying creditor of the debtor is to pursue any remedy for the recovery of a qualifying debt, unless—

    (a) regulations provide otherwise, or

    (b) the creditor has the permission of a county court.

(3) A county court may give permission for the purposes of subsection (2)(b) subject to such conditions as it thinks fit.

(4) This section does not have any effect in relation to bankruptcy proceedings.

117 Charging of interest etc

(1) This section applies in relation to a non-business debtor during a period of protection.

(2) No qualifying creditor is to charge any sum by way of interest, fee or other charge in respect of a qualifying debt, unless—

    (a) regulations provide otherwise, or

       (b)   the creditor has the permission of a county court.

  (3)   A county court may give permission for the purposes of subsection (2)(b) subject to such conditions as it thinks fit.

118   Stopping supplies of gas or electricity

  (1)   This section applies in relation to a non-business debtor during a period of protection.

  (2)   In relation to the debtor, a domestic utility creditor is any person who—

       (a)   provides the debtor with a supply of mains gas or mains electricity for the debtor's own domestic purposes, and

       (b)   is a creditor under a qualifying debt that relates to the provision of that supply.

  (3)   No domestic utility creditor is to stop the supply of gas or electricity, or the supply of any associated services, except in the cases in subsections (4) to (7).

  (4)   The first case is where the reason for stopping a supply relates to the non-payment by the debtor of charges incurred in connection with that supply after the start of the period of protection.

  (5)   The second case is where the reason for stopping a supply is unconnected with the non-payment by the debtor of any charges incurred in connection with—

       (a)   that supply, or

       (b)   any other supply of mains gas or mains electricity, or of associated services, that is provided by the domestic utility creditor.

  (6)   The third case is where regulations allow the supply to be stopped.

  (7)   The fourth case is where a county court gives permission to stop a supply.

  (8)   A county court may give permission for the purposes of subsection (7) subject to such conditions as it thinks fit.

  (9)   A supply of mains gas is a supply of the kind mentioned in section 5(1)(b) of the Gas Act 1986.

  (10) A supply of mains electricity is a supply of the kind mentioned in section 4(1)(c) of the Electricity Act 1989.

119   Existing county court proceedings to be stayed

  (1)   This section applies if these conditions are met—

       (a)   a debt repayment plan is arranged for a non-business debtor in accordance with an approved scheme;

       (b)   proceedings in a county court (other than bankruptcy proceedings) are pending against the debtor in respect of a qualifying debt;

       (c)   by virtue of section 116, the creditor under the qualifying debt is not entitled to continue the proceedings in respect of the debt;

       (d)   the county court receives notice of the debt repayment plan.

  (2)   The county court must stay the proceedings.

  (3)   The court may allow costs already incurred by the creditor.

  (4)   Subsection (5) applies if—

       (a)   the court allows such costs, and

       (b)   the qualifying debt is a specified debt.

  (5)   The operator of the approved scheme may, if requested to do so by—

       (a)   the non-business debtor, or

       (b)   the creditor under the qualifying debt,

      add the costs to the amount specified in the plan in respect of the debt.

  (6)   But the operator may not add the costs under subsection (5) if, under the terms of the approved scheme, the operator is under a duty to terminate the plan.

120   Registration of plans

  (1)   Regulations may make provision about the registration of either or both of the following—

       (a)   any request made to the operator of an approved scheme for a debt repayment plan to be arranged in accordance with the scheme;

       (b)   any debt repayment plan arranged for a non-business debtor in accordance with an approved scheme.

(2) In subsection (1) "registration" means registration in the register maintained under section 98 of the Courts Act 2003 (the register of judgments and orders etc).

(3) Regulations under this section may amend section 98 of the 2003 Act.

121 Other debt management arrangements in force

(1) This section applies if—

    (a) a debt repayment plan is arranged for a debtor in accordance with an approved scheme, and

    (b) immediately before the plan is arranged, other debt management arrangements are in force in respect of the debtor.

(2) The plan is not to come into effect unless the other debt management arrangements cease to be in force.

(3) Any provision (whether in the plan or elsewhere) about when the plan is to come into effect is subject to subsection (2).

(4) If the operator of the approved scheme is aware of the other debt management arrangements, the operator must give the relevant authority notice that the plan has been arranged.

(5) In a case where the operator is aware of other debt management arrangements at the time the plan is arranged, it must give the notice as soon as practicable after the plan is arranged.

(6) In a case where the operator becomes aware of those arrangements after the plan is arranged, it must give the notice as soon as practicable after becoming aware of them.

(7) "Other debt management arrangements" means any of the following—

    (a) an administration order under Part 6 of the County Courts Act 1984;

    (b) an enforcement restriction order under Part 6A of the County Courts Act 1984;

    (c) a debt relief order under Part 7A of the Insolvency Act 1986.

(8) "The relevant authority" means—

    (a) in relation to an administration order: the proper county court (within the meaning of Part 6 of the County Courts Act 1984);

    (b) in relation to an enforcement restriction order: the proper county court (within the meaning of Part 6A of the County Courts Act 1984);

    (c) in relation to a debt relief order: the official receiver.

(9) For the purposes of this section a debt relief order is "in force" if the moratorium applicable to the order under section 251H of the Insolvency Act 1986 has not yet ended.

Appeals

122 Right of appeal

(1) This section applies if a debt repayment plan is arranged for a debtor in accordance with an approved scheme.

(2) An affected creditor may appeal to a county court against any of the following—

    (a) the fact that the plan has been arranged;

    (b) the fact that a debt owed to the affected creditor has been specified in the plan;

    (c) the terms of the plan (including any provision included in the plan in accordance with section 110(3)).

(3) Subsection (2)(c) does not allow an affected creditor to appeal against the fact that a debt owed to any other creditor has been specified in the plan.

(4) In this section "affected creditor" means the creditor under any debt which is specified in the plan.

123 Dealing with appeals

(1) This section applies if an appeal is made to a county court under section 122.

(2) The county court may determine the appeal in any way that it thinks fit.

(3) The county court may make such orders as may be necessary to give effect to the determination of the appeal.

(4) The county court may, in particular, order the scheme operator to do any of the following—

    (a) to reconsider the decision to arrange the plan;

       (b)   to reconsider any decision about the terms of the plan;
       (c)   to modify the debt repayment plan;
       (d)   to revoke the debt repayment plan.

(5) The county court may make such interim provision as it thinks fit in relation to the period before the appeal is determined.

(6) The county court is the county court to which the appeal is made.

Approved schemes: charging

124 Charges by operator of approved scheme

(1) The operator of an approved scheme may recover its costs by charging debtors or affected creditors (or both).

(2) In this section—

"costs" means the costs which the operator incurs, taking one year with another, in connection with the approved scheme, so far as those costs are reasonable;

"debtors" means—

       (a)   debtors who make requests for debt repayment plans to be arranged in accordance with the approved scheme, and

       (b)   debtors for whom debt repayment plans are arranged in accordance with the approved scheme.

Termination of approval

125 Procedure for termination

(1) Regulations may specify a procedure for terminating the approval of a debt management scheme.

(2) Regulations under this section may, in particular, specify a procedure that requires any or all of the following—

       (a)   notice of, or the reasons for, an intended termination to be given (whether to the supervising authority, the scheme operator, the Lord Chancellor or any other person);

       (b)   conditions to be met before a termination takes effect;

       (c)   a particular period of time to elapse before a termination takes effect.

126 Terminating an approval

The approval of a debt management scheme may be terminated only if the termination is in accordance with all of the following (so far as they are relevant)—

(a) any terms to which the approval is subject by virtue of section 113;

(b) any provision made in regulations under section 125;

(c) any other provision made in other regulations under this Chapter.

...

Effects of end of approval

128 Effects of end of approval

(1) Regulations may make provision about the effects if the approval of a debt management scheme comes to an end.

(2) Regulations under this section may, in particular, make provision about the treatment of debt repayment plans arranged for non-business debtors before the scheme came to an end.

(3) That includes provision to treat a plan—

       (a)   as though the approval had not come to an end, or

       (b)   as though the plan had been made in accordance with a different approved scheme.

(4) Regulations under this section may, in particular, make provision about cases where, at the time the scheme comes to an end, the scheme operator is in breach of a relevant obligation.

(5) That includes provision to ensure that the operator is not released from the relevant obligation by virtue of the termination.

(6) In subsections (4) and (5) "relevant obligation" means any obligation (including a requirement or condition) however arising, that relates to—

(a)   the scheme in question (including its operation),

(b)   the approval of that scheme, or

(c)   the termination of that approval.

The supervising authority

129   The supervising authority

(1)   The supervising authority is—

(a)   the Lord Chancellor, or

(b)   any person that the Lord Chancellor has authorised to approve debt management schemes under section 111.

(2)   Subsections (3) and (4) apply in any case where an authorisation under subsection (1)(b) starts or ends.

(3)   The start or end of the authorisation does not affect the validity of an approval that is in force at the relevant time.

(4)   The new supervising authority may exercise all of its functions in relation to an approval that is in force at the relevant time as though it had given the approval itself.

(5)   In this section—

"approval" means an approval of a debt management scheme given under section 111;

"relevant time" means the time when an authorisation starts or ends.

Various

...

131   Main definitions

(1)   In this Chapter—

"affected creditor" has the meaning given by section 122;

"approved scheme" means a debt management scheme that is approved under section 111;

"debt management scheme" has the meaning given by section 109;

"debt repayment plan" has the meaning given by section 110;

"non-business debtor" means any individual who—

(a)   is a debtor under one or more qualifying debts, but

(b)   is not a debtor under any business debts;

"period of protection" has the meaning given by section 133;

"qualifying creditor" means a creditor under a qualifying debt;

"scheme operator" means the body that operates a debt management scheme;

"specified debt" means a debt specified in a debt repayment plan;

"supervising authority" has the meaning given by section 129.

(2)   Any reference to a county court is subject to rules of court as to the venue for, and transfer of, proceedings in county courts.

132   Expressions relating to debts

(1)   All debts are qualifying debts, except the following—

(a)   any debt secured against an asset;

(b)   in relation to a debt repayment plan which has been requested or arranged, any debt which could not, by virtue of the terms of the debt management scheme, be specified in the plan.

(2)   A business debt is any debt (whether or not a qualifying debt) which is incurred by a person in the course of a business.

133   Periods of protection

(1)   A "period of protection", in relation to a non-business debtor, is a period which begins and ends as specified in this section.

(2)   The period begins if, and when, the debtor makes a request to the operator of an approved scheme for a debt repayment plan to be arranged in accordance with the scheme.

(3)   The period ends as follows—

(a) if a debt repayment plan is not arranged in consequence of the request: when the decision is made not to arrange the plan;

(b) if a debt repayment plan is arranged in consequence of the request: when that plan ceases to have effect.

(4) But if other debt management arrangements are in force in relation to debtor immediately before he makes the request, the period does not begin unless, and until, a debt repayment plan—

(a) is arranged in consequence of the request, and

(b) comes into effect in accordance with section 121(2).

(5) In this section the reference to other debt management arrangements which are in force has the same meaning as such references in section 121.

...

SCHEDULE 17
PART 7A OF THE INSOLVENCY ACT 1986

"PART 7A DEBT RELIEF ORDERS

Preliminary

251A   Debt relief orders

(1) An individual who is unable to pay his debts may apply for an order under this Part ("a debt relief order") to be made in respect of his qualifying debts.

(2) In this Part "qualifying debt" means (subject to subsection (3)) a debt which—

(a) is for a liquidated sum payable either immediately or at some certain future time; and

(b) is not an excluded debt.

(3) A debt is not a qualifying debt to the extent that it is secured.

(4) In this Part "excluded debt" means a debt of any description prescribed for the purposes of this subsection.

Applications for a debt relief order

251B   Making of application

(1) An application for a debt relief order must be made to the official receiver through an approved intermediary.

(2) The application must include—

(a) a list of the debts to which the debtor is subject at the date of the application, specifying the amount of each debt (including any interest, penalty or other sum that has become payable in relation to that debt on or before that date) and the creditor to whom it is owed;

(b) details of any security held in respect of any of those debts; and

(c) such other information about the debtor's affairs (including his creditors, debts and liabilities and his income and assets) as may be prescribed.

(3) The rules may make further provision as to—

(a) the form of an application for a debt relief order;

(b) the manner in which an application is to be made; and

(c) information and documents to be supplied in support of an application.

(4) For the purposes of this Part an application is not to be regarded as having been made until—

(a) the application has been submitted to the official receiver; and

(b) any fee required in connection with the application by an order under section 415 has been paid to such person as the order may specify.

251C   Duty of official receiver to consider and determine application

(1)   This section applies where an application for a debt relief order is made.

(2)   The official receiver may stay consideration of the application until he has received answers to any queries raised with the debtor in relation to anything connected with the application.

(3)   The official receiver must determine the application by—

(a)   deciding whether to refuse the application;

(b)   if he does not refuse it, by making a debt relief order in relation to the specified debts he is satisfied were qualifying debts of the debtor at the application date;

but he may only refuse the application if he is authorised or required to do so by any of the following provisions of this section.

(4)   The official receiver may refuse the application if he considers that—

(a)   the application does not meet all the requirements imposed by or under section 251B;

(b)   any queries raised with the debtor have not been answered to the satisfaction of the official receiver within such time as he may specify when they are raised;

(c)   the debtor has made any false representation or omission in making the application or on supplying any information or documents in support of it.

(5)   The official receiver must refuse the application if he is not satisfied that—

(a)   the debtor is an individual who is unable to pay his debts;

(b)   at least one of the specified debts was a qualifying debt of the debtor at the application date;

(c)   each of the conditions set out in Part 1 of Schedule 4ZA is met.

(6)   The official receiver may refuse the application if he is not satisfied that each condition specified in Part 2 of Schedule 4ZA is met.

(7)   If the official receiver refuses an application he must give reasons for his refusal to the debtor in the prescribed manner.

...

251D   Presumptions applicable to the determination of an application

(1)   The following presumptions are to apply to the determination of an application for a debt relief order.

(2)   The official receiver must presume that the debtor is an individual who is unable to pay his debts at the determination date if—

(a)   that appears to the official receiver to be the case at the application date from the information supplied in the application and he has no reason to believe that the information supplied is incomplete or inaccurate; and

(b)   he has no reason to believe that, by virtue of a change in the debtor's financial circumstances since the application date, the debtor may be able to pay his debts.

(3)   The official receiver must presume that a specified debt (of the amount specified in the application and owed to the creditor so specified) is a qualifying debt at the application date if—

(a)   that appears to him to be the case from the information supplied in the application; and

(b)   he has no reason to believe that the information supplied is incomplete or inaccurate.

(4)   The official receiver must presume that the condition specified in paragraph 1 of Schedule 4ZA is met if—

(a)   that appears to him to be the case from the information supplied in the application;

(b)   any prescribed verification checks relating to the condition have been made; and

(c)   he has no reason to believe that the information supplied is incomplete or inaccurate.

...

Making and effect of debt relief order

251E   Making of debt relief orders

(1)   This section applies where the official receiver makes a debt relief order on determining an application under section 251C.

(2)   The order must be made in the prescribed form.

(3)   The order must include a list of the debts which the official receiver is satisfied were qualifying debts of the debtor at the application date, specifying the amount of the debt at that time and the creditor to whom it was then owed.

(4)   The official receiver must—

(a)   give a copy of the order to the debtor; and

(b)   make an entry for the order in the register containing the prescribed information about the order or the debtor.

(5)   The rules may make provision as to other steps to be taken by the official receiver or the debtor on the making of the order.

(6)   Those steps may include in particular notifying each creditor to whom a qualifying debt specified in the order is owed of—

(a)   the making of the order and its effect,

(b)   the grounds on which a creditor may object under section 251K, and

(c)   any other prescribed information.

(7)   In this Part the date on which an entry relating to the making of a debt relief order is first made in the register is referred to as "the effective date".

251F   Effect of debt relief order on other debt management arrangements

(1)   This section applies if—

(a)   a debt relief order is made, and

(b)   immediately before the order is made, other debt management arrangements are in force in respect of the debtor.

(2)   The other debt management arrangements cease to be in force when the debt relief order is made.

(3)   In this section "other debt management arrangements" means—

(a)   an administration order under Part 6 of the County Courts Act 1984;

(b)   an enforcement restriction order under Part 6A of that Act;

(c)   a debt repayment plan arranged in accordance with a debt management scheme that is approved under Chapter 4 of Part 5 of the Tribunals, Courts and Enforcement Act 2007.

251G   Moratorium from qualifying debts

(1)   A moratorium commences on the effective date for a debt relief order in relation to each qualifying debt specified in the order ("a specified qualifying debt").

(2)   During the moratorium, the creditor to whom a specified qualifying debt is owed—

(a)   has no remedy in respect of the debt, and

(b)   may not—

(i)   commence a creditor's petition in respect of the debt, or

(ii)   otherwise commence any action or other legal proceedings against the debtor for the debt, except with the permission of the court and on such terms as the court may impose.

(3) If on the effective date a creditor to whom a specified qualifying debt is owed has any such petition, action or other proceeding as mentioned in subsection (2)(b) pending in any court, the court may—

    (a) stay the proceedings on the petition, action or other proceedings (as the case may be), or

    (b) allow them to continue on such terms as the court thinks fit.

(4) In subsection (2)(a) and (b) references to the debt include a reference to any interest, penalty or other sum that becomes payable in relation to that debt after the application date.

(5) Nothing in this section affects the right of a secured creditor of the debtor to enforce his security.

251H   The moratorium period

(1) The moratorium relating to the qualifying debts specified in a debt relief order continues for the period of one year beginning with the effective date for the order, unless—

    (a) the moratorium terminates early; or

    (b) the moratorium period is extended by the official receiver under this section or by the court under section 251M.

(2) The official receiver may only extend the moratorium period for the purpose of—

    (a) carrying out or completing an investigation under section 251K;

    (b) taking any action he considers necessary (whether as a result of an investigation or otherwise) in relation to the order; or

    (c) in a case where he has decided to revoke the order, providing the debtor with the opportunity to make arrangements for making payments towards his debts.

(3) The official receiver may not extend the moratorium period for the purpose mentioned in subsection (2)(a) without the permission of the court.

(4) The official receiver may not extend the moratorium period beyond the end of the period of three months beginning after the end of the initial period of one year mentioned in subsection (1).

(5) The moratorium period may be extended more than once, but any extension (whether by the official receiver or by the court) must be made before the moratorium would otherwise end.

(6) References in this Part to a moratorium terminating early are to its terminating before the end of what would otherwise be the moratorium period, whether on the revocation of the order or by virtue of any other enactment.

251I   Discharge from qualifying debts

(1) Subject as follows, at the end of the moratorium applicable to a debt relief order the debtor is discharged from all the qualifying debts specified in the order (including all interest, penalties and other sums which may have become payable in relation to those debts since the application date).

(2) Subsection (1) does not apply if the moratorium terminates early.

(3) Subsection (1) does not apply in relation to any qualifying debt which the debtor incurred in respect of any fraud or fraudulent breach of trust to which the debtor was a party.

(4) The discharge of the debtor under subsection (1) does not release any other person from—

    (a) any liability (whether as partner or co-trustee of the debtor or otherwise) from which the debtor is released by the discharge; or

(b)   any liability as surety for the debtor or as a person in the nature of such a surety.

(5)   If the order is revoked by the court under section 251M after the end of the moratorium period, the qualifying debts specified in the order shall (so far as practicable) be treated as though subsection (1) had never applied to them.

Duties of debtor

251J   Providing assistance to official receiver etc

(1)   The duties in this section apply to a debtor at any time after the making of an application by him for a debt relief order.

(2)   The debtor must—
     (a)   give to the official receiver such information as to his affairs,
     (b)   attend on the official receiver at such times, and
     (c)   do all such other things,
     as the official receiver may reasonably require for the purpose of carrying out his functions in relation to the application or, as the case may be, the debt relief order made as a result of the application.

(3)   The debtor must notify the official receiver as soon as reasonably practicable if he becomes aware of—
     (a)   any error in, or omission from, the information supplied to the official receiver in, or in support of, the application;
     (b)   any change in his circumstances between the application date and the determination date that would affect (or would have affected) the determination of the application.

(4)   The duties under subsections (2) and (3) apply after (as well as before) the determination of the application, for as long as the official receiver is able to exercise functions of the kind mentioned in subsection (2).

(5)   If a debt relief order is made as a result of the application, the debtor must notify the official receiver as soon as reasonably practicable if—
     (a)   there is an increase in his income during the moratorium period applicable to the order;
     (b)   he acquires any property or any property is devolved upon him during that period;
     (c)   he becomes aware of any error in or omission from any information supplied
     by him to the official receiver after the determination date.

(6)   A notification under subsection (3) or (5) must give the prescribed particulars (if any) of the matter being notified.

Objections, investigations and revocation

251K   Objections and investigations

(1)   Any person specified in a debt relief order as a creditor to whom a specified qualifying debt is owed may object to—
     (a)   the making of the order;
     (b)   the inclusion of the debt in the list of the debtor's qualifying debts; or
     (c)   the details of the debt specified in the order.

(2)   An objection under subsection (1) must be—
     (a)   made during the moratorium period relating to the order and within the prescribed period for objections;
     (b)   made to the official receiver in the prescribed manner;
     (c)   based on a prescribed ground;
     (d)   supported by any information and documents as may be prescribed;

and the prescribed period mentioned in paragraph (a) must not be less than 28 days after the creditor in question has been notified of the making of the order.

(3) The official receiver must consider every objection made to him under this section.

(4) The official receiver may—

    (a) as part of his consideration of an objection, or

    (b) on his own initiative,

carry out an investigation of any matter that appears to the official receiver to be relevant to the making of any decision mentioned in subsection (5) in relation to a debt relief order or the debtor.

(5) The decisions to which an investigation may be directed are—

    (a) whether the order should be revoked or amended under section 251L;

    (b) whether an application should be made to the court under section 251M; or

    (c) whether any other steps should be taken in relation to the debtor.

(6) The power to carry out an investigation under this section is exercisable after (as well as during) the moratorium relating to the order.

(7) The official receiver may require any person to give him such information and assistance as he may reasonably require in connection with an investigation under this section.

(8) Subject to anything prescribed in the rules as to the procedure to be followed in carrying out an investigation under this section, an investigation may be carried out by the official receiver in such manner as he thinks fit.

251L   **Power of official receiver to revoke or amend a debt relief order**

(1) The official receiver may revoke or amend a debt relief order during the applicable moratorium period in the circumstances provided for by this section.

(2) The official receiver may revoke the order on the ground that—

    (a) any information supplied to him by the debtor—

        (i) in, or in support of, the application, or

        (ii) after the determination date,

    was incomplete, incorrect or otherwise misleading;

    (b) the debtor has failed to comply with a duty under section 251J;

    (c) a bankruptcy order has been made in relation to the debtor; or

    (d) the debtor has made a proposal under Part 8 (or has notified the official receiver of his intention to do so).

(3) The official receiver may revoke the order on the ground that he should not have been satisfied—

    (a) that the debts specified in the order were qualifying debts of the debtor as at the application date;

    (b) that the conditions specified in Part 1 of Schedule 4ZA were met;

    (c) that the conditions specified in Part 2 of that Schedule were met or that any failure to meet such a condition did not prevent his making the order.

…

Role of the court

251M   **Powers of court in relation to debt relief orders**

(1) Any person may make an application to the court if he is dissatisfied by any act, omission or decision of the official receiver in connection with a debt relief order or an application for such an order.

(2) The official receiver may make an application to the court for directions or an order in relation to any matter arising in connection with a debt relief order or an application for such an order.

(3) The matters referred to in subsection (2) include, among other things, matters relating to the debtor's compliance with any duty arising under section 251J.

(4) An application under this section may, subject to anything in the rules, be made at any time.

(5) The court may extend the moratorium period applicable to a debt relief order for the purposes of determining an application under this section.

(6) On an application under this section the court may dismiss the application or do one or more of the following—

(a) quash the whole or part of any act or decision of the official receiver;

(b) give the official receiver directions (including a direction that he reconsider any matter in relation to which his act or decision has been quashed under paragraph (a));

(c) make an order for the enforcement of any obligation on the debtor arising by virtue of a duty under section 251J;

(d) extend the moratorium period applicable to the debt relief order;

(e) make an order revoking or amending the debt relief order;

(f) make an order under section 251N; or

(g) make such other order as the court thinks fit.

...

251N   Inquiry into debtor's dealings and property

(1) An order under this section may be made by the court on the application of the official receiver.

(2) An order under this section is an order summoning any of the following persons to appear before the court—

(a) the debtor;

(b) the debtor's spouse or former spouse or the debtor's civil partner or former civil partner;

(c) any person appearing to the court to be able to give information or assistance concerning the debtor or his dealings, affairs and property.

(3) The court may require a person falling within subsection (2)(c)—

(a) to provide a written account of his dealings with the debtor; or

(b) to produce any documents in his possession or under his control relating to the debtor or to the debtor's dealings, affairs or property.

(4) Subsection (5) applies where a person fails without reasonable excuse to appear before the court when he is summoned to do so by an order under this section.

(5) The court may cause a warrant to be issued to a constable or prescribed officer of the court—

(a) for the arrest of that person, and

(b) for the seizure of any records or other documents in that person's possession.

(6) The court may authorise a person arrested under such a warrant to be kept in custody, and anything seized under such a warrant to be held, in accordance with the rules, until that person is brought before the court under the warrant or until such other time as the court may order.

Offences

251O   False representations and omissions

(1) A person who makes an application for a debt relief order is guilty of an offence if he knowingly or recklessly makes any false representation or

omission in making the application or providing any information or documents to the official receiver in support of the application.

(2) A person who makes an application for a debt relief order is guilty of an offence if—

    (a) he intentionally fails to comply with a duty under section 251J(3) in connection with the application; or

    (b) he knowingly or recklessly makes any false representation or omission in providing any information to the official receiver in connection with such a duty or otherwise in connection with the application.

(3) It is immaterial for the purposes of an offence under subsection (1) or (2) whether or not a debt relief order is made as a result of the application.

(4) A person in respect of whom a debt relief order is made is guilty of an offence if—

    (a) he intentionally fails to comply with a duty under section 251J(5) in connection with the order; or

    (b) he knowingly or recklessly makes any false representation or omission in providing information to the official receiver in connection with such a duty or otherwise in connection with the performance by the official receiver of functions in relation to the order.

(5) It is immaterial for the purposes of an offence under subsection (4)—

    (a) whether the offence is committed during or after the moratorium period; and

    (b) whether or not the order is revoked after the conduct constituting the offence takes place.

...

251Q   Fraudulent disposal of property

(1) A person in respect of whom a debt relief order is made is guilty of an offence if he made or caused to be made any gift or transfer of his property during the period between—

    (a) the start of the period of two years ending with the application date; and

    (b) the end of the moratorium period.

(2) The reference in subsection (1) to making a transfer of any property includes causing or conniving at the levying of any execution against that property.

(3) A person is not guilty of an offence under this section if he proves that, in respect of the conduct constituting the offence, he had no intent to defraud or to conceal the state of his affairs.

(4) For the purposes of subsection (3) a person is to be taken to have proved that he had no such intent if—

    (a) sufficient evidence is adduced to raise an issue as to whether he had such intent; and

    (b) the contrary is not proved beyond reasonable doubt.

(5) It is immaterial for the purposes of this section whether or not the debt relief order in question is revoked after the conduct constituting an offence takes place (but no offence is committed by virtue of conduct occurring after the order is revoked).

251R   Fraudulent dealing with property obtained on credit

(1) A person in respect of whom a debt relief order is made is guilty of an offence if during the relevant period he disposed of any property which he had obtained on credit and, at the time he disposed of it, had not paid for it.

(2) Any other person is guilty of an offence if during the relevant period he acquired or received property from a person in respect of whom a debt relief order was made (the "debtor") knowing or believing—

  (a) that the debtor owed money in respect of the property, and

  (b) that the debtor did not intend, or was unlikely to be able, to pay the money he so owed.

(3) In subsections (1) and (2) "relevant period" means the period between—

  (a) the start of the period of two years ending with the application date; and

  (b) the determination date.

(4) A person is not guilty of an offence under subsection (1) or (2) if the disposal, acquisition or receipt of the property was in the ordinary course of a business carried on by the debtor at the time of the disposal, acquisition or receipt.

(5) In determining for the purposes of subsection (4) whether any property is disposed of, acquired or received in the ordinary course of a business carried on by the debtor, regard may be had, in particular, to the price paid for the property.

(6) A person is not guilty of an offence under subsection (1) if he proves that, in respect of the conduct constituting the offence, he had no intent to defraud or to conceal the state of his affairs.

(7) In this section references to disposing of property include pawning or pledging it; and references to acquiring or receiving property shall be read accordingly.

(8) It is immaterial for the purposes of this section whether or not the debt relief order in question is revoked after the conduct constituting an offence takes place (but no offence is committed by virtue of conduct occurring after the order is revoked).

251S Obtaining credit or engaging in business

(1) A person in respect of whom a debt relief order is made is guilty of an offence if, during the relevant period—

  (a) he obtains credit (either alone or jointly with any other person) without giving the person from whom he obtains the credit the relevant information about his status; or

  (b) he engages directly or indirectly in any business under a name other than that in which the order was made without disclosing to all persons with whom he enters into any business transaction the name in which the order was made.

(2) For the purposes of subsection (1)(a) the relevant information about a person's status is the information that—

  (a) a moratorium is in force in relation to the debt relief order,

  (b) a debt relief restrictions order is in force in respect of him, or

  (c) both a moratorium and a debt relief restrictions order is in force,

  as the case may be.

(3) In subsection (1) "relevant period" means—

  (a) the moratorium period relating to the debt relief order, or

  (b) the period for which a debt relief restrictions order is in force in respect of the person in respect of whom the debt relief order is made,

  as the case may be.

(4) Subsection (1)(a) does not apply if the amount of the credit is less than the prescribed amount (if any).

(5) The reference in subsection (1)(a) to a person obtaining credit includes the following cases—

        (a)   where goods are bailed to him under a hire-purchase agreement, or agreed to be sold to him under a conditional sale agreement;

        (b)   where he is paid in advance (in money or otherwise) for the supply of goods or services.

..."

SCHEDULE 18
SCHEDULE 4ZA TO THE INSOLVENCY ACT 1986

"SCHEDULE 4ZA CONDITIONS FOR MAKING A DEBT RELIEF ORDER

PART 1
CONDITIONS WHICH MUST BE MET

Connection with England and Wales

1.— (1) The debtor—
    (a)   is domiciled in England and Wales on the application date; or
    (b)   at any time during the period of three years ending with that date—
        (i)   was ordinarily resident, or had a place of residence, in England and Wales; or
        (ii) carried on business in England and Wales.
   (2) The reference in sub-paragraph (1)(b)(ii) to the debtor carrying on business includes—
    (a)   the carrying on of business by a firm or partnership of which he is a member;
    (b)   the carrying on of business by an agent or manager for him or for such a firm or partnership.

Debtor's previous insolvency history

2. The debtor is not, on the determination date—
    (a)   an undischarged bankrupt;
    (b)   subject to an interim order or voluntary arrangement under Part 8; or
    (c)   subject to a bankruptcy restrictions order or a debt relief restrictions order.
3. A debtor's petition for the debtor's bankruptcy under Part 9—
    (a)   has not been presented by the debtor before the determination date;
    (b)   has been so presented, but proceedings on the petition have been finally disposed of before that date; or
    (c)   has been so presented and proceedings in relation to the petition remain before the court at that date, but the court has referred the debtor under section 274A(2) for the purposes of making an application for a debt relief order.
4. A creditor's petition for the debtor's bankruptcy under Part 9—
    (a)   has not been presented against the debtor at any time before the determination date;
    (b)   has been so presented, but proceedings on the petition have been finally disposed of before that date; or
    (c)   has been so presented and proceedings in relation to the petition remain before the court at that date, but the person who presented the petition has consented to the making of an application for a debt relief order.
5. A debt relief order has not been made in relation to the debtor in the period of six years ending with the determination date.

Limit on debtor's overall indebtedness

6.— (1) The total amount of the debtor's debts on the determination date, other than unliquidated debts and excluded debts, does not exceed the prescribed amount.
   (2) For this purpose an unliquidated debt is a debt that is not for a liquidated sum payable to a creditor either immediately or at some future certain time.

Limit on debtor's monthly surplus income

7.— (1) The debtor's monthly surplus income (if any) on the determination date does not exceed the prescribed amount.

(2)   For this purpose "monthly surplus income" is the amount by which a person's monthly income exceeds the amount necessary for the reasonable domestic needs of himself and his family.

(3)   The rules may—

    (a)   make provision as to how the debtor's monthly surplus income is to be determined;

    (b)   provide that particular descriptions of income are to be excluded for the purposes of this paragraph.

Limit on value of debtor's property

8.—   (1)   The total value of the debtor's property on the determination date does not exceed the prescribed amount.

    (2)   The rules may—

        (a)   make provision as to how the value of a person's property is to be determined;

        (b)   provide that particular descriptions of property are to be excluded for the purposes of this paragraph.

PART 2
OTHER CONDITIONS

9.—   (1)   The debtor has not entered into a transaction with any person at an undervalue during the period between—

    (a)   the start of the period of two years ending with the application date; and

    (b)   the determination date.

    (2)   For this purpose a debtor enters into a transaction with a person at an undervalue if—

        (a)   he makes a gift to that person or he otherwise enters into a transaction with that person on terms that provide for him to receive no consideration;

        (b)   he enters into a transaction with that person in consideration of marriage or the formation of a civil partnership; or

        (c)   he enters into a transaction with that person for a consideration the value of which, in money or money's worth, is significantly less than the value, in money or money's worth, of the consideration provided by the individual.

10.—   (1)   The debtor has not given a preference to any person during the period between—

    (a)   the start of the period of two years ending with the application date; and

    (b)   the determination date.

    (2)   For this purpose a debtor gives a preference to a person if—

        (a)   that person is one of the debtor's creditors to whom a qualifying debt is owed or is a surety or guarantor for any such debt, and

        (b)   the debtor does anything or suffers anything to be done which (in either case) has the effect of putting that person into a position which, in the event that a debt relief order is made in relation to the debtor, will be better than the position he would have been in if that thing had not been done."

PART TWO: RULES

INSOLVENCY RULES 1986
(SI 1986 No 1925)[1]

PART 1
COMPANY VOLUNTARY ARRANGEMENTS

...

PART 2
PROPOSAL BY DIRECTORS

1.3   Contents of proposal

(1)   The directors' proposal shall provide a short explanation why, in their opinion, a voluntary arrangement under Part I of the Act is desirable, and give reasons why the company's creditors may be expected to concur with such an arrangement.

(2)   The following matters shall be stated, or otherwise dealt with, in the directors' proposal—

    (a)   the following matters, so far as within the directors' immediate knowledge—

        (i)   the company's assets, with an estimate of their respective values,

        (ii)   the extent (if any) to which the assets are charged in favour of creditors,

        (iii)   the extent (if any) to which particular assets are to be excluded from the voluntary arrangement;

    (b)   particulars of any property, other than assets of the company itself, which is proposed to be included in the arrangement, the source of such property and the terms on which it is to be made available for inclusion;

    (c)   the nature and amount of the company's liabilities (so far as within the directors' immediate knowledge), the manner in which they are proposed to be met, modified, postponed or otherwise dealt with by means of the arrangement, and (in particular)—

        (i)   how it is proposed to deal with preferential creditors (defined in section 4(7)) and creditors who are, or claim to be, secured,

        (ii)   how persons connected with the company (being creditors) are proposed to be treated under the arrangement, and

        (iii)   whether there are, to the directors' knowledge, any circumstances giving rise to the possibility, in the event that the company should go into liquidation, of claims under—

        section 238 (transactions at an undervalue),

        section 239 (preferences),

        section 244 (extortionate credit transactions), or

        section 245 (floating charges invalid);

1.5   Statement of affairs

(1)   The directors shall, within 7 days after their proposal is delivered to the nominee, or within such longer time as he may allow, deliver to him a statement of the company's affairs.

(2)   The statement shall comprise the following particulars (supplementing or amplifying, so far as is necessary for clarifying the state of the company's affairs, those already given in the directors' proposal)—

    (a)   a list of the company's assets, divided into such categories as are appropriate for easy identification, with estimated values assigned to each category;

    (b)   in the case of any property on which a claim against the company is wholly or partly secured, particulars of the claim and its amount, and of how and when the security was created;

---

1.   The Insolvency Rules 1986 are voluminous and are included here only as a brief edited sample. The most frequently used and cited rules are included as well as others of general interest. To view them in full see: www.statutelaw.gov.uk/Home.aspx. The rules will be replaced on 1 October 2009 with an entirely new set of Insolvency Rules. These will be reproduced in any subsequent edition of this work in an edited form. In the interim see further: http://www.insolvency.gov.uk/insolvencyprofessionandlegislation/consolidation/updatefeb08.htm.

(c) the names and addresses of the company's preferential creditors (defined in section 4(7)), with the amounts of their respective claims;

(d) the names and addresses of the company's unsecured creditors, with the amounts of their respective claims;

(e) particulars of any debts owed by or to the company to or by persons connected with it;

(f) the names and addresses of the company's members, with details of their respective shareholdings;

(g) such other particulars (if any) as the nominee may in writing require to be furnished for the purposes of making his report to the court on the directors' proposal.

PART 2
ADMINISTRATION PROCEDURE

PART 2
APPOINTMENT OF ADMINISTRATOR BY COURT

2.2   Affidavit in support of administration application

(1) Where it is proposed to apply to the court for an administration order to be made in relation to a company, the administration application shall be in Form 2.1B and an affidavit complying with Rule 2.4 must be prepared and sworn, with a view to its being filed with the court in support of the application.

(2) If the administration application is to be made by the company or by the directors, the affidavit shall be made by one of the directors, or the secretary of the company, stating himself to make it on behalf of the company or, as the case may be, on behalf of the directors.

(3) If the application is to be made by creditors, the affidavit shall be made by a person acting under the authority of them all, whether or not himself one of their number. In any case there must be stated in the affidavit the nature of his authority and the means of his knowledge of the matters to which the affidavit relates.

(4) If the application is to be made by the supervisor of a voluntary arrangement under Part I of the Act, it is to be treated as if it were an application by the company.

PART 10
DISTRIBUTIONS TO CREDITORS

SECTION B
MACHINERY OF PROVING A DEBT

2.72   Proving a debt

(1) A person claiming to be a creditor of the company and wishing to recover his debt in whole or in part must (subject to any order of the court to the contrary) submit his claim in writing to the administrator.

(2) A creditor who claims is referred to as "proving" for his debt and a document by which he seeks to establish his claim is his "proof".

(3) Subject to the next paragraph, a proof must–

(a) be made out by, or under the direction of, the creditor and signed by him or a person authorised in that behalf; and

(b) state the following matters–

(i) the creditor's name and address;

(ii) the total amount of his claim as at the date on which the company entered administration, less any payments that have been made to him after that date in respect of his claim and any adjustment by way of set-off in accordance with Rule 2.85;

(iii) whether or not the claim includes outstanding uncapitalised interest;

(iv) whether or not the claim includes value added tax;

(v) whether the whole or any part of the debt falls within any, and if so, which categories of preferential debts under section 386;

(vi) particulars of how and when the debt was incurred by the company;

        (vii) particulars of any security held, the date on which it was given and the value which the creditor puts on it;

       (viii) details of any reservation of title in respect of goods to which the debt refers; and

       (ix)   the name, address and authority of the person signing the proof (if other than the creditor himself).

(4)   There shall be specified in the proof details of any documents by reference to which the debt can be substantiated; but (subject as follows) it is not essential that such document be attached to the proof or submitted with it.

(5)   The administrator may call for any document or other evidence to be produced to him, where he thinks it necessary for the purpose of substantiating the whole or any part of the claim made in the proof.

PART 3
ADMINISTRATIVE RECEIVERSHIP

PART1
APPOINTMENT OF ADMINISTRATIVE RECEIVER

3.1   Acceptance and confirmation of acceptance of appointment

(1)   Where two or more persons are appointed as joint receivers or managers of a company's property under powers contained in an instrument, the acceptance of such an appointment shall be made by each of them in accordance with section 33 as if that person were a sole appointee, but the joint appointment takes effect only when all such persons have so accepted and is then deemed to have been made at the time at which the instrument of appointment was received by or on behalf of all such persons.

(2)   Subject to the next paragraph, where a person is appointed as the sole or joint receiver of a company's property under powers contained in an instrument, the appointee shall, if he accepts the appointment, within 7 days confirm his acceptance in writing to the person appointing him.

(3)   Paragraph (2) does not apply where an appointment is accepted in writing.

(4)   Any acceptance or confirmation of acceptance of appointment as a receiver or manager of a company's property, whether under the Act or the Rules, may be given by any person (including, in the case of a joint appointment, any joint appointee) duly authorised for that purpose on behalf of the receiver or manager.

PART 4
COMPANIES WINDING UP

PART 2
THE STATUTORY DEMAND (NO CVL APPLICATION)

4.5   Form and content of statutory demand

(1)   The statutory demand must state the amount of the debt and the consideration for it (or, if there is no consideration, the way in which it arises).

(2)   If the amount claimed in the demand includes—

    (a)   any charge by way of interest not previously notified to the company as included in its liability, or

    (b)   any other charge accruing from time to time,

    the amount or rate of the charge must be separately identified, and the grounds on which payment of it is claimed must be stated.

    In either case the amount claimed must be limited to that which has accrued due at the date of the demand.

4.6   Information to be given in statutory demand

(1)   The statutory demand must include an explanation to the company of the following matters—

    (a)   the purpose of the demand, and the fact that, if the demand is not complied with, proceedings may be instituted for the winding up of the company;

     (b)   the time within which it must be complied with, if that consequence is to be avoided; and

     (c)   the methods of compliance which are open to the company.

  (2)   Information must be provided for the company as to how an officer or representative of it may enter into communication with one or more named individuals, with a view to securing or compounding for the debt to the creditor's satisfaction.

     In the case of any individual so named in the demand, his address and telephone number (if any) must be given.

PART 4
COMPANIES WINDING UP

PART 9
PROOF OF DEBTS IN A LIQUIDATION

SECTION A
PROCEDURE FOR PROVING

4.73   Meaning of "prove"

  (1)   Where a company is being wound up by the court, a person claiming to be a creditor of the company and wishing to recover his debt in whole or in part must (subject to any order of the court under Rule 4.67(2)) submit his claim in writing to the liquidator. (NO CVL APPLICATION)

  (2-CVL)   In a voluntary winding up (whether members' or creditors') the liquidator may require a person claiming to be a creditor of the company and wishing to recover his debt in whole or in part, to submit the claim in writing to him.

  (3)   A creditor who claims (whether or not in writing) is referred to as "proving" for his debt; and a document by which he seeks to establish his claim is his "proof".

  (4)   Subject to the next paragraph, a proof must be in the form known as "proof of debt" (whether the form prescribed by the Rules, or a substantially similar form), which shall be made out by or under the directions of the creditor, and signed by him or a person authorised in that behalf. (NO CVL APPLICATION)

  (5)   Where a debt is due to a Minister of the Crown or a Government Department, the proof need not be in that form, provided that there are shown all such particulars of the debt as are required in the form used by other creditors, and as are relevant in the circumstances. (NO CVL APPLICATION)

  (6-CVL)   The creditor's proof may be in any form.

  (7)   In certain circumstances, specified below in this Chapter, the proof must be in the form of an affidavit.

  (8)   Where a winding up is immediately preceded by an administration, a creditor proving in the administration shall be deemed to have proved in the winding up.

SECTION B
QUANTIFICATION OF CLAIM

4.90   Mutual credits and set-off

  (1)   This Rule applies where, before the company goes into liquidation there have been mutual credits, mutual debts or other mutual dealings between the company and any creditor of the company proving or claiming to prove for a debt in the liquidation.

  (2)   The reference in paragraph (1) to mutual credits, mutual debts or other mutual dealings does not include—

     (a)   any debt arising out of an obligation incurred at a time when the creditor had notice that—

         (i)   a meeting of creditors had been summoned under section 98; or

         (ii)   a petition for the winding up of the company was pending;

     (b)   any debt arising out of an obligation where—

         (i)   the liquidation was immediately preceded by an administration; and

(ii)   at the time the obligation was incurred the creditor had notice that an application for an administration order was pending or a person had given notice of intention to appoint an administrator;

(c)   any debt arising out of an obligation incurred during an administration which immediately preceded the liquidation; or

(d)   any debt which has been acquired by a creditor by assignment or otherwise, pursuant to an agreement between the creditor and any other party where that agreement was entered into—

    (i)   after the company went into liquidation;

    (ii)   at a time when the creditor had notice that a meeting of creditors had been summoned under section 98;

    (iii)   at a time when the creditor had notice that a winding up petition was pending;

    (iv)   where the liquidation was immediately preceded by an administration, at a time when the creditor had notice that an application for an administration order was pending or a person had given notice of intention to appoint an administrator; or

    (v)   during an administration which immediately preceded the liquidation.

(3)   An account shall be taken of what is due from each party to the other in respect of the mutual dealings, and the sums due from one party shall be set off against the sums due from the other.

(4)   A sum shall be regarded as being due to or from the company for the purposes of paragraph (3) whether—

(a)   it is payable at present or in the future;

(b)   the obligation by virtue of which it is payable is certain or contingent; or

(c)   its amount is fixed or liquidated, or is capable of being ascertained by fixed rules or as a matter of opinion.

(5)   Rule 4.86 shall also apply for the purposes of this Rule to any obligation to or from the company which, by reason of its being subject to any contingency or for any other reason, does not bear a certain value.

(6)   Rules 4.91 to 4.93 shall apply for the purposes of this Rule in relation to any sums due to the company which—

(a)   are payable in a currency other than sterling;

(b)   are of a periodical nature; or

(c)   bear interest.

(7)   Rule 11.13 shall apply for the purposes of this Rule to any sum due to or from the company which is payable in the future.

(8)   Only the balance (if any) of the account owed to the creditor is provable in the liquidation. Alternatively the balance (if any) owed to the company shall be paid to the liquidator as part of the assets except where all or part of the balance results from a contingent or prospective debt owed by the creditor and in such a case the balance (or that part of it which results from the contingent or prospective debt) shall be paid if and when that debt becomes due and payable.

(9)   In this Rule "obligation" means an obligation however arising, whether by virtue of an agreement, rule of law or otherwise.

PART 11
THE LIQUIDATOR

SECTION G
RULES APPLYING IN EVERY WINDING UP, WHETHER VOLUNTARY OR BY THE COURT

4.149 Power of court to set aside certain transactions

(1)   If in the administration of the estate the liquidator enters into any transaction with a person who is an associate of his, the court may, on the application of any person interested, set the transaction aside and order the liquidator to compensate the company for any loss suffered in consequence of it.

(2)   This does not apply if either—

(a)   the transaction was entered into with the prior consent of the court, or

(b)   it is shown to the court's satisfaction that the transaction was for value, and that it was entered into by the liquidator without knowing, or having any reason to suppose, that the person concerned was an associate.

(3)   Nothing in this Rule is to be taken as prejudicing the operation of any rule of law or equity with respect to a liquidator's dealings with trust property, or the fiduciary obligations of any person.

PART 14
COLLECTION AND DISTRIBUTION OF COMPANY'S ASSETS BY LIQUIDATOR

4.181   Debts of insolvent company to rank equally

(NO CVL APPLICATION)

(1)   Debts other than preferential debts rank equally between themselves in the winding up and, after the preferential debts, shall be paid in full unless the assets are insufficient for meeting them, in which case they abate in equal proportions between themselves.

(2)   Paragraph (1) applies whether or not the company is unable to pay its debts.

PART 19
PUBLIC EXAMINATION OF COMPANY OFFICERS AND OTHERS

4.211   Order for public examination

(1)   If the official receiver applies to the court under section 133 for the public examination of any person, a copy of the court's order shall, forthwith after its making, be served on that person.

(2)   Where the application relates to a person falling within section 133(1)(c) (promoters, past managers, etc.), it shall be accompanied by a report by the official receiver indicating—

(a)   the grounds on which the person is supposed to fall within that paragraph, and

(b)   whether, in the official receiver's opinion, it is likely that service of the order on the person can be effected by post at a known address.

(3)   If in his report the official receiver gives it as his opinion that, in a case to which paragraph (2) applies, there is no reasonable certainty that service by post will be effective, the court may direct that the order be served by some means other than, or in addition to, post.

(4)   In a case to which paragraphs (2) and (3) apply, the court shall rescind the order if satisfied by the person to whom it is directed that he does not fall within section 133(1)(c).

PART 20
ORDER OF PAYMENT OF COSTS, ETC., OUT OF ASSETS

4.218   General rule as to priority

(1)   All fees, costs, charges and other expenses incurred in the course of the liquidation are to be regarded as expenses of the liquidation.

…

(2)   The expenses of the liquidation are payable out of—

(a)   assets of the company available for the payment of general creditors, which shall be taken to include proceeds—

(i)   of any legal action which the liquidator has power to bring in his own name or in the name of the company, or

(ii)   arising from any award made under any arbitration or other dispute resolution procedure which the liquidator has power to bring in his own name or in the name of the company, which shall, for the purposes of this subparagraph, also include—

(iii) any payments made under any compromise or other agreement intended to avoid legal action or recourse to arbitration or to any other dispute resolution procedure, and

(iv)   payments made as a result of a settlement of any such action, arrangement or procedure in lieu of or prior to any judgment being given or award being made;

(b)   subject as provided in Rules 4.218A to 4.218E, property comprised in or subject to a floating charge created by the company.

(3) Subject as provided in Rules 4.218A to 4.218E, the expenses are payable in the following order of priority—

(a) expenses which—

    (i) are properly chargeable or incurred by the provisional liquidator in carrying out the functions conferred on him by the court;

    (ii) are properly chargeable or incurred by the official receiver or the liquidator in preserving, realising or getting in any of the assets of the company or otherwise in the preparation or conduct of any legal proceedings, arbitration or other dispute resolution procedures, which he has power to bring in his own name or bring or defend in the name of the company or in the preparation or conduct of any negotiations intended to lead or leading to a settlement or compromise of any legal action or dispute to which the proceedings or procedures relate;

    (iii) relate to the employment of a shorthand writer, if appointed by an order of the court made at the instance of the official receiver in connection with an examination; or

    (iv) are incurred in holding an examination under Rule 4.214 (examinee unfit) where the application for it was made by the official receiver;

(b) any other expenses incurred or disbursements made by the official receiver or under his authority, including those incurred or made in carrying on the business of the company;

(c) the fees payable under any order made under section 414 or section 415A, including those payable to the official receiver (other than the fee referred to in sub-paragraph (d)(i) below), and any remuneration payable to him under general regulations;

(d) (i) the fee payable under any order made under section 414 for the performance by the official receiver of his general duties as official receiver;

    (ii) any repayable deposit lodged under any such order as security for the fee mentioned in sub-paragraph (i);

(e) the cost of any security provided by a provisional liquidator, liquidator or special manager in accordance with the Act or the Rules;

(f) the remuneration of the provisional liquidator (if any);

(g) any deposit lodged on an application for the appointment of a provisional liquidator;

(h) the costs of the petitioner, and of any person appearing on the petition whose costs are allowed by the court;

(j) the remuneration of the special manager (if any);

(k) any amount payable to a person employed or authorised, under Chapter 6 of this Part of the Rules, to assist in the preparation of a statement of affairs or of accounts;

(l) any allowance made, by order of the court, towards costs on an application for release from the obligation to submit a statement of affairs, or for an extension of time for submitting such a statement;

(la) the costs of employing a shorthand writer in any case other than one appointed by an order of the court at the instance of the official receiver in connection with an examination;

(m) any necessary disbursements by the liquidator in the course of his administration (including any expenses incurred by members of the liquidation committee or their representatives and allowed by the liquidator under Rule 4.169, but not including any payment of corporation tax in circumstances referred to in sub-paragraph (p) below);

(n) the remuneration or emoluments of any person who has been employed by the liquidator to perform any services for the company, as required or authorised by or under the Act or the Rules;

(o) the remuneration of the liquidator, up to any amount not exceeding that which is payable under Schedule 6;

(p) the amount of any corporation tax on chargeable gains accruing on the realisation of any asset of the company (without regard to whether the realisation is effected by the liquidator, a secured creditor, or a receiver or manager appointed to deal with a security);

(q)   the balance, after payment of any sums due under sub-paragraph (o) above, of any remuneration due to the liquidator;

(r)   any other expenses properly chargeable by the liquidator in carrying out his functions in the liquidation

PART 6
BANKRUPTCY

PART 16A
INCOME PAYMENTS AGREEMENTS

6.193A   Approval of income payments agreements

(1)   An income payments agreement can only be entered into prior to the discharge of the bankrupt.

(2)   Where an income payments agreement is to be entered into between the official receiver or trustee and the bankrupt under section 310A(1), the official receiver or trustee shall provide an income payments agreement to the bankrupt for his approval.

(3)   Within 14 days or such longer period as may be specified by the official receiver or trustee (whichever is appropriate) from the date on which the income payments agreement was sent, the bankrupt shall—

(a)   if he decides to approve the draft income payments agreement, sign the agreement and return it to the official receiver or trustee (whichever is appropriate); or

(b)   if he decides not to approve the agreement, notify the official receiver or trustee (whichever is appropriate) in writing of his decision.

PART 20
LEAVE TO ACT AS DIRECTOR, ETC.

6.203   Application for leave

(1)   An application by the bankrupt for leave, under section 11 of the Company Directors Disqualification Act 1986, to act as director of, or to take part or be concerned in the promotion, formation or management of a company, shall be supported by an affidavit complying with this Rule.

(2)   The affidavit must identify the company and specify—

(a)   the nature of its business or intended business, and the place or places where that business is, or is to be, carried on,

(b)   whether it is, or is to be, a private or a public company,

(c)   the persons who are, or are to be, principally responsible for the conduct of its affairs (whether as directors, shadow directors, managers or otherwise),

(d)   the manner and capacity in which the applicant proposes to take part or be concerned in the promotion or formation of the company or, as the case may be, its management, and

(e)   the emoluments and other benefits to be obtained from the directorship.

(3)   If the company is already in existence, the affidavit must specify the date of its incorporation and the amount of its nominal and issued share capital; and if not, it must specify the amount, or approximate amount, of its proposed commencing share capital, and the sources from which that capital is to be obtained.

(4)   Where the bankrupt intends to take part or be concerned in the promotion or formation of a company, the affidavit must contain an undertaking by him that he will, within not less than 7 days of the company being incorporated, file in court a copy of its memorandum of association and certificate of incorporation under section 13 of the Companies Act.

(5)   The court shall fix a venue for the hearing of the bankrupt's application, and give notice to him accordingly.

PART 6A
INDIVIDUAL INSOLVENCY REGISTER

6A.2   Entry of information onto the individual insolvency register — individual voluntary arrangements

    (1)   The Secretary of State shall enter onto the individual insolvency register—

        (a)   as regards any voluntary arrangement other than a voluntary arrangement under section 263A any information—

            (i)   that was required to be held on the register of individual voluntary arrangements maintained by the Secretary of State immediately prior to the coming into force of this Rule and which relates to a voluntary arrangement which has not been completed or has not terminated on or before the date on which this Rule comes into force; or

            (ii)   that is sent to him in pursuance of Rule 5.29 or Rule 5.34; and

        (b)   as regards any voluntary arrangement under section 263A of which notice is given to him pursuant to Rule 5.45—

            (i)   the name and address of the debtor;

            (ii)   the date on which the arrangement was approved by the creditors; and

            (iii)   the court in which the official receiver's report has been filed; and,

        (c)   in the circumstances set out in (a) and (b) above, the debtor's gender, date of birth and any name by which he was known, not being the name in which he has entered into the voluntary arrangement.

    (2)   This Rule is subject to Rule 6A.3.

PART 7
COURT PROCEDURE AND PRACTICE

PART 9
GENERAL

7.55   Formal defects

No insolvency proceedings shall be invalidated by any formal defect or by any irregularity, unless the court before which objection is made considers that substantial injustice has been caused by the defect or irregularity, and that the injustice cannot be remedied by any order of the court.

PART 11
EC REGULATION—MEMBER STATE LIQUIDATOR

7.64   Interpretation of creditor

    (1)   This Rule applies where a member State liquidator has been appointed in relation to a person subject to insolvency proceedings.

    (2)   For the purposes of the Rules referred to in paragraph (3) a member State liquidator appointed in main proceedings is deemed to be a creditor.

    (3)   The Rules referred to in paragraph (2) are Rules 7.31(1) (right to inspect court file) and 7.53(1) (right of attendance).

    (4)   Paragraphs (2) and (3) are without prejudice to the generality of the right to participate referred to in paragraph 3 of Article 32 of the EC Regulation (exercise of creditor's rights).

COUNCIL REGULATION (EC) No 1346/2000 of 29 May 2000
on Insolvency Proceedings

Having regard to the Treaty establishing the European Community, and in particular Articles 61(c) and 67(1) thereof ...

(1)   The European Union has set out the aim of establishing an area of freedom, security and justice.

(2)   The proper functioning of the internal market requires that cross-border insolvency proceedings should operate efficiently and effectively and this Regulation needs to be adopted in order to achieve this objective ...

(3)   The activities of undertakings have more and more cross-border effects and are therefore increasingly being regulated by Community law. While the insolvency of such undertakings also affects the proper functioning of the internal market, there is a need for a Community act requiring coordination of the measures to be taken regarding an insolvent debtor's assets.

(4)   It is necessary for the proper functioning of the internal market to avoid incentives for the parties to transfer assets or judicial proceedings from one Member State to another, seeking to obtain a more favourable legal position (forum shopping).

(5)   These objectives cannot be achieved to a sufficient degree at national level and action at Community level is therefore justified.

(6)   In accordance with the principle of proportionality this Regulation should be confined to provisions governing jurisdiction for opening insolvency proceedings and judgments which are delivered directly on the basis of the insolvency proceedings and are closely connected with such proceedings. In addition, this Regulation should contain provisions regarding the recognition of those judgments and the applicable law which also satisfy that principle.

(7)   Insolvency proceedings relating to the winding-up of insolvent companies or other legal persons, judicial arrangements, compositions and analogous proceedings are excluded from the scope of the 1968 Brussels Convention on jurisdiction and the Enforcement of judgments in Civil and Commercial Matters ... as amended by the Conventions on Accession to this Convention ...

(8)   In order to achieve the aim of improving the efficiency and effectiveness of insolvency proceedings having cross-border effects, it is necessary, and appropriate, that the provisions on jurisdiction, recognition and applicable law in this area should be contained in a Community law measure which is binding and directly applicable in Member States.

(9)   This Regulation should apply to insolvency proceedings, whether the debtor is a natural person or a legal person, a trader or an individual. The insolvency proceedings to which this Regulation applies are listed in the Annexes. Insolvency proceedings concerning insurance undertakings, credit institutions, investment undertakings holding funds or securities for third parties and collective investment undertakings should be excluded from the scope of this Regulation. Such undertakings should not be covered by this Regulation since they are subject to special arrangements and, to some extent, the national supervisory authorities have extremely wide-ranging powers of intervention.

(10)   Insolvency proceedings do not necessarily involve the intervention of a judicial authority; the expression "court" in this Regulation should be given a broad meaning and include a person or body empowered by national law to open insolvency proceedings. In order for this Regulation to apply, proceedings (comprising acts and formalities set down in law) should not only have to comply with the provisions of this Regulation, but they should also be officially recognised and legally effective in the Member State in which the insolvency proceedings are opened and should be collective insolvency proceedings which entail the partial or total divestment of the debtor and the appointment of a liquidator.

(11)   This Regulation acknowledges the fact that as a result of widely differing substantive laws it is not practical to introduce insolvency proceedings with universal scope in the entire Community. The application without exception of the law of the State of opening of proceedings would, against this background, frequently lead to difficulties. This applies, for example, to the widely differing laws on security interests to be found in the Community. Furthermore, the preferential rights enjoyed by some creditors in the insolvency proceedings are, in some cases, completely different. This Regulation should take account of this in two different ways. On the one hand,

provision should be made for special rules on applicable law in the case of particularly significant rights and legal relationships (eg rights *in rem* and contracts of employment). On the other hand, national proceedings covering only assets situated in the State of opening should also be allowed alongside main insolvency proceedings with universal scope.

(12)   This Regulation enables the main insolvency proceedings to be opened in the Member State where the debtor has the centre of his main interests. These proceedings have universal scope and aim at encompassing all the debtor's assets. To protect the diversity of interests, this Regulation permits secondary proceedings to be opened to run in parallel with the main proceedings. Secondary proceedings may be opened in the Member State where the debtor has an establishment. The effects of secondary proceedings are limited to the assets located in that State. Mandatory rules of coordination with the main proceedings satisfy the need for unity in the Community.

(13)   The "centre of main interests" should correspond to the place where the debtor conducts the administration of his interests on a regular basis and is therefore ascertainable by third parties.

(14)   This Regulation applies only to proceedings where the centre of the debtor's main interests is located in the Community.

(15)   The rules of jurisdiction set out in this Regulation establish only international jurisdiction, that is to say, they designate the Member State the courts of which may open insolvency proceedings. Territorial jurisdiction within that Member State must be established by the national law of the Member State concerned.

(16)   The court having jurisdiction to open the main insolvency proceedings should be enabled to order provisional and protective measures from the time of the request to open proceedings. Preservation measures both prior to and after the commencement of the insolvency proceedings are very important to guarantee the effectiveness of the insolvency proceedings. In that connection this Regulation should afford different possibilities. On the one hand, the court competent for the main insolvency proceedings should be able also to order provisional protective measures covering assets situated in the territory of other Member States. On the other hand, a liquidator temporarily appointed prior to the opening of the main insolvency proceedings should be able, in the Member States in which an establishment belonging to the debtor is to be found, to apply for the preservation measures which are possible under the law of those States.

(17)   Prior to the opening of the main insolvency proceedings, the right to request the opening of insolvency proceedings in the Member State where the debtor has an establishment should be limited to local creditors and creditors of the local establishment or to cases where main proceedings cannot be opened under the law of the Member State where the debtor has the centre of his main interest. The reason for this restriction is that cases where territorial insolvency proceedings are requested before the main insolvency proceedings are intended to be limited to what is absolutely necessary. If the main insolvency proceedings are opened, the territorial proceedings become secondary.

(18)   Following the opening of the main insolvency proceedings, the right to request the opening of insolvency proceedings in a Member State where the debtor has an establishment is not restricted by this Regulation. The liquidator in the main proceedings or any other person empowered under the national law of that Member State may request the opening of secondary insolvency proceedings.

(19)   Secondary insolvency proceedings may serve different purposes, besides the protection of local interests. Cases may arise where the estate of the debtor is too complex to administer as a unit or where differences in the legal systems concerned are so great that difficulties may arise from the extension of effects deriving from the law of the State of the opening to the other States where the assets are located. For this reason the liquidator in the main proceedings may request the opening of secondary proceedings when the efficient administration of the estate so requires.

(20)   Main insolvency proceedings and secondary proceedings can, however, contribute to the effective realisation of the total assets only if all the concurrent proceedings pending are coordinated. The main condition here is that the various liquidators must cooperate closely, in particular by exchanging a sufficient amount of information. In order to ensure the dominant role of the main insolvency proceedings, the liquidator in such proceedings should be given several

possibilities for intervening in secondary insolvency proceedings which are pending at the same time. For example, he should be able to propose a restructuring plan or composition or apply for realisation of the assets in the secondary insolvency proceedings to be suspended.

(21) Every creditor, who has his habitual residence, domicile or registered office in the Community, should have the right to lodge his claims in each of the insolvency proceedings pending in the Community relating to the debtor's assets. This should also apply to tax authorities and social insurance institutions. However, in order to ensure equal treatment of creditors, the distribution of proceeds must be coordinated. Every creditor should be able to keep what he has received in the course of insolvency proceedings but should be entitled only to participate in the distribution of total assets in other proceedings if creditors with the same standing have obtained the same proportion of their claims.

(22) This Regulation should provide for immediate recognition of judgments concerning the opening, conduct and closure of insolvency proceedings which come within its scope and of judgments handed down in direct connection with such insolvency proceedings. Automatic recognition should therefore mean that the effects attributed to the proceedings by the law of the State in which the proceedings were opened extend to all other Member States. Recognition of judgments delivered by the courts of the Member States should be based on the principle of mutual trust. To that end, grounds for non-recognition should be reduced to the minimum necessary. This is also the basis on which any dispute should be resolved where the courts of two Member States both claim competence to open the main insolvency proceedings. The decision of the first court to open proceedings should be recognised in the other Member States without those Member States having the power to scrutinise the court's decision.

(23) This Regulation should set out, for the matters covered by it, uniform rules on conflict of laws which replace, within their scope of application, national rules of private international law. Unless otherwise stated, the law of the Member State of the opening of the proceedings should be applicable (*lex concursus*). This rule on conflict of laws should be valid both for the main proceedings and for local proceedings; the *lex concursus* determines all the effects of the insolvency proceedings, both procedural and substantive, on the persons and legal relations concerned. It governs all the conditions for the opening, conduct and closure of the insolvency proceedings.

(24) Automatic recognition of insolvency proceedings to which the law of the opening State normally applies may interfere with the rules under which transactions are carried out in other Member States. To protect legitimate expectations and the certainty of transactions in Member States other than that in which proceedings are opened, provisions should be made for a number of exceptions to the general rule.

(25) There is a particular need for a special reference diverging from the law of the opening State in the case of rights *in rem*, since these are of considerable importance for the granting of credit. The basis, validity and extent of such a right in rem should therefore normally be determined according to the *lex situs* and not be affected by the opening of insolvency proceedings. The proprietor of the right *in rem* should therefore be able to continue to assert his right to segregation or separate settlement of the collateral security. Where assets are subject to rights *in rem* under the *lex situs* in one Member State but the main proceedings are being carried out in another Member State, the liquidator in the main proceedings should be able to request the opening of secondary proceedings in the jurisdiction where the rights *in rem* arise if the debtor has an establishment there. If a secondary proceeding is not opened, the surplus on sale of the asset covered by rights *in rem* must be paid to the liquidator in the main proceedings.

(26) If a set-off is not permitted under the law of the opening State, a creditor should nevertheless be entitled to the setoff if it is possible under the law applicable to the claim of the insolvent debtor. In this way, set-off will acquire a kind of guarantee function based on legal provisions on which the creditor concerned can rely at the time when the claim arises.

(27) There is also a need for special protection in the case of payment systems and financial markets. This applies for example to the position-closing agreements and netting agreements to be found in such systems as well as to the sale of securities and to the guarantees provided for such transactions as governed in particular by Directive 98/26/EC of the European Parliament and of

the Council of 19 May 1998 on settlement finality in payment and securities settlement systems. For such transactions, the only law which is material should thus be that applicable to the system or market concerned. This provision is intended to prevent the possibility of mechanisms for the payment and settlement of transactions provided for in the payment and set-off systems or on the regulated financial markets of the Member States being altered in the case of insolvency of a business partner. Directive 98/26/EC contains special provisions which should take precedence over the general rules in this Regulation.

(28)   In order to protect employees and jobs, the effects of insolvency proceedings on the continuation or termination of employment and on the rights and obligations of all parties to such employment must be determined by the law applicable to the agreement in accordance with the general rules on conflict of law. Any other insolvency law questions, such as whether the employees' claims are protected by preferential rights and what status such preferential rights may have, should be determined by the law of the opening State.

(29)   For business considerations, the main content of the decision opening the proceedings should be published in the other Member States at the request of the liquidator. If there is an establishment in the Member State concerned, there may be a requirement that publication is compulsory. In neither case, however, should publication be a prior condition for recognition of the foreign proceedings.

(30)   It may be the case that some of the persons concerned are not in fact aware that proceedings have been opened and act in good faith in a way that conflicts with the new situation. In order to protect such persons who make a payment to the debtor because they are unaware that foreign proceedings have been opened when they should in fact have made the payment to the foreign liquidator, it should be provided that such a payment is to have a debt-discharging effect.

(31)   This Regulation should include Annexes relating to the organisation of insolvency proceedings. As these Annexes relate exclusively to the legislation of Member States, there are specific and substantiated reasons for the Council to reserve the right to amend these Annexes in order to take account of any amendments to the domestic law of the Member States.

(32)   The United Kingdom and Ireland, in accordance with Article 3 of the Protocol on the position of the United Kingdom and Ireland annexed to the Treaty on European Union and the Treaty establishing the European Community, have given notice of their wish to take part in the adoption and application of this Regulation.

...

CHAPTER I
GENERAL PROVISIONS

Article 1 – Scope
1.   This Regulation shall apply to collective insolvency proceedings which entail the partial or total divestment of a debtor and the appointment of a liquidator.
2.   This Regulation shall not apply to insolvency proceedings concerning insurance undertakings, credit institutions, investment undertakings which provide services involving the holding of funds or securities for third parties, or to collective investment undertakings.

Article 2 – Definitions
For the purposes of this Regulation:
(a)   "insolvency proceedings" shall mean the collective proceedings referred to in Article 1 (1). These proceedings are listed in Annex A;
(b)   "liquidator" shall mean any person or body whose function is to administer or liquidate assets of which the debtor has been divested or to supervise the administration of his affairs. Those persons and bodies are listed in Annex C;
(c)   "winding-up proceedings" shall mean insolvency proceedings within the meaning of point (a) involving realising the assets of the debtor, including where the proceedings have been closed by a composition or other measure terminating the insolvency, or closed by reason of the insufficiency of the assets. Those proceedings are listed in Annex B;
(d)   "court" shall mean the judicial body or any other competent body of a Member State empowered to open insolvency proceedings or to take decisions in the course of such proceedings;

(e)   "judgment" in relation to the opening of insolvency proceedings or the appointment of a liquidator shall include the decision of any court empowered to open such proceedings or to appoint a liquidator;

(f)   "the time of the opening of proceedings" shall mean the time at which the judgment opening proceedings becomes effective, whether it is a final judgment or not;

(g)   "the Member State in which assets are situated" shall mean, in the case of:
  –   tangible property, the Member State within the territory of which the property is situated,
  –   property and rights ownership of or entitlement to which must be entered in a public register, the Member State under the authority of which the register is kept,
  –   claims, the Member State within the territory of which the third party required to meet them has the centre of his main interests, as determined in Article 3(1);

(h)   "establishment" shall mean any place of operations where the debtor carries out a non-transitory economic activity with human means and goods.

Article 3 – International jurisdiction

1.   The courts of the Member State within the territory of which the centre of a debtor's main interests is situated shall have jurisdiction to open insolvency proceedings. In the case of a company or legal person, the place of the registered office shall be presumed to be the centre of its main interests in the absence of proof to the contrary.

2.   Where the centre of a debtor's main interests is situated within the territory of a Member State, the courts of another Member State shall have jurisdiction to open insolvency proceedings against that debtor only if he possesses an establishment within the territory of that other Member State. The effects of those proceedings shall be restricted to the assets of the debtor situated in the territory of the latter Member State.

3.   Where insolvency proceedings have been opened under paragraph 1, any proceedings opened subsequently under paragraph 2 shall be secondary proceedings. These latter proceedings must be winding-up proceedings.

4.   Territorial insolvency proceedings referred to in paragraph 2 may be opened prior to the opening of main insolvency proceedings in accordance with paragraph 1 only:
  (a)   where insolvency proceedings under paragraph 1 cannot be opened because of the conditions laid down by the law of the Member State within the territory of which the centre of the debtor's main interests is situated; or
  (b)   where the opening of territorial insolvency proceedings is requested by a creditor who has his domicile, habitual residence or registered office in the Member State within the territory of which the establishment is situated, or whose claim arises from the operation of that establishment.

Article 4 – Law applicable

1.   Save as otherwise provided in this Regulation, the law applicable to insolvency proceedings and their effects shall be that of the Member State within the territory of which such proceedings are opened, hereafter referred to as the "State of the opening of proceedings".

2.   The law of the State of the opening of proceedings shall determine the conditions for the opening of those proceedings, their conduct and their closure. It shall determine in particular:
  (a)   against which debtors insolvency proceedings may be brought on account of their capacity;
  (b)   the assets which form part of the estate and the treatment of assets acquired by or devolving on the debtor after the opening of the insolvency proceedings;
  (c)   the respective powers of the debtor and the liquidator;
  (d)   the conditions under which set-offs may be invoked;
  (e)   the effects of insolvency proceedings on current contracts to which the debtor is party;
  (f)   the effects of the insolvency proceedings on proceedings brought by individual creditors, with the exception of lawsuits pending;
  (g)   the claims which are to be lodged against the debtor's estate and the treatment of claims arising after the opening of insolvency proceedings;
  (h)   the rules governing the lodging, verification and admission of claims;

(i)   the rules governing the distribution of proceeds from the realisation of assets, the ranking of claims and the rights of creditors who have obtained partial satisfaction after the opening of insolvency proceedings by virtue of a right in rem or through a set-off;

(j)   the conditions for and the effects of closure of insolvency proceedings, in particular by composition;

(k)   creditors' rights after the closure of insolvency proceedings;

(l)   who is to bear the costs and expenses incurred in the insolvency proceedings;

(m) the rules relating to the voidness, voidability or unenforceability of legal acts detrimental to all the creditors.

Article 5 – Third parties' rights *in rem*

1.   The opening of insolvency proceedings shall not affect the rights in rem of creditors or third parties in respect of tangible or intangible, moveable or immoveable assets - both specific assets and collections of indefinite assets as a whole which change from time to time - belonging to the debtor which are situated within the territory of another Member State at the time of the opening of proceedings.

2.   The rights referred to in paragraph 1 shall in particular mean:

(a)   the right to dispose of assets or have them disposed of and to obtain satisfaction from the proceeds of or income from those assets, in particular by virtue of a lien or a mortgage;

(b)   the exclusive right to have a claim met, in particular a right guaranteed by a lien in respect of the claim or by assignment of the claim by way of a guarantee;

(c)   the right to demand the assets from, and/or to require restitution by, anyone having possession or use of them contrary to the wishes of the party so entitled;

(d)   a right in rem to the beneficial use of assets.

3.   The right, recorded in a public register and enforceable against third parties, under which a right in rem within the meaning of paragraph 1 may be obtained, shall be considered a right in rem.

4.   Paragraph 1 shall not preclude actions for voidness, voidability or unenforceability as referred to in Article 4(2)(m).

Article 6 – Set-off

1.   The opening of insolvency proceedings shall not affect the right of creditors to demand the set-off of their claims against the claims of the debtor, where such a set-off is permitted by the law applicable to the insolvent debtor's claim.

2.   Paragraph 1 shall not preclude actions for voidness, voidability or unenforceability as referred to in Article 4(2)(m).

Article 7 – Reservation of title

1.   The opening of insolvency proceedings against the purchaser of an asset shall not affect the seller's rights based on a reservation of title where at the time of the opening of proceedings the asset is situated within the territory of a Member State other than the State of opening of proceedings.

2.   The opening of insolvency proceedings against the seller of an asset, after delivery of the asset, shall not constitute grounds for rescinding or terminating the sale and shall not prevent the purchaser from acquiring title where at the time of the opening of proceedings the asset sold is situated within the territory of a Member State other than the State of the opening of proceedings.

3.   Paragraphs 1 and 2 shall not preclude actions for voidness, voidability or unenforceability as referred to in Article 4(2)(m).

Article 8 – Contracts relating to immoveable property

The effects of insolvency proceedings on a contract conferring the right to acquire or make use of immoveable property shall be governed solely by the law of the Member State within the territory of which the immoveable property is situated.

Article 9 – Payment systems and financial markets

1.   Without prejudice to Article 5, the effects of insolvency proceedings on the rights and obligations of the parties to a payment or settlement system or to a financial market shall be governed solely by the law of the Member State applicable to that system or market.

2.   Paragraph 1 shall not preclude any action for voidness, voidability or unenforceability which may be taken to set aside payments or transactions under the law applicable to the relevant payment system or financial market.

Article 10 – Contracts of employment

The effects of insolvency proceedings on employment contracts and relationships shall be governed solely by the law of the Member State applicable to the contract of employment.

Article 11 – Effects on rights subject to registration

The effects of insolvency proceedings on the rights of the debtor in immoveable property, a ship or an aircraft subject to registration in a public register shall be determined by the law of the Member State under the authority of which the register is kept.

Article 12 – Community patents and trade marks

For the purposes of this Regulation, a Community patent, a Community trade mark or any other similar right established by Community law may be included only in the proceedings referred to in Article 3(1).

Article 13 – Detrimental acts

Article 4(2)(m) shall not apply where the person who benefited from an act detrimental to all the creditors provides proof that:

–   the said act is subject to the law of a Member State other than that of the State of the opening of proceedings, and
–   that law does not allow any means of challenging that act in the relevant case.

Article 14 – Protection of third-party purchasers

Where, by an act concluded after the opening of insolvency proceedings, the debtor disposes, for consideration, of.

–   an immoveable asset, or
–   a ship or an aircraft subject to registration in a public register, or
–   securities whose existence presupposes registration in a register laid down by law,

the validity of that act shall be governed by the law of the State within the territory of which the immoveable asset is situated or under the authority of which the register is kept.

Article 15 – Effects of insolvency proceedings on lawsuits pending

The effects of insolvency proceedings on a lawsuit pending concerning an asset or a right of which the debtor has been divested shall be governed solely by the law of the Member State in which that lawsuit is pending.

CHAPTER II
RECOGNITION OF INSOLVENCY PROCEEDINGS

Article 16 – Principle

1.   Any judgment opening insolvency proceedings handed down by a court of a Member State which has jurisdiction pursuant to Article 3 shall be recognised in all the other Member States from the time that it becomes effective in the State of the opening of proceedings.

        This rule shall also apply where, on account of his capacity, insolvency proceedings cannot be brought against the debtor in other Member States.

2.   Recognition of the proceedings referred to in Article 3(1) shall not preclude the opening of the proceedings referred to in Article 3(2) by a court in another Member State. The latter proceedings shall be secondary insolvency proceedings within the meaning of Chapter III.

Article 17 – Effects of recognition

1.   The judgment opening the proceedings referred to in Article 3(1) shall, with no further formalities, produce the same effects in any other Member State as under this law of the State of the opening of proceedings, unless this Regulation provides otherwise and as long as no proceedings referred to in Article 3(2) are opened in that other Member State.

2.   The effects of the proceedings referred to in Article 3(2) may not be challenged in other Member States. Any restriction of the creditors' rights, in particular a stay or discharge, shall produce

effects vis-à-vis assets situated within the territory of another Member State only in the case of those creditors who have given their consent.

Article 18 – Powers of the liquidator

1.   The liquidator appointed by a court which has jurisdiction pursuant to Article 3(1) may exercise all the powers conferred on him by the law of the State of the opening of proceedings in another Member State, as long as no other insolvency proceedings have been opened there nor any preservation measure to the contrary has been taken there further to a request for the opening of insolvency proceedings in that State. He may in particular remove the debtor's assets from the territory of the Member State in which they are situated, subject to Articles 5 and 7.

2.   The liquidator appointed by a court which has jurisdiction pursuant to Article 3(2) may in any other Member State claim through the courts or out of court that moveable property was removed from the territory of the State of the opening of proceedings to the territory of that other Member State after the opening of the insolvency proceedings. He may also bring any action to set aside which is in the interests of the creditors.

3.   In exercising his powers, the liquidator shall comply with the law of the Member State within the territory of which he intends to take action, in particular with regard to procedures for the realisation of assets. Those powers may not include coercive measures or the right to rule on legal proceedings or disputes.

Article 19 – Proof of the liquidator's appointment

The liquidator's appointment shall be evidenced by a certified copy of the original decision appointing him or by any other certificate issued by the court which has jurisdiction.

A translation into the official language or one of the official languages of the Member State within the territory of which he intends to act may be required. No legalisation or other similar formality shall be required.

Article 20 – Return and imputation

1.   A creditor who, after the opening of the proceedings referred to in Article 3(1) obtains by any means, in particular through enforcement, total or partial satisfaction of his claim on the assets belonging to the debtor situated within the territory of another Member State, shall return what he has obtained to the liquidator, subject to Articles 5 and 7.

2.   In order to ensure equal treatment of creditors a creditor who has, in the course of insolvency proceedings, obtained a dividend on his claim shall share in distributions made in other proceedings only where creditors of the same ranking or category have, in those other proceedings, obtained an equivalent dividend.

Article 21 – Publication

1.   The liquidator may request that notice of the judgment opening insolvency proceedings and, where appropriate, the decision appointing him, be published in any other Member State in accordance with the publication procedures provided for in that State. Such publication shall also specify the liquidator appointed and whether the jurisdiction rule applied is that pursuant to Article 3(1) or Article 3(2).

2.   However, any Member State within the territory of which the debtor has an establishment may require mandatory publication. In such cases, the liquidator or any authority empowered to that effect in the Member State where the proceedings referred to in Article 3(1) are opened shall take all necessary measures to ensure such publication.

Article 22 – Registration in a public register

1.   The liquidator may request that the judgment opening the proceedings referred to in Article 3(1) be registered in the land register, the trade register and any other public register kept in the other Member States.

2.   However, any Member State may require mandatory registration. In such cases, the liquidator or any authority empowered to that effect in the Member State where the proceedings referred to in Article 3(1) have been opened shall take all necessary measures to ensure such registration.

Article 23 – Costs

The costs of the publication and registration provided for in Articles 21 and 22 shall be regarded as costs and expenses incurred in the proceedings.

Article 24 – Honouring of an obligation to a debtor

1.   Where an obligation has been honoured in a Member State for the benefit of a debtor who is subject to insolvency proceedings opened in another Member State, when it should have been honoured for the benefit of the liquidator in those proceedings, the person honouring the obligation shall be deemed to have discharged it if he was unaware of the opening of proceedings.

2.   Where such an obligation is honoured before the publication provided for in Article 21 has been effected, the person honouring the obligation shall be presumed, in the absence of proof to the contrary, to have been unaware of the opening of insolvency proceedings; where the obligation is honoured after such publication has been effected, the person honouring the obligation shall be presumed, in the absence of proof to the contrary, to have been aware of the opening of proceedings.

Article 25 – Recognition and enforceability of other judgments

1.   Judgments handed down by a court whose judgment concerning the opening of proceedings is recognised in accordance with Article 16 and which concern the course and closure of insolvency proceedings, and compositions approved by that court shall also be recognised with no further formalities. Such judgments shall be enforced in accordance with Articles 31 to 51, with the exception of Article 34(2), of the Brussels Convention on jurisdiction and the Enforcement of judgments in Civil and Commercial Matters, as amended by the Conventions of Accession to this Convention.

The first subparagraph shall also apply to judgments deriving directly from the insolvency proceedings and which are closely linked with them, even if they were handed down by another court.

The first subparagraph shall also apply to judgments relating to preservation measures taken after the request for the opening of insolvency proceedings.

2.   The recognition and enforcement of judgments other than those referred to in paragraph 1 shall be governed by the Convention referred to in paragraph 1, provided that that Convention is applicable.

3.   The Member States shall not be obliged to recognise or enforce a judgment referred to in paragraph 1 which might result in a limitation of personal freedom or postal secrecy.

Article 26 – Public policy

Any Member State may refuse to recognise insolvency proceedings opened in another Member State or to enforce a judgment handed down in the context of such proceedings where the effects of such recognition or enforcement would be manifestly contrary to that State's public policy, in particular its fundamental principles or the constitutional rights and liberties of the individual.

CHAPTER III

SECONDARY INSOLVENCY PROCEEDINGS

Article 27 – Opening of proceedings

The opening of the proceedings referred to in Article 3(1) by a court of a Member State and which is recognised in another Member State (main proceedings) shall permit the opening in that other Member State, a court of which has jurisdiction pursuant to Article 3(2), of secondary insolvency proceedings without the debtor's insolvency being examined in that other State. These latter proceedings must be among the proceedings listed in Annex B. Their effects shall be restricted to the assets of the debtor situated within the territory of that other Member State.

Article 28 – Applicable law

Save as otherwise provided in this Regulation, the law applicable to secondary proceedings shall be that of the Member State within the territory of which the secondary proceedings are opened.

Article 29 – Right to request the opening of proceedings

The opening of secondary proceedings may be requested by:

(a)   the liquidator in the main proceedings;

(b)   any other person or authority empowered to request the opening of insolvency proceedings under the law of the Member State within the territory of which the opening of secondary proceedings is requested.

Article 30 – Advance payment of costs and expenses

Where the law of the Member State in which the opening of secondary proceedings is requested requires that the debtor's assets be sufficient to cover in whole or in part the costs and expenses of the proceedings, the court may, when it receives such a request, require the applicant to make an advance payment of costs or to provide appropriate security.

Article 31 – Duty to cooperate and communicate information

1.   Subject to the rules restricting the communication of information, the liquidator in the main proceedings and the liquidators in the secondary proceedings shall be duty bound to communicate information to each other. They shall immediately communicate any information which may be relevant to the other proceedings, in particular the progress made in lodging and verifying claims and all measures aimed at terminating the proceedings.

2.   Subject to the rules applicable to each of the proceedings, the liquidator in the main proceedings and the liquidators in the secondary proceedings shall be duty bound to cooperate with each other.

3.   The liquidator in the secondary proceedings shall give the liquidator in the main proceedings an early opportunity of submitting proposals on the liquidation or use of the assets in the secondary proceedings.

Article 32 – Exercise of creditors' rights

1.   Any creditor may lodge his claim in the main proceedings and in any secondary proceedings.

2.   The liquidators in the main and any secondary proceedings shall lodge in other proceedings claims which have already been lodged in the proceedings for which they were appointed, provided that the interests of creditors in the latter proceedings are served thereby, subject to the right of creditors to oppose that or to withdraw the lodgement of their claims where the law applicable so provides.

3.   The liquidator in the main or secondary proceedings shall be empowered to participate in other proceedings on the same basis as a creditor, in particular by attending creditors' meetings.

Article 33 – Stay of liquidation

1.   The court, which opened the secondary proceedings, shall stay the process of liquidation in whole or in part on receipt of a request from the liquidator in the main proceedings, provided that in that event it may require the liquidator in the main proceedings to take any suitable measure to guarantee the interests of the creditors in the secondary proceedings and of individual classes of creditors. Such a request from the liquidator may be rejected only if it is manifestly of no interest to the creditors in the main proceedings. Such a stay of the process of liquidation may be ordered for up to three months. It may be continued or renewed for similar periods.

2.   The court referred to in paragraph 1 shall terminate the stay of the process of liquidation:
   –   at the request of the liquidator in the main proceedings,
   –   of its own motion, at the request of a creditor or at the request of the liquidator in the secondary proceedings if that measure no longer appears justified, in particular, by the interests of creditors in the main proceedings or in the secondary proceedings.

Article 34 – Measures ending secondary insolvency proceedings

1.   Where the law applicable to secondary proceedings allows for such proceedings to be closed without liquidation by a rescue plan, a composition or a comparable measure, the liquidator in the main proceedings shall be empowered to propose such a measure himself

   Closure of the secondary proceedings by a measure referred to in the first subparagraph shall not become final without the consent of the liquidator in the main proceedings; failing his agreement, however, it may become final if the financial interests of the creditors in the main proceedings are not affected by the measure proposed.

2.   Any restriction of creditors' rights arising from a measure referred to in paragraph 1 which is proposed in secondary proceedings, such as a stay of payment or discharge of debt, may not have

effect in respect of the debtor's assets not covered by those proceedings without the consent of all the creditors having an interest.

3.   During a stay of the process of liquidation ordered pursuant to Article 33, only the liquidator in the main proceedings or the debtor, with the former's consent, may propose measures laid down in paragraph 1 of this Article in the secondary proceedings; no other proposal for such a measure shall be put to the vote or approved.

Article 35 – Assets remaining in the secondary proceedings

If by the liquidation of assets in the secondary proceedings it is possible to meet all claims allowed under those proceedings, the liquidator appointed in those proceedings shall immediately transfer any assets remaining to the liquidator in the main proceedings.

Article 36 – Subsequent opening of the main proceedings

Where the proceedings referred to in Article 3(1) are opened following the opening of the proceedings referred to in Article 3(2) in another Member State, Articles 31 to 35 shall apply to those opened first, in so far as the progress of those proceedings so permits.

Article 37 – Conversion of earlier proceedings

The liquidator in the main proceedings may request that proceedings listed in Annex A previously opened in another Member State be converted into winding-up proceedings if this proves to be in the interests of the creditors in the main proceedings.

The court with jurisdiction under Article 3(2) shall order conversion into one of the proceedings listed in Annex B.

Article 38 – Preservation measures

Where the court of a Member State which has jurisdiction pursuant to Article 3(1) appoints a temporary administrator in order to ensure the preservation of the debtor's assets, that temporary administrator shall be empowered to request any measures to secure and preserve any of the debtor's assets situated in another Member State, provided for under the law of that State, for the period between the request for the opening of insolvency proceedings and the judgment opening the proceedings.

CHAPTER IV
PROVISION OF INFORMATION FOR CREDITORS AND LODGEMENT OF THEIR CLAIMS

Article 39 – Right to lodge claims

Any creditor who has his habitual residence, domicile or registered office in a Member State other than the State of the opening of proceedings, including the tax authorities and social security authorities of Member States, shall have the right to lodge claims in the insolvency proceedings in writing.

Article 40 – Duty to inform creditors

1.   As soon as insolvency proceedings are opened in a Member State, the court of that State having jurisdiction or the liquidator appointed by it shall immediately inform known creditors who have their habitual residences, domiciles or registered offices in the other Member States.

2.   That information, provided by an individual notice, shall in particular include time limits, the penalties laid down in regard to those time limits, the body or authority empowered to accept the lodgement of claims and the other measures laid down. Such notice shall also indicate whether creditors whose claims are preferential or secured in rem need lodge their claims.

Article 41 – Content of the lodgement of a claim

A creditor shall send copies of supporting documents, if any, and shall indicate the nature of the claim, the date on which it arose and its amount, as well as whether he alleges preference, security *in rem* or a reservation of title in respect of the claim and what assets are covered by the guarantee he is invoking.

Article 42 – Languages

1.   The information provided for in Article 40 shall be provided in the official language or one of the official languages of the State of the opening of proceedings. For that purpose a form shall be used bearing the heading "Invitation to lodge a claim. Time limits to be observed" in all the official languages of the institutions of the European Union.

2.   Any creditor who has his habitual residence, domicile or registered office in a Member State other than the State of the opening of proceedings may lodge his claim in the official language or

one of the official languages of that other State. In that event, however, the lodgement of his claim shall bear the heading "Lodgement of claim" in the official language or one of the official languages of the State of the opening of proceedings. In addition, he may be required to provide a translation into the official language or one of the official languages of the State of the opening of proceedings.

CHAPTER V
TRANSITIONAL AND FINAL PROVISIONS

Article 43 – Applicability in time

The provisions of this Regulation shall apply only to insolvency proceedings opened after its entry into force. Acts done by a debtor before the entry into force of this Regulation shall continue to be governed by the law which was applicable to them at the time they were done.

Article 44 – Relationship to Conventions

1. After its entry into force, this Regulation replaces, in respect of the matters referred to therein, in the relations between Member States, the Conventions concluded between two or more Member States, in particular:

    (a) the Convention between Belgium and France on jurisdiction and the Validity and Enforcement of judgments, Arbitration Awards and Authentic Instruments, signed at Paris on 8 July 1899;

    (b) the Convention between Belgium and Austria on Bankruptcy, Winding-up, Arrangements, Compositions and Suspension of Payments (with Additional Protocol of 13 June 1973), signed at Brussels on 16 July 1969;

    (c) the Convention between Belgium and the Netherlands on Territorial Jurisdiction, Bankruptcy and the Validity and Enforcement of Judgments, Arbitration Awards and Authentic Instruments, signed at Brussels on 28 March 1925;

    (d) the Treaty between Germany and Austria on Bankruptcy, Winding-up, Arrangements and Compositions, signed at Vienna on 25 May 1979;

    (e) the Convention between France and Austria on jurisdiction, Recognition and Enforcement of judgments on Bankruptcy, signed at Vienna on 27 February 1979;

    (f) the Convention between France and Italy on the Enforcement of judgments in Civil and Commercial Matters, signed at Rome on 3 June 1930;

    (g) the Convention between Italy and Austria on Bankruptcy, Winding-up, Arrangements and Compositions, signed at Rome on 12 July 1977;

    (h) the Convention between the Kingdom of the Netherlands and the Federal Republic of Germany on the Mutual Recognition and Enforcement of judgments and other Enforceable instruments in Civil and Commercial Matters, signed at The Hague on 30 August 1962;

    (i) the Convention between the United Kingdom and the Kingdom of Belgium providing for the Reciprocal Enforcement of judgments in Civil and Commercial Matters, with Protocol, signed at Brussels on 2 May 1934;

    (j) the Convention between Denmark, Finland, Norway, Sweden and Iceland on Bankruptcy, signed at Copenhagen on 7 November 1933;

    (k) the European Convention on Certain International Aspects of Bankruptcy, signed at Istanbul on 5 June 1990.

2. The Conventions referred to in paragraph 1 shall continue to have effect with regard to proceedings opened before the entry into force of this Regulation.

3. This Regulation shall not apply:

    (a) in any Member State, to the extent that it is irreconcilable with the obligations arising in relation to bankruptcy from a convention concluded by that State with one or more third countries before the entry into force of this Regulation;

    (b) in the United Kingdom of Great Britain and Northern Ireland, to the extent that is irreconcilable with the obligations arising in relation to bankruptcy and the winding-up of insolvent companies from any arrangements with the Commonwealth existing at the time this Regulation enters into force.

...

INDEX